Discourse and Social l

DISCOURSE AND SOCIAL LIFE

Edited by
SRIKANT SARANGI
AND
MALCOLM COULTHARD

An imprint of **Pearson Education**

Harlow, England · London · New York · Reading, Massachusetts · San Francisco
Toronto · Don Mills, Ontario · Sydney · Tokyo · Singapore · Hong Kong · Seoul
Taipei · Cape Town · Madrid · Mexico City · Amsterdam · Munich · Paris · Milan

Pearson Education Limited
Edinburgh Gate
Harlow
Essex CM20 2JE
England

and Associated Companies throughout the world

Visit us on the World Wide Web at:
www.pearsoneduc.com

First published 2000

© Pearson Education Limited 2000

ISBN 0-582-40469-X CSD
ISBN 0-582-40468-1 PPR

British Library Cataloguing-in-Publication Data

A catalogue record for this book is available from the British Library

Library of Congress Cataloging-in-Publication Data

Discourse and social life / edited by Srikant Sarangi and Malcolm Coulthard.
    p. cm.
  Includes bibliographical references and index.
  ISBN 0–582–40468–1 — ISBN 0–582–40469–X
  1. Discourse analysis—Social aspects. I. Sarangi, Srikant, 1956– .
II. Coulthard, Malcolm.

  P302.84.D573   2000
  401'.41—dc21   99–089711

Set by 35 in 10/12pt Palatino
Printed and bound in Great Britain by
T.J. International Ltd, Padstow, Cornwall

DISCOURSE AND SOCIAL LIFE

is dedicated to

Chris Candlin

on the occasion of his 60th Birthday

in order to celebrate his major contribution to the discipline of Applied Linguistics.

Chris has contributed significantly in two ways – firstly, as the editor of several major book series of inestimable importance, and secondly, as an individual and team researcher. For this reason we chose *Discourse and Social Life* as the title of this book both to echo that of his Longman Series 'Language in Social Life', and as an appropriate label for much of his own very varied research output.

Over the past three decades Chris has played a significant role in building the bridge between discourse study and its social relevance, while at the same time being a forceful leader in the move to extend the remit of Applied Linguistics beyond language education and into professional settings. For him, discourse analysis is essentially a socially relevant enterprise and his unfailing endeavour to keep to this brief is clearly reflected in his very successful series editorships at Longman and in the establishment of Centres for Language and Social Life at both Lancaster University, UK and Macquarie University, Australia. His initiatives have fostered quality research and significant teaching provision in the broad area of Discourse and Social Life in three continents.

It is a great privilege for us to have been ratified participants on two levels – playing a role in his discourse crusade and being part of his rich social life. On behalf of both the contributors to this book and the production and commissioning team at Longman,

We wish Chris a very fruitful and social future.

This dedication, like the book itself, would be incomplete without an expression of appreciation to Sally Candlin for the various discourses she had to devise and perform 'back-to-back' (including the Text pretext and the Inspector Morse script) in order to succeed in preserving the Candlin social life, while at the same time acting as midwife during the gestation and delivery of the project.

31 March 2000
Cardiff

Srikant Sarangi
Malcolm Coulthard

Contents

CONTENTS

Contributors

Sally Candlin is Adjunct Associate Professor at the University of Western Sydney. Her professional experience in nursing informs her research activities in discourse analysis. Her major publications focus on the transcultural aspects of nursing practice, and on the issue of power relations in nurse-patient encounters. She is currently working on *English for Nurses* (with K. Keobke).

Malcolm Coulthard is Professor of English Language and Linguistics at the University of Birmingham. He is best known for his work on spoken and written discourse. His current research is in the area of Forensic Linguistics. He was founding President of the International Association of Forensic Linguists and is editor of the journal *Forensic Linguistics* where two recent publications 'A failed appeal' (1997) and 'Tools for the trade' (1998) appeared.

Justine Coupland is Senior Lecturer at the Centre for Language and Communication Research at Cardiff University. Her research interests are in social interaction, discourse analysis and interpersonal communication. She has an edited book on *Small Talk* (2000) and has recently published papers on dating advertisements as texts of identity in *Discourse & Society* and the *Journal of Sociolinguistics*.

Nikolas Coupland is Professor and Director at the Centre for Language and Communication Research, Cardiff University. He is founding editor of the *Journal of Sociolinguistics* (with A. Bell). He has recently co-edited *The Discourse Reader* (1999, with A. Jaworski).

Norman Fairclough is Professor of Language in Social Life at Lancaster University. He is the major articulator of Critical Discourse Analysis. His most recent books are *Discourse in Late Modernity* (1999, with L. Chouliaraki) and *New Labour, New Language* (2000). He is currently working on the theme of language in the new capitalism.

CONTRIBUTORS

Ruqaiya Hasan is Professor Emeritus at Macquarie University in Sydney. Her areas of interest are stylistics, discourse analysis and sociolinguistics, with particular emphasis on semantic variation and ideology. Two of her recent publications are 'Speaking with reference to context' in *Text and Context in Functional Linguistics* (1999, edited by M. Ghadessy) and 'The disempowerment game: Bourdieu and language in literacy' in *Linguistics and Education* (1999).

Robert B. Kaplan is Emeritus Professor of Applied Linguistics in the Department of Linguistics, University of Southern California. He is best known for his research in the broad area of contrastive rhetoric, intercultural communication and cross-linguistic text analysis. His work has been extensively applied to foreign language teaching and language education policy.

Geoffrey Leech is Research Professor of English Linguistics at Lancaster University. His interests range from advertising and stylistics through pragmatics and semantics to English grammar. He is probably best known for his contribution to the *Comprehensive Grammar of the English Language* and his most recent publication is the mould-breaking *Longman Grammar of Spoken and Written English* (1999, with D. Biber, S. Johansson, S. Conrad and E. Finegan).

Yon Maley is Honorary Associate in Linguistics (formerly Senior Lecturer) at Macquarie University in Sydney. She has published widely on various genres of legal language, both written and spoken. With Chris Candlin, she has published several papers on discourse of mediation and alternative dispute resolution in the workplace, most recently in *Talk, Work and Institutional Order* (1999, edited by S. Sarangi and C. Roberts).

Greg Myers is Senior Lecturer in the Department of Linguistics and Modern English Language at Lancaster University, UK. He is author of *Writing Biology* (1990), *Words in Ads* (1994), and *Ad Worlds* (1999), and is now working on a study of the expression of opinion in interaction.

Celia Roberts is Senior Research Fellow at Kings College, London. Her research interests are in interactional sociolinguistics and institutional and urban ethnography. Her major publications are *Language and Discrimination* (1992, with E. Davies and T. Jupp), *Achieving Understanding: Discourse in Intercultural Encounters* (1996, with K. Bremer et al.), and *Talk, Work and Institutional Order: Discourse in Medical, Mediation and Management Settings* (1999, with S. Sarangi).

Srikant Sarangi is Reader in Language and Communication and Director of the Health Communication Research Centre at Cardiff University. His recent publications include *Language, Bureaucracy and Social Control* (1996, with S. Slembrouck), *Talk, Work and Institutional Order: Discourse in Medical, Mediation and Management Settings* (1999, with C. Roberts). He is currently editor (with J. Wilson) of *TEXT: An Interdisciplinary Journal for the Study of Discourse*, and series editor (with C. N. Candlin) of *Advances in Applied Linguistics*.

Ron Scollon is Professor of Linguistics in the Department of Linguistics and Asian Sociocultural Research Projects at Georgetown University, Washington DC. His research interests are mediated discourse, the sociolinguistics of literacy and new literacy studies, and multimodal discourse. He is author of *Mediated Discourse as Social Interaction* (1998) and *Intercultural Communication* (1995, with S. Wong Scollon).

Henry Widdowson is Professor of English Linguistics at the University of Vienna. His major publications are in the areas of linguistics stylistics and the theory and practice of language teaching. In a number of recent publications, he has turned his attention to the work of critical linguists and while acknowledging the social significance of their work, has questioned their procedures of analysis and interpretation.

Theo van Leeuwen is Professor of Language and Communication at Cardiff University. His main research interests are media discourse, critical discourse analysis and multimodality. His books include *The Media Interview: Confession, Contest, Conversation* (1994, with P. Bell), *Reading Images: The Grammar of Visual Design* (1996, with G. Kress) and *Speech, Music, Sound* (1999).

Ruth Wodak is Professor of Applied Linguistics and Discourse Analysis at the University of Vienna. Her main areas of research are organizational discourse and the discursive construction of identities along the lines of gender, race and anti-Semitism. Her most recent books in English are *Disorders of Discourse* (1996), *Gender and Discourse* (1997), *Communicating Gender in Context* (1997, with H. Kotthoff) and *The Discursive Construction of National Identity* (1999, with R. de Cillia, M. Reisigl and K. Liebhart).

Publisher's Acknowledgements

We are grateful to the following for permission to reproduce copyright material:

The Chief Justice NSW for extracts from the case *Broken Bay Protection Committee and Peter Helman v Byron Council and Another*' March–May, 1994, *'Potoroo'* trial; The Controller of Her Majesty's Stationery Office for extracts from various 'Trial' transcripts and Times Newspapers Ltd for the obituary to 'Annabella' in *The Times* 23.9.96 © Times Newspapers Ltd 23rd September 1996.

Whilst every effort has been made to trace the owners of copyright material, in a few cases this has proved impossible and we take this opportunity to offer our apologies to any copyright holders whose rights we may have unwittingly infringed.

Discourse as topic, resource and social practice: An introduction

Srikant Sarangi and Malcolm Coulthard

Our purpose in organising this collection was to offer a mapping of the current field of discourse studies by inviting leading 'discourse practitioners' to situate themselves in this growing intellectual landscape and to illustrate their concerns with data of their choice.[1] All contributors, working within their chosen tradition, mark their points of departure and indicate how they legitimate their choice of theory, data sites and analytic preferences. They share, explicitly or implicitly, a view of discourse as social practice, and make it their topic of study. We do not propose, in this introduction, to detail the complex web of similarities, nor all the fruitful contrasts and/or conflicts, between the individual contributions – rather we invite you the reader to make those links and to draw the parallels.

It is important to emphasise that this volume is not about discourse as such, but rather about the relationship between discourse and social life. The book's cover design, an original painting by Donald Friend,[2] entitled *Conversations*, captures these two key concepts. What combines the two, and the conjunction *and* is crucial, is the focus on interaction and dialogism. It aligns with a broad view of discourse succinctly summarised by Candlin (1997: viii):

> Discourse is a means of talking and writing about and acting upon worlds, a means which both constructs and is constructed by a set of social practices within these worlds, and in so doing both reproduces and constructs afresh particular social-discursive practices, constrained or encouraged by more macro movements in the overarching social formation.

At first glance, all the characters in the painting seem to be engaged in localised 'social-discursive practices'. Given the complexity of the action sequences, we can see how some of the characters appear disoriented, thus cueing different 'participation frameworks' (Goffman 1981): we see someone posing as a bystander at one point and as a ratified participant at another point in the interactional routine. Even without cues from talk bubbles giving partial insight into topics, we can label some of these as two-party, some as multi-party interactions and some as more focussed than others (as suggested through extralinguistic markers such as posture and gesture). In general, the painting alludes to the fact that social encounters lubricate our relational positioning in society. By a similar token, they can bracket off people on the basis of dominant or subtle categorisations. In a given society, over time, certain social formations achieve normative status, and thus become constraining for one group while encouraging another as far as participation is concerned. The birds in the picture, cast as onlookers, not only provide a contrastive backdrop, but also serve to emphasise that social interaction is multi-faceted. To repeat the words of Simmel (1950: 54) from Myers' chapter in this volume: 'The more profound, [and] double sense of "social game" is that not only is the game played in society (as its external medium) but [also] that, with its help, people actually "play" "society" '. This 'playing of society' equates with our view about the interrelationship between discourse and social life. Put differently, discourse becomes the means through which social life is played out.

It is not only people, in the everyday sense, who play society. Over the years, scholars in the humanities and social sciences have made everyday social life a focus of their study. Let us begin with a brief overview of linguistics and then chart the discursive turn in our neighbouring fields, in particular, philosophy, anthropology, history, sociology and psychology. A detailed historical account is beyond the remit of this introduction, but we will try to indicate when and where linguistics was a borrower from, and where a lender to, other disciplines.

The discursive turn in linguistics

Within linguistics, the view of discourse is not only diverse; it even has an anti-discourse beginning. Historically speaking, Saussure ([1916] 1966: 14) proposed a distinction between *langue* ('the social side of language, outside the individual') and *parole* ('the individual side of language, the individual act'), and called for linguistic activity to concentrate on *langue* and not *parole*. For him, the primary task of linguistics as a new discipline was 'to delimit and define itself'. But as early as 1935, Firth anticipated how conversation (i.e., *parole* in Saussure's terminology) would become central to a linguistic enterprise, although he himself did not deal with any conversational data in his work:

> Conversation is much more of a roughly prescribed ritual than most people think. Once someone speaks to you, you are in a relatively determined context and you are not free just to say what you please. We are born individuals. But to satisfy our needs we have to become social persons . . . it is [in] the study of conversation . . . that we shall find the key to a better understanding of what language really is and how it works. (cited in Stubbs 1993: 19)

Chomskyan linguistics (e.g., Chomsky 1957), based on Saussure, however, further undermined the study of performance, conversation or otherwise, as a legitimate linguistic activity. In other words, linguistic performance was designated an unsuitable topic of study. In reviewing and discarding Skinner's (1957) behaviourism, Chomsky (1959) set up linguistic competence and creativity as an alternative. But this marks a refusal to address the question of how language is intimately linked to communication and information exchange systems, although it must be admitted that the then contemporary model of information flow (Shannon and Weaver 1949) did not offer an adequate basis for accommodating linguistic insights. In participation-structure terms, the Chomskyan tradition has constrained linguists to refrain from taking a scholarly interest in how language mediates social life. This is all the more surprising when one considers that, wearing his other, political, hat, one of Chomsky's main concerns is with the analysis of the misleading discourse of politicians, a concern which one might think would ally him academically with critical discourse analysts.

In the structural, descriptive linguistic tradition, the focus was on the sentence as a unit of linguistic description. Also, the sentences analysed were mainly constructed intuitively by the analyst, rather than those produced by speakers in real communicative situations. Zellig Harris (1952), in his seminal paper 'Discourse Analysis', only expands the boundaries of the paradigm as far as including supra-sentential structure; he does not envisage analysing real discourse corpora:[3]

> One can approach discourse analysis from two types of problem, which turn out to be related. The first is the problem of continuing descriptive linguistics beyond the limits of a single sentence at a time. The other is the question of correlating 'culture' and language (i.e. non-linguistic and linguistic behaviour). (Harris: 1952: 1)

Thus his main preoccupation remained that of treating discourse as a linguistic object, 'as fertile soil for the methods of descriptive linguistics, since these methods study the relative distribution of elements within a connected stretch of speech' (1952: 3). The second rationale accommodates the work of Sapir and Whorf on the interrelation of grammar and thought patterns. As Tannen (1990: 110) rightly points out: 'Some of the work of Jakobson, Sapir, and Whorf, were they working today, would be considered discourse analysis. The term was not needed in their time because linguistics did not then exclude any of the kinds of linguistic analysis they did'.

Paradoxically, the beginnings of discourse analysis as we know it were in the neighbouring discipline of philosophy where the speech act theoreticians (Austin 1962, Searle 1969 and Grice 1975, in particular) put forward a view of language as social action. The means by which representations of truth, sincerity etc are achieved in linguistic performance and the fit between the word and the world became a central concern in this tradition (see Rose 1960 on the 'world as a worded entity'). However, just like Harris, the speech act analysts do not deal with real discourse data, even in the more recent statement (Searle 1995), and the approach has many drawbacks for those hoping to adapt it to investigate naturally-occurring data.

Pratt (1981: 8), for instance, draws our attention to the ideological basis of the speech act model, because too much emphasis is given to individual beliefs and intentions, and 'speech situations in which speakers speak for and through other people look like marked or abnormal cases'. Others (e.g., Turner 1971, Levinson 1983) dispute the claim that there is a one-to-one correspondence between utterance and illocutionary force and point out that the model overemphasises the role of verbs and leaves out other aspects of social action. Rather than content himself with criticising the speech act model in its own terms, Hymes (1986: 55) draws attention to its limited application, on the grounds that it does not take into account the speech community let alone the speech event in which speech acts are embedded.

There have been within linguistics at least three important and unrelated moves to widen the discipline to include discourse features. The first, and perhaps theoretically the most important, is Hymes' work on communicative competence. Working within a tradition of linguistic anthropology, both Hymes (1964) and Gumperz (see Gumperz and Hymes 1972) account for a range of sociolinguistic and ethnographic variables underlying linguistic performance. Hymes (1964) identifies eight variables in his framework: setting, participants, ends, act sequences, key, instrumentalities, norms and genre (with the acronym SPEAKING). From a vantage point 35 years later this taxonomic model seems rather descriptive and perhaps fails to account for how participants in a given situation prioritise one variable over another. However, the model did provide a strong basis for much of the subsequent work in context analysis, sociolinguistics, pragmatics and discourse analysis.

The second tradition is associated with the work of Labov and Fanshel (1977) who devised an elaborate model of discourse comprehension to cope with authentic data from the psychotherapeutic interviews. Their prime interest lay in uncovering rules of discourse production and interpretation involving the two levels of 'what is said' and 'what is done', and their analysis was based in part on what they called A, B, and A/B events. 'A' events refer to information which is known to the speaker, 'B' events refer to information which is known to the addressee and 'A/B' events refer to information known to both parties.[4] Using these categories they were able to offer one explanation for declarative clauses being heard as questioning – *If X makes a statement about a B event this will be heard by Y as a Request for Confirmation.*

The third tradition is better known as the Birmingham school of discourse analysis (Sinclair and Coulthard 1975), which is one of the earliest attempts at identifying routine structural features of discourse based on authentic, transcribed data (here, interaction between teachers and pupils in the classroom setting). Sinclair and Coulthard base their work on the Hallidayan systemic-functional approach to language use, when they look at 'the organisation of linguistic units above the rank of clause'. What this analysis does not account for is the dynamics of the teacher-pupil relational frame, or shifting participant structures, as Goffman would have it. In addition, as Stubbs (1993) points out, the work of the Birmingham school had two different audiences, educational and linguistic, and in its historical context did not quite satisfy either camp's expectations.

Discourse as language in context and as social interaction

Over the last three decades, the notion of context has been a prime target of language and interaction analysis, not just something to be recognised and glossed over as did Harris (1952). In addition to the work of Hymes and Gumperz, Halliday's (1978) view of language as a social semiotic with its ideational, interpersonal and textual properties has been instrumental in shifting our attention from *syntactic structures* in the abstract sense to *meaning potential* in communicative settings. Duranti and Goodwin (1992) attest at least four layers of context which can impinge on meaning making: (i) physical/social setting; (ii) behavioural context, including nonverbal communication and use of space; (iii) language and its indexical function, and (iv) extra-situational context. As Sarangi argues in his chapter, an activity type framework would cut across all these four levels of context, as participants shift between different contexts, mainly signalled through a deployment of different 'discourse types' (Fairclough 1992a) or 'contextualisation cues' (Gumperz 1982). Relevant here is Cicourel's (1992) ecological view of context, or what he calls the 'interpenetration of communicative contexts', as a necessary basis for unpacking what constitutes an understanding of social phenomena.

In the same way that a multi-layered notion of context is an integral part of discourse study,[5] so a differentiated notion of speaker-hearer is equally relevant to understanding participation structure and shifts in footing and frames vis-à-vis activity-specific constraints. In his analytical framework for participant structure, Goffman (1981) challenges the traditional concepts of speaker and hearer as being too global, and argues in favour of a differentiated account of production and reception formats, e.g., spokesperson, mouthpiece, bystander, overhearer etc. Slippages between and across footings and frames allow participants to turn context-specific constraints into interactional resources in their pursuit of communicative goals.

The primacy of discourse: discursive turns within and across disciplinary boundaries

As is evident, discourse – both as context and as social interaction – is not the prerogative of the discipline of linguistics. Other allied disciplines have contributed immensely to our understanding of how communication works. In what follows we allude to the discursive turns within some of these disciplines by picking out the main threads and key figures.

Starting with *Philosophy*, the breakaway from an analytic tradition (based on truth, values and abstraction) to a hermeneutic one (based on human understanding as in the case of e.g., Heidegger, Gadamar, Schutz, Wittgenstein) marks a discursive turn. First, Wittgenstein (1958: 12) underlined philosophy's anti-positivistic stance, with his proposal of the notion of language games to 'bring into prominence the fact that speaking a language is part of an activity, or of a form of life'. For him, the meaning of an utterance is a matter of use, and therefore our understanding of social action and utterance must always involve an awareness of the appropriate 'form of life' in which the utterance is situated. This resonates with Voloshinov's ([1929] 1986) emphasis on the social and intersubjective dimensions of language use – that parole is not an individual but rather a social phenomenon (Rommetveit 1974).

Gadamar (1975) argues that our understanding of social action amounts to interpreting a text, and adds that we understand parts in terms of the whole and vice versa. In other words, understanding is not a simple matter of adding together the meanings of individual words. Viewed from our linguistic perspective this may not seem to have been telling us anything significantly new even at the time, but such developments within philosophy can be connected to relevant schools of thinking within linguistics and elsewhere. The view that the overall context of the utterance influences meaning-making resonates with Jakobson ([1960] 1990: 114):

> A systematic consideration of multiform whole-part relations broadly extends the scope of our science; it allows a systematic analysis of verbal messages with respect both to the code and to the context; it uncovers the complex interaction of the various levels of language, from the largest to the smallest units, and the constant interplay of diverse verbal functions ... Indeed a rich scale of tensions between wholes and parts is involved in the constitution of language where *the part for the whole and, on the other hand, the whole for the part, the genus for the species, and the species for the individual* are the fundamental devices. (his emphasis)

Even for Habermas (1984, 1987), who is mainly preoccupied with a universalist pragmatics, the social conditioning of meaning remains a paramount feature of his theory of communicative action.

A discursive turn in *Cultural Anthropology* is presupposed in Geertz's (1973) conceptualisation of culture as interpretation, or 'thick description', while Sherzer (1987) draws explicitly on the works of Hymes and Gumperz in his advocacy of a discourse view of culture. This move has to be seen against the backdrop of the anthropological linguistics of Sapir (see Mandelbaum 1958) and Whorf (1956), which, as we saw above, had much earlier suggested a link between grammar (in the narrow sense of the term) and culturally salient thought patterns. Sherzer argues:

> Instead of asking such questions as 'does grammar reflect culture' or 'is culture determined by grammar', or 'are there isomorphisms between grammar and culture', we [should] rather start with discourse, which is the nexus, the actual and

concrete expression of the language-culture-society relationship. It is discourse which creates, recreates, focuses, modifies, and transmits both culture and language and their intersection. (Sherzer 1987: 296)

Both linguists and anthropologists have traditionally treated discourse as an invisible glass through which the researcher perceives the reality of grammar, social relations, ecological practices, and belief systems. But the glass itself, discourse and its structure, the actual medium through which knowledge (linguistic and cultural) is produced, conceived, transmitted, and acquired, by members of societies and by researchers, is given little attention. (Sherzer 1987: 305)

There are two main points which need our attention. First, grammar is seen as distinct from discourse: grammar is narrowly conceived of as a set of abstract rules, whereas discourse is equated with actual practice. Second, in calling for attention to discourse, Sherzer is alluding to the well-known dilemma of topic vs resource in social science (see below). Sherzer's own study of 'verbal-duel bargaining' and 'echo words' in their interactional environment foregrounds the relevance of the context-based interpretation of everyday practice. In other words, lived everyday practice becomes an object of study in its own right. Likewise, Moerman's (1988) work on the ethnic identity of the Lau stands as a good example of a discursive, interactional approach to the study of another culture, however defined. Scollon (this volume) argues for combining ethnography and discourse analysis in the study of another community – in his case, the Hong Kong Chinese student community. Nevertheless, such an integrated framework, he goes on to show, still offers only a partial understanding of social life, as Labov and Fanshel (1977) had attested earlier.

Within *History*, we note that Foucault (1971, 1972) underlines the importance of discourse for an understanding of social change in its historical context – an observation which has, in the past decade, influenced the field of critical discourse analysis. For Foucault, discourse is best understood as a system of the possibility of knowledge – enabling us, and at the same time constraining us, to do things. He draws attention to how individuals occupy certain 'subject positions' in both senses of the term: they produce discourse as well as being products of their own discourses. Philp (1985: 69) formulates Foucault's position as follows:

[T]he rules of a discourse are not rules which individuals consciously follow; a discourse is not a method or canon of enquiry. Rather, these rules provide the necessary preconditions for the formation of statements, and as such they operate 'behind the backs' of speakers of a discourse. Indeed, the place, function and character of the 'knowers', authors and audiences of discourse are also a function of these discursive rules.

We can see here a juxtaposition to the mainstream linguistic view of discourse as a method (in the sense of looking beyond the sentence in order to find coherence in message structure, patterns of turn-taking etc). For

Foucault, however, discourse is a topic to be investigated by an array of methodological tools such as 'ethnology' and 'the monument'.

Such a broad conceptualisation of discourse poses problems about its operationalisation for analytic purposes (Kendall and Wickham 1999, Prior 1997). Critical discourse analysts, especially Fairclough (passim), draw our attention to the ways in which textual analysis can be integrated with social analysis (see Fairclough 1992b, Sarangi and Slembrouck 1996).[6] As Cicourel (1981), among others, sees it, the relation between the micro and the macro should be the main concern of text and discourse analysis.

Armed with sophisticated analytic tools, any thematic focus would yield social evaluations. In this volume, most of the contributors provide a link between the micro and macro levels of social analysis: Coupland/Coupland focus on pronominal referencing in discussions in geriatric clinics against the backdrop of patient-centred medical care (see also Fairclough's analysis of the pronoun 'we' and the conjunction 'and' in discourses of politics and governance); Sarangi looks at information and advice sequences in genetic counselling and relates such practices to professional concerns about non-directiveness; Roberts scrutinises the subtle role of prosody and arrhythmia in intercultural encounters and the extent to which mismatches at this level can potentially contribute to discrimination and social exclusion; Candlin examines the thematic structure of messages in nurse-patient encounters and relates this analysis to the apparent empowerment of patients; Van Leeuwen focuses on the grammatical realisation of purpose and links it to the ways in which school text books construct parent-child role-relationships in our society. Even the microscopic forensic analysis of texts which Coulthard undertakes in the last chapter, is very much part of a broader social and institutional process. So most of the analytic stances espoused here are related to broader socio-political issues: patient autonomy, institutional discrimination, miscarriage of justice etc. When it comes to linking micro discourse analysis with socio-political structures, we need to see discourse not as a unit beyond the sentence, but as social practice.

Social life and interaction as a topic for sociological analysis

The other discipline which has close ties with language and interaction analysis is *Sociology*. As Douglas (1971: 4) rightly points out, the Durkheimian (sociologistic) adage that 'the social must be explained socially' in order to avoid the reductionism associated with micro-level analysis, misses the point that all macro-level analysis of social structure is based on one's understanding of everyday life in its localised settings. This is a turn away from those macro studies which focus on members' practices and orientations to how social order is maintained and displayed. Interaction is the resource through which members sustain social order and what we regard as society. So, study of social interaction in detail is not reductionist; rather it is the study of 'the interaction order' which is a resource for us to understand what social structures are. Indeed within phenomenological sociology, the microanalysis of social interaction is the only way to study the broad fabric of social structure.[7] Rather than seeing the macro and micro interests being divisive and oppositional, long range perspectives and microscopic perspectives can potentially be reconciled within social analysis.

In the social anthropological tradition, we notice this in Bailey's (1971: 2–3) commitment to the study of what he calls the 'small politics' of everyday life: 'reputations and gossip are the small beer of small people and are worthy of intellectual attention'. He (ibid: 3) clearly states that 'if our object is to explore regular patterns in social behaviour, the activities of small people provide evidence no less useful than the actions of statesmen'. As he goes on to show in the small village of Valloire in the French Alps, when a woman appears in the public arena wearing an apron, it is a way of signalling that she has pressing domestic tasks to return to and so cannot stop for gossiping. That the woman is politically 'off-stage' can only be understood by paying attention to the local everyday practices. If a particular community goes about conducting their lives by using specific communicative resources (such as the apron in this case), then an analyst needs to turn the members' resource/method into a topic of investigation in its own right. In other words, the 'social' cannot be taken as a given to explain the meaning of human activity.

Analysing the social game: topic or resource?

In many of our neighbouring disciplines as discussed above, discourse seems to have been a resource for understanding social life and human action. In the past few decades, within sociology, we notice a drift towards studying social action in its own right, rather than as a simple manifestation of social structure. In particular Goffman (1964), in his influential paper titled 'the neglected situation' calls for a foregrounding of 'the interaction order' in the analysis of social performance.

The confounding of topic/resource is characteristic of sociological analysis, prior to the arrival of Schutz's (1962) phenomenology. As Douglas (1971: 11) boldly puts it:

> *Any scientific understanding of human action, at whatever level of ordering or generality, must begin with and be built upon an understanding of the everyday life of the members performing those actions.* (To fail to see this and to act in accord with it is to commit what we might call the *fallacy of abstractionism*, that is, the fallacy of believing that you can know in a more abstract form what you do not know in the particular form.) (his emphasis)

He goes on to label this as the 'natural stance' in opposition to the 'absolutist stance' while acknowledging that '[W]e must continue to do macro analysis for very pressing practical reasons' (1971: 11).

In more recent years this 'natural stance' has become the bedrock of the domain of those working within ethnomethodology, and later conversation analysis, as they seek to 'describe methods persons use in doing social life' (Sacks 1984: 21). 'Doing social life' here suggests a move away from grand theories about social structure towards studying mundane, local, everyday activities in their own right. This is echoed by Zimmerman and Pollner (1971: 82–3):

> Through one technique or another, the received social world is available as a topic of investigation. The social world is attended to as a domain whose stable properties are discoverable by *some* method . . . The topic then would consist not in the social order as ordinarily conceived, but rather in the ways in which members assemble particular scenes so as to provide for one another evidences of a social order as-ordinarily-conceived. (their emphasis)

The analytic job thus resembles what ordinary members do (which is what Douglas above refers to as the natural stance). Sacks (1984: 21) offers a blueprint for this methodology:

> The detailed ways in which actual, naturally occurring social activities occur are subjectable to formal description.
>
> Social activities – actual, singular sequences of them – are methodical occurrences. That is, their description consists of the description of sets of formal procedures persons employ.
>
> The methods persons employ to produce their activities permit formal description of singular occurrences that are generalisable in intuitively nonapparent ways and are highly reproducibly usable.

What Sacks points to here is that in examining ordinariness we are bound to discover orderliness 'at all points'. Conversation analysis thus aims to 'transform, in an almost literal, physical sense, our view of "what happened", from a matter of a particular interaction done by particular people, to a matter of interactions as products of a machinery' (1984: 26). Elsewhere, Sacks (1985: 15) explicitly states:

> A first rule of procedure in doing analysis, a rule that you absolutely must use or you can't do the work, is this: In setting up what it is that seems to have happened, preparatory to solving the problem, do not let your notion of what could conceivably happen decide for you what must have happened.

The topic/resource dilemma is thus recast as a problematic in keeping analysts' interpretive method distinct from participants' own methods of commonsense making. This is echoed by Schegloff (1997) when he insists that a technical analysis of text, which privileges the participants' perspective, is the only possible starting point. Cicourel (1980: 101), however, is more cautious when it comes to equating participants' reasoning with analytic reasoning:

> Forms of reasoning are viewed as central to the researcher's understanding of the way speakers and hearers presumably understand each other. The forms of

reasoning we attribute to the participants of discourse parallel the reasoning we employ as researchers in making sense of the speech acts we record and listen to in arriving at some form of analysis. But as researchers we can, of course, specify formal aspects of discourse, produce systematic descriptions, and note emergent properties of the interaction. Yet we cannot attribute such properties unequivocally to the knowledge base of the participants.

A discursive turn is now also evident in *Psychology* under the label 'discursive psychology' (see especially Edwards and Potter 1992, Harré and Stearns 1995). This tradition draws heavily on work in another discipline, that of the conversation analysts who view social actions, feelings, emotions etc as interactional productions. There is thus a move away from speculating about the internal states of the mind, as well as from the confines of the natural scientific methodology associated with the experimental laboratory set-up. But as Sarangi and Wilson (1998: 2) note:

> [T]hey are a new breed of psychologists (rather than a new breed of discourse analysts) who use discourse to understand core psychological issues, and in doing so challenge the orthodoxy of specific cognitive and experimental approaches to central psycho-cognitive phenomena.

The topic/resource dichotomy in discourse study: structure and function as frames of analysis

Discourse forces one to look closely at social life, so one discovers patterns and nuances in social activities. Social life, like language, is assembled according to a grammar. This is the grammar of social interaction, or the 'organisation of practices . . . which underlie the organisation of social life' (Schegloff et al. 1996: 2). Social life as a topic presents itself for decoding and we need a method as well as a rationale for doing so. We have already discussed how the topic/resource dichotomy pervades sociological analysis. Let us now consider the same problematic with regard to discourse scholarship.

Turning to discourse as a topic of study,[8] Schiffrin (1990: 98) summarises the two-fold focus:

> Discourse itself has often been viewed as both structure, i.e. a unit of language that is larger than the sentence, and as the realisation of functions, i.e. as the use of language for social, expressive, and referential purposes . . . These two different definitions of discourse can lead to radically different descriptions and analyses of the same text because they define the task in such different ways.

As we saw earlier, Harris (1952) was interested in analysing discourse in structural and sequential terms, with a focus on the relative distributional relations among elements. His analysis attends to the structural representation through what he calls a 'double array' consisting of a horizontal axis and a vertical axis. This is a rigorous model, empirically feasible, which can potentially be used for finding correlations: 'that the discourses of a particular person, social group, style, or subject-matter exhibit not only particular meanings (in their selection of morphemes) but also characteristic formal features' (1952: 3). Such formal findings, Harris goes on to argue, can then form a basis for further interpretative work (such as what the text producer and receiver might intend or read into a particular text). Corpus-based studies on spoken and written grammar (e.g., Leech in this volume) see texts as objective linguistic phenomena which can be subjected to empirical analysis.[9]

Other strands of discourse analysis (e.g., Sinclair and Coulthard 1975, Labov and Fanshel 1977) also focus on discourse structure beyond the level of the sentence and the turn. The IRF (initiation-response-feedback) sequence is identified as characteristic of teacher-pupil interaction and forms a basis for understanding other possible patterns such as that of court-room interaction which is formulated as Q-A (question-answer) sequences, or casual conversation where we find elaborate inserted sequences, which follow neither the IRF sequence nor the Q-A sequence. These studies are not only structural, they also take a functionalist perspective: what functions are routinely served by, say, questions in a given setting. Such a goal for finding patterns in talk and text (see in particular the developments in genre analysis) may be seen as favouring the analyst's perspective to the participants' perspective.

The topic/resource dichotomy comes to the fore in Myers' (this volume) analysis of interactional patterns in focus groups. Unlike the way in which traditional sociological research would use focus groups for formulating public choice and decisions, Myers' approach puts the focus on how the participants interactionally orient to belonging to this group – a highly social activity, beyond or even at the expense of the very research purpose which brought about this group's existence. This is also where a sociological research instrument becomes a topic of discourse analysis.

The book's scope, structure and content

One way of understanding the value of discourse in social life is to expand both the analytic frameworks and the range of data types and sites: spoken, written, institutional, conversational etc. This edited collection attempts a wide coverage in order to illustrate the similarities and differences which constitute the field of discourse study. The book comprises fifteen chapters, but they defy any clear sequential or thematic structure. One could block them in terms of written text analysis (examples include Fairclough, Widdowson, Wodak, van Leeuwen etc) as opposed to talk analysis (Candlin, Coupland/Coupland, Hasan, Maley, Myers, Roberts, Sarangi etc). But such a dichotomisation would presuppose that a distinction between talk and text is a given. Other possible criteria for organising the chapters would have been on the basis of micro or macro contextual analysis or in terms of the home domain vs the public domain. But, like all other binary divisions, that would be to impose an artificial order. As Hymes (1986: 50) suggests:

> Such dichotomies do us the service of naming diversity. They do us the disservice of reducing diversity to polar opposites. Such oppositions recurrently invite evaluation, so that one is seen as good and the other bad, or one as complex and the other simple, or one as systematic, explicit, ordered, or rational, and the other not.

Our view is that the various data types and settings impact upon each other, and that the reading of any given chapter becomes much richer when it is read alongside another which treats a similar type of data or uses a similar methodology. Although we have organised the chapters in a particular sequence in the contents page, there is no particular reason to read them in that sequence. In fact we are breaking the rule ourselves now by offering a different coherence as we introduce the chapters.

The volume opens with a broad characterisation of the interrelationship between language and context. **Srikant Sarangi** brings together two key dimensions of discourse analysis – activity types and discourse types – and argues for the seminal concept of hybridity to account for actual interactional routines. He takes genetic counselling as both a discourse type and an activity type, and analyses the three critical moments that constitute counselling: information giving, advice giving and negotiating decisions about predictive testing. Sarangi begins by reviewing studies of counselling in other contexts, which have been mainly studied in terms of turn design and the packaging of information and advice. He argues that in the genetic counselling setting, the information-as-explanation sequence allows counsellors to turn 'advice seeking' into 'information giving' routines, and thereby maintain their non-directive stance. He suggests that hybridity, i.e., shifts between activity types and discourse types, is routinely observable in institutional encounters, and he goes on to demonstrate how both professionals and their clients strategically manipulate the sequential patterns within the constraints of an activity type in order to achieve differential communicative outcomes.

Two other chapters – Candlin and Coupland/Coupland – also deal with the medical site. **Sally Candlin** offers an account of nurse-patient encounters, an area that has been neglected in medical discourse research. Most of the sociolinguistic and disocurse analytic studies of the medical setting have focused on doctor-patient encounters, even though patients spend much less time with doctors. Candlin argues that often the quality of care the patient receives depends crucially on the quality of nurse-patient interaction. The quality of interaction, in turn, will partly depend on the level of training and experience the nurse practitioner brings to the encounter. Candlin begins with a diversified model of what constitutes nursing practice and pitches her analysis against the backdrop of broader changes in patient empowerment and patient-centred medical care. Any such changes must have an impact at the discourse level – see Coupland/Coupland for a discussion of a similar linkage between the institutional and interactional level – but Candlin's analysis suggests that, despite the appearance of democratisation, with patients offering long self-narratives, the interactional asymmetry persists.

Nik Coupland and Justine Coupland focus on data in the area of gerontology and, following Candlin (1997), foreground discourse analysis as a sound basis for getting at institutional and social practices. They bring together the ideological underpinning of the geriatric clinic – committed to patient autonomy – and the dynamics of multi-party conversation. The problem they examine is that many patients have an accompanying son or daughter who often acts as a (self-selected) spokesperson and the very presence of this third party threatens the ideological basis of care for the patient. The relational frames are ambivalent to start with, and are open to negotiation as talk proceeds. Coupland/Coupland focus in detail on the use of pronouns and the interactional work they do in endorsing or contesting various relational frames. The pronominal references, with their turn design potential, make the relational frame more complex in the process of establishing 'entitlements' and 'responsibilities'. They draw our attention to how the discursive manifestation of relational ambivalence signals the reconfiguration of role-relationships associated with chronic illness in our society.

The similarities and difference between the chapters by Coupland/Coupland and Hasan are striking. In the former we have an institutional site with role-relations being redefined in social terms, where the 'child' often speaks on behalf of the elderly parent/patient; in the latter we see the mother using discourse strategies to manipulate the child. **Ruqaiya Hasan** begins with the topic of 'contextual shifts' and the way young children learn to manage them. By contextual shift she means that the ongoing topic may suddenly change and the context suddenly be re-classified – so, for example, participants who were in a discussion about friends or clothes may suddenly find themselves in an argument – although, as Hasan emphasises, a contextual shift does not necessarily represent a complete break; it may simply become 'a subtext to the ongoing text, playing some part in its management'. Her research claim is that 'the disposition to entertain shifting boundaries in discursive situations is something that is very likely to have been inculcated early' in childhood. She goes on to illustrate from her data that there are significant differences in children's experience of the management of contextual shifts – one mother is seen to encourage, another to actively discourage shifts – and argues that this will result in a differential ability to handle contextual shifts in later life.

In commenting on data collected from a mother who encourages shifts, Hasan draws attention to the absence of disjunction – talk on one topic is seen to merge seamlessly into talk on another, which in itself is not a surprising or novel finding. However, what is fascinating is the observation that these seamless shifts are a way of the mother controlling the child. The shifts are away from a context concerned with a conflictual topic and serve to distract the child from her objections to the mother's plans. Hasan generalises: 'when . . . talk appears to move away from the particular ongoing context to something apparently unrelated to the business in hand, this shift . . . contributes significantly to the carrying out of the primary activity'. She notes that the continuity across the shift is maintained semantically and lexicogrammatically in the form of cohesive chains and suggests that, when such cohesion is lacking, the talk is typically 'not perceived as being part of the same ongoing text'.

Looked at from a slightly different angle, the notion of socialisation through language use is central to Hasan's analysis of mother-child interaction. The child learns his/her way into becoming a legitimate member of the society. **Greg Myers** shares a similar concern when he looks at the interactional fabric of the 'focus group' in order to examine how sociability emerges through talk. By bringing together Goffman and Simmel, he draws our attention to a hitherto neglected aspect of language and interaction – that of sociability. Myers rightly questions the over-indulgence of discourse analysts with the strategic, goal-orientedness nature of communication (see our earlier discussion Bailey's call to study 'small politics' in this regard). A further point of departure for him is that we should not take speech communities for granted, but instead examine how language plays a part in bringing about socialisation at the interactional plane. For his analysis, Myers chooses the focus group to explicate members' socialisation practices. As we know, focus groups are made up artificially: these are individuals brought along for a specific purpose (unlike natural groups of friends or colleagues). It is unlike studying existing speech communities where 'groupness' is taken as an analytic given. Myers argues that although focus groups are mainly formed for sampling public opinions and attitudes, the participating members of these groups gel together and 'play relations' through exchanging agreement tokens, maintaining topics while signalling disagreement etc. Different interaction patterns however emerge across different focus group communities, as we see here with regard to the 'small business group' and the 'new Europeans'. Even these individual groups do not inhabit a shared relational history, yet a society emerges in interactional terms as language permeates social cohesion.

Socialisation is also at the heart of **Celia Roberts'** focus on gatekeeping encounters and on how insider/outsider role-relations are worked up in interactional moments. She conceptualises interviews as gatekeeping, in that they reflect divides but also mask the purpose. She notes that the objectivity and efficiency of interviews is questioned in diverse, multicultural societies, because certain ways of saying and doing things become central to defining who is 'one of us'. This is where, Roberts argues, a sophisticated analysis of interaction will help to uncover cultural differences in relation to the construction of performed/situated identities. Her theoretical basis is formed by integrating Gumperz's tradition of interactional sociolinguistics and

Erickson's micro-ethnography. Using data from a medical oral examination setting, Roberts demonstrates that intentionality is interactionally accomplished and analysable, a factor which has been ignored by CA. Like Myers, she shows how an interactional basis can be provided for looking at inferencing and, in addition, she establishes a link between interactional discomfort and social/institutional exclusion. Thus there may be some association between micro interactional patterns and their negative evaluation, leading to potential discrimination in stratified multicultural societies. Roberts acknowledges that certain aspects (e.g. prosody) become fossilised with secondary socialisation, and can contribute to a reification of discriminatory practices. Discourse analysts in a way can make minute disocurse features transparent and raise awareness about their inferencing potential on both sides of the 'gate'.

Robert Kaplan is also interested in the intercultural communication setting, but his focus is on the different patterning in text realisation across cultural groups. With regard to different patterning of textual organisations, what one group might regard as linear and straightforward may not seem so to another group. Kaplan offers a historical overview of the Contrastive Rhetoric (CR) tradition and contextualises it with regard to its practice and application. He acknowledges the potential drawbacks of earlier studies in CR and goes on to provide a revised model by drawing our attention to new subtleties. Kaplan is particularly interested in language learning programmes across linguistic and cultural differences and underlines how what he refers to as 'blank spaces' in each language system pose difficulties when we attempt to translate and interpret one language/culture system on the basis of our knowledge of another. The blank spaces, he notes, are identifiable at all levels: lexical, syntactic as well as rhetorical. As we can see, the roots of the CR tradition can be traced to the earlier work of Sapir and Whorf on linguistic relativity. The focus on variations across language systems and users is a move away from the Chomskyan paradigm of Universal Grammar. In CR work, the linguistic resource and its lack within specific groups of language users becomes the topic of study.

One of the major current research paradigms is that of critical discourse analysis (CDA), developing from work by Roger Fowler, Bob Hodge, Gunther Kress and Tony Trew at the University of East Anglia in the late '70s (Fowler et al. 1979). More recently the theory has been principally developed and exemplified by Norman Fairclough in a series of books (1989, 1992a, 1995). This work has aroused strong emotions in a normally phlegmatic profession and has produced groups of fiercely loyal supporters and aggressively outspoken critics. In this book we include contributions from four of the major figures in the debate. First, Widdowson argues the case for the prosecution and then follow chapters by Fairclough, Wodak and Van Leeuwen.

Henry Widdowson begins by distinguishing the two meanings of 'critical': he suggests that in literary criticism the purpose is to appreciate aesthetic effect, whereas in CDA it is rather to uncover covert ideological intent. Widdowson points out that CDA in fact has its origins in literary criticism and highlights the similarities between the two enterprises: 'both assume a privileged authority to provide an exegesis and reveal to unenlightened readers covert meanings which would otherwise escape their notice.' The importance of the comparison, Widdowson asserts, is that the two kinds of texts in fact need *different* reading practices – as for a work of literature there is no objective, real world co-reference, every nuance of meaning must be explored. Whereas in real world texts the co-operative principle comes into play and authors know they can be held accountable for their text(s) as they can be tested for accuracy and truthfulness against the real world.

Essentially, Widdowson's criticism of CDA is that the analyst assumes the stance of a privileged reader who focuses on a small number of textual features, but

a) gives no methodology for deciding which features ought to be focused on;

b) argues for the ideological effect of a given isolated feature like nominalization, personification or passivisation, without demonstrating the validity of that interpretation either by reference to the same feature functioning in other texts or by testing the text on a series of readers to confirm that the feature does indeed have this communicative effect;

c) chooses to analyse (parts of) texts without full reference to the outside world to which they refer;

d) insists on taking up a deliberately non-co-operative reading position.

Widdowson's chapter provides a context for readers to engage with those of Wodak and Fairclough. They do not, nor were they asked to, reply to Widdowson, nor do they in these chapters undertake the kind of interpretative microanalysis of texts that Widdowson attacks so strongly – instead they provide two examples of the range of work currently being undertaken within the CDA paradigm.

Norman Fairclough focuses on two orders of discourse, *governance* and *politics*, which, he argues, are 'based on contrary logics' and 'in a relationship of tension and struggle'. He sees the regime of governance as trying to marginalise and suppress disagreement, whereas politics sets out to disagree and open governance to scrutiny in order to expose this marginalisation and suppression. To exemplify he focuses on the discourse of the British New Labour party, currently in government, in order to show how dialogue is squeezed out. Focusing on extracts from two speeches, Fairclough shows how Prime Minister Blair uses *and* to link concepts that were previously thought to be incompatible so as to illustrate his political innovation, the 'Third Way', in action. In addition, he illustrates how *we* functions to paper over the cracks of inconsistencies.

Later, examining a Green Paper on welfare reform, Fairclough notes how most political voices are excluded most of the time – while we are told that 'the vast majority of single parents want to work', we are not told either how the report writer knows, or what are the views and reasoning of the minority and we hear nothing at all about the views of welfare professionals and experts. He goes on to analyse the structure and reception of the Green Paper to demonstrate how most questioning and debate is circumvented and how those questions which are offered to the reader presuppose a pre-acceptance of the main political assumptions whose questioning might otherwise have been the reader's natural reaction. Fairclough concludes by offering a set of necessary properties of democratic dialogue and asserting the need for 'a better understanding of how and why interactions fail as democratic dialogue' and of 'what hitherto un- or under-realised potentials for democratic dialogue can be discerned . . . within them'.

Ruth Wodak starts from the standpoint that 'it is through discursive interaction that meanings are produced and transmitted, that institutional roles are constructed and power relations developed and maintained'. Her data come from E.U. meetings about employment policies and her interest is in recontextualisation, in how ideas and their expression change as they are transformed from written to oral and back again and how they reflect attempts to express and reconcile conflicts of interest. She distinguishes four types of transformation: addition, deletion, substitution and rearrangement and uses these to chart the changes from one draft to another. In one place she notes a re-arrangement to change emphasis, in another an addition to give voice to a trade union view, in a third a substitution of 'people' for 'public opinion' to emphasise the actor, in another deletion to clarify the title of the whole document. Looking at the wider canvas Wodak finds that these devices are the linguistic realisations of four contradictory recontextualisation tendencies in the data: static versus dynamic; simplicity versus complexity; precision versus vagueness; argumentation versus statement and generalising claims. In concluding she argues for a broader analytic approach, asserting that critical discourse analysis alone is insufficient, it needs to be complemented by an interdisciplinary, applied linguistic approach.

In his chapter **Theo van Leeuwen** first creates one more tool for the critical analysis of texts – a new description of a small part of the grammar of English, the grammar of purpose – and then applies it to a small set of texts. The data he chooses is all concerned with 'going to school for the first time', and ranges from story-books for young children through newspaper articles for parents to teacher-training textbooks, the majority of which he finds to be 'continually constructing purposes'. As most purpose is realised grammatically in the clause, most of the examples he uses for exemplificatory purposes in presenting his analysis are isolated sentences, but in the final section of the chapter he demonstrates one way of using the methodology insightfully in the analysis of whole texts. He begins by pointing out that the discursive construction of purposeful action requires three elements – a purpose, a purposeful action, and a link between the two – which may be explicit or implicit. He suggests that purposes may be 'goal-oriented', typically realised by "in order to", 'means-oriented', typically realised by "by means of", or 'effective' in which case it is the outcome that is emphasised. Once he has set up the framework, Van Leeuwen uses it to compare and contrast in interesting ways two of the story-books, *Mary Kate and the School Bus*, a children's Penguin and *Mark and Mandy* a mass-market book sold through newsagents and supermarkets. Mary Kate is found to be 'constantly represented as engaged in intentional goal-oriented actions', whereas what Mark and Mandy do is represented as the 'effect of physical states and emotions'. There were similar findings for two factual texts: *And so to School*, a specialist publication for teachers, had large numbers of goal- and means-oriented purpose constructions, whereas *Your Child and Success at School*, a magazine format booklet for parents and, like *Mark and Mandy* sold through newsagents, contained very few goal- and means-oriented actions performed by either parents or children.

These are admittedly pilot findings, but the indications are clear – children in a book which is aimed at the middle class market and which focuses on a middle class child attending a middle class school are 'endowed with purposefulness', while in the mass-market publication children are represented as 'acting on impulse' or as reacting to 'authoritative commands'. An obvious question for the reader is how far these books can be seen as reflecting and how far as helping to condition the situation. But, as Van Leeuwen concludes, 'clearly the discursive distribution of purposefulness has everything to do with the distribution of power in concrete social practices and in society generally'. This new analytic tool makes it easier for readers and critical discourse analysts alike to externalise their perceptions of what is happening.

Many analyses of discourse rely on a detailed consideration of grammatical features. As we have seen both Candlin and Wodak focus on theme and rheme, while Fairclough and Coupland/Coupland discuss the significance of pronoun selection. All such analyses, irrespective of whether the data is written or spoken, rely on grammatical descriptions which were essentially designed for written text. **Geoffrey Leech**, in his chapter, takes up the question of how far one needs different grammatical descriptions to handle spoken and written texts. After considering two more radical proposals, his own conclusion is that the same basic descriptive apparatus can be used for both spoken and written texts, but that there are interesting and significant differences in terms of the relative distribution of grammatical and lexical features. These findings, which are presented in detail in the newly published *Longman Grammar of Spoken and Written English* (1999), confirm the validity of using the same grammatical categories for analysing both types of text, while at the same time giving those interested in comparing and contrasting written and spoken texts a way of doing so. Two areas of application are Fairclough's concern with the 'conversationalisation' of written texts and Coulthard's with testing the authenticity of disputed contemporaneous records of interaction made by the police, when the appearance of features of written grammar can be diagnostic of fabrication.

Ron Scollon suggests how discourse analysis can be aided by ethnography. He takes up the issue of ethnographic understanding – as an aspect of discourse study – but argues that ethnography, by nature, is fundamentally unfinalisable. By extension, discourse analysis cannot claim to be an enterprise in omniscience. Scollon combines aspects of literacy practices with multi-modal analysis of social life. A photograph of a street in Hong Kong at the critical moment in the handover of Hong Kong to China shows the embedding of different discourses. Even the size of lettering and the choice of dialect can be analysed – 'the discourse of the transition of political sovereignty are legible here'. Our social belonging is partly constituted in road names, store names etc.: in Moerman's (1988) terms, it's like 'a world in a grain of rice'.

Scollon's interest in public discourse provides a basis for drawing on various strands of analysis. He draws on the works of Barthes and Bakhtin, as well as scholars in communication studies, to illustrate how these public discourses capture the sentiment of the times. An investigation of textual practices can always uncover dominant sociopolitical trends since texts are inherently addressee-oriented. The central question which concerns Scollon is: to what extent can we discern reading practices from the way the text is produced and displayed? He raises the issue of methodological interdiscursivity since analysts' and participants' interpretations are bound to be different. The irony is that a different discourse in the end misrepresents the discourse of social life. The problem about the authenticity and authority of ethnographic texts is however a long standing one (see Clifford and Marcus 1986). To illustrate the methodological issues, Scollon narrates the life history of a research project – academic writing practices of university students in Hong Kong – and the bearing different public discourses and their readings have on their academic practices. The research subjects, out of necessity, turn into co-researchers on the project. Also, in the focus group Scollon, like Myers, notices differential interpretations of the social world as different age groups are bounded by their own readings of what constitutes 'revolution' and 'reformation'.

Despite Scollon's caution about unfinalisability, there is an application dimension to discourse analytic work – we have already seen how Roberts, Kaplan and Leech, among others, see that description of language can serve practical ends. **Yon Maley** comes from a different perspective and presents research conducted in an entirely different discourse site, that where a subject specialist is performing as expert witness. However, like Hasan, she is concerned with the way that control of the discourse can be used to restrict options and like Fairclough, with the way in which the recontextualisation of the contributions of other participants can be used to mis-represent their intentions. Maley's data comes from a court case involving an endangered species, the Australian long-nosed Potoroo, whose judged presence or absence in a particular piece of land will determine whether or not that land can be exploited for quarrying.

Maley shows how the Opening Addresses by both sets of lawyers frame the rest of the case and delimit the area of disagreement. She then exemplifies the two major strategies lawyers have for handling the other side's expert evidence – they can set out to destroy the credibility of the witnesses and with it the value of their evidence, or they can highlight those aspects of the evidence which favour their own case. She shows how a major skill of the lawyer lies in *recontextualising* evidence and how in this case exactly the same piece of evidence from one of the expert witnesses, the discovery of potoroo hair, was used by both sides, one to argue that all that had been found was one potoroo hair, which probably did not indicate residence, the other to assert that not only was it/they resident, but also 'definitely . . . likely to be affected by the development'. Through this analysis Maley is able to demonstrate why so many expert witnesses leave court dissatisfied because they feel they have not been allowed to tell 'their story' and/or angry that what they said has been twisted, misunderstood or even ignored. Even those who do understand how the system works are still often very disgruntled when their evidence is (mis)used to tell another story, a story which they may not even believe or let alone support.

The volume ends with **Malcolm Coulthard** exploring what the linguist can say about individual style and authorship and exemplifying his observations with texts drawn in the main from real court cases where authorship has been disputed. The first three cases, all of which resulted in convictions based on verbal evidence and all of which were later referred to the Court of Appeal, are instances where the accused disputed police records of statements and/or interviews. In each case the linguistic evidence supported the accused and demonstrated that there was police involvement in the authorship of texts which had been represented to the Court as having been produced solely by the accused.

The chapter moves on to look at plagiarism and presents an analysis based on interesting findings about the degree of novelty and lexical uniqueness that one can expect to find in texts which have been produced independently though on the same topic. Methods for detecting student plagiarism automatically are also outlined. Next comes a discussion of the case of the Unabomber, Kaczynski, who was captured because his brother and sister-in-law recognised his style and who was then convicted because linguistic analysis was able to demonstrate the basis of their intuitive identification. Interestingly, this case gives some new support to the currently unfashionable concept of idiolect. The chapter ends, somewhat speculatively, by examining a new and promising technique for analysing individual style in terms two pervasive stylistic choices which are very much under the control of the author – sentence length and the degree of lexical innovativeness displayed by the author.

Conclusion: Discourse study as a community of practice

Earlier we characterised the contributors to this volume as 'discourse practitioners', but there was no intention to represent discourse as a unified, monolithic concept, as if what makes for the differences are the types of practitioner and their respective toolboxes. Again, Douglas (1971: 13) draws our attention to a crucial turning point in analysing everyday life:

> The first important point to note is that, instead of allowing our methods to determine our stance toward everyday life, we allow our stance to determine our methods.

The issue of observability is a moot methodological point, and it continues to be central to the analytic enterprise. Applied to corpus based studies of the kind Leech reports in this volume, the stance to an extent determines how texts should be sampled and whether a mapping of distribution patterns will reveal differences between written and spoken grammar. In this brand of text/discourse analysis, a main priority is to engage with real data, but without taking 'turn' or 'message' as the unit of analysis. Still for many of the contributors who deal with spoken interaction the 'turn' remains the basic unit of analysis.[10] Hasan, however, uses the semantic unit, referred to as 'message', instead of the structural unit 'turn', in order to identify the 'con/textual shifts' which are characteristic of much of her interactional data. Again, message structure can be kept analytically separate from the prosodic and intonational import of a given message. Roberts, as we saw, draws on Gumperz's (1982) notion of 'contextualisation cues' to account for such extralinguistic variables vis-a-vis 'coversational inferencing'.

If discourse analysis is to be seen as a method, it will mean challenging the received wisdom of linguistic fencing. The dimensions of discourse and pragmatics are not just add-ons, indeed there is a displacement of cumulative analysis by analysts explicitly suggesting their preferences and prioritising their theoretical standpoints and analytic categories. In fact, what we are dealing with here is 'discourses', very much in the way that culture was pluralised at the turn of the nineteenth century. Discourse study is without doubt an interdisciplinary domain and is currently known by different names and forms. As Tannen (1990: 110) puts it, 'if 'discourse' is nothing less than language itself, and 'discourse analysis' attempts to admit a broad range of research to the analysis of language, then it is by nature interdisciplinary'. However, interdisciplinarity, warns Widdowson (1988: 185–86), comes with a price:

> The conventions of the paradigm not only determine which topics are relevant. They determine too the approved manner of dealing with them: what counts as data, evidence and the inference of fact; what can be allowed as axiomatic, what needs to be substantiated by argument or empirical proof. The paradigm, therefore, is a sort of cultural construct. So it is that the disciplines which concern themselves with language, from their different epistemological perspectives, con-

stitute different cultures, different ways of conceiving language phenomena and different ways of using language to convey their conceptions . . . This means that those who try to promote cross-cultural relations by being inter-disciplinary are likely to be ostracised by both sides and to be stigmatised twice over as amateur and mountebank.

What we have in this volume is a range of different approaches to the analysis of talk, text and interaction, but even so we would argue that the contributors here, and elsewhere, form a community of practice in terms of what constitutes data, accountability to subjects/informants and a form of reflexivity. For all practitioners, discourse analysis can be viewed as activity-specific interpretation of social life, although this is not to deny substantial degrees of variation within and across particular discourse analytic traditions.[11] As Candlin (1997: x) alerts us: 'In identifying this collectivity . . . it is important not to homogenise diversity and lose the characteristic inter-discursivity emphasised by Bourdieu . . . , which is not only interpersonal within the community, but also intrapersonal within the ideological constitution of the individual'.

References

Austin, J. L. (1962) *How to Do Things with Words*. Oxford: Clarendon Press.

Bailey, F. G. (ed.) (1971) *Gifts and Poison: The Politics of Reputation*. Oxford: Basil Blackwell.

Brown, G. and Yule, G. (1983) *Discourse Analysis*. Cambridge: Cambridge University Press.

Caldas-Coulthard, C. R. and Coulthard, M. (eds) (1996) *Texts and Practices: Readings in Critical Discourse Analysis*. London: Routledge.

Candlin, C. N. (1997) General editor's preface. In B-L. Gunnarsson, P. Linell and B. Nordberg (eds) *The Construction of Professional Discourse*. London: Longman, viii–xiv.

Chomsky, N. (1957) *Syntactic Structures*. The Hague: Mouton.

Chomsky, N. (1959) Review of Verbal Behaviour by B. F. Skinner. *Language* 35, 26–58.

Cicourel, A. V. (1980) Three models of discourse analysis: the role of social structure. *Discourse Processes* 3, 101–132.

Cicourel, A. V. (1981) Notes on the integration of micro- and macro-levels of analysis. In K. Knor Cetina and A. V. Cicourel (eds) *Advances in Social Theory and Methodology*. London: Routledge, 51–80.

Cicourel, A. V. (1992) The interpenetration of communicative contexts: examples from medical encounters. In A. Duranti and C. Goodwin (eds), 291–310.

Clifford, J. and Marcus, G. E. (eds) (1986) *Writing Culture: The Poetics and Politics of Ethnography*. Berkeley: University of California Press.

Coulthard, M. (1977) *An Introduction to Discourse Analyses*. London: Longman.

Douglas, J. D. (ed.) (1971) *Understanding Everyday Life: Toward the Reconstruction of Sociological Knowledge*. London: Routledge and Kegan Paul.

Douglas, J. D. (1971) Understanding everyday life. In J. D. Douglas (ed.), 3–44.

Drew, P. and Heritage, J. (eds) (1992) *Talk at Work: Interaction in Institutional Settings.* Cambridge: Cambridge University Press.

Duranti, A. and Goodwin, C. (eds) (1992) *Rethinking Context: Language as an Interactive Phenomenon.* Cambridge: Cambridge University Press.

Edelsky, C. (1981) Who's got the floor? *Language in Society* 10, 383–421.

Edwards, D. and Potter, J. (1992) *Discursive Psychology.* London: Sage.

Fairclough, N. (1989) *Language and Power.* London: Longman.

Fairclough, N. (1992a) *Discourse and Social Change.* Cambridge: Polity Press.

Fairclough, N. (1992b) Discourse and text: linguistic and intertextual analysis within discourse analysis. *Discourse & Society* 3, 193–217.

Fairclough, N. (1995) *Critical Discourse Analysis.* London: Longman.

Foucault, M. (1971) *L'ordre du discours.* Paris: Gallimard.

Foucalut, M. (1972) *The Archaeology of Knowledge.* Trans. A. Sheridan-Smith. London: Tavistock.

Fowler, R., Hodge, R., Kress, G. and Trew, T. (1979) *Language and Control.* London: Routledge and Kegan Paul.

Gadamar, F. G. (1975) *Truth and Method.* Trans. G. Barden and J. Cumming. New York: Seabury Press.

Geertz, C. (1973) *The Interpretation of Cultures.* New York: Basic Books.

Goffman, G. (1964) The neglected situation. *American Anthropologist* 66 (Part II, Special Issue), 133–136.

Goffman, G. (1981) *Forms of Talk.* Oxford: Blackwell.

Grice, H. P. (1975) Logic and conversation. In P. Cole and J. L. Morgan (eds) *Syntax and Semantics, Vol. III: Speech Acts.* New York: Academic Press, 41–58.

Gumperz, J. J. (1982) *Discourse Strategies.* Cambridge: Cambridge University Press.

Gumperz, J. J. and Hymes, D. (eds) (1972) *Directions in Sociolinguistics: The Ethnography of Communication.* New York: Holt, Rinehart and Winston.

Habermas, J. (1984) *The Thory of Communicative Action (vol. I): Reason and the Rationalization of Society.* Cambridge: Polity Press.

Habermas, J. (1987) *The Theory of Communicative Action (vol. II): The Critique of Functionalist Reason.* Cambridge: Polity Press.

Halliday, M. A. K. (1978) *Language as Social Semiotic.* London: Edward Arnold.

Harré, R. and Stearne, P. (eds) (1995) *Discursive Psychology in Practice.* London: Sage.

Harris, Z. (1952) Discourse analysis. *Language* 28, 1, 1–30.

Hymes, D. (1964) Introduction: toward ethnography of communication. *American Anthropologist* 66, 2, 12–25.

Hymes, D. (1986) Discourse: scope without depth. *International Journal of the Sociology of Language* 57, 49–89.

Jakobson, R. ([1966] 1990) *On Language.* Edited by L. R. Wangh and M. Monville-Burston. Cambridge Mass: Harvard University Press.

Kendall, G. and Wickham, G. (1999) *Using Foucault's Methods.* London: Sage.

Labov, W. and Fanshel, D. (1977) *Therapeutic Discourse: Psychotherapy as Conversation.* New York: Academic Press.

Labov, W. and Waletzky, J. (1967) Narrative analysis: oral versions of personal experience. In J. Helms (ed.) *Essays in Verbal and Visual Arts.* Seattle: University of Washington Press, 12–44.

Lave, J. (1988) *Cognition in Practice: Mind, Mathematics and Culture in Everyday Life.* Cambridge: Cambridge University Press.

Levinson, S. (1983) *Pragmatics.* Cambridge: Cambridge University Press.

Mandelbaum, E. (ed.) (1958) *Selected Writing of Edward Sapir in Language, Culture and Personality*. Berkeley: University of California Press.

Moerman, M. (1988) *Talking Culture: Ethnography and Conversation Analysis*. Philadelphia: Pennsylvania University Press.

Ochs, E., Schegloff, E. and Thompson, S. (eds) (1996) *Interaction and Grammar*. Cambridge: Cambridge University Press.

Philp, M. (1985) Michel Foucault. In Q. Skinner (ed.) *The Return of the Grand Theory in the Human Sciences*. Cambridge: Cambridge University Press, 65–82.

Pratt, M. L. (1981) The ideology of speech act theory. *Centrum (New Series)* 1, 5–18.

Prior, L. (1997) Following in Foucault's footsteps: text and context in qualitative research. In D. Silverman (ed.) *Qualitative Research: Theory, Method and Practice*. London: Sage.

Roberts, C. and Sarangi, S. (1999) Hybridity ingatekeeping discourse: issues of practical relevance for the researcher. In S. Sarangi and C. Roberts (eds), 473–503.

Rommetveit, R. (1974) *On Message Structure: A Framework for the Study of Language and Communication*. London: John Wiley and Sons.

Rose, E. (1960) The English record of a natural sociology. *American Sociological Review* XXV (April), 193–208.

Sacks, H. (1984) Notes on methodology. In J. M. Atkinson and J. Heritage (eds) *Structures in Social Action: Studies in Conversation Analysis*. Cambridge: Cambridge University Press, 21–27.

Sacks, H. (1985) The inference-making machine: notes on observability. In T. van Dijk (ed.) *Handbook of Discourse Analysis, vol.3*. London: Academic Press.

Sarangi, S. and Roberts, C. (eds) (1999) *Talk, Work and Institutional Order: Discourse in Medical, Mediation and Management Settings*. Berlin: Mouton de Gruyter.

Sarangi, S. and Slembrouck, S. (1996) *Language, Bureaucracy and Social Control*. London: Longman.

Sarangi, S. and Wilson, J. (1998) Editorial. *Text* 18, 1, 1–6.

Saussure, F. ([1916] 1966) *Course in General Linguistics*. Trans. W. Baskin. New York: McGraw Hill.

Schegloff, E. A. (1997) Whose text? Whose context? *Discourse & Society* 8, 165–187.

Schegloff, E. A., Ochs, E. and Thompson, S. A. (1996) Introduction. In E. Ochs, E. A. Schegloff and S. A. Thompson (eds), 1–51.

Schiffrin, D. (1990) The language of discourse: connections inside and out. *Text* 10, 1/2, 97–100.

Schutz, A. (1962) *Collected Papers I: The Problem of Social Reality*. The Hague: Martinus Nijhoff.

Searle, J. R. (1969) *Speech Acts: An Essay in the Philosophy of Language*. Cambridge: Cambridge University Press.

Searle, J. R. (1995) *The Construction of Social Reality*. London: Penguin.

Shannon, C. and Weaver, W. (1949) *The Mathematical Theory of Communication*. Urbana, IL: University of Illinois Press.

Sherzer, J. (1987) A discourse-centred approach to language and culture. *American Anthropologist* 89, 295–309.

Simmel, G. ([1917] 1950) Sociability: an example of pure, or formal, sociology. In K. H. Wolff ed., *The Sociology of Georg Simmel*. New York: The Free Press, 40–57.

Sinclair, J. McH and Coulthard, M. (1975) *Towards an Analysis of Discourse: The English Used by Teachers and Pupils*. Oxford: Oxford University Press.

Skinner, B. F. (1957) *Verbal Behaviour*. New York: Appleton-Century-Crofts.

Stubbs, M. (1983) *Discourse Analysis*. Oxford: Basil Blackwell.

Stubbs, M. (1993) British traditions in text analysis: from Firth to Sinclair. In M. Baker, G. Francis and E.Tognini-Bonelli (eds) *Text and Technology: In Honour of John Sinclair*. Amsterdam: John Benjamins, 1–33.

Tannen, D. (ed.) (1982) *Analysing Discourse: Text and Talk*. Washington D.C.: Georgetown University Press.

Tannen, D. (1990) Discourse analysis: the excitement of diversity. *Text* 10, 1/2, 109–111.

Turner, R. (1971) Words, utterances and activities. In J. Douglas ed., 165–187.

Van Dijk, T. (ed.) (1985) *Handbook of Discourse Analysis (4 vols)*. London: Academic Press.

Van Dijk, T. (ed.) (1997) *Discourse Studies: A Multidisciplinary Introduction (2 vols)*. London: Sage.

Voloshinov, V. N. (1986 [1929]) *Marxism and the Philosophy of Language*. Trans. L. Matjeka and I. R. Titunik. Cambridge: Harvard University Press.

Wetherell, M. (1998) Positioning and interpretative repertoires: conversation analysis and post-structuralism in dialogue. *Discourse & Society* 9, 3, 387–412.

Whorf, B. L. (1956) *Language, Thought and Reality*. Cambridge, MA: MIT Press.

Widdowson, H. G. (1988) Poetry and pedagogy. In D. Tannen (ed.) *Linguistics in Context: Connecting Observation and Understanding*. Norwood, NJ: Ablex, 185–197.

Wittgenstein, L. (1958) *Philosophical Investigations*. Oxford: Blackwell.

Zimmerman, D. and Pollner, M. (1971) The everyday world as a phenomenon. In J. D. Douglas (ed.), 80–103.

Notes

1. Several overviews of Discourse Analysis are available. See, among others, Coulthard (1977), Tannen (1982), Brown and Yule (1983), Stubbs (1983), van Dijk (1985, 1997), Drew and Heritage (1992), Schiffrin (1993), Caldas-Coulthard and Coulthard (1996).

2. Donald Friend (1915–1989) is acclaimed as one of 'the most gifted figure draughtsmen in Australian art'.

3. In this paper Harris even acknowledges Noam Chomsky as a collaborator on the project.

4. It is perhaps worth mentioning Labov and Waletzky's (1967) work on narrative structure which has had a durable impact on the study of discourse production.

5. Lave (1988) points to a dialectic of 'setting', 'activity' and 'arena' in her analysis of the supermarket. For her, a setting is generated out of one's activity (a particular shelf may not exist for one shopper). This view of setting-activity relation is similar to what in ethnomethodological terms amounts to the orientation of participants through action, in preference to analysts' imposition of activity-specific norms.

6. See the recent debate about how to connect the micro and macro levels, especially Schegloff (1997) and Wetherell (1998). For a detailed treatment of this tension in workplace-based studies, see Sarangi and Roberts (1999).

7. This turn could be seen as a parallel to how discourse has become a topic and resource in mainstream sociolinguistic studies.

8. Note that topic in mainstream linguistic discourse analysis refers to 'what is being talked about', i.e., what is being topicalised by the participants – how topic shifts are managed, negotiated etc. Here we are interested in discourse as topic.

9. One can, however, notice here the seeds of genre analysis and stylistics, including the recent work in forensic linguistics as illustrated in the final chapter by Coulthard. In returning to the topic/resource dilemma, we can see how discourse as a topic of investigation can align with resource for discourse analysts. The topic/resource dilemma in the field of discourse study and sociolinguistics needs an altogether different reading than it has in allied social science disciplines.

10. Edelsky (1981) argues for a further distinction between 'turn' and 'floor' in the analysis of spoken discourse.

11. Even contributors in this volume differ in their use of transcript conventions, citation systems etc. Scollon rightly points out the unfinalisable aspects of analysis. Indeed Roberts' transcription and analysis of a piece of data used earlier by Roberts and Sarangi (1999) underscores this methodological point.

Chapter 1

Activity types, discourse types and interactional hybridity: the case of genetic counselling

Srikant Sarangi

1 Introduction

Just over twenty years ago, in 1979, Levinson published a seminal paper titled 'Activity types and language', which has since provided an analytic frame of reference for scholars working in the traditions of interactional pragmatics and discourse analysis. In a sense, its publication is comparable to those of Sacks et al.'s (1974) 'A simplest systematics for the organisation of turn-taking in conversation', or Grice's (1975) 'Logic and conversation', or even Austin's (1962) *How to Do Things with Words*. Indeed Levinson situates his paper in relation to an array of analytic traditions: ethnomethodology and conversation analysis, philosophy of language, artificial intelligence – not to mention the formalist school of linguistics. Its recent republication (Drew and Heritage 1992) under the same title signals a continuing interest in Levinson's proposal, especially in the context of analysing talk and text in institutional settings. Although not many conversation analytic 'studies of work' draw explicitly on the notion of activity type, at least there is now a recognition of the limitations of applying the generic, sequential rules of conversation to institutional interaction (Psathas 1995) as well as a call for combining sequential analysis and categorisation analysis in the study of talk-in-interaction generally (Watson 1996).

In this chapter I offer a reappraisal of the notion of activity type with special reference to institutional/professional domains of language use. I argue that because activity types (e.g., job interviews, committee meetings, court hearings) are durable entities, it allows language analysts to study not only durable patterns, but also aspects of social change. In order to account for the dynamics inherent in activity types, in the second part, I draw upon a related notion, i.e., discourse type, broadly defined as specific manifestations of language form in their interactional contexts (e.g., ranging from utterance types such as 'how are you?', 'what are we doing here?' to the sequential organisation of questions and answers as in a cross-examination, to stylistic features as in promotional talk). While activity type is a means of character-ising settings (e.g., a medical consultation, a service encounter, a university seminar), discourse type is a way of characterising the forms of talk (e.g., medical history taking, promotional talk, interrogation, troubles telling, etc.). The overlap between activity types and discourse types, as I shall show, is most apparent when we deal with counselling and therapy, as they con-stitute both a type of activity and a form of discourse. In other words, what we regard as counselling talk or therapy talk may occur in a number of activity types and, similarly, therapy and counselling sessions will draw on different discourse types (e.g., advising, troubles telling). This leads me to suggest that activity types and discourse types (re)configure in various ways, and that both participants and analysts need to be sensitive to this 'inter-actional hybridity'. I also go on to argue that the hybridity between activity types and discourse types is most noticeable at the interactional level. So, interactional hybridity, in both senses of the term as I am using it here, can account for continuity and variations within and across activity types. In the final part I examine how different discourse types (e.g., informing, ad-vising and decision-making) are interactionally managed in the context of genetic counselling. In doing so, I try to combine my ongoing advocacy for activity analysis over the last ten years with my current interest in genetic counselling as a discursive site.[1]

2   Levinson and activity types

Levinson (1979: 368) sees activity type as 'a fuzzy category whose focal members are goal-defined, socially constituted, bounded events with con-straints on participants, settings and so on, but above all on the kind of allowable contributions'. If we were to regard medical consultation as an activity type, then we could work out the constraints that will normally apply for participation. For instance, in a clinical setting, when the doctor opens the consultation with '*how are you?*', the patient interprets this as a request to talk about his/her state of health rather than as a ritual greeting to talk about the weather or something else. This is not to suggest that patients cannot respond to doctors' '*how are you?*' in interpersonal terms. Indeed, by treating this utterance as a greeting and by entering into a 'small talk' frame, patients can signal their relational histories with doctors. What is less likely, however, is for the patient to open the consultation with a '*how are you?*' ques-tion directed at the doctor, and for the doctor, in turn, to respond with a catalogue of his/her illnesses and work-related stress. So, the talk format such as '*how are you?*' derives its meaning from the activity type in which it is embedded, and, by a similar token, it can be responded to in several ways as a basis for (re)defining the role-relations between participants as well as the very boundaries of an activity type. Since everyday members have access to its use in more than one interactional setting they can impute its inference without difficulty. More generally, if participants are not aware of the range of situations in which a certain linguistic form can occur, they are more likely to impose a wrong interpretation.[2]

Levinson's paper celebrates the role of context in inferencing, with particular reference to the function of questions in a variety of institutional settings. Of course Levinson is not claiming new grounds with regard to meaning being context dependent. Many scholars before him (e.g., Hymes 1964, Jakobson 1976, Leont'ev 1978, Rommetveit 1974, Voloshinov 1986 [1929], and Wittgenstein 1958) have made this point in strong terms, mainly as a reaction to linguistic formalism and generative grammar, and to Saussure's (1966) langue/parole, code/message distinctions (for a comprehensive review, see Linell 1998). Roman Jakobson (1976), for instance, suggests that the notion of 'speech event' (a variant of 'activity type' in Levinson's sense) comprises the six factors shown in Figure 1.1.

| | Context | |
Addresser	Message	Addressee
	Contact	
	Code	

Figure 1.1 Jakobson's model of a 'speech event'

Hymes (1964) extends this to include as many as eight variables in his framework of Ethnography of Speaking. Further insights on the notion of 'context' (Cicourel 1992, Duranti and Goodwin 1992, Gumperz 1982) and on the notion of 'participant structure' (Goffman 1974, 1981) have contributed significantly towards our understanding of activity-specific language use. As Voloshinov (1986: 86) puts it: 'The word is a two-sided act. It is determined equally by whose word it is and for whom it is meant.' This view clearly coincides with the Bakhtinian focus on 'addressivity'.

What Levinson offers in his paper as new is a robust analytic framework for analysing talk-in-context, based on the view that language use is primarily indexical and that meaning is dependent on its context of production (Bar-Hillel 1957).[3] The main strength of the activity framework is its openness to accommodate a wide range of concepts as they operate at different levels of language production and interpretation. This can be represented as in Figure 1.2.

2.1 Activity-specificity as a constraint on communicative practice?

In focusing on how inferencing is activity-specific, Levinson takes on board the structural, stylistic and interactional dimensions of language use. He offers a middle ground (or, a third way, to use a currently fashionable piece of rhetoric!) between the broad Gricean maxims of language behaviour and

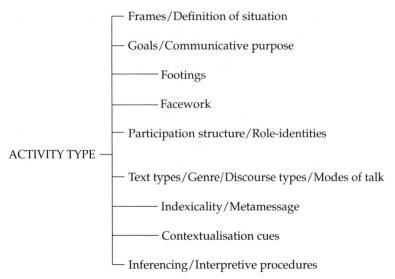

Figure 1.2 Integrated model of activity analysis

the too-specific frameworks of inference (as in artificial intelligence). For Levinson (1979: 373):

> The knowledge that is required to make appropriate inferences is clearly not provided by Grice's maxims alone, for these are (implicitly) supposed to hold across different kinds of activity. Nor is it provided by the general structural expectations that have on the whole been the focus of work by Sacks, Schegloff and their colleagues. The knowledge in question rather seems to be a distinct and further kind of structural expectation that lies behind inference in discourse.

He argues in favour of a manageable explanatory framework which takes into account speaker intentionality and audience design. Levinson (1979: 393) underscores his point about 'activity-specific rules of inference' as follows:

> [T]ypes of activity, social episodes if one prefers, play a central role in language usage. They do this in two ways especially: on the one hand, they constrain what will count as an allowable contribution to each activity; and on the other hand, they help to determine how what one says will be 'taken' – that is, what kinds of inferences will be made from what is said. Both of these issues are of some theoretical and practical interest.

Let me draw attention to the two main points that Levinson is making here. First of all, he says that there are constraints on 'allowable contributions'. By this he does not mean that participants in a given activity will behave as 'judgemental dopes' (Garfinkel 1967) by not being able to say what they like, and when they like. My activity-specific reading of what he says suggests that there is a likelihood that participants will generally not do so. Here we have overtones of the Gricean universal maxims in action, but it is quite possible to see such cooperative behaviour as a form of 'habitus' – a way of acting and interacting – in the Bourdieuan sense. In arguing for a move from rules to strategies in sociological analysis, what Bourdieu (1994: 63) says is relevant here:

> . . . the constraints and demands of the game, although they are not restricted to a code of rules, *impose themselves* on those people – and those people alone – who, because they have a feel for the game, a feel, that is, for the immanent necessity of the game, are prepared to perceive them and carry them out. (His emphasis)

It seems then that there is an element of agency involved in playing the game, and that people are cautious in exercising their creativity in view of a necessary 'feel for the game' and desirable outcomes. Also, within an activity type or language game, we can uncover the strategic (as opposed to rule-governed) behaviour. Consider here Goffman's (1969) distinction between 'expressing information' and 'communicating information' in the context of spying. The actual words spoken are not to be interpreted literally but in activity-specific terms, given that such statements may have been made under direct scrutiny of the enemy.

Levinson's second point relates to inferencing and interpretative procedures which are based on shared knowledge about the world. When participants go beyond what is 'allowable', their contributions will be regarded as 'marked' and these will be subject to activity-specific inferencing by their co-participants. In other words, transgressions are possible, but with such transgressions come specific inferences (cf. Grice's implicature associated with flouting).

We can notice interesting parallels here with the ethnomethodological tradition, and social constructionism generally. Of direct relevance here is Garfinkel's (1967: 78) formulation of what Mannheim originally conceptualised as the 'documentary method of interpretation':

> The method consists of treating an actual appearance as 'the document of,' as 'pointing to,' as 'standing on behalf of' a presupposed underlying pattern. Not only is the underlying pattern derived from its individual documentary evidences, but the individual documentary evidences, in their turn, are interpreted on the basis of 'what is known' about the underlying pattern. Each is used to elaborate the other.

One of Garfinkel's so-called breaching experiments brings home the point about common interpretative procedures that members routinely rely on in everyday settings. In an experimental counselling set-up, Garfinkel asked the actor-counsellors to provide random yes/no responses to subjects' (i.e., student counsellees') questions. The subjects nonetheless interpreted the counsellors' answers on the basis of their background expectations about counselling as a social encounter. As Wilson (1971: 68) puts it: 'documentary interpretations are retrospective and prospective'. This is what participants do in a given interaction, and following from this, Wilson (1971: 69–70) urges that 'the researcher must engage in documentary interpretation, and in particular he [sic] must do so in order to identify what action is performed at any given moment'. As I see it, the activity type framework allows for a convergence of participants' and analysts' perspectives in understanding (inter)action.

Another way of framing this debate would be to draw on type-token or whole-part reasoning (Jakobson 1990), to see how this aids our understanding of activity-specific inferencing. In their influential work on the social construction of reality, Berger and Luckmann (1967: 89–90) suggest:

> That is, there will be the recognition not only of a particular actor performing an action of type X, but of type-X action as being performable by *any* actor to whom the relevance structure in question can be plausibly imputed . . . The typification of forms of action requires that these have an objective sense, which in turn requires a linguistic objectification. That is, there will be a vocabulary referring to these forms of action (such as 'nephew-thrashing', which will belong to a much larger linguistic structuring of kinship and its various rights and obligations).

It is very much the case that activity-specific norms are culture-specific, a point Levinson also puts forward in his paper. What constitutes 'nephew-thrashing' in one culture may not be the same elsewhere, or even non-existent in another. Even within a given socio-cultural order an activity type may not constitute a homogeneous entity with determinate structures and interactional routines. To make things more complex, activity-specific norms may have their origin, and realisations, beyond the narrow linguistic parameters made accessible to analysts.

Perhaps the term 'type' suggests a blend of 'idealism' and 'determinism'. With regard to idealism, one could draw attention to Weber's (1949 [1904]) suggestion that the ideal type is necessary for our understanding of social events and processes *in situ*. As far as determinism is concerned, Fairclough (1995: 45) argues that the activity type model 'regards properties of a particular type of interaction as determined by the perceived social functions of that type of interaction (its "goal"), thus representing the relationship between discourse and its determinants as transparent to those taking part'. Such a criticism, which exposes the analytic bias in interpreting activity-specific performance in a normative way, can be redressed if we foreground what participants themselves orient to as a recognisable type-token relation based on their experience of the world. Sacks (1985: 20), among others, draws our attention to the routine and generic nature of human conduct:

> . . . how it is that persons learn that the activities they have gone through are observable by virtue of their appearances, where, again, this observability is not specific to each activity but is learned as a general phenomenon.

To summarise, the notion of activity type appeals for various reasons: it takes into account cognitive, historical and genealogical dimensions, as it links these to interactional patterns and structural configurations. Unlike behaviourist or cognitive models which focus on the individual performance and mental scripts, activity type analysis removes the burden from the individual. However, agency – or 'improvisation', to use Erickson and Shultz's (1982) term – is very much a part of Levinson's own definition of activity type as being fuzzy. Against the backdrop of prototype theory, Levinson moves away from an either/or categorisation, towards a categorisation of entities based on more/less along a continuum. For instance, not all legal proceedings or medical consultations are conducted in exactly the same way, but there is a prototypical form from which other versions can deviate, but not without activity-specific inferences/implicatures attached to such deviations. A notion of normality is thus presupposed in activity-specific behaviour, but this does not amount to fixedness or rigidity. Deviations from the focal points only make us rethink the potential boundaries and crossings between activity types.

2.2 Categorisation as definition of situation

A key notion associated with activity types is categorisation – both for participants and analysts. Following Sacks (1985: 17), we may say that all categorisation work is activity-specific. A case in point is Heritage and Lindstrom's (1998) account of how health visitors discuss fact-sheet data with their clients. A typical interview with a teenage-mother will begin something like 'now first the particulars they want to know th' baby's father's age'. Here the formulation already presupposes what counts as part of the activity and how this is brought along (they want to know, and it's my job to ask you). Beyond this is the categorisation work: here the use of the term 'baby's father' instead of 'husband' or 'boyfriend' (the latter may be seen as pejorative, signalling illegitimacy). This categorisation – 'baby's father' – may appear as an on-the-spot lexical choice, but it is also possible to argue that such instructions may be coming down from above – i.e., what institutionally ratified categories should be used on these occasions? So, the use of one set of categories instead of others contributes towards defining the situation and the attendant role-relations.

Because participants may bring their own discourse styles and expectations to an activity – and they may have competing goals in mind – there will be an attempt on their part to define and redefine the situation. As McHugh (1968) points out, the two parameters of 'defining the situation' are: emergence and relativity. Generally, members participating in an activity type draw implicitly on their background knowledge, but, when necessary, they may resort to explicit definition of the situation in an emergent fashion. Consider the following example, which is taken from a medical oral examination setting. As an activity type, this setting is close to what we might call a 'selection interview' or a 'gatekeeping encounter', with the interviewer/gatekeeper controlling the topics and the interaction. In this activity type, as we know, interviewers do not usually make the force of their questions explicit, because guessing what lies behind a question is as much a display of interviewee competence as the answer itself (Roberts 1985, Sarangi 1994).

In Example 1 below,[4] the candidate is asked about his suitability for medical practice – a rather threatening question which requires a balanced act of self-presentation. Our concern here is to see how the candidate handles this question in activity-specific terms. As we shall see, he offers an explicit 'definition of situation' as a way of signalling how the activity itself constrains what he wants to say, and by extension, why his co-participant (i.e., the examiner) should share this definition of situation and adopt a reciprocal frame of interpretation.

Example 1

01 E: ok how does personality affect one's work as a doctor – the doctor's personality

02 C: [sighs and long pause] ok [pause] well personality [pause] maybe I am trying to think of er in the literature to supplement my erm my answer that's what you are looking at

03 E: erm your thoughts on it – not necessarily literature

04 C: ok personality affects [laughs] how many (. . .) patients you have – research shows that doctor's perception of workload erm time pressure family pressure – maybe qualifications affect the number of (. . .) patients you are having – the problems we're having erm with patients your personality – bad in communication – you are bad communicator – you get in trouble with patients and patients will get into troubles – it would of course affect your practice – bad communication is [laughs] bad thing basically – your personality is (.) a major factor in how you establish communication erm (.) your personality depends on your attitude towards education further education – are you being updated or just (. .) so confident and do you think that it is unnecessary (. . .) what caused by you (. . .) just so much behind

05 E: what about your own er personality – do you think that's ideally suited for for general practice

06 C: well of course that's why I chose general practice

07 E: good

08 C: general practice er er

09 E: good what what are the features of your personality that you think that suits general practice

10 C: (.) it's very difficult for somebody to praise himself – but I am in an exam and I have to give you a firm | answer

11 E: yes

12 C: and that's what I am going to do

13 E: good

14 C: I am a highly qualified person – I have postgraduate qualification apart from the medical degree | I am

15 E: | ok just just just the personality factor

16 C: personality erm evidence-based medicine study hard work hard good communicator I understand my patients empathise with my patients I have compassion I communicate well and I have feelings for other peoples I come from a mixed background so I have understanding of all ethnic minorities and local population – I am adaptable (. . .) allow to do this I

    always criticise myself and keep changing my attitude my thinking my clinical performance | and I always

17   E: | right that's that's great (.) what what about negative sides – are there any any blemishes

18   C: (.) again it's not it's not wise for me to [laughs] say much otherwise I score negatively in such an exam

19   E: [laughs]

20   C: so you have put me a very difficult question – but just to be honest erm sometimes recently (. .) in my family life – it's being sorted out – I am married and have got a child sometimes I feel (.) caution myself – am I doing much (.) what am I – I just get this on erm have more time with my family – I am trying all my weekends and everything and spending with my family so this is almost my family – again its sports and I have stopped doing it – it's a bad thing and I am starting

Both participants come to this activity with the knowledge that this is an oral examination, scheduled in terms of time, place and participation structure. Hence my characterisation of them above as examiner and candidate, as they orient to this activity by taking on the roles of questioner and answerer respectively. This is in preference to other available categorisations (e.g., they are fellow doctors). In turn 10 we have an explicit definition of situation and this is occasioned by interactional trouble (note the initial sigh and long pause in turn 02 and the negotiation routine that follows). Why has it become necessary for C to offer an explicit definition of situation?

In turn 01, E asks the question about personality as part of his agenda.[5] What C says in turn 02 is framed as 'thinking aloud', followed by a confirmation check. Strategically, he buys time to organise his thoughts, because, for him, combing for relevant literature to 'supplement' his answer would coincide with what he perceives E's expectations might be (i.e., C should display an adequate grasp of relevant literature on the subject). Once the examiner clarifies that 'your thoughts' would do (without any reference to literature), in turn 04, C comes up with a long, fluid response mainly consisting of a check-list of how personality is at stake (note in particular the formulations using the impersonal 'you'). C's assumption here is that this would suffice as an appropriate response to the examiner's general question *'how does personality affect ONE'S work as a doctor?'*. But in turn 05, E tries to elicit a more specific answer to find out the extent to which C sees himself suitable for general practice. C's response in turn 06 only answers the second part of E's question in the previous turn.[6] As in many selection interviews, such a minimalist response may be regarded as an inadequate basis for the interviewer to form a judgement about a candidate's fit. We thus notice the more specific directive in turn 09: *'what are the features of YOUR personality that you think that suits general practice?'*. Given the selection activity type, this specificity was to be inferred from the very first question in turn 01, but the candidate had so far failed to impute the exact inference by not displaying his own personal abilities as a doctor. This may also explain how and why E redefines the question to make it more activity-specific, and in doing so he signals that they are in an interview situation and that the topic of the candidate's suitability will be sustained until a specific response is forthcoming.

In turns 10–13, C offers an explicit definition of the situation ('*I am in an exam*'), and this framing now allows him to package his specific response as a 'firm answer'. Within this activity type, and following E's specific question and C's definition of situation so far, the contribution in turn 16 is likely to be interpreted as an 'appropriate' response rather than a boastful display of 'self-praise' and 'self-promotion'. In the turns that follow, the examiner moves to the negative aspects of the candidate's personality, and once again C offers an explicit definition of the difficult situation he finds himself in: '*it's not wise for me to say much [about negative sides] otherwise I score negatively in such an exam*'. So, what we see here is that the candidate makes constant reference to the exam activity, and its potential outcomes, by competently displaying his knowledge that language production and inferencing are context-specific. This perhaps lies behind C's strategic avoidance of the situational trap unless cornered further, given the threatening nature of the questions. The language game is being played out on a moment-by-moment basis, and neither party is prepared to give away more than what is seen as necessary.

From the above example we may conclude that explicit definitions of situation are called for at times of interactional trouble, especially in the institutional gatekeeping encounters. As Erickson (1976) suggests, hyper-questions, and here hyper-answers, are indicative of ambivalence and uncertainty. The interactional negotiation of such uncertainty signals how participants make manifest their understanding of the 'how and why' of language games.

3 Activity types, discourse types and interactional hybridity

In the previous example we categorised the activity as an oral examination and the participants as examiner and candidate. Such an initial categorisation no doubt influenced our analysis of the interaction, especially in imputing the force and value of the utterances in their interactional context. Let us consider the following extract without any categorisation of what the activity is and who the participants are and see how far we, as analysts, can go with our inferencing scheme.

Example 2
01 A: Are there any other problems?
02 B: Well, he chews cigarette ends . . . [laughs] . . . . It's very difficult to stop him.
03 A: Why are you laughing? Do you think it's funny?
04 B: No, I don't think it's funny.

05 A: Well, why did you laugh then; do you always laugh at this?
        [. . .]
06 A: So you entirely ignore it when he starts chewing cigarettes?
07 B: No, I don't.
08 A: Well, why did you say you did?
09 B: I didn't.

Without any initial categorisation and definition of the situation, what can we infer from the language form and its interactional organisation? Here we have a question–answer sequence, as in the previous example. There is also evidence of hyper-questioning on the part of A (note the back-to-back questions in turns 03 and 05), as B gets increasingly defensive in his/her responses. To some extent, the question–answer sequence resembles cross-examination in a court-room setting; it is perhaps also characteristic of how parents deal with unruly children. There is very little cue here to suggest that this interaction takes place between a doctor and a mother. In fact, I have taken this extract from Philip Strong's (1979) classic *The Ceremonial Order of the Clinic*, although he admits that such confrontational routines are rather untypical of his doctor–patient corpus. Now that we have this additional contextual knowledge about the activity and the participants, we can infer where and how deviations occur, as demonstrated by the participants themselves.

The very first turn is recognisable as a doctor's query about B's state of health/illness. In turn 02, the mother reports a problem with her son, which suggests that B's interpretation of A's question is activity-specific. However her response is marked with an individualistic style which includes laughter. And this light-hearted response is seen as deviant by A. In turn 03, we see the doctor orienting himself to the interpersonal dimension of the encounter as he shifts focus from the cigarette-chewing son to the mother's lack of seriousness and concern. In doing so, A is simultaneously orienting to his medical identity and the consultation activity. As Strong points out, the doctor here is doing 'character work' which has moral overtones. The mother is subjected to a kind of cross-examination to prove that she is lying and contradicting herself – against the general assumption that mothers tell the truth in these activity types.

In its untypicality, this episode shows that cross-examination as a discourse type can be appropriated into a range of activity types (into consultations as is the case here, but also into classroom interaction, mother–child interaction, etc.). Although such appropriations may signal interactional problems, they can be recruited as strategic moves by powerful participants in order to (re)establish a normative interaction order. The doctor, through his questioning of the mother's demeanour, carries out an implicit definition of the clinic situation, and points to what constitutes allowable contributions within it. An allowable contribution thus comprises not only 'what is said' but also 'how something is said, when and where'.

3.1 Embedding of discourse types in activity types

This brings me to the notion of discourse types and how they are embedded in activity types. Fairclough (1992: 124) uses the label 'discourse type' as an umbrella term to include a range of concepts such as genre, style, register, discourse (as in 'interview genre', 'conversational style', 'register of cookery books', 'scientific medical discourse'). The term 'discourse type' in its broadest sense coincides with 'discourse practice' and 'orders of discourse'. According to Fairclough (1989: 39), '. . . discourse (and practice generally) draws upon discourse types rather than mechanically implementing them . . . [D]iscourse types are a resource for subjects, but the activity of combining them in ways that meet the ever-changing demands and contradictions of real social situations is a creative one' (see our earlier discussion of determinism, and also Hasan, this volume, on 'genre combination').

In Fairclough's (1992) work, the notion of discourse type is emphasised as a basis for a critical analysis of the recurrence of the same discourse form, for instance cross-examination, across a range of settings. Tendencies of intertextuality help to highlight which discourse types are becoming dominant and prolific in our discourse practice *vis-à-vis* activity types. What Fairclough refers to as 'conversationalisation' – the simulation of conversational forms in institutional settings to manifest equality – is a case in point. There are strategic motivations behind appropriations and transfers of different discourse types, and we need to appeal to sociopolitical changes to account for them. However, I would argue that such shifts at the intertextual and interdiscursive levels are premised upon the notion of activity types and are therefore understood better – both by participants and analysts – within a framework of activity type. In other words, we can draw upon 'interactional hybridity' in order to understand how certain discourse types are overlaid within and across activity types. At what point do certain discourse types become peripheral or cease to belong to one activity type and occupy a focal point in another? This is a difficult question to answer, partly because no discourse type, not even a single utterance, can be attributed one single function, location and value.

Let us consider the therapeutic context, where therapy is both an activity type and a form of discourse. In group therapy sessions, as Turner (1972) shows, statements such as *'why are we here?'* are made frequently by clients. When clients ask this question as 'first action', the therapist is not supposed to occupy 'the second action' position. This can be regarded as a constraint on allowable contributions, to use Levinson's terminology. In other words, as far as the therapist is concerned, *'why are we here?'* does not function as a question requiring an immediate answer, even if the therapist does seem to have a ready-made answer. The basis of such inferencing is that if s/he answered the client's question in her/his next turn, it would no longer be regarded as a therapy activity. Rather than becoming a constraint, however, the client's question is utilised by the therapist as an interactional resource as s/he redirects it to the clients themselves. The received wisdom in the therapeutic circle is that clients should be encouraged to find solutions to their questions through introspection and self-reflection. So, the therapist's position as an active listener (realised in sequential terms) comes to be regarded as one of the definitional properties of this activity as therapy.[7]

Like therapy, counselling is both an activity and a form of discourse. Jefferson and Lee (1981) discuss how troubles telling and service encounter talk may collide (see also, Miller and Silverman 1995). When someone narrates a trouble-telling, the other participant is supposed to take the position of recipient of troubles talk (as in the case of therapy sessions above). If the listener offers advice prematurely, it is more likely to be rejected. In a typical service encounter, however, explicit advice giving may be in place, because the focus here is on the problem and its properties, unlike in troubles-telling where the focus lies on the teller and his/her experience. As we shall see in the genetic counselling activity, there is a combination of these discourse types: counsellors take on a position whereby the lifeworld experiences of the client are listened to, but they also volunteer information about specific genetic conditions and the kinds of health service provisions (e.g., predictive tests) available for clients.

In both contexts of therapy and counselling, hybridity is occasioned by a conflation of activity types (e.g., troubles-telling and service encounter) and discourse types (e.g., advising and informing). A further aspect of hybridity may be observable at the structural level. We can take 'advising' as a discourse type which occurs in a range of activity types, with specific sequential structures. As Heritage and Sefi (1992) point out, there are five steps which constitute an advice-giving sequence in encounters between health visitors (HVs) and new parents:

step 1: Initial inquiry by HV
step 2: Potential problem-implicating response by Mother
step 3: Focusing inquiry into the problem by HV
step 4: Response detailing
step 5: Advice giving

Variations of this sequence are realised as:

initial inquiry → 'no problem' response → advice giving on 'possible problems'

initial inquiry → problem indicative response → advice giving

Heritage and Sefi are quick to point out that such a sequence (including the alternatives) is easily disrupted at the interactional level. Whatever the interactional sequence, any contribution made by the HV is likely to be taken up as potential advice/complaint by the mothers (see our earlier discussion on context-specific inferencing with regard to Garfinkel's breaching experiment). In order to understand why this might be the case, we need to appeal to the wider socio-political context. In the UK, home rounds by HVs constitute part of surveillance: the HV is there to help inexperienced mothers as well as monitor good mothering practices.

From our discussion so far, it is clear that the same discourse type can occur in different activity types and may receive differential treatment. For example, the question *'what are we doing here?'* can have a different function in, say, the activity type of academic seminar, where the question would be regarded as an information-seeking move. This means that permeability at the level of discourse types anticipates fuzziness at the level of activity types. We have also seen how certain discourse types (defined broadly to include stylistic, sequential and structural properties) can occupy focal positions in specific activity types. The case of therapeutic indifference (i.e., the decision that the client's question is not answered immediately in the next turn) and the case of delayed advice giving (i.e., the realisation that the offer of premature advice may be rejected) are just a few examples. It remains difficult to draw boundaries around what we might call therapeutic, counselling and service encounters, despite their emergent definitional properties.

4   Genetic counselling as an activity type or a hybrid discourse type?

Over the past two decades there has been a growing interest in the study of counselling/therapeutic discourse across a range of professional sites. One can begin with Labov and Fanshel's (1977) study, which has more do with rules of discourse coherence and their linguistic/pragmatic manifestations than with what I would see as an activity-specific analysis of therapy. A clear improvement upon Labov and Fanshel's study is Candlin and Lucas's (1986) account of family planning discourse as a continuum, based on pragmatic principles, discoursal structures and linguistic features. They point out that 'modes of advising' are realised *vis-à-vis* communicative frames of 'interview', 'education' and 'counselling'. Because counsellors have to offer information as well as education, they might 'produce discourse which fluctuated along a continuum, the poles of which were information-giving and seeking on the one hand, and the specifying of contra-indicating behaviour on the other (Candlin and Lucas 1986: 14). Figure 1.3 is a reproduction of their model.

According to Candlin and Lucas (1986: 23), 'as the counsellor moves along the continuum from Pole A in the direction of Pole B, her discourse takes on the characteristics of *advice'*. In other words, contra-indicative statements are likely to be heard by clients as potential advice. There is also a division of labour in this setting between family therapy counsellors and medical practitioners, as it is only the latter who can issue directives.[8] A general point here is that counsellors in many interactional contexts have to manage the tensions between being objectively rational on the one hand, and being an advocate of clients' interest on the other hand (Erickson and Shultz 1982).

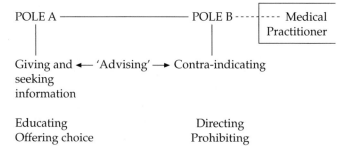

Figure 1.3   The counselling Continuum (Candlin and Lucas 1986)

In more recent years a number of counselling sites have been studied in detail: HIV/AIDS (Peräkylä 1995, Silverman 1997), divorce mediation (Greatbatch and Dingwall 1999) and family therapy (Gale 1991). Silverman, for instance, points out that 'communicative formats' in HIV/AIDS counselling are accomplished interactionally via two discourse types (in our sense of the term): informing and advising. He draws our attention to how (factual, medical) information is packaged in order to signal an advising frame. This is done via turn design, where the patient is put in a recipient position, although it is equally possible to deliver advice via interview sequences made up of questions and answers as in the history-taking phase of the consultation. It is perhaps reasonable to assume that the counselling situation is a highly charged advice giving scenario (as we have seen in the case of health visitor practice), and it is likely that messages intended as information may be taken up as potential advice. In divorce mediation, as Greatbatch and Dingwall (1999) suggest, the mediators design their speaking turns in ways which allow them to refrain from (i) directly giving opinions and (ii) overtly displaying affiliation or disaffiliation. In other words, it is through strategic turn design that the professionals are able to maintain a neutralistic stance. Against this backdrop, let us see how genetic counselling as an activity type differs not only from its first and second counselling cousins (i.e., counselling in other contexts), but also from its parent (i.e., the prototypical doctor–patient encounter), in both structure and substance.

4.1   Structural variables in genetic counselling activity

ten Have (1989), following Byrne and Long (1976), proposes that medical consultation may be viewed as a genre (in the activity type sense as we are discussing here), which is organised structurally as: complaint, physical examination, diagnosis, treatment.[9] Each stage will give salience to a particular discourse type: for instance at the complaint stage the patient will answer the series of questions asked by the doctor, and elaborate, in a narrative mode, on aspects s/he perceives as relevant. Whereas at the diagnosis and treatment stages, it is the doctor who does more explaining and it is the patient who offers minimal acknowledgement tokens. Also, it is possible that at the stage of delivery of diagnosis, there may be hypothetical for-mulations and mitigations resembling counselling talk. The different stages will thus foreground different interactional and discoursal configurations. In terms of activity-specific constraints, a patient, if s/he so wishes, can volun-teer information in complaining mode at the treatment phase, but such information may be too late to make a difference to the diagnosis or treat-ment options.

This structural sequence, however, is not typical of genetic counselling. History-taking in genetic clinics follows a significantly different course. Mainly structured around information on family trees, it pervades the entire counselling process (especially when such information has not been gathered during previous home visits).[10] Also what constitutes physical examination in genetic counselling, which may or may not be undertaken in the clinic, is different. Similarly, diagnosis and treatment phases may be absent altogether, since for many genetic disorders there is no available treatment, and in some cases even a diagnosis is not possible. Indeed much of genetic counsel-ling work is around prognosis, risk assessment and coping, in addition to the routine information gathering activity surrounding family networks and it may focus on reproductive choices.

At the interactional level, any 'token' of the genetic counselling activity 'type' is realised differently. There are, no doubt, some structural and rhetor-ical similarities across counselling sessions, but a host of factors can account for each session being unique. These can include: the genetic disorder in question, medical facts and treatment options known to be (un)available, clients'/patients' level of genetic awareness, the family members poten-tially affected, the prevailing kinship and family ties, the ethical and legal implications around decision-making, and even the family members present in the clinic.

4.2 Modes of genetic explanation: some examples

Genetic counselling, by definition, is an information-rich environment where different modes of explanation take centre stage. As Wolff and Jung (1995) put it, it is a situation where one 'provides information about information'. This focus on information and explanation brings to the fore why genetic counselling is equated with non-directiveness in the professional circle.[11] However, given the nature of genetic risk involved, any information offered by counsellors in situated encounters has the potential for being taken up as advice by clients/patients. In what follows I select three critical moments of the genetic counselling activity for further analysis: (i) giving information, (ii) seeking advice and (iii) negotiating decisions about predictive tests. Let us first consider an information-giving sequence, as in Example 3 below.

Data Example 3
[D = Doctor; P = Patient]

01 D: =yeah (.) .hhhhh okay, ehm:::::: (.) ((tats)) so (.5) so we've got this informa-
        tion .hhhhh ehm (.) I think (.) the best thing to do would be fo– for me
        to– (.) just– to tell you a little about (.) the condition that we think that you
        have (.) .hhhh and most it means what the implications are for your chil-
        dren (.) .hhh and (.) what we can do (.) .hhhh and at some stage I wouldn't
        mind having a a quick look at you |if that's alright
02 P: |yeah
03 D: = we'll do that at the end ehm just to see (.) how many (of tho–) lumps you
        have
04 P: =mmh mmh(.)
05 D: .hhhh ehm (.) so (.) this condition is called neurofibromatosis that's quite a
        long word (.) and what it means is that ehm (.) neuron– (.) on the nerves (.)
        [(that's what it means)] and (.) ehm (.) fib-fibromas are swellings |within
06 P: |mmh mmh right
07 D: the nerves (.) so– (.) it's really describing eh these sort of |lumps yes so
08 P: |ehmmh
09 D: and these are– (.5) th– that lump is is actually here eh– is actually a nerve
        running (in the skin) (.) eh (.) and the swelling is due to eh ehm the the
        growth in in in th– in the sheath covers surrounding the nerv (.) which is
        eh called the fibroma (.5) so the name just describes (.) what's happening in
        the |skin basically
10 P: |mmh
11 D: so these lumps are called neurofibromas (.) and the condition is called
        neurofibromatosis(1.0)
12 D: there are actually two types (.) ehm and we abbreviate to NF one NF for
        neurofibromatosis (.) NF one and NF two (.) .hhhh NF one is very common
        (.) ehm and that's not the one that you have you've got NF two (.) which is
        a lot rarer (.) ehm (.) and (.5) it's characterised by these by causing these
        kind of swellings in the in the |[^^^^^]
13 P: |mmh
14 D: and that's very (.) characteristic of NF two (.)
15 D: okay? (.) .hhh but – (.5) if you're reading up up about neurofibromatosis (.)
        you always– they always talk about NF first and there's always much more
        space devoted to NF one because it's so much more common (.) okay but
        it's important not to be confused |'cause they're different
16 P: |right(.)
17 D: .hhhhhh e::hm (.5) [does] that all make |sense to you? yeah
18 P: |ugh– yeah alright
19 D: =okay (.) .hhh ehm (.) the condition is due to an alteration in the gene
20 P: =right
21 D: =okay(.)
22 D: .hhh ehm and that gene (.) is (.) is found in– in NF two it's found chromo-
        some twenty-two (.5) .hhh genes are the (.) instructions (.) the basic instruc-
        tions that we inherit from our parents which determine how we develop and
        how we're made up we have genes for all sorts of things (.) like eye colour,
        ^^^^, all our basic characteristics basically (.) .hhhhhhhhhh ehm (.) and the

17

the chromosomes are actually the packages where the genes are carried on so we have ehm (.) the twenty-three pairs of chromosomes [^^^^^] and that's just one of the packages where the genes are carried on. over a hundred thousand genes. (.5) so like ehm (.) you can look at it (.) like ehm genes– you can see genes as being recipes for all (.) parts of the body and chromosomes are the cookbooks ehm which hold the recipes together (.5) ehm (.5) so we– we're talking about one particular alteration in one gene (.) basically

23 P: yeah(.)
24 D: which is f– which is causing the |(.) NF two
25 P: |yeah yeah(.5)
26 D: .hhh ehm (.5) and we have– [^^] the genes actually come in pairs 'cause we've one from our mum and one |from our father so we've two copies
27 P: |mmh yeah
28 D: of each gene (.) .hhhhhhhh so you have a normal copy of the gene (.) and an altered copy of the gene (.) and the altered copy is the one that's causing the prolems (.) .hhhh even though you've got a normal copy (.) and (.) for some reason that we not– we don't understand fully (.) the problem lies with the fact that you have one altered copy of a gene (.) that's what's causing the problem. the– but– (.) the problems basically.

What we see in the above extract is a typical information-giving sequence, framed as such by D in turn 01 to announce what will follow. In other words, D has information which P is seen as not having. If information were to be regarded as a commodity, then we have here a service encounter. Considering the quality and quantity of information provided, it seems to fit into the educational end of the counselling continuum that Candlin and Lucas (1986) talk about. There are chunks of monologue from the doctor (see turns 05, 09, 12, 15, 22 and 28), interspersed with minimal acknowledgement tokens from the patient. Even the monologic bits sound as if they are being read out from a medical text book.

Such explicit and 'qualified' information giving is rarely a feature of mainstream doctor–patient interaction. In fact, the counselling activity is constructed more as an academic lecture/seminar than as a consultation in the clinic. The interaction flows smoothly, as the role-relation between D and P get reconfigured as one between a lecturer and a student. P mainly provides acknowledgement tokens and at several points D asks clarification check questions, as one would expect in an educational setting. There is also the allusion to 'further readings' (turn 15). The doctor here draws on his knowledge that patients often access websites and available literature on the genetic condition that affects them or other family members.

What is striking about this discourse type is that it is not a simple information giving exercise. All information is structurally packaged into 'modes of explanation'. Note, for instance, the repertoire of describing and explaining D is drawing upon: there are ontological statements (e.g., *this condition is called neurofibromatosis*, turn 05); classificatory and taxonomic details (e.g., *there are actually two types*, turn 12); causal relations (e.g., *the swelling is due to the the growth in in in th– in the sheath covers surrounding the nerve*, turn 09) and use of lifeworld metaphors (e.g. *'you can see genes as being recipes . . . and chromosomes are the cookbooks'*, turn 22). Also, we notice that D explains the category to which this patient does not belong (turn 12). It reminds us of Candlin and Lucas's (1986) notion of contra-indication, and this may be a salient aspect of genetic counselling, given that population risk figures are often used for purposes of comparison. In educational terms, information about both categories – NF1 and NF2 – is relevant, even if the patient does not belong to the former category. In this case the category to which P belongs is the rarer one (NF2) as opposed to the common one (NF1), and such a contra-indication (or, contrast) may implicitly suggest the serious-ness of the case in hand. The information, as we can see, is formulated as explanation, and may be taken up as advice when making decisions in the future. It makes the point that there is no such thing as value-free informa-tion in the counselling setting, genetics or otherwise.

Staying within the activity type of genetic counselling, in the next example, let us consider an explicit advice seeking sequence. The case concerns a mother in her mid-30s, who has had a brain tumour (meningioma) removed two years ago. The husband and wife are now seeking advice as to whether a future pregnancy will carry further risks. The extract occurs towards the end of the consultation where the husband asks what is often referred to as 'the famous infamous question' in genetic counselling. What has gone before is a great deal of 'explaining' which seems not to have led to any resolution of the key question – whether or not to go ahead with pregnancy.

Data Example 4
[D = Doctor; H = Husband; W = Wife]

01	H:	so it it eh– to cut a long story short, if eh your wife was in this position God forbid (.5) eh and you wanted another child would you say (.) the chances are so minute (.5) we can go ahead with one (.5)
02	H:	|it was your–
03	D:	|you're asking– (.) you're asking (.) two separate questions.
04	H:	if you were me or–
05	D:	yeah
06	H:	=well yeah
07	D:	but you're– you are asking two separate questions
08	H:	mmh
09	D:	you see there's the (.) the (.) the you know what you're saying one is (.) eh (.) is there a chance of eh (.) say of a child having a tendency to get meningiomas? (.5)
10	H:	[^^^^^] (.) well I know I know it's like it would be the same chances as some [^^^^^]
11	D:	yes that's very very unlikely
12	H:	|unlikely
13	D:	|so there's that question. and then there is the question of
14	H:	mhm

15 D: of would the pregnancy cause another tumour
(1.0)
16 D: and (.) I think the answer |to that
17 H: |that's (unclear)
18 D: =well I think (.) the pregnancy itself wouldn't cause another tumour. (.) if
there is a small recurrence eh that (.) was not identified on the scan (.) then
I suppose a pregnancy could perhaps influence that rate of growth but (.)
it's not going to make the difference between (.) the tumour coming back
or not coming back. (.5) it (.5) could make a (.) a difference to when it
shows itself
19 H: mmh
20 D: but it would show itself anyway. (.) but ehm::::
21 W: =I mean I'm going to have MRI scans– regular MRI scans (.) each year? (.)
and eh–

We may consider H's opening turn as an advice-seeking move because H is
not requesting information as such. In fact he already has the information
about low risk (see turns 10, 12 and 17). With the hypothetical formulation,
H invites D to take on his (i.e., H's) position as the husband of a wife who
has had a brain tumour removed, and who now considers a further pregnancy. As we can see, D does not take up this hypothetical husband role,
nor does he offer any explicit advice. In Labov and Fanshel's (1977) terms,
here we have a request for advice followed by a put-off and refusal rather
than compliance. A piece of somewhat direct advice here would read something like 'if I were you, I would go ahead with the pregnancy because the
risks are very minute'. Even any other vaguely formulated opinion to H's
question may run the risk of being taken up as potential advice. Instead D
turns the 'advice seeking' into an 'information giving' sequence. In sequential
terms, this strategy resembles that of therapists who avoid answering direct
questions like 'why are we here' and posit them instead as occasions for self-
reflection by clients (see our earlier discussion of group therapy in section 3).

D's formulation in turn 07 ('*you are asking two separate questions*') now
prepares the ground for him to offer expert explanations about the nature
of risk associated with a recurrence of the tumour in the wife's brain, or
with the baby inheriting a tumour. A decision – shared or otherwise – about
pregnancy clearly falls outside the remit of genetic counselling. Instead D
creates the interactional space, through turn design, for an information-as-
explanation sequence. In fact, we notice that a hyper-explanation follows,
which is suggestive of interactional difficulty and ambivalent role expectations. To an extent, the sequential transformation of an advice seeking move
into an information-as-explanation giving sequence may be regarded as a
characteristic feature of genetic counselling. It is, however, quite possible
to imagine that the husband and wife may read D's explanation as advice
or as (dis)confirmation of views they held prior to attending the clinic.
This reading will coincide with Silverman's (1997) idea about packaging
information-as-advice. In order to understand why D is reluctant to offer

H any explicit expert advice, we need to bear in mind the emphasis on non-directiveness in genetic counselling (see Sarangi and Clarke 1999 for an extended transcript and a fuller account of this case).

The final critical moment in genetic counselling is the negotiation of decisions about predictive tests involving children. The ethical and legal issues are paramount here as the counsellor needs to balance what is 'in the best interest of the child' and what constitutes the parental right to genetic information about their children. In the following example, the mother wants to test her elder son's carrier status with regard to a chromosome trans-location which runs in the family. Her younger child was tested when he was very young and he is in the clear. There are now sensitive issues around getting the elder son tested, including informed consent, provision for disclosure of test results if the test were to be carried out and the results were to be positive (for an extended transcript and a detailed discussion, see Sarangi and Clarke 1998). The mother suggests that a blood sample could be taken under some other pretext (e.g., being anaemic because of nose bleeds). The extract here opens with the doctor raising his concerns about 'doing something surreptitiously':

Data Example 5
[D: geneticist; M: mother]

01 D: yeah (.) oh well we could certainly do that of course (.) I I have (.5) I've got a (.) just a slight sort of (.5) eh::::: (.) question mark in my mind about doing something too surreptitiously you know
02 M: =mmh
03 D: =I mean if if (.) if that's what we did (.) and (.) eh (.5) (the result) came back clear it wouldn't be a problem (.) wouldn't have to say anything at this stage but if (1.0) but if one did it and it did show the chromosome thing
04 M: =mmh
05 D: =so (.) you'd be then having to think well (.5) when's the best time to raise it and how do we do it (.) it would (.5) it might then mean having to say to him that you know that blood test we took a couple of years ago (.)
06 M: mmh yeah
07 D: that that wasn't really for (.5) ehm you know to check if you're anaemic 'cause of the nose bleeds (.) eh:::: (.5) it was actually for something different
08 M: =mmh mmh
09 D: =and and (.) do you think that would be hard? (.) to (.5) to say to him would (.)
10 D: |ehm [slight laugh]
11 M: |ehm I see your point
12 D: =I– I don't know him so I'm not– I don't know how he'd take–
13 M: =He's a very sensitve (.) may be sensitive 'cause he's going through a lot of trauma at the moment 'cause my father is quite ill (.) so he's very weepy anyway at this stage [laughing]
14 D: =right
15 M: =but ehm (.) I guess that's part of I think he would accept having a blood test done and the I think you know the only thing is is to say well we

checked for anaemia but also they've checked for other bits and pieces as well (.) at the same time and (.) tell it that way at least that way you're covering yourself (.)

16 D: yeah

17 M: and ehm– (.5)

18 D: we–

19 M: and we can bring it up say in a year or so's time then because (.) they started to cover genes and things like that now

20 D: =it's in the national curriculum isn't it now

21 M: =biology and they just go into it so we could always broach ehm because he has started to ask questions now about (.) Down syndrome children and

22 D: =right

23 M: =how that happens so::::: ehm (.) you know he's (.) he's quite an in– for his age he is ehm very intelligent ehm

24 D: =yeah

25 M: =I'm not saying it because he is mine

26 D: [laughing]

27 M: =but everybody the teachers in school said well he's way beyond his years really but

28 D: =yeah

29 M: I think something like this will play on his mind for (.5) a long time you know and there's no real need

This extract differs significantly from the earlier two instances of information-giving and advice-seeking, as both parties pursue their ethical and utilitarian concerns with the help of different modes of explanation and justification. Both seem to be framing their explanations 'in the best interest of the child', but the warrants for their justification seem to be located in different domains. D happens to be more concerned about the ethical principles surrounding genetic tests of children and disclosure of results *vis-à-vis* parents' right to know. He paints the alternative scenario (turns 03, 05 and 07) where the test results might be positive, and invites M to put herself in the position of handling the information-giving activity to her son (cf. Maynard (1991) on perspective display sequence for delivery of bad news). This interaction is also complex because of the prevalence of hypothetical action scenarios embedded within one another (Peräkylä 1995). Projections into the future are inevitable when a discussion centres around predictive tests. But note that the formulation of hypothetical projections by D makes use of contra-indications (realised as *'if one did it and it did show the chromosome thing'*; *'it might then mean having to say . . . it [the blood test] was actually for something different'*). These contra-indications serve to highlight the doctor's reluctance in agreeing to the mother's request for the predictive test and for withholding the test result if it is positive.

Following M's remark in turn 11 (*'I see your point'*), turn 12 marks an interesting transition. M now seizes the floor to forward her argument in favour of the test and for not disclosing the results. It's not only that M differs from D in her outlook, but also that her warrants for justification come from the emotional and educational domains: the child is sensitive and he is not yet ready, despite being intelligent, to understand how genetics works (see turns 13ff). When the testing involves children, even if they are not co-present, their voices and perspectives are constantly brought to bear on the decision-making process. In most clinics concerned with childhood testing, the consultations are characterisable as multi-party interaction even if there are only two participants (doctor and parent) who are co-present. The cumulative manipulation of different voices while offering explanations and justifications may be seen as yet another distinctive aspect of genetic counselling activity.

5 Summary and concluding remarks

In this chapter I have revisited Levinson's notion of 'activity types', which developed the idea that language analysis needs to be done in context as it is done by participants *in situ*. I have argued that the activity type framework has a stronger explanatory power to account for the differential functions that 'discourse types' serve in communicative practices, both contemporaneously and historically. Discourse types are, however, not imported into activity types willy nilly, and therefore a systematic examination of what I have called 'interactional hybridity' *vis-à-vis* specific activity types can be useful. I have also suggested that, in the light of the multiple levels at which activity types and discourse types configure in talk and text, hybridity is most likely to be manifest at the interactional level. So, hybridity in itself is not an indication of the failure of the activity type framework. On the contrary, hybridity is recognisable, both by participants and analysts, only against an idealised activity type (following the Darwinian thesis on the relation between hybridism and sterility).

In an exploratory way I have drawn attention to genetic counselling as an emergent activity type and have focused my analysis on how various discourse types are embedded within this activity. I have put forward the view that genetic counselling is constituted in three critical moments: information giving, advice seeking and decision making. Talk primarily plays an informational, and perhaps hyper-explanatory, role as genetic counsellors account for relevant aspects of why a particular genetic condition has happened or might happen. It is the dual informational and explanatory modes of talk in genetic counselling which distinguish it from other forms of therapy talk and counselling talk.

Let me conclude this chapter, in the same manner as Levinson, by returning to Wittgenstein's (1958: I.23) statement that 'language games' and 'language types' are not fixed: 'new types of language, new language-games, as we may say, come into existence, and others become obsolete and get forgotten'. It is perhaps not an overstatement to claim that genetic counselling is a new 'language game' (i.e., activity type), accompanied by 'new types of language' (i.e., discourse types) and that the hybridity between the two poses a challenge for both participants and discourse analysts.

Notes

1. I would like to acknowledge the financial support of the Leverhulme Trust (RF&G/2/9800687) for my ongoing study of 'risk communication in genetic counselling'.
2. It is worth mentioning the inherent problem in speech act models as they attempt to establish linkage between utterances and activities, without taking into account the interactional location of the utterance (see Turner 1971 for a detailed account).
3. Levinson's activity paper should be read together with his other (1988) influential paper on roles, the latter drawing heavily on Goffman's participant-structure. It foregrounds a shift from language to talk-in-interaction, and is quite appropriately titled 'putting linguistics on a proper footing'. Levinson, however, does not refer to Goffman's work in the activity type paper.
4. The following transcription conventions have been followed in this paper: dots or numbers between round brackets denote pause; texts within square brackets are glosses; vertical line (|) signals overlaps; equal sign (=) means latching; extended colons (:::) stand for lengthened sound and untranscribable segments are signalled by [^^^^]. I am grateful to the Royal College of General Practitioners, London, for giving their kind permission for the use of Example 1.
5. Prior to the oral, the examiners decide on the topic areas to be covered during the interview. The exact formulation of a question may or may not have been written down (for more details, see Roberts and Sarangi 1999).
6. This is a case of an 'institutional' response which aligns with what the interviewer would like to hear and then let it pass (see Roberts and Sarangi 1999, Sarangi (forthcoming), on a distinction between institutional, professional and personal experience modes in interview talk).
7. See Gaik (1992) for an interesting discussion of radio talk-shows as therapeutic.
8. This is relevant for us because genetic counselling is offered in various formats in various places. In some instances, it is offered by trained counsellors, whereas in my clinical site the counsellors happen to be medical practitioners, including clinical genetic consultants.
9. It is worth noting that this is a biased characterisation of the clinic since the doctor's action sequence is taken as the organising principle of the activity type.
10. In the site where I am studying these clinics, a home visit by a genetic specialist nurse usually precedes the clinic activity. The main purpose of such visits is to alert patients/clients about what to expect from the clinic, given that it is so different from their experience of mainstream doctor–patient encounters. It also allows the nurse to elicit relevant information about the family tree and to address issues of consent for review of medical records. The following brief extract from a home visit reflects this:

> Nurse: the form is fairly explanatory there (.) it's just (.) asking his permission if we may look at his notes . . . the idea is that we would then have done some homework before you come to the clinic (.) so that we're able to give you better information . . .

11. There is an ongoing debate about the desirability and feasibility of non-directiveness in genetic counselling (see Clarke 1991, 1997, Mitchie et al. 1997, Wolff and Jung 1995). Also, very little is known about the interactional management of (non)directiveness in the clinical setting.

References

Austin, J.L. (1962) *How to Do Things with Words*. Oxford: Clarendon Press.

Bar-Hillel, Y. (1957) Three methodological remarks on 'fundamentals of language'. *Word* 13, 323–335.

Berger, P. and Luckmann, T. (1967) *The Social Construction of Reality: A Treaty in the Sociology of Knowledge*. Harmondsworth: Penguin.

Bourdieu, P. (1994) *In Other Words: Essays towards a Reflexive Sociology*. Cambridge: Polity Press.

Byrne, P.S. and Long, B.E.L. (1976) *Doctors Talking to Patients: A Study of the Verbal Behaviour of General Practitioners Consulting in their Surgeries*. London: HMSO.

Candlin, C.N. and Lucas, J. (1986) Interpretations and explanations in discourse: modes of 'advising' in family planning. In T. Ensink et al. (eds), *Discourse Analysis and Public Life*. Dordrecht: Foris, 13–38.

Cicourel, A.V. (1992) The interpenetration of communicative contexts: examples from medical encounters. In A. Duranti and C. Goodwin (eds), 291–310.

Clarke, A. (1991) Is non-directive genetic counselling possible? *Lancet* 338, 998–1001.

Clarke, A. (1997) The process of genetic counselling: beyond non-directiveness. In P.S. Harper and A.J. Clarke (eds), *Genetics, Society and Clinical Practice*. Oxford: Bios Scientific Publishers, 179–200.

Douglas, J. (ed.) (1971) *Understanding Everyday Life: Toward the Reconstruction of Sociological Knowledge*. London: Routledge & Kegan Paul.

Drew, P. and Heritage, J. (eds) (1992) *Talk at Work: Interaction in Institutional Settings*. Cambridge: Cambridge University Press.

Duranti, A. and Goodwin, C. (eds) (1992) *Rethinking Context: Language as an Interactive Phenomenon*. Cambridge: Cambridge University Press.

Erickson, F. (1976) Gatekeeping encounters: a social selection process. In P.R. Sanday (ed.), *Anthropology and Public Interest*. New York: Academic Press, 111–145.

Erickson, F. and Shultz, J. (1982) *The Counsellor as Gatekeeper: Social Interaction in Interviews*. New York: Academic Press.

Fairclough, N. (1989) *Language and Power*. London: Longman.

Fairclough, N. (1992) *Discourse and Social Change*. Cambridge: Polity Press.

Fairclough, N. (1995) *Critical Discourse Analysis*. London: Longman.

Gaik, F. (1992) Radio talk-show therapy and the pragmatics of possible worlds. In A. Duranti and C. Goodwin (eds), 271–289.

Gale, J.E. (1991) *Conversation Analysis of Therapeutic Discourse: The Pursuit of a Therapeutic Agenda*. Norwood, NJ: Ablex.

Garfinkel, H. (1967) *Studies in Ethnomethodology*. Engelwood Cliffs, NJ: Prentice Hall.

Goffman, E. (1969) *Strategic Interaction*. Philadelphia: University of Philadelphia Press.

Goffman, E. (1974) *Frame Analysis*. New York: Harper & Row.

Goffman, E. (1981) *Forms of Talk*. Oxford: Blackwell.

Greatbatch, D. and Dingwall, R. (1999) Professional neutralism in family mediation. In S. Sarangi and C. Roberts (eds), 271–292.

Grice, H.P. (1975) Logic and conversation. In P. Cole and J.L. Morgan (eds), *Syntax and Semantics, Vol. III: Speech Acts*. New York: Academic Press, 41–58.

Gumperz, J.J. (1982) *Discourse Strategies*. Cambridge: Cambridge University Press.

Heritage, J. and Lindström, A. (1998) Motherhood, medicine and morality: scenes from a medical encounter. *Research on Language and Social Interaction* 31, 397–438.

Heritage, J. and Sefi, S. (1992) Dilemmas of advice: aspects of the delivery and reception of advice in interactions between health visitors and first-time mothers. In P. Drew and J. Heritage (eds), 359–417.

Hymes, D. (1964) *Language in Culture and Society*. New York: Harper & Row.

Jakobson, R. (1976) Metalanguage as a linguistic problem. In *Selected Writings VII*. Berlin: Mouton de Gruyter, 113–121.

Jakobson, R. (1990) *On Language*. Edited by L.R. Waugh and M. Monville-Burston. Cambridge, Mass.: Harvard University Press.

Jefferson, G. and Lee, J. (1981) The rejection of advice: managing the problematic convergence of a 'troubles-telling' and a service encounter. *Journal of Pragmatics* 5, 399–422.

Labov, W. and Fanshel, D. (1977) *Therapeutic Discourse: Psychotherapy as Conversation*. New York: Academic Press.

Leont'ev, A.N. (1978) *Activity, Consciousness, and Personality*. Trans M.J. Hall. Englewood Cliffs, NJ: Prentice Hall.

Levinson, S. (1979) Activity types and language. *Linguistics* 17, 356–399. Reprinted in P. Drew and J. Heritage (eds), 66–100.

Levinson, S. (1988) Putting linguistics on a proper footing: explorations in Goffman's concepts of participation. In P. Drew and A.J. Wootton (eds), *Erving Goffman: Exploring the Interaction Order*. Cambridge: Cambridge University Press, 161–227.

Linell, P. (1998) *Approaching Dialogue: Talk, Interaction and Contexts in Dialogical Perspectives*. Amsterdam: John Benjamins.

McHugh, P. (1968) *Defining the Situation: The Organisation of Meaning in Social Interaction*. Indianapolis: Bobbs-Merrill.

Maynard, D. (1991) Perspective-display sequences and the delivery and receipt of diagnostic news. In D. Boden and D.H. Zimmerman (eds), *Talk and Social Structure*. Cambridge: Polity Press, 164–192.

Michie, S., Bron, F., Bobrow, M. and Marteau, T.M. (1997) Nondirectiveness in genetic counseling: an empirical study. *American Journal of Human Genetics* 60, 40–47.

Miller, G. and Silverman, D. (1995) Troubles talk and counselling discourse: a comparative study. *Sociological Quarterly* 36, 4, 725–747.

Peräkylä, A. (1995) *AIDS Counselling: Institutional Interaction and Clinical Practice*. Cambridge: Cambridge University Press.

Psathas, G. (1995) 'Talk and social structure' and 'studies of work'. *Human Studies* 18, 139–155.

Roberts, C. (1985) *The Interview Game, Interview Training and Housing*. Broadcast by BBC between 5 and 19 January 1986.

Roberts, C. and Sarangi, S. (1999) Hybridity in gatekeeping discourse: issues of practical relevance for the researcher. In S. Sarangi and C. Roberts (eds), 473–503.

Rommetveit, R. (1974) *On Message Structure: A Framework for the Study of Language and Communication*. London: John Wiley & Sons.

Sacks, H. (1985) The inference-making machine: notes on observability. In T. van Dijk (ed.), *Handbook of Discourse Analysis*, Vol. 3. London: Academic Press, 13–23.

Sacks, H., Schegloff, E. and Jefferson, G. (1974) A simplest systematics for the organisation of turn-taking in conversation. *Language* 50, 4, 696–735.

Sarangi, S. (1994) Accounting for mismatches in intercultural selection interviews. *Multilingua* 13, 1/2, 163–194.

Sarangi, S. (forthcoming) Institutional, professional and lifeworld frames in interview talk. In M. Wetherell, H. van den Berg and H. Houtkoop-Steenstra (eds), *Analysing Interviews on Racial Issues*. Cambridge University Press.

Sarangi, S. and Clarke, A.J. (1998) Constructing an account by contrast in childhood genetic testing. Paper presented at the *International Pragmatics Conference*, Reims, 17–24 July.

Sarangi, S. and Clarke, A.J. (1999) Appeals to expertise and authority in genetics risk communication. Paper at the International Association for Dialogue Analysis, University of Birmingham, 8–10 April 1999.

Sarangi, S. and Roberts, C. (1999) *Talk, Work and Institutional Order: Discourse in Medical, Mediation and Management Settings*. Berlin: Mouton de Gruyter.

Saussure, F. (1966) *Course in General Linguistics*, trans. W. Baskin. New York: McGraw-Hill.

Silverman, D. (1997) *Discourses of Counselling: HIV Counselling as Social Interaction*. London: Sage.

Strong, P.M. (1979) *The Ceremonial Order of the Clinic: Parents, Doctors and Medical Bureaucracies*. London: Routledge & Kegan Paul.

Ten Have, P. (1989) The consultation as a genre. In B. Torode (ed.), *Text and Talk as Social Practice: Discourse Difference and Division in Speech and Writing*. Dordrecht: Foris Publications, 115–135.

Turner, R. (1971) Words, utterances and activities. In J. Douglas (ed.), 165–187.

Turner, R. (1972) Some formal properties of therapy talk. In D. Sudnow (ed.) *Studies in Social Interaction*. New York: Free Press, 367–396.

Voloshinov, V.N. (1986 [1929]) *Marxism and the Philosophy of Language*. Trans. L. Matjeka and I.R. Titunik. Cambridge: Harvard University Press.

Watson, R. (1996) Some general reflections on 'categorisation' and 'sequence' in the analysis of conversation. In S. Hester and P. Eglin (eds), *Culture in Action: Studies in Membership Categorisation Analysis*. Lanham, MD and London: International Institute for Ethnomethodology and University Press of America, 49–78.

Weber, M. (1949 [1904]) *The Methodology of the Social Sciences*. Glencoe: Free Press.

Wilson, T. (1971) Normative and interpretative paradigms in sociology. In J. Douglas, (ed.), 57–79.

Wittgenstein, L. (1958) *Philosophical Investigations*. Oxford: Blackwell.

Wolff, G. and Jung, C. (1995) Nondirectiveness and genetic counselling. *Journal of Genetic Counseling* 4, 1, 3–25.

Chapter 2

The uses of talk

Ruqaiya Hasan

1   Introduction: learning how to play power games

Does the neonate have intimations of power? When it screams because it is in need of some attention from an other, is it engaged in the active exercise of power? When it searches for the mother's breast without any realisation of what exactly it is searching for, does it have a sense of being dependent? One might dismiss such questions lightly as fanciful, clearly calling for a negative answer. But then how do we account for the fact that this same neonate grown taller does engage in power games, sometimes as the one who exercises it, sometimes as the one who undergoes its exercise by others? I will ignore explanations that appeal to inherent elements in the neonate's personality which some might imagine grows naturally with the physically growing baby. I do not wish to imply by this rejection that there is no bio-genetic foundation to human personality, but I do wish to assert that the appeal to inherent personality traits is far from sufficient if for the simple reason that engagement in power games is in one respect something like engagement in conversation: sometimes you give, sometimes you receive; no one is always at the giving end, and no one always at the receiving end. Which means of course that typically both power and dependence combine in the same personality – by and by, the neonate must come to know how and when it is 'the done thing' to dominate and how and when it is 'wise' to submit to domination. We know that the problem of how the management of this game becomes second nature has, one way or another, occupied sociologists, anthropologists and psychologists for a long time. Which goes to show that the ramifications of the problem implicate every aspect of the living of life. My intention is not to engage in a discussion of this wide range of phenomena, but simply to examine one facet of apprenticeship to life which appears to be deeply implicated in turning the innocent neonate into a fully fledged participant in the power games prevalent in a society.

   The facet I have in mind concerns an unavoidable aspect of human life, namely participation in talk with others. Although very much stronger claims can be made about the role of languaging in the construal of social power,

I will again, for lack of space, ignore these wider and more fundamental considerations. Instead, I will simply postulate what seems to me the weakest hypothesis: namely that fashions of talking vary in the extent to which speaking subjects are able to position the interacting other in ways that contribute to the success of their own agenda. Not surprisingly, the ability to manage talk as it were on one's feet is often viewed as a measure of control over the discursive situation. Recent studies of asymmetrical talk, especially in the institutionalised environments of workplace, such as job interviews, clinical consultations or committee meetings, all show that moving with the movement of talk and making the talk move to suit one's own purposes is one way of holding one's own in various categories of discursive power games.[1] It seems to me that underlying this property of movement in talk – which is often subsumed under what is currently known as 'hybridity', a term applied to the mixing of the recognised properties of different pre-existing genres – is speakers' readiness to constantly reclassify discursive situations. With apologies for oversimplification due to lack of space, let me explain briefly what I mean by the expression *reclassification of discursive situations*.

1.1 Reclassification of con/text

After decades of disdain, most linguists have come to agree with Malinowski about the relevance of context of situation to language use (Malinowski 1923, 1935), though many still deny its relevance to language system. The properties of discursive situations which by tacit consent most linguists have found relevant to language may be worded, with apologies to Fishman (1965), as *who says what to whom where when and how*. Identifying the foci in this slogan, we theorise the ARC of discursive context as embracing the three parameters of Action, Relation and Contact – what social activity is being performed by persons in what social relation and what is the mode of their contact.[2] Any one occasion of talk 'is a' configuration of some specific type of action, relation and contact; and in most cases the continuity of discourse implies that the interactants have reached a sufficiently congruent reading of these specifics to allow a reasonable pursuit of joint activity. But a discursive situation so established is not, as it were, carved in stone: under certain circumstances, the specifics of the parameters might shift as the talk continues.[3] For example, what in informal talk we perceive as a quarrel very often does not begin as a quarrel; rather, it develops in the course of the talk occurring *a propos* some action the interactants are already engaged in. In turn, this quarrel is indicative of a *con/textual shift*: that is to say, at that textual point where the quarrel 'happens', there occurs a shift in the text's design. So, if with Halliday (1977) we think of *text* as language occurring *a propos* some social activity, clearly the quarrel-talk would not be seen as occurring *a propos* that particular activity which the interactants had been engaged in before they started quarrelling: whatever the generic/registral

29

requirements of that previous discourse, they must be at least suspended, if not totally abandoned. At the same time, by virtue of the dialectic of context and text, there is a shift in the context as well, in the sense that the interactants are no longer engaged in the activity which they were performing previously: they are fighting, not doing whatever they were doing before. Their mutual relation too is now different: they are antagonists, having suspended/abandoned their previous personae, whatever those might have been, and so on. So in one sense, what happens is that the ongoing con/text is *reclassified* which is what I mean by saying things like *the discourse has moved* or *the con/text has shifted*. In one respect, con/textual shift is something like Gumperz' (metaphorical) code switching, minus the switching of codes! In metaphorical code switching, two things change: speakers switch to another language/dialect and this, as it were, becomes an indicator of change of context (Blom and Gumperz 1972); in talk of code switching, attention has not been specifically drawn to genre/register switch. By comparison, in what I am calling con/textual shift, speakers use their language differently from how they were using it before: they have 'done' a register/genre switch without necessarily engaging in a change of language or dialect: in other words the con/text has been reclassified. And yet, to leave the matter at this point would be misleading. An interesting feature of con/textual shift is that such a shift does not necessarily represent a complete break from the previous genre/register. Quite often the talk that is indicative of the con/textual reclassification ends up playing a part in the management of whatever discourse was in process previously: the shift thus becomes a *sub-text* to an ongoing text, playing some part in its management. In Goffman's (1974) terminology, we have frames within frames, though I am suggesting that there is always a functional relation between the text and the sub-text. I will draw attention to some of these details in the discussion below. The skill with which one is able to manage such shifts to as it were 'contain' their disruptive influence is of considerable consequence in controlling the course of interaction.

1.2   Con/textual shift and the management of discursive control

I want to suggest that the disposition to entertain shifting boundaries in discursive situations is something that is very likely to have been inculcated early in children, precisely because the apprehension of such shifts has to be rooted in the experience of semiosis. The ability to perceive these abstract shifts and to actively manage them makes an important contribution to gaining ground in social encounters of various kinds which are ostensibly democratically organised but which can be often turned to one's own advantage if one knows how to exploit this strategy. In the rest of this chapter I want to do two things. First, evidence from research (Cloran 1994, 1999a; Williams 1995) points to the fact that there is systematic variation in children's early experience of the management of con/textual shifts. I want to examine some instances of mother–child dialogues that demonstrate the ways in which the early recognition of such shifts is encouraged or discouraged in everyday talk (sections 2–4). A condition for success in the invisible inculcation of attitudes to the reclassification of con/text is precisely that the entire procedure should appear completely natural: the shift in discourse should not be heard as a form of disjunction, but simply as a natural continuation of talk. This raises the question: how is this seamlessness of the con/textual shifts created and maintained. Secondly, I want to suggest an answer to this question, which will call for a functional explanation of what these con/textual shifts do in the ongoing discourse. The chapter will close with a brief comment on the use of the term 'hybridity', focusing particularly on what is implied in the use of this metaphor for describing a massively prevalent property of talk (section 5).

The mother–child dialogues (segments of which are presented and discussed below) form part of an extensive database collected for a sociolinguistic research at Macquarie University.[4] The 24 mother–child dyads who participated in the research are native speakers of English from areas around Sydney. The mean age of the children was three years eight months. The recording was done by the mothers themselves, each of whom recorded in the privacy of her home approximately 5 hours of talk with the subject child; the recording was spread over some 4–6 weeks, and it was done while the mother was engaged in chores which she would typically carry out in her everyday living of life. The contextual ambience of the data may thus be described in general terms as relevant to the living of life in families with small children. Since the main purpose of my research was to carry out a quantitative analysis of certain aspects of the semantic content of discourse, I decided to segment the data into messages[5] rather than turns. A message is the smallest semantic unit capable of functioning as a discursive stage or an element of the generic structure of text, call it what you will. A message itself is realised lexicogrammatically as a clause and thus expresses, among other information, some state of affairs and some rhetorical stance through the choices of transitivity and mood respectively. As such, the kind of work a message does in the structuring of texts, as well as the kind of information it carries in its own make up, are matters that are somewhat more unambiguous than can be claimed for the notion of turn taking, not forgetting the fact that the latter is also limited in its application to only dialogic discourse, with the result that the comparison of dialogic and monologic discourse poses a problem if the analysis of dialogue is in terms of turn taking. So far as the discussion in this chapter is concerned, the message numbers act as a convenient means of identifying the points in the segment where some significant reclassification of con/text is being negotiated. The scope of the chapter does not allow the presentation of the analysis of the various subtexts as rhetorical units, which would further highlight the merits of treating message as the unit of analysis.[6]

2   Moving with the movement of talk

With this brief introduction let us turn to dialogue 1.1, where Kristy's mother is trying to get a more than reluctant Kristy to get ready to go to a play group while at the same time she is attending to the needs of Kristy's toddler sister, Ruth.[7] The recording opens as follows:

Dialogue 1.1

Kristy: (1) what about I fold the cardboard (2) and then ≪(3) if I want some pieces≫ um—

Mother: (4) well how about I get you dressed instead?

Kristy: (5) no don't want to go out today (CRIES)

Mother: (6) you'll have a lovely day pet (7) I won't be late home either (8) I'll probably be home about the same time as Dee's big kids get home . . maybe a little bit later, may be a little bit earlier (KRISTY CONTINUES CRYING) (9) oh dear oh dear . . I don't think you are really upset about me going (10) I think you're upset (11) because the [?] wasn't working (RUTH CALLS OUT TO MOTHER) (12) Ruth wants to go on the potty

Kristy: (13) I don't want to [?go away] (CRYING ALL THE WHILE)

Mother: (14) come on . . oh dear oh dear

Kristy: (15) mummy I don't want to go away from you

Mother: (16) you go away from me to kinder,[8] don't you?

Kristy: (17) **yeah but—

Mother: (18) **and you like going away from me sometimes

Kristy: (19) yeah but then I don't meet so many kids at kinder (20) and there's not only a big room

Mother: (21) you mean you want to go to kinder (22) but you don't want to go to Dee's?

Kristy: (23) yeah (24) (PEEVISHLY TO RUTH) don't!

Mother: (25) oh she's trying to be nice (26) don't get cranky

And here is another extract from the same dialogue:

Dialogue 1.3

Mother: (94) but you often call people a goose (95) if they're silly

Kristy: (96) hmm

Mother: (97) you know ≪(98) if you eat too much≫ I say you're a little pig (99) you're a little piggy-wig

Kristy: (100) yeah (LAUGHING)

Mother: (101) well ≪(102) if people are silly≫ you say 'silly goose!' (103) and sometimes you can say they're a donkey (104) 'you silly donkey!'

Kristy: (105) silly donkey! (LAUGHS)

Mother: (106) and ≪(107) if they are fussy≫ what do you say?** (108) I think you'd say they're a hen . . or a mother hen

Dialogue 1.1 quite unambiguously declares the mother's concern with getting both her children ready to embark on the business of the day. Embedded within this materially accomplishable activity is the semiotic activity of persuading Kristy to get ready to go to Dee's. Dialogue 1.3, on the other hand, just as unambiguously shows the mother engaged in instructing Kristy on an aspect of language[9]; and this context appears to have nothing to do with what was going on in 1.1, though both are parts of the same dialogue. How did the discourse of the desirability of going or not going to Dee's in dialogue 1.1 turn, in dialogue 1.3, into a discourse of instruction on the use of metaphors?

This, as a matter of fact, is an analyst's question: for the interactants in the dialogue the shifts are naturalised as a normal feature of the flow of ordinary everyday talk. Here, there is no perceptible point of discontinuity, as does happen sometimes when a completely different conversation is struck in the course of the same dialogue.[10] By contrast, what happens in con/textual shifts is perhaps best described as a 'gradual becoming', where the discourse of one thing merges into the discourse of another – which is precisely the case with respect to our two examples. Following dialogue 1.1, in between attending to Ruth's needs, the mother has humoured Kristy into allowing herself to start getting dressed, but tears and tantrums are not far away: Kristy's co-operation is still precarious. Fights with Ruth have broken out. Kristy is fully aware that she is being manoeuvred, and that her preferred plan is being thwarted despite the spate of 'legitimate reasons' she has offered against the mother's agenda of sending her to Dee's. She knows it is a contest in which she is likely to lose, and at every point she is anxious to reveal to the mother something that might be a cause for concern in sending her away. This brings us to the following point in the dialogue:[11]

Dialogue 1.2

Kristy: (61) mummy I think I'm going to get cold today

Mother: (62) I have no idea what the weather is going to be like today (63) I'll send your sweatshirt or your cardigan or your jumper or whatever you'd like over too

Kristy: (64) I want— I want a short-sleeved cardigan— a long-sleeved one (65) if it goes hot (66) I'll have to wear a short-sleeved one so**—

Mother: (67) **yep (68) well see yesterday I thought it was going to be cold (69) and you were really hot by the end of the day (70) so I think the best thing is to put a short-sleeved tee-shirt on you and a cardigan

Kristy: (71) yeah (72) I think we don't know what day its going to be

Mother: (73) no (74) it's a bit [?   ] in spring and autumn, isn't it? (75) stand up straight (76) so I can get your duds on (77) in winter it is cold (78) and in the summer it's hot (79) and in the spring and the autumn it's funny (RUTH IS HEARD CRYING) (80) oh Ruth! . . (81) (TO KRISTY) she's jammed her fingers in the sewing box (82) [?put] her hand on top of the [?lid] . . (83) silly monkey!

Kristy: (84) silly monkey!

Mother: (85) she had her hand in [?the box]

Kristy: (86) yeah

Mother: (87) and she had the other hand on top (88) pushing it down (89) squashing her hand (KRISTY LAUGHS) (90) oh you're a goose Ruth!

Kristy: (91) oh you're a goose! (92) do goosies do that?

Mother: (93) no no (94) *but you often call people a goose* (95) *if they're silly*

Kristy: (96) *hmm*

As will be noted, the italicised messages of dialogue 1.2 are in fact the opening messages of dialogue 1.3: it is the response to Ruth's antics that evokes 'silly monkey!' and 'silly goose!'. The talk has thus moved to the explication of metaphors via attention to Ruth, which is itself an integral part of the original concern. The mother appears to grasp this opportunity to inform Kristy about the ways of saying and meaning typical to some members of her community.

3 Protecting an established con/text

There is no exaggeration in the claim that in all naturally occurring everyday dialogue, openings for textual shifts of one kind or another present themselves. Whether these 'opportunities' will develop sufficiently to claim the status of an established shift depends a good deal on the readiness of the interactants to re-classify the context of their interaction – to move with the movement of talk without letting go of the primary concern. However, the readiness to re-classify the discursive situation is not a uniform characteristic of talk everywhere: as I have implied above speakers vary in the extent to which they will entertain con/textual shifts. We thus have a paradox: on the one hand, *all* informal everyday talk is potentially open to the possibility of these con/textual shifts; on the other hand, *not all* speakers are equally willing to re-classify the discursive situation. How does this paradox manifest itself in discourse? I will use a dialogue between Karen and her mother to answer this question. This dialogue occurs at mealtime and the recording opens with Karen requesting first some sauce on her food, then some lemonade. The mother attends to these requests and reminds Karen of the need to observe her 'linguistic table manners', asking her to say *please!* and commenting *I didn't hear a thank you from you*. With these niceties observed, we come to the following point:

Dialogue 2.1

Mother: (32) come on, eat your tea please . .
Karen: (33) could you put some more[12] in there? . .
Mother: (34) (WARNINGLY) Karen! . . (35) give me it (36) eat your tea
Karen: (37) [?   ]
Mother: (38) mm?
Karen: (39) [?put] lemon in it
Mother: (40) well, eat some tea (41) or you don't get nothing
Karen: (42) I see how many [?   ] there are (TALKS TO HERSELF AS MOTHER POURS DRINK)
Mother: (43) quick . . (44) want the lid on it?
Karen: (45) no
Mother: (46) come on, eat your tea (47) less drink (48) and more eat . . (49) did you hear what I said Karen?
Karen: (50) mm
Mother: (51) well, do it

Dialogue 2.1 construes a context where the mother's primary concern is to get Karen to *eat her tea*. Anything that interrupts this activity is seen as disruptive. The mother has defined the parameters of the discursive context and she is going to insist on the inviolability of that classification. Within a dialogue lasting some 20 minutes, the mother produces the injunction to *eat your tea* over 20 times. There certainly occur brief moments in the discourse which bear a nascent possibility of move to some other discursive path but the mother does not entertain these possibilities. Here is one such example, which follows shortly after dialogue 2.1:

Dialogue 2.2

Karen:	(81) mummy that haven't got no sauce on it
Mother:	(82) oh you've got plenty of sauce there now (83) now eat it
Karen:	(84) on here
Mother:	(85) oh there's plenty of sauce on your plate Karen (86) you don't need it on every single drop of tea
Karen:	(87) eh?
Mother:	(88) you don't need it on every little bit
Karen:	(89) [?of tea]?
Mother:	(90) mm
Karen:	(91) is that [?tea]?
Mother:	(92) that's sauce
Karen:	(93) mm hot sauce
Mother:	(94) no, mint sauce
Karen:	(95) mince? . . (96) why do you put mince sauce on here for?
Mother:	(97) 'mint' not 'mince'
Karen:	(98) mint (99) this mint?
Mother:	(100) use your spoon or your fork
Karen:	(101) 'Country Practice' is on now?
Mother:	(102) no
Karen:	(103) 'Sons and Daughters'?
Mother:	(104) no, the news
Karen:	(105) oh . .
Mother:	(106) that's why I said use a spoon . . (107) now sit up (108) and use a spoon

In dialogue 2.2, Karen has initiated many different openings for a discursive shift. For example, at (91) she raises the question of the referential scope of the word *tea*. The mother's response is certainly locally adequate: what Karen was pointing to was not strictly speaking *tea*; it was *sauce*. But note that the mother has been instructing the child to *eat her tea*, and some elaboration of the reference of the term *tea* would not have been irrelevant. This elaboration is not entertained presumably because it would have been a divergence from the actual business in hand. Karen's enquiry at (96) *why do you put mince sauce on here for?* is handled in the same way: it is used as an occasion for a local correction of the child's pronunciation, rather than an explanation the girl was after. That explanation too would have taken the discourse in a rather different direction. Finally, Karen's reference to a couple of TV programmes – *Country Practice* and *Sons and Daughters* – offers a chance to move in a direction that would be far removed from any mention of food/eating. The mother 'naturally' does not welcome those openings either, though clearly it is feasible to eat one's tea and talk of unrelated things such as *Country Practice*. Compare Karen's mother's uncompromising devotion to the primary and established context with Stephen's mother's discursive orientation: she too is engaged primarily in attending to her child's meal:

Dialogue 3.2

Mother:	(17) ok . . right . . peanut butter sandwich?
Stephen:	(18) yeah . .
Mother:	(19) you go to the table (20) and I'll bring it in . . (21) there aren't many passionfruits out there at the moment
Stephen:	(22) why?
Mother:	(23) because passionfruit usually come (24) when its warm (25) here, you sit here in nana's seat
Stephen:	**(26) why—
Mother:	**(27) I'll put—
Stephen:	(28) why does Nana like to sit here?
Mother:	(29) oh, its easy for her to get up (30) if she's sitting there . . (31) we have to go to Chatswood this afternoon Stephen
Stephen:	(32) why?

As I have pointed out earlier, the average age of children on this research project was three years eight months, an age where *why?* is one of their commonest utterances. One mother entertains the enquiry in the midst of attending to the child's meal: the mealtime context is thus reclassified as an informative context. Another mother behaves as if the enquiry had never been made, or that it is simply a disruption of the context already defined by her. For Karen's mother, all discourse on this occasion of talk, within this established frame, must pertain to what concerns the eating of tea: talk about sauce, lemonade, spoon and fork is acceptable since it is relevant to the 'right' context; other things which do not directly contribute to the activity of eating here and now are not to be recognised. The effort to keep the child within the bounds of the activity of eating as the only legitimate context leads to the following scenario:

Dialogue 2.3

Mother:	(156) give me your spoon (157) and I'll feed you, like a big baby (158) come on, baby! give me your spoon
Karen:	(159) (SCANDALISED TONE) no
Mother:	(160) well sit up properly (161) and eat your tea . . (162) Karen! (WARNING TONE)
Karen:	(163) I'm falling down (i.e. OFF THE CHAIR)
Mother:	(164) you're not falling down
Karen:	(165) yes I am (166) I always fall down . . (167) **I am falling down
Mother:	(168) **eat your tea
Karen:	(169) I am falling down
Mother:	(170) sit up (171) before I get a stick (172) and smack you

Dialogues 2.1–2.3 probably illustrate quite adequately how the reclassification of a previously established situation might be discouraged. Like much of what we do in language use, the orientation toward the rejection of discursive shifts is entirely naturalised. So far as Karen's mother is concerned 'eat when you are supposed to be eating' is, therefore, logically a desirable principle that needs to be impressed on the growing child: from her perspective, the rejection of con/textual reclassification is entirely rational.[13] And simply because this discursive orientation is naturalised as entirely 'rational', it will manifest itself in nearly every possible discursive environment. Participation in discourse will thus become a massive validation of this rationality, whereby discursive shifts are to be avoided. I suggest that the habitus for the management of an ongoing situation takes shape by participating in myriads of entirely insignificant seeming interactions of the kind exemplified here. Which would be one explanation why some might avoid the reclassification of con/text, while others are hardly aware of weaving in and out of so many different discourses in the same interaction.

But then, does this mean that Karen's mother never entertains con/textual shifts? Strictly speaking this is not true. 'Never' is not a word that can ever be applied comfortably to language either as system or as process! Consider dialogue 2.4, which occurs in the same dialogue after mother and daughter have half seriously exchanged threats to 'hurt' each other under certain conditions:

Dialogue 2.4

Mother:	(266) I'm bigger than you (267) I can hurt more
Karen:	(268) and I could too
Mother:	(269) no you can't
Karen:	(270) yes **I—
Mother:	(271) **you are only a little girl who is becoming a very cheeky little girl
Karen:	(272) no I not
Mother:	(273) and if you don't stop it**
Karen:	(274) **Christine is a naughty girl and spiteful
Mother:	(275) and so are you (276) you're a spiteful little girl (277) when you want to be (278) you can't talk about anybody else (279) if you don't stop it (i.e. DOING OTHER THINGS THAN EATING) (280) you are going to go into bed (281) and you'll never see anybody (282) 'cause I won't let you see any of your friends
Karen:	(283) [?] I will sneak out
Mother:	(284) no you won't sneak out (285) now sit up on that chair (286) and eat your tea
Karen:	(287) yes I will (i.e. SNEAK OUT)
Mother:	(288) Karen . . I am not playing games
Karen:	(289) mum . . Oh mummy (CUDDLING UP TO THE MOTHER)
. . .	
Mother:	(290) no go away (291) don't come crawling to me (292) go away (293) go away (294) I don't want you (295) until you sit down (296) and eat your tea . . (297) go away . . (298) go away (299) Karen leave me alone please

(300) now sit down (301) and eat your tea (302) I won't talk to you (303) until you eat it (304) no I don't want no cuddles (305) no I don't want a cuddle off of you (306) no, no kisses either (307) no I don't want – (308) oh you kiss me (309) I am not kissing you back . . (310) Karen (WARNING TONE)

Karen: (311) it doesn't matter

Mother: (312) it will matter in a minute (313) now stop crawling (314) and sit down (315) and eat your tea

Much of the mother's discourse in dialogue 2.4 construes a regulative context embedded within the tea-eating context just as in the Kristy dialogue the discussion of reasons for or against visiting Dee is embedded within the context of getting ready for the day. In dialogue 2.4 Karen's mother issues the threat of banishing the child from maternal favour – and much worse – unless Karen eats her tea. In other words, somewhat ironically, the con/textual shift has to be used for pointing out the undesirability of entertaining con/textual shift: in this environment it construes a context of control which declares con/textual reclassification to be an illegitimate act.

4   Turning the tide: discursive moves

The last two sections have exemplified two different ways of coping with the onset of con/textual shifts – two different attitudes to the possible reclassification of an already established and ongoing con/text. As I hope to show in the following section one of these two discursive orientations is relatively more conducive to 'getting round people', which, it would not be wrong to say, is the active manifestation of power in play where everyday interaction is concerned. In a curious way, the power that Kristy's mother exercises on Kristy is a classic case of invisible control, where Kristy is literally left resourceless in pushing her own perspective. I now want to turn to the second announced concern of this paper, namely, what accounts for the seamlessness of a discourse that is so full of seams. But, before that it would be appropriate to say a few words on matters relating to the first concern.

The question of the etiology of these discursive orientations – or discursive habitus, if you prefer that term – is complex and deserves a separate discussion. But I want to emphasize quite explicitly that discursive orientation, whatever its etiology, is not static, imbibed once for all never to change. However there seems to be a consensus that the orientations developed in the early years of the life of a social agent are 'self-perpetuating' and not easily modified.[14] It would not be surprising if, as a response to massive participation in discourses of the type which actively encourage or discourage that practice in the early years of life, one developed a predisposition for or an antipathy against moving with the movement of talk. And if power games are played by the use of strategies for managing the movement of discourse which helps one to get round people and to turn the tide of discourse to one's own advantage, then obviously an orientation which shuns con/textual shifts may be expected to position one as a loser in those games. It has become fashionable these days to ask in the presence of such variation: *what should be done?* It seems to me that there are perhaps two ways of struggling against this situation. First, one might somehow ensure that the use of this strategy is banned from asymmetrical talk especially in publicly institutional environments; and secondly, one might through analysis reveal the invidious nature of the uses to which we put these 'subtle', 'flexible' and 'dynamic' modes of talk. However, as those who have reflected seriously on the nature of social power might agree, neither of these solutions will actually suffice to extirpate power games from society, though our expressed concern with such issues might succeed in establishing our *bona fide* as socially responsible academics, which is not a mean achievement. On this somewhat dismal note, I turn to the second part of this chapter, concerned with the elaboration of the notion of con/textual integration.

5   Con/textual integration: a seamless conjunction of disjunction

In tracing the progress of the dialogue between Kristy and her mother, I drew attention to the absence of discursive disjunction: talk of one thing gradually and seamlessly merged into talk of something else; the same is true, of course, of dialogue 1.2. The secret of this seamlessness lies, on the one hand, in what the discursive shift does for the ongoing con/text and, on the other, in how the shift itself is construed by the ongoing acts of languaging. It is these aspects – concerned more directly with the construing power of language – that I will discuss in this section.

To take the first point: what the discursive shift does for the ongoing con/text may be described at two dialectically related levels – that of text as a semantic unit and that of context of situation as an instantiation of culture, a recognised frame of social activity within which talk is embedded. We observed earlier that in dialogue 1.1 the metaphor of *silly goose* first arose out of what is still part of the care-giving situation, and that the mother seized this chance given opportunity to instruct her child on the use of other similar metaphors. However, it would be a mistake to imagine that language instruction is all there is to that discourse.[15] Although the occasion for the use of the metaphor was adventitious, the mother's exploitation of it is functional: she uses it to suit her own purposes. This should not surprise: after all, the *raison d'être* for the progress of the dynamic moves – as opposed to their onset in discourse – lies in their functional pertinence. Kristy's mother uses the metaphors as a strategy for humouring her rather disgruntled daughter. Note the way that by her dramatic narration of what Ruth was doing, the mother manages to get Kristy to laugh, which is also true of her skilful selection of metaphorical expressions, such as *piggy-wig*: given the child's age the latter were bound to amuse. The laughter obliterates – at least for a while – the tension created by the tussle over going to Dee's. A renewal of goodwill and solidarity is achieved, albeit at the cost of Ruth who, fortunately for the mother, is not mature enough to recognize, much less resent, this fact. That by these devices the mother did succeed in winning Kristy's co-operation is evident from the segment below, which follows almost immediately after the last message of dialogue 1.3:

Dialogue 1.4
Mother: (110) you haven't got your panties on, have we? (111) where are they? (112) goodness me, I put them out (113) there they are! (114) the blue ones
Kristy: (115) hello [?fussy hen]
Mother: (116) OK Ruth . . We've nearly got Kristy dressed (117) we'll get you dressed after her (118) (TO KRISTY) stand up pet! (119) put your hands on my shoulder (120) so you don't fall over

So in the midst of explaining some of the animal aspects of human behaviour, the mother has 'nearly got Kristy dressed'; not only that, but also for the time being at least, Kristy's distress at having to go to Dee's is pushed into the background. In fact throughout this dialogue, the mother employs two major strategies for 'bringing Kristy round': persuasion or diversion. In dialogue 1.1, we encountered a variety of persuasion, with the mother reassuring Kristy about the visit to Dee's and pointing out the – to her – unreasonable nature of Kristy's objections against that plan. In the segment just prior to dialogue 1.2, she had commented *we'll have to make you more blouses, won't we?* – a formulation that demanded Kristy's involvement in this discourse. I take this as an attempt to divert Kristy's attention to things not immediately connected with the contentious issue of going to Dee's. The difficulty of deciding what clothes to send with Kristy is another possible distracter. These are highly skilful strategies for manoeuvring the daughter to fit in with the mother's plans: at no point does the mother relinquish the assumption of Kristy's going to Dee's and yet by exploiting the possibilities of discursive shifts, she is able to distract the child's attention from that issue, while inch by inch undermining the daughter's desire. Within this environment then, I interpret the mother's instructions on the use of metaphors as an 'over blown' example of the same strategy of diversion, which is not to say that it does not teach language at the same time. An outstanding feature of most human talk is that it can be simultaneously used in diverse ways without necessarily displaying any discursive disjunction; in fact without this property talk would be unable to assist in shaping the unself-conscious contours of our ideological affiliations. In the Kristy dialogue, the discourses of persuasion by reasoning, of discussion of the waywardness of weather, and of the explication of metaphor all have a dual status. On the one hand, each strand is itself: discussion of clothes, weather, and metaphors each in its own make-up recalls the properties of a self-sufficient discourse. Viewed localistically, each is a (fragment of a) register/genre in its own right in that it is language in use operative in a context of situation. On the other hand, each strand of the discourse is channelled towards the accomplishment of the same practical goal – namely to get the child ready and willing to go to Dee's: in this respect each strand is functionally integrated with the primary con/text, and each acts as a subtext – an auxiliary to the accomplishment of the activity of the primary con/text.[16] Viewed functionally, dialogues 1.1–1.4 form (part of) a complex text.

What integrates each discursive shift into the primary text is not any intrinsic quality of that part of the discourse itself; rather the secret lies in what that discourse does in the ongoing con/text. In general terms, it is by resetting the values of the parameters of the ongoing context that a discursive shift gets perceived as integrated into the primary text. For example, the shifts illustrated so far in this discussion act on the specific nature of interactant relation. Human relations are axiomatically enacted and maintained in the co-participation of some activity; this is true whether or not language has been involved in the performance of that act. But linguistic semiosis is, however, a crucial amplifier of how the co-acting agents see themselves in relation to each other, and within linguistic semiosis, shifts of the type exemplified above have a special role. When in the performance of some activity such as putting food on the table, of getting clothes on the backs of children, of teaching them something etc. talk appears to move away from the particular ongoing context to something apparently unrelated to the business in hand, this shift has a significant bearing on the relations of the interactants: by acting on the interpersonal relations of the social agents involved in the activity, it contributes significantly to the carrying out of the primary activity, making it a pleasant or unpleasant pursuit. Elsewhere (Hasan, 1999) I have referred to this contribution as a tone-setting function of discursive shifts, thereby implying that the emotional tone of the activity is set by how these shifts are developed in discourse. Con/textual integration by tone setting is an impressive way of using talk for the creation and maintenance of human relations: as Cloran (1999a) has pointed out it represents an aspect of the *framing* of discourse (Bernstein 1990, 1996) in action. In general terms, what Bernstein means by framing is 'various forms of the principles of communication' (Bernstein 1990: 36)[17]; Bernstein uses this notion to account for variation in forms of communication. So consider that in dialogues 1.1–1.4 the framing is relatively weak: we witness a tone-setting function that is co-operative; there is a tone we would normally refer to as one of mutual negotiation. The nature of the relationship between Kristy and her mother shifts during the interaction from tense to relatively relaxed: we begin with Kristy in a recalcitrant mood, throwing tantrums and being generally unco-operative; we finish with Kristy laughing and reconciled to pursuing the mother's agenda. By contrast, in dialogues 2.1–2.4 the tone-setting function is conflictual; the framing of the interaction is relatively strong; the mother is persistent in maintaining what she considers the legitimate activity in that situation; the daughter's role is to conform. The nature of their relation shifts from an even tenor to a relatively hostile one. In both cases the nature of the tone setting acts on the primary activity being performed.

Not all con/textual integration is based on the tone-setting function. A discursive shift may reset the parameter of ongoing action, as the following extract from another dyad shows:

Dialogue 3.1

Mother: (1) now Stephen, do you want a sandwich for lunch?
Stephen: (2) yes (3) and some passionfruit
Mother: (4) and some passionfruit (5) where is the passionfruit?
Stephen: (6) um . . um the passionfruit is um . . um [?] (7) do you know where the passionfruit is?
Mother: (8) no (9) you were walking around with it (10) what did you do with it?
Stephen: (11) I don't remember
Mother: (12) is it on the table?
Stephen: (13) let me see . . it is under the table
Mother: (14) under the table!
Stephen: (15) yes . . (16) here it is
Mother: (17) ok . . right . . peanut butter sandwich?

In dialogue 3.1 from message (5) through to (16) the talk represents a shift: the mother and son are no longer discussing what the son will have for lunch. They are in fact engaged in locating one of the items supposed to be on the menu; the menu itself cannot be supplied without the subsidiary action of locating the passionfruit. I have referred to this as a *facilitative* function of a discursive shift: it concerns an action that is subsidiary to the practical activity of providing lunch. In this respect it resembles what in the analysis of dialogue is known as *side sequence* (Goffman 1981), a term that highlights the subsidiary nature of the subtext without offering a functional description, unlike the term *facilitative* used here.

Whereas a tone-setting move contributes to the primary concern by acting on the subjectivity of the participants, a facilitative move contributes by helping achieve some objective requirement of the activity mooted in the primary context. Despite this difference, the two modes of integration are identical in two important ways.[18] First, both reset the value of some parameter of the ongoing context. It is in this sense that discursive shifts involve a reclassification of the ongoing context. The second respect in which both modes of integration are identical is intrinsic to 'how the language comes', and this has to do with the relations of cohesion and cohesive harmony.[19]

The fact that the discursive shift arises 'naturally' in the course of referring to an ongoing concern means that semantically and lexicogrammatically there is a continuity. This continuity manifests itself in the form of cohesive chains, each link of which is either co-referentially or co-classificationally related to the others. Further, the chains interact with each other in a systematic manner, thus creating cohesive harmony in the staging of the discourse. Simplifying the analysis greatly, in dialogues 1.1–1.4, reference to Ruth is the major link forging continuity between the discourse of care giving and of the explication of metaphors. Ruth acted in a silly way; Ruth is a silly goose. Ruth is thus instantially co-referential with silly goose. When people act in a silly way they are, or they are called/may be referred to as, silly goose; Ruth is a member of the same class as people. When people act greedily they are called greedy pig. At a particular level of delicacy, geese and pigs belong to the same class, namely animal, and so on. This informal account of how relations of co-referentiality and co-classification create co-hesive chains, and how the chains in turn interact might give an indication of the linguistic devices whereby the threads of continuity are construed.[20] When a disjunctive move in talk lacks this kind of continuity, it is typically not perceived as part of the same ongoing text; an example of this kind is discussed in Hasan (1999) and in Cloran (1999b). Underlying the seamless-ness of discourses of the type presented here is, thus, a rich orchestration of wording, meaning and context.

This discussion of con/textual integration furnishes the basis for a brief look into the final concern of this chapter, namely the metaphors by which we refer to what I am calling con/textual integration. Implicit in the discus-sion of what the shift does for the con/text is the overwhelmingly semiotic nature of discursive context. If one of the things that a discursive shift is capable of doing is to reset the values of some parameter of the context of discourse to, as it were, define the frame within which the talk is embedded, then clearly language is an active force in the construal of context; at the same time, given the dialectic of realisation (Halliday 1992; Hasan 1996), the acknowledgement of a context puts certain meanings at risk. In speaking naturally, speakers respond to their sense of the occasion of talk, and the conduct of the talk in its turn constructs the identity of the ongoing context for the interactants.[21] In a rather important sense, in normal everyday dis-course speakers do not have a sense of 'speaking' a genre/register; their concern seems to be simply to fashion their language according to the ongo-ing context.[22] And this language in use is what provides the basis for the discourse analyst to make objective, after the fact generalisations about who says what to whom where, when and how – the subject matter for the delin-eation of genre. But first and foremost, register/genre refers to language in use, which is not a static entity, but a process of fashioning one's mean-ings in keeping with one's perception of what 'goes' on a particular occa-sion of talk. Even in those cases (see note 22) where a self-conscious regard for a template is present, the fact that the nature of language in use is active implies that departures from the template can be made; this has to be the case, otherwise specialised genres such as essays, sermons, bureaucratic missives would remain unchanged over time. From this point of view, the metaphor of *genre combination* as also that of *hybridity* appears less than desirable, since both imply an unfortunate reification of the process of re-gister, as if what is happening is simply a co-location or a fusion of two (or more) already existing recognisable objects. Registers/genres are not peaches and plums that can be hybridised into nectarines. And though con/textual integration may seem like a hybrid since it combines different discourses into one complex discourse, it should be obvious from the above discussion that each discursive shifts has a dual character: it is responsive to the context both as itself, and as auxiliary to whatever was going on prior to the shift. The metaphor of hybridity or of genre combination is incapable of invoking this complexity, whereby the discourse presents itself in its protean fluidity. It may be said that essentially both in the kind of analysis presented here and in the kind where one talks of genre combination or of hybrids, there is the same recognition of textual disjunction; and that our concern should not be with the label but rather with the analysis itself. I would disagree. As Wittgenstein (1953: 109) remarked 'An unsuitable type of expression is a sure means of remaining in a state of confusion. It as it were bars the way out.' The metaphor of genre combination and hybridity inherently discourages reflection on the ways in which 'these different things' are fused into one, while retaining their own character. I hope that the discussion presented here has amply demonstrated that it is not simply that predetermined qualities of genres are being mixed, combined, hybridized: the fact of the matter is that by these devices people extend, elaborate and reclassify their discursive contexts. Derrida's celebrated claim that one cannot not mix genres should really be rephrased as contexts of life cannot but be permeable; the rest follows by the dialectic of language and discursive situations.

Notes

1. See, for example, Roberts and Sarangi (1999) for one such account.
2. In the systemic functional framework, these three properties are known as field, tenor and mode, respectively.
3. For a specification of some of these circumstances, see Hasan (1999).
4. The research, directed by myself, was funded by Macquarie University Research Grant Scheme and the national Australian Research Council.
5. For details of this research see Hasan and Cloran (1990); Hasan (1989, 1992), etc.
6. See Cloran (1994, 1995) for such an analysis.
7. The transcription conventions used here are as below:

(15)	= counted consecutively, this is message number 15 in the dialogue;
(CAPITALS)	= situational comment, based on analyst's listening to audio-recording;
[?go away]	= segment not intelligible; best guess on the basis of context;
[?]	= segment unintelligible; co-textual clues insufficient to allow guess;
≪3 abc≫	= enclosed message(s), i.e. 3 interrupts the message surrounding ≪ ≫.
?**	= no time allowed for response after this question;
abc—	= message *abc* left incomplete;
abc . .	= a (longer than usual) pause at this point;
**abc	
**def	= paired asterisks indicate turn overlap.

8. 'kinder' stands for 'kindergarten'.

9. Which belies the view, popular in language acquisition studies (e.g. Brown 1973) that mothers will often teach their children about the world but seldom will they teach language. (For an interesting discussion, see Butt 1989.)

10. For the discussion of an instance of such a sudden and clear break, see Hasan (in press).

11. It is with regret that, for lack of space, I have decided not to include the entire dialogue here.

12. On the basis of the preceding dialogue, it would appear that Karen is referring to some sauce.

13. That speakers are entirely rational in their discourse as Grice (1975) maintained can hardly be questioned; however, contra Grice, the shape of rationality in a society is far from uniform as a comparison of the discourses presented here suggests.

14. For an elaboration of this claim see, for example, Bernstein (1971, 1973, 1990, 1996), Bourdieu (1990, 1991) and Bourdieu et al. (1994).

15. The way in which some mothers use these con/textual shifts to assimilate it into an instructional context is discussed in Cloran (1999), where the idea of con/textual reclassification is also developed.

16. The notion of con/textual integration (Hasan, in press) attempts to account for some of the phenomena referred to as 'genre combination' (Martin 1992) or 'hybridity'. For the elaboration of terms such as *subtext, primary text,* etc., see Hasan (in press).

17. In this sense Bernstein's term *framing* is much more specific than the term *frame* as used by Goffman following Bateson. For the latter, the term *frame* is almost synonymous with what I have called *contextual configuration,* i.e. some set of the values of action, relation and contact whose configuration 'is a' particular occasion of talk. By contrast, Bernstein's concept of *framing* applies largely to the vector of relation. It is theses relations of the interactants that are 'translated' into principles of communication, for communicative acts are of necessity coloured by human relation.

18. I do not wish to imply that there are only two kinds of moves; how many kinds there are might well depend on the delicacy of the analysis.

19. On cohesive harmony see Hasan (1984, 1994; in press), Butt (1988) and Cloran (1994; 1999b).

20. For lack of space the actual analysis of cohesive chains and their interaction cannot be included in this chapter. The point at issue is that what the eye, the ear, and the reading brain apprehend as seamlessness is largely created by these linguistic devices.

21. Naturally I do not mean to deny the significance of material attributes in the recognition of a context, but there certainly are many types of context the specific character of which can be recognised only on the basis of the meanings being meant, e.g. presentation and revision lessons, etc.

22. This is in contrast to language use that is not extempore but produced with planning and deliberation such as for example the writing of this chapter. The latter kind of activities tend to pertain to what I have called 'specialised' sphere of activity. In such non-quotidian activities, the sense of the 'type of discourse', i.e. the 'appropriate' register/genre with its somewhat stylised and stilted situation, is typically present to the speakers' awareness: in fact the conscious presence of a template is a necessary point of departure.

45

References

Bernstein, Basil (1971) *Class, Codes and Control*, Vol. 1: *Theoretical Studies towards a Sociology of Language*. London: Routledge & Kegan Paul.

Bernstein, Basil (1973) *Class, Codes and Control*, Vol. 3: *Towards a Theory of Educational Transmission*, 2nd edn. London: Routledge & Kegan Paul.

Bernstein, Basil (1990) *The Structuring of Pedagogic Discourse: Class, Codes and Control*, Vol. 4. London: Routledge & Kegan Paul.

Bernstein, Basil (1996) *Pedagogy, Symbolic Control and Identity: Theory, Research, Critique*. London: Taylor & Francis.

Blom, Jan-Petter and Gumperz, John J. (1972) Social meaning in linguistic structures: Code-switching in Norway. In *Directions in Sociolinguistics: The Ethnography of Communication*, edited by John J. Gumperz and Dell Hymes. New York: Holt, Reinhart & Winston.

Bourdieu, Pierre (1990) *The Logic of Practice* (tr., Richard Nice). London: Polity Press.

Bourdieu, Pierre (1991) *Language and Symbolic Power* (ed., John B. Thompson, tr., Gino Raymond and Matthew Adamson). London: Polity Press.

Bourdieu, Pierre, Passeron, Jean-Claude and de Saint Martin, Monique (1994) *Academic Discourse: Linguistic Misunderstanding and Professional Power* (translated by Richard Teese). London: Polity Press.

Brown, Roger (1973) *A First Language: The Early Stages*. Cambridge, MA: Harvard University Press.

Butt, David (1988) Randomness, order and the latent patterning of text. In *Functions of Style*, edited by David Birch and Michael O'Toole. London: Pinter.

Butt, David (1989) The object of language. In *Language Development: Learning Language, Learning Culture*, edited by Ruqaiya Hasan and J.R. Martin. Norwood, NJ: Ablex.

Cloran, Carmel (1994) *Rhetorical Units and Decontextualisation: An Enquiry into Some Relations of Context, Meaning and Grammar*. Monographs in Systemic Linguistics, No 6. Nottingham: Department of English, Nottingham University.

Cloran, Carmel (1995) Defining and relating text segments. In *On Subject and Theme: From a Discourse Functional Perspective*, edited by Ruqaiya Hasan and Peter H. Fries. Amsterdam: Benjamins.

Cloran, Carmel (1999a) Contexts for learning. In *Pedagogy and the Shaping of Consciousness: Linguistic and Social Processes*, edited by Frances Christie. London: Cassell.

Cloran, Carmel (1999b) Context, material situation and text. In *Text and Context: A Functional Perspective*, edited by Mohsen Ghadessy. Amsterdam: Benjamins.

Fishman, J.A. (1965) The relationship between micro- and macro-sociolinguistics in the study of who speaks what language to whom when. *La Linguistique*, **2**: 67–88.

Goffman, Erving (1974) *Frame Analysis*. New York: Harper & Row.

Goffman, Erving (1981) *Forms of Talk*. Philadelphia: University of Pennsylvania Press.

Grice, H.P. (1975) Logic and conversation. In *Syntax and Semantics*, Vol. III, edited by P. Cole and J.P. Morgan. New York: Academic.

Halliday, M.A.K. (1977) Text as a semantic choice in social contexts. In *Grammars and Descriptions*, edited by Teun A. van Dijk and János Petöfi. Berlin: Mouton de Gruyter.

Halliday, M.A.K. (1992) How do you mean? In *Advances in Systemic Linguistics: Recent Theory and Practice*, edited by Martin Davies and Louise Ravelli. London: Pinter.

Hasan, Ruqaiya (1984) Coherence and cohesive harmony. In *Understanding Reading Comprehension: Cognition, Language and the Structure of Prose*, edited by J. Flood. Newark, Delaware: International Reading Association.

Hasan, Ruqaiya (1989) Semantic variation and sociolinguistics. *Australian Journal of Linguistics*, **9**: 221–75.

Hasan, Ruqaiya (1992) Rationality in everyday talk: from process to system. In *Directions in Corpus Linguistics, Proceedings of Nobel Symposium 82, Stockholm, 4–8 Aug. 1991*, edited by Jan Svartvik. Berlin: Mouton de Gruyter.

Hasan, Ruqaiya (1994) Situation and the definition of genre. In *What's Going On Here? Complementary Studies of Professional Talk* (Vol. 2 of the Multiple Analysis Project), edited by Allen D. Grimshaw. Norwood, NJ: Ablex.

Hasan, Ruqaiya (1996) Semantic networks: A tool for the analysis of meaning. In *Ways of Saying: Ways of Meaning*, edited by Carmel Cloran, David Butt and Geoff Williams. London: Cassell.

Hasan, Ruqaiya (1999) Speaking with reference to context. In *Text and Context: A Functional Perspective*, edited by Mohsen Ghadessy. Amsterdam: Benjamins.

Hasan, Ruqaiya and Cloran, Carmel (1990) A sociolinguistic interpretation of everyday talk between mothers and children. In *Learning, Keeping and Using Language, I: Selected Papers from the 8th World Congress of Applied Linguistics, Sydney, 16–21 August 1987*, edited by M.A.K. Halliday, John Gibbons and Howard Nicholas. Amsterdam: Benjamins.

Malinowski, B. (1923) The problem of meaning in primitive languages. Supplement 1, in *The Meaning of Meaning*, C.K. Ogden and I.A. Richards. New York: Harcourt Brace.

Malinowski, B. (1935) An ethnographic theory of language. Part IV in *Coral Gardens and Their Magic*, Vol. II. London: Allen & Unwin.

Martin, J.R. (1992) English Text: System and Structure. Amsterdam: Benjamins.

Roberts, Celia and Sarangi, Srikant (1999) Hybridity in gatekeeping discourse: issues of practical relevance for the researcher. In *Talk, Work and the Institutional Order: Discourse in Medical, Mediation and Management Settings*. Berlin: Mouton de Gruyter.

Williams, Geoff (1995) *Joint book-reading and literacy pedagogy: A socio-semantic interpretation*. Ph.D. dissertation (unpub.), Linguistics, Macquarie University, Australia.

Wittgenstein, Ludwig (1953) *Philosophical Investigations* (tr. G.E.M. Anscombe). Oxford: Basil Blackwell.

Chapter 3

Same grammar or different grammar? Contrasting approaches to the grammar of spoken English discourse

Geoffrey Leech

1 Introduction

In the last few years, attention has increasingly turned to the observable characteristics of spoken English. There have been two main reasons for this: (a) the need to know more about spoken English, because of the increasing focus on oral communication in language use, learning and education; and (b) the opportunity of satisfying that need that has recently arisen, through the availability of electronic corpora of spoken discourse. In the study of English grammar, which is the subject of this chapter, a justifiable tendency has been to propose that a completely fresh look at grammar is needed when one turns to examine the grammatical characteristics of speech. Both the traditional and modern linguistic traditions of grammar scholarship have been too much bound to the written language, so that they have failed to reflect adequately the dynamic and interactive nature of spoken discourse.

1.1 The impact of corpora of spoken English

This reappraisal has arisen from a sudden growth, since the 1970s, in the compilation of corpora of spoken English. Some of the largest of these have been created by English dictionary publishers, who have often been rather restrictive (unsurprisingly so) in allowing others access to them. These are (a) the spoken component of the COBUILD Corpus – now over 20 million words; (b) the CANCODE Corpus created by CUP with the help of Nottingham University; (c) the Longman Corpus of Spoken American English; and others. A particular exception to this restricted availability is the 10-million-word spoken component of the British National Corpus, which (although created by publishers – in this case Longman) is available to those who have paid a reasonably modest licensing fee and signed a licence agreement.[1]

There is thus a wealth of data in electronic form, covering the whole gamut of spoken English, available to be analysed. To some extent analysis can be aided by automatic processing by computer, but there is still the requirement of painstaking involvement with the data: quantitative analysis goes hand in hand with qualitative analysis in most corpus studies. These can take several years if one accepts seriously the challenge to engage with a large spoken corpus, with all its variety and detail. The wide range of data available in such corpora is an important platform for the accumulation of fresh knowledge and insight (whereas previous studies can often be criticised for concentrating on one or two restricted varieties of spoken discourse, and treating them as somehow paradigmatic). On the other hand, quantity of data in itself can be overvalued, and results, equally useful in the short run, can be obtained by sampling procedures which enable the researcher to select from the large body of data a much smaller though representative subset.[2] It has been pointed out, for example, that a smallish sample can be as valuable as a large one, if the characteristics of speech that one is studying are relatively common. Certainly it is true that many grammatical aspects of spoken language can be studied on the basis of a relatively small amount of data – say of a quarter of a million words – if sufficiently broadly sampled.

1.2 Recent corpus-oriented approaches to spoken grammar

Pioneers in spoken English corpus research were the team at Lund University (Svartvik, Aijmer, Altenberg and others), who examined the grammatical, lexical, prosodic and discoursal features of the London–Lund Corpus (LLC) in extenso.[3] More recently, three or four significant corpus studies of spoken English grammar have been taking place:

1. The late David Brazil's *A Grammar of Speech* (1995), although corpus-based in only a limited way (using a small collection of oral narratives as data), takes a highly original approach. Brazil argues that there is a fundamental difference between spoken and written grammar, rejecting 'sentence grammar' and the grammar of mainstream constituent-structure analysis, implicitly based on the study of written language, in favour of a linear, process-oriented approach.
2. The writings[4] on spoken grammar by Carter, McCarthy and Hughes have been based on their examination of samples of the CANCODE corpus. Their arguments, like those of Brazil, are that the apparatus of traditional and theoretical grammars, or even of 'mainstream' corpus-informed grammars like Quirk et al.'s (1985) *A Comprehensive Grammar of the English Language (CGEL)*, have been too much under the influence of the written-grammar tradition. By focusing on the CANCODE spoken data, they show how corpus studies can illuminate the study of spoken grammar with a new confrontation with reality: no longer are we bound by the time-honoured frameworks of 'sentence grammar', but instead we can examine spoken grammar in its own terms, observing characteristics whose importance has been ignored or undervalued in the past.

Both Brazil and (to a lesser extent) Carter, Hughes and McCarthy emphasise the 'dynamic' or 'linear' nature of spoken grammar, in contrast to written grammar. The fact that spoken utterances are constructed and interpreted in real time, by on-line processing, has important implications for the workings of spoken grammar and for how spoken grammar is to be described. This dynamism, together with the fact that spoken utterances are typically interactive, means that our frameworks for discussing and describing spoken grammar need to be thoroughly overhauled. The 'Nottingham school' of spoken grammar (as I will henceforth refer to the combined work of Carter, McCarthy and Hughes) does this by stressing the integration of grammar with discourse analysis.

3. Douglas Biber and his associates have examined spoken grammar from a somewhat different angle. In the later 1980s, Biber developed a technique for statistically analysing a corpus of both written and spoken texts to determine the dimensions of grammatical and lexical variation observable in language use (see especially Biber 1986, 1988a). This multi-feature multi-dimensional analysis has been extensively tried out on different research domains, being applied to register and dialect variation, also to historical and developmental variation, and even across languages (see Biber 1988b, 1991, 1995; Biber and Finegan 1997). Broadly, Biber's methodology has identified, by computational means, the frequency of occurrence of a large number of linguistic features, mostly grammatical or lexical, across a broad range of spoken and written genres. Through statistical techniques such as factor analysis, this method has revealed that, in place of a simplistic division between spoken and written varieties of discourse, there are actually several relevant scales of variation, such as informative–involved and narrative–non-narrative. More recently, Biber has focused more particularly on grammar, and, with an international authorial team (of which I am a member), has produced a new extensive corpus-based study of English grammar (Biber et al. (1999), *Longman Grammar of Spoken and Written English*). This work has made pervasive use of frequency counts of grammatical phenomena to characterise the similarities and differences between four major registers: conversation, fiction writing, news writing and academic writing. In practice, it is the distinction between conversation (as a 'prototypical' spoken register) and the other three (written) registers that is most likely to capture interest in this book.

Implicitly, the major principle which distinguish these studies from those of the Nottingham School is that both spoken and written data are considered essential to the characterisation of conversational English grammar. In other words, to describe spoken grammar without investigating written grammar is to omit the key contrastive dimension needed for its characterisation. Another principle taken for granted in the Biberian approach is that both spoken and written grammar can be (largely) characterised in terms of the same descriptive apparatus of categories, structures, and rules.

In terms of the 'same grammar' vs 'different grammar' distinction mentioned above, we may therefore characterise Biber et al.'s approach as an example of the 'same grammar' view, and Brazil's approach as an example of the 'different grammar' view of the spoken/written opposition. That is, the Biberian approach takes it for granted that, for practical purposes at least, there is a single 'English grammar', which can be differently implemented in different registers, whether in spoken or written varieties of the language. The Brazil approach is to concentrate only on the spoken language, as a variety which manifestly has not been described adequately up to now, and to describe it 'in its own terms', in ways which are clearly appropriate to spoken rather than written discourse. The Carter and McCarthy approach can be seen as intermediate between the 'same grammar' and 'different grammar' positions. While recognising the likelihood of considerable overlap between spoken and written grammars, they argue that traditional 'sentence grammar' has failed to do justice to the peculiar features of grammar applied to the spoken language and so, like Brazil, emphasise the need to escape from the trammels of conventional grammar and to give an account of the grammar of speech *in its own terms* (see especially McCarthy 1988: 47, 90).

1.3   There is nothing new . . .

Actually, the 'same grammar' and 'different grammar' approaches can be traced back to earlier traditions of English grammar writing. For example, Biber et al.'s, in a sense, goes back to the 'Quirk grammars', notably Quirk et al. (1972) (*GCE*) and Quirk et al. (1985) (*CGEL*), which were informed by the original Survey of English Usage corpus (Quirk 1960), a pre-computer compilation equally composed of spoken and written data. The Quirk grammars in general apply the same descriptive categories to both spoken and written language – e.g. spoken and written English both need adjectives, noun phrases, appositives, past tenses, and so on – virtually the whole standard paraphernalia of English grammar. Where special consideration of categories for spoken grammar was needed – e.g. in accounting for so-called 'left- and right-dislocation' or 'situational ellipsis',[5] these were provided and flagged, just as were categories more or less restricted to written language. Those who have used the 'Quirk grammars' and have noted the extent to which spoken features such as stress and intonation are used in illustrations and examples can scarcely argue that they neglect the spoken language, and indeed they represented a considerable shift of emphasis towards the spoken language, when compared with other grammars in the mainstream descriptive tradition (such as Jespersen, Kruisinga and Poutsma). However, they are firmly wedded to the view that a single 'integrated' approach to English grammar can account for its use in both writing and speech. Carter and McCarthy make the reasonable criticism that the authors of the Quirk grammars did not always sufficiently escape the frameworks of 'sentence grammar' with its implicit bias towards written language. In hindsight, they could also have done more to redress the balance between speech and writing if they had followed the policy of Biber et al. (1999) in using authentic corpus examples throughout – a policy less easy to follow in those days of when corpora were stored in filing cabinets rather than on disks.

Similarly, if we look back in the ELT grammar tradition, the antecedents of the 'different grammar' approach are to be found in the highly original contributions of H.E. Palmer (see Palmer's *A Grammar of Spoken English*, 1924),[6] who avowedly adopted a speech-oriented approach to the grammar of English, as well as to language teaching in general. Another landmark figure to be mentioned is C.C. Fries, whose revolutionary, though flawed, account of syntax in *The Structure of English* (1952) adopted a radically new metalanguage for grammatical description, based on spoken English data (in actual fact, a limited corpus of telephone conversations).

2   The 'different grammar' approach: Brazil

My aim in the remainder of this chapter is to evaluate the two approaches I have called 'same grammar' and 'different grammar',[7] together with the third 'in-between' model of the Nottingham School. We begin with Brazil's 'different grammar' model.

Brazil presents his 'grammar of speech' as a radical departure from grammatical tradition, which he sees as following a tradition of constituent structure (or phrase structure) grammar appropriate (if at all) only to the written language. He starts by assuming 'that the mechanisms whereby words are assembled to make bigger units will be revealed to us if we begin by thinking of speakers as pursuing some useful communicative purpose and as aiming, at any one time, at the successful accomplishment of that purpose' (p. 2). While admitting that his approach is 'exploratory' rather than authoritative (p. 1), Brazil follows this insight wholeheartedly, stating in conclusion the following guiding principles[8]:

1. Begin with the 'speaker's perception' of 'communicative need'.
2. 'Interactants cannot always co-operate successfully' but 'the repair of breakdowns' is achieved by special use of syntactic mechanisms.
3. Focus on 'the increment', i.e. 'something that satisfies a perceived communicative need' at a given point in the speech chain.[9]
4. 'Each increment progresses from an Initial State to a Target State', adding 'one element to another along a time continuum'.
5. Start with 'a subset of the rules which operate in a strictly linear way and result in the production of simple chains'. These may be supplemented by 'extensions' and 'suspensions', the latter permitting 'the production of certain elements "out of order" '.
6. No reference is to be made to 'sentence grammar' with immediate constituents: hence one cannot admit relations among elements which cannot be shown in terms of 'temporal sequence'.

7. The grammatical choices which in 'sentence grammar' are described in terms of constituent structure are to be explained, in the grammar of speech, by reference to different communicative needs the speaker has to satisfy.
8. Indeterminacy, although pervasive to human language, is tolerable because both speaker and hearer can rely on apprehension of communicative need.
9. This resolution of indeterminacy applies both to the interpretation of single words, and to the relations between different parts of the speech chain.
10. 'Knowing the (grammar of a) language', in this framework, is not a matter of knowing the rules of how to generate sentences, but of knowing 'how to satisfy all the communicative needs one may encounter'.

One may sympathise profoundly with the thrust of Brazil's argument, without coming to his radical conclusion – that the tradition of constituent-structure grammar should be thrown away when one comes to spoken language, and replaced by something close to what grammatical theorists have called a *finite-state grammar*. The basic idea – that an understanding of spoken grammar depends on seeing 'grammar in action', dynamically and interactively – is sound. Moreover, Brazil's bold pursuit of this theme leads to many fresh insights. But the approach also has weaknesses, due to a conflation of several distinctions which linguistics has regarded as important, including lumping together under the title of 'sentence grammar' an assortment of trends he is opposed to. First, there are different types of grammar which take a general sentence-based, tree-structure approach. But constituent-structure grammar doesn't necessarily go with the habit of abstraction which sees sentences as isolated from their context: there are functional as well as formal approaches which accept the constituent structure model as basic. Secondly, Brazil appears not to accept that context and meaning are separate, though interrelated, in the interpretation of grammar. For example, a past tense verb has a meaning which can be understood out of context, as well as within context. In practice, he conflates in the study of grammar the three separate levels of syntax, semantics and pragmatics. Pragmatics is the driving force of his grammar, in that he requires the whole of syntax to be answerable to 'communicative need', whereas 'sentence grammar', as he sees it, looks at grammatical sentences as complete formal entities in isolation, as in the Chomskyan tradition.

My inclination here is to question not the involvement of grammar with communication, but rather the tendency to see this as a one-way street, with communicative need determining grammar. If one takes this to its logical conclusion, then one cannot analyse grammar without having a prior knowledge of 'communicate need', which is on the whole a much more vague and problematic thing to characterise than the observable formal patterns of grammar.

Along with the conflation of form, meaning and use, there is another conflation: that of utterances/sentences as process and as product. Brazil sees grammar in speech as entirely a matter of process: the product material-ises only if one is looking at written sentences on the page. I believe there is an important philosophical issue here. Computationally, syntactic parsers and generators often analyse sentences sequentially, working from start to finish (or left to right). In this respect, such programs behave like Brazil's process grammar. But they rely on the existence of a 'declarative' grammar independent of the process: a formal characterisation of the potential for building and interpreting sentences. To go back to the old analogy of lan-guage and a game of chess, I believe that by focusing exclusively on the process of producing or interpreting grammatical sequences, Brazil is rather like a chess player who denies that the rules of chess have an existence independent of this or that game, seen as a sequence of moves. Putting this in terms of the Chomskyan distinction between competence and performance, Brazil's position is to interpret grammar in terms of only performance (or language use), ignoring the level of generality represented by competence: the grammatical system we carry around in our heads.

Since it is easy to misunderstand these issues, my own position should be clarified: as a corpus grammarian, I am deeply wedded to the study of performance – since, after all, a corpus is nothing other than a record of linguistic performance. But I do not believe that a focus on performance – what Chomsky (e.g. in Chomsky 1987) has called 'externalised grammar' – should ignore the existence of competence ('internalised grammar'). In fact, the link between competence and performance is to my mind an explana-tion of why, in general, the same system of grammatical categories can be applied both to spoken and written language. It is obvious that the abilities to speak English and to write English are not unconnected, and surely they must be connected in the mind of the native speaker.

Another issue on which misunderstanding should be avoided is the use of the term 'sentence'. Biber et al. (1999) agree with Brazil and Carter and McCarthy (and others) that the term 'sentence' is not helpful when we turn to the grammar of spoken language. It is too much tied to the written medium, and to the use of punctuation marks such as full-stops and ques-tion marks. On the other hand, in reference to spoken data there is no difficulty in applying such terms as 'clause' and 'phrase' – these units being recognisable in precisely the same way that they are recognisable in writ-ing. To reject the 'sentence' is not to reject the whole of constituent structure grammar.

Yet a further misunderstanding should be avoided. Brazil's grammar of speech is remarkably similar to finite-state networks, through which one progresses from 'start' to 'end'. I think that here he captures an important insight: that, indeed, a surprisingly large proportion of spoken utterances can be syntactically parsed in the word-by-word way of the finite-state network, since spoken grammatical performance relies necessarily on the fact that a speaker has a severely limited short-term memory[10] with which to construct the grammatical shape of on-line utterances. For example, the way in which spoken grammatical performance is shaped to the limitations of working memory shows up, in the comparison between informal speech and written registers, in the very high frequency in conversation of one-word subjects (typically pronouns) of clauses.[11] A single-word subject minimises the amount of storage one has to use in planning a clause before one gets to the main verb. But the word-by-word analysis doesn't always work well: for example, in conversation there is a surprisingly high frequency of *if*-clauses which precede the subject of the main clause.[12] These make considerably more use of working memory, before one gets to the main clause verb, than a single-word subject beginning the utterance. So, whereas I believe that on-line production exerts a strong influence in shaping the likelihoods of spoken grammar, the evidence of spoken transcription shows that speakers can elaborate more complex grammatical constructions than the finite-state model would suggest. These are the phenomena that Brazil handles in terms of suspensions and extensions of the simple word-by-word model with which he operates.

Having criticised Brazil's conception of the grammar of speech, I will end with an important point in his favour. Unlike the other two approaches, that of Brazil (whose extensive work on intonation is well known) recognizes the importance of the prosodic basis in the processing of spoken grammar.

3   The 'Nottingham School': grammar as discourse

The 'Nottingham School' of Carter, McCarthy and Hughes adopts a more balanced stance in the debate of whether spoken grammar should be treated as a 'separate grammar' or the 'same grammar' as that of written English. Whereas Brazil thinks spoken grammar needs a radically new approach, disassociated from the traditional architectural influence of written grammar, Carter and colleagues take a less extreme view, insisting that spoken grammar should be dealt with 'in its own terms', while at the same time recognising that the same grammatical categories often apply to both media. McCarthy (1998: 3) sees two opposite dangers:

> (a) that we may rush off and assume that everything is different in spoken grammar and nothing we say about written language has any validity for the description and the teaching of spoken language, or (b) equally dangerously, that we should assume that descriptions of the written grammar can simply be imported wholesale into spoken grammars.

In practice, the second danger is the one that most concerns them: they point out that both pedagogical and descriptive grammars in the past have tended to overlook the features of spoken grammar, importing the apparatus appropriate to written grammar wholesale into the spoken medium. They bring many persuasive examples to bear on the issue, showing how spoken grammatical phenomena, such as situational ellipsis, left dislocation, tails,[13] have been generally underplayed in the grammatical tradition. One of the advantages of studying even a small corpus of speech, from their point of view, is that such features, which are common in speech, are given their due weight, and are not treated as some kind of aberration from a written norm. Another advantage is that grammatical features can be explained by their role in their discoursal context, thus enabling the grammarian not only to describe but also to explain them in terms of their functional importance in speech. Even features which are considered to be well described in existing grammars, such as the tenses and aspects of the verb, can be seen to have significant discoursal patterns when one examines them in an extended transcription of the spoken word.[14] It is this combination of advantages that leads the Nottingham School to take a new look at 'grammar as discourse'.

The CANCODE corpus, on which this research depends, is far larger and more varied than the 'mini-corpus' of narratives employed by Brazil. The corpus is designed to represent a broad range of spoken English, taking a genre-oriented approach. Thus, the corpus consists of samples of such speech varieties as:

Transactional discourse (goal-oriented as in service encounters)
Professional discourse   Socialising discourse
Pedagogical discourse   Intimate discourse

The constructional aspect of grammar is also given fresh attention. The clause, as a key unit both for spoken and written grammar, has a special elaboration in speech, since it can be preceded by a *topic* element (as in 'left-dislocation' above) and can be followed by a *tail* element (as in retrospectively added noun phrases or predicates).[15] For my own analysis of the syntax of spoken discourse this tripartite scheme has proved extremely useful, and yet, on the other hand, I should mention that topics and tails are not so frequent in the construction of speech syntax as the occurrence of stand-alone non-clausal elements, which cannot convincingly be linked to any clause, and which account for more than one-third of the syntactically independent units in speech (Biber et al. 1999: 1071). Given that one abandons the sentence, the clause, even with variable pre-extensions and post-extensions, cannot be treated as *the* canonical unit of spoken grammar.

One of the Nottingham School's main concerns has been with giving a new impetus to the teaching and learning of spoken grammar, and they have shown convincingly that a corpus-based study of spoken English, away from the influence of the written word, can rearrange the paradigms of more orthodox sentence grammar, and reveal the characteristics of speech syntax in its own terms. Their study of grammar in its discoursal environment is a particularly valuable contribution.

4 The 'same grammar' approach: Biber et al.

In spite of the advantages of looking at spoken grammar 'in its own terms', I shall argue in this next section that there is still a great deal to be gained from looking at spoken grammar in terms of the CONTRAST between the grammars of speech and of writing. It is relevant first to describe briefly the corpus used by Biber et al.

There are two different ways of designing a spoken corpus in order to achieve 'representativeness'. One is to select recordings of speech to represent the various activity types, contexts, and genres into which spoken discourse can be classified. This may be called a *genre-based* sampling. A second method is to sample across the population of the speech community one wishes to represent, in terms of sampling across variables such as region, gender, age, and socio-economic group, so as to represent a balanced cross-section of the population of the relevant speech community. This may be called a *demographic* sampling.

In the *Longman Grammar of Spoken and Written English*, Biber et al. do not rely mainly on a genre-based corpus of speech. The corpus they use (the Longman Spoken and Written English Corpus) is sampled, in part, from genre-based data (*c.* 6 million words), similar to CANCODE. But the main spoken corpus analysed is a combination of demographically sampled transcriptions (*c.* 4 million words each) from British and American speakers. The demographic sampling method, as used for the BNC, involved identifying a stratified sample of individuals to represent a demographically balanced cross-section of British and American speakers. These 'guinea pigs' were handed a high-quality walkman, which they carried around with them for a period of up to a week. They switched on the walkman and recorded any spoken discourse in which they engaged in their day-to-day life, whether at work or in the home. Hence, in calling this a 'conversational corpus', we take an inclusively pragmatic definition of conversation: that conversation is a broad range of impromptu (usually private) discourse between two or more interactants, such as is captured by the sampling method just described. In practice (with over 300 respondents, and over 1,000 speakers) the range of conversational settings is enormous. 'Conversation', so captured, is a broad but typical sampling of spoken English. Although there are some types of speech (especially planned and/or public discourse) which are not included, it can be convincingly maintained that such varieties, being to a greater or lesser extent influenced by the written medium, are less characteristic and central to spoken discourse than is conversation. The conversational subcorpus, as noted earlier, was compared with equivalently large corpora of three written registers: fiction writing, news writing, and academic writing. The Biber method was to work in the opposite direction from Brazil, from formal distribution to communicative function. First, the comparisons of registers yielded relative frequencies for each grammatical feature studied (all major features of English grammar were studied in this way), then the differences were explained in terms of functional factors such as the on-line processing constraint of speech. There was no straightforward binary comparison between spoken and written material, as this distinction of medium, on the basis of previous research (e.g. Biber 1988a), in itself would not be so crucial as other factors, such as the spontaneity and private nature of conversation. In the comparison between conversation and the other three registers, however, a striking though not unsurprising pattern emerged. There was a very strong tendency for conversation to show the lowest or highest frequency of the four registers in the occurrence of grammatical features. This could be roughly and readily checked by looking at the 57 bar charts in the book which compared frequency in the four varieties: even though they were chosen to illustrate a wide range of grammatical topics from many different chapters of the book, about 75 per cent of these bar charts show conversation as having the highest frequency or the lowest frequency of the feature(s) being examined. An example of such charts is given in Figure 3.1, showing a stepwise increase in frequency of postmodifiers (both prepositional phrases and others) as one moves from conversation through the written registers to academic prose.

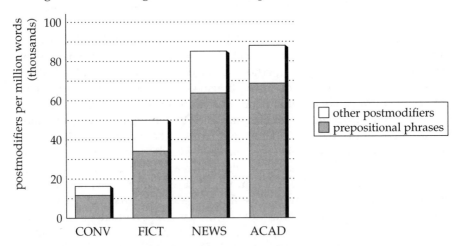

Figure 3.1 Prepositional v. other postmodification across registers

We could therefore say that, in the comparison of grammatical perform-ance in the four varieties, conversation typically occurs at the extremity of a scale. (Wherever the four varieties were plotted on a bar chart, there was also a tendency for academic writing to occur at the opposite end of the scale from conversation, as the 'least conversational' of the three written registers analysed, with fiction and news in intermediate positions. This happened, however, in only 39 per cent of the bar graphs in question.)

The discovery that, in conversation, as compared with the three written registers, there are strikingly different probabilities of encountering particular grammatical features is, on the one hand, interesting though not surprising.

On the other hand, it should also not be overlooked that in a minority of cases (about 25 per cent) conversation is in the middle ground of frequency, with different written registers showing greater and lesser likelihood of the occurrence of the feature in question. For example, in four-register comparisons such as that illustrated in Figure 3.1, conversation comes second to news in frequency of the present perfect tense, and second to fiction in the frequency of adverbials. Such cases are particularly persuasive in favour of the 'same grammar' approach, since they show that, even in frequency terms, the characteristics of conversation are not always polarised away from written language in one direction or another. More generally, the fact that virtually all major features of grammar can be compared on the basis of the same set of categories (even though conversation is typically clearly differentiated in frequency from the written varieties) gives no support to the idea that conversation and written language operate with radically different grammars, but rather the opposite. From the frequency analysis of a large and varied corpus like the LSWE Corpus we learn

(a) that (for all practical purposes) conversational and written varieties of English can be studied in terms of the same grammar;
(b) that, in terms of frequency, the use the grammatical resources is strikingly different in conversation and writing.

We conclude, then, that conversational grammar and written grammar can be contrasted in terms of frequency of use of the same repertoire, rather than in terms of different grammatical repertoires. Empirically, it is probably difficult, in principle, to argue that there are formal differences *in kind*, in addition to *quantitative* differences, between the repertoires of spoken and written grammar. Even if a feature is so biased in its distribution that it does not occur at all in the written or the spoken subcorpus, it is unwise to conclude that it could *never* occur in that variety, since an enlargement of the corpus could give the lie to this conclusion. Even features of disfluency, which seem utterly characteristic of unplanned spoken language, can also occur in written language – for example, in simulations of speech in fiction, as in this case:

'I er that is to say we er feel that we well, that we can't go on like this.'

As a further illustration, I looked through a random set of 500 examples of *for* from the spoken part of the LSWE Corpus, but found no examples of the conjunction *for*. It seems that this conjunction of cause/reason is alien to spoken discourse, but there is no guarantee that a search through a larger random sample would not have unearthed one or more instances. In any case, in a frequency or probability model of language use, even proportions near or even at 0 or 100 per cent occurring in a spoken corpus can be accommodated as extremes of the scale of likelihood.

The **internal** grammatical analysis of corpora, as indicated above, is (in the Biberian scheme of things) a preliminary to an **external** analysis, understood as a functional or discoursal explanation of the frequency phenomena that have been uncovered. Such an explanation normally requires some careful qualitative analysis of the data which has been shown to be quantitatively salient. Unlike Brazil's method, Biber et al.'s method involves starting with the observable grammatical characteristics of corpora, including frequency characteristics, and using those as the basis for explaining the observed patterns in functional terms.

4.1 Functional explanations of high-frequency grammatical features of spoken discourse

In this section, I will give a brief list of features of grammar which are of much higher frequency in conversation than in the written registers. These features will be classified functionally, in terms of the assumed reasons for their high-frequency occurrence in conversation. In effect, this will lead from a starting point in observed frequency to a conclusion in terms of a set of interconnected functional or contextual constraints, which mould the conversational use of grammar. These are:

1. *Taking place in a shared context.*
2. *Avoiding elaboration or specification of meaning.*
3. *Interactiveness.*
4. *Expressing personal meanings of emotion, politeness and attitude.*
5. *Taking place in real time.*
6. *Having a restricted and repetitive repertoire.*[16]

Under the headings of these six functional characteristics of conversation, the following are some of the grammatical features, which are outstandingly frequent in conversation:

1. **Frequent on account of: Taking place in a shared context:** personal pronouns; substitute forms (e.g. *one, do it*); situational ellipsis; grammatical isolates (or **inserts**) such as *Yes, Okay*; non-clausal material such as *About two ticks, ya. Alright.*
2. **Frequent on account of: Avoidance of elaboration or specification of meaning:** simple noun phrases (without modifiers); elliptical genitives; hedges or imprecision adverbials.
3. **Frequent on account of: Interactiveness:** *I, we* and *you*; peripheral adverbials such as stance adverbials and discoursal adverbials; vocatives; questions and imperatives; negatives; adversative *but*; certain types of inserts (attention signals such as *hey*, response forms such as *yeah*, greetings such as *hi, bye*), backchannels such as *uh huh*, discourse markers such as *well, I mean*).
4. **Frequent on account of: Personal meanings: emotion, attitude and politeness:** *can, could, will* and *would* in questions (expressing indirectness e.g. in requests); polite formulae such as *thank you, sorry, please*; familiarising vocatives such as *honey, mum, guys, dude, Rosy*; interjections such as

oh, ah, aha, oops, huh; expletives such as *God, my gosh, hell, geez*; exclamatory utterances such as *what a rip off; the bastard; good boy.*

5. **Frequent on account of: Processing taking place in real time:** disfluency features (e.g. pauses and hesitation fillers such as *um*); repeats, retrace-and-repair sequences; grammatically incomplete utterances; simple phrases especially in pre-verbal and medial positions; auxiliary omission, as in *you better . . . , what you doing? We gonna . . .* ; negative and verb contractions such as *isn't, didn't, you'll, I'd.* Topics and tails (as discussed by Carter and McCarthy 1995).

6. **Frequent on account of: A restricted and repetitive repertoire in speech:** repeated use of conversational routines, especially at the beginning of a clause (e.g. *Can I have a . . . ; Do you know what . . .*); tendency to use a few favourite lexical items in particular constructions, e.g. favourite subordinators (*if, because/cos, when*); favourite modals (*can, will, would, could*); favourite adverbs: *there, just, so, then, anyway, though, now*). Conversation shows a stronger tendency to use such 'favourite' lexico-grammatical choices than do the other registers.

4.2 Points in favour of the 'one grammar' approach

I argue that there is an advantage in characterising spoken grammar through a contrasting analysis of both spoken and written grammar, applying the same sets of categories to both. The argument is that the analysis highlights precisely those features of grammar which are characteristic of spoken grammar, including those which would not necessarily occur to the analyst, in terms of high, or for that matter, low frequency. This is a better and more objective basis for identifying what is 'different' about spoken grammar than reliance on what the analyst notices in a spoken corpus. There is also an advantage in having a corpus, both of speech and writing, which is large and varied enough to have a representative function, so that this comparison can be made properly. For example, McCarthy (1998: 124–5) presents the construction *tend to* as being particularly common in speech, saying that it appears to be developing a function as a 'habituality' marker in spoken English, and that this fact has been overlooked by previous studies. He reaches this conclusion on the basis of a small corpus of 100,000 words of speech and 100,000 words of writing. However, in the much larger and (presumably) more varied LSWE Corpus of more than 20 million words, analysis of *tend to* indicates that this verb complex is less frequent in conversation than in written English, when figures are averaged across the three written registers. Also, that *tend to* is actually much more frequent in academic writing than in conversation, news or fiction.[17] Hence, while it may be true that *tend to* is developing a specialised function as a 'habitual' marker, the issues to be investigated include why this form is particularly frequent in two registers (conversation and academic writing) which elsewhere seem to be so strikingly different from one another.

Table 3.1 Three approaches to spoken grammar

(Brazil 1995)	(Nottingham School 1998)	(Biber et al. 1999)
Two different grammars	Two different grammars, but with considerable overlap	One grammar, with probabilistic differences between speech and writing (the probabilities reaching 0% or 100% in extreme cases)

5 Conclusion

In conclusion, Table 3.1 summarises the three approaches to spoken grammar discussed in this chapter, placing them in relation to the 'same grammar' – 'different grammar' debate.

I have argued that the corpus-oriented description of spoken grammar 'in its own terms', as by David Brazil and the Nottingham School, is a valuable corrective to the tradition whereby the grammar of spoken discourse is described in terms of a framework informed primarily by written language use. On the other hand, I also argue that the analysis of a *general* corpus broadly representative of BOTH spoken AND written language is a corrective to the description of spoken grammar 'in its own terms': the general corpus enables us to provide a contrastive 'frequency map' of the language, showing where spoken grammar differs significantly from written grammar. It also shows, implicitly, that the same framework of grammatical categories can be applied both to spoken and written discourse.

Notes

1. Further details of the British National Corpus and its availability can be found on the BNC website: http//info.ox.ac.uk/bnc/. There are also other spoken corpora which are publicly obtainable, although of more limited size: one is a 2-million-word sample of the BNC (including 1 million words of speech), known as the Sampler Corpus. Others include the London–Lund Corpus (LLC), the IBM/Lancaster Spoken English Corpus, and the spoken component of the British part of the International Corpus of English (ICE-GB). These corpora can be obtained from the Norwegian Computing Centre for the Humanities, Bergen or (in the case of the ICE-GB) from University College London. Details can be found on the following websites: http://www.hd.uib.no/corpora.html and http//www.ucl.ac.uk/english-usage/ice.htm.

2. Two relevant quotations here are the following. 'For many common grammatical features . . . counts are relatively stable across 1,000-word samples from a text. However, some grammatical features are so rare . . . that they would require much larger samples for quantitative comparisons' (Biber et al. 1999: 249). 'Even

very small corpora, if properly targeted and approached with an open mind and careful observation, can yield recurring patterns of grammar that are not fully . . . described in conventional grammars' (Carter and McCarthy 1995: 154). On the issue of representativeness of corpora, see Biber (1993).

3. The LLC in its original version consisted of 435,000 words of spoken material from the pre-computer Survey of English Usage corpus collected by Randolph Quirk and his associates at University College London. Later the corpus was completed by the addition of a further 65,000 words. On the composition of the LLC, see Greenbaum and Svartvik (1990).

4. For the topics covered in this chapter, see especially Carter and McCarthy (1995) and McCarthy (1998). Some other relevant publications by these three authors are listed in the references.

5. Situational ellipsis (e.g. omission of an initial unstressed subject and/or auxiliary as in *Know what I mean?*) is discussed in *CGEL* (Quirk et al. 1985), pp. 895–9. So-called left- and right-dislocation are also discussed in *CGEL* (pp. 510, 1416–17) under the headings 'postponed and anticipated identification' and 'proxy pronouns'. Examples (respectively from the BNC and from *CGEL*) are: *This little shop – it's lovely* and *They're all the same, these politicians*.

6. However, Palmer's claim to deal with spoken English grammar largely rested on his principle that the learning of grammar should be closely associated with the learning of pronunciation, including segmental phonetics and prosody. His treatment of grammar *per se* relied heavily on model sentence types, and was not notably sensitive to the features characterising spontaneous spoken language.

7. At the outset I have to admit that I have a personal interest in this issue, being a co-author of Biber et al. (1999), and the main author of the final chapter entitled 'The grammar of conversation'.

8. The following list is a simplification of the list on pages 222–5 of Brazil's book (1995).

9. In Brazil's focus on the incremental satisfaction of communicative need in context, one might see overtones of Relevance Theory (Sperber and Wilson 1986, especially pp. 60–4 on *communicative intention*). However, unlike Sperber and Wilson, Brazil sees things predominantly from the speaker's point of view, and also does not make a distinction between the linguistic code and the inferential model of communication. For Brazil, communication and the linguistic code (including phonology, grammar and semantics) are thoroughly integrated.

10. Also termed 'working memory' or 'short-term store' (Atkinson and Shiffrin 1968; Clark and Clark 1977: 135–41). See Miller (1956) for the 'magical number seven, plus or minus two' as a guide to the limitations on short-term memory.

11. The percentage figure (derived from data in Table 17.124, Quirk et al. 1985: 1351) is as follows: 87.75 per cent of subject noun phrases in a sizeable corpus sample were single-word (pronoun or name) noun phrases. The corresponding figure for a larger sample of 17,000 noun phrases roughly equally divided between speech and writing was 73.7 per cent. A contrasting result was provided for scientific writing, where the percentage of pronoun/name noun phrases as subjects was less than 40 per cent. (These figures exclude occasional single-word noun phrases of other kinds – e.g. an uncountable common noun like *music*.)

12. Examples such as the following (from the Longman Corpus of Spoken American English) seem typical:

    > *If they'd have asked* I probably would have said no.
    > *If it has tires or testicles* you're going to have trouble with it.
    > *If there's no market* they're not gonna have anything to shop for.

13. So-called 'left dislocation' is illustrated in Note 5 above, and tails in Note 15 below.

14. Particularly relevant here is Chapter 5 of McCarthy (1998), dealing with the discoursal patterns associated with apparently competing English verb constructions, such as the present perfect vs the past simple, or *used to* vs *would* as expressions of past habitual meaning.

15. See Aijmer (1989) with reference to 'themes' and 'tails', as well as Carter and McCarthy (1995). Biber et al. (1999: 1080–2) use the term 'tag' for a similar range of phenomena, and provide a survey of these features of conversational syntax. Examples of 'tail' elements are italicised in the examples below (from the Longman Spoken and Written English Corpus (LSWE Corpus)):

    > Mm I wouldn't go into Armada Close *I don't think.*
    > Depends on what you want most *don't it I suppose.*
    > I mean she never liked that car. *Ever.*
    > He's had a blind put up . . . *a special blind that that leads straight across the fanlight.*
    > I mean it was the only one with a . . . with its own kitchen, *the one I was gonna have.*
    > That'll be a bit crispy, *that bit.*

16. For fuller details of these functional factors and their grammatical correlates, see Biber et al. (1999: 1049–50).

17. The frequency figures for the LSWE Corpus (including the different inflectional forms *tend, tends, tended*, etc.) for *tend* + infinitive *to* are as follows:

Conversation	Fiction writing	News writing	Academic writing
35 per million words	14 per million	33 per million	185 per million

References

Aijmer, K. (1989) Themes and tails: the discourse functions of dislocated elements. *Nordic Journal of Linguistics* 12: 137–54.

Aijmer, K. (1996) *Conversational Routines in English: Convention and Creativity.* London: Longman.

Atkinson, R.C. and Shiffrin, R.M. (1968) Human memory: a proposed system and its control processes. In K.W. Spence and J.T. Spence (eds), *The Psychology of Learning and Motivation.* New York: Academic Press, 2: 92–122; 191–5.

Biber, D. (1986) Spoken and written textual dimensions in English: Resolving the contradictory findings. *Language* 62: 384–414.

Biber, D. (1988a) *Variation across Speech and Writing.* Cambridge: Cambridge University Press.

Biber, D. (1988b) A textual comparison of British and American writing. *American Speech* 62: 99–119.

Biber, D. (1991) Oral and literate characteristics of selected primary school reading materials. *Text* 11: 73–96.

Biber, D. (1993) Representativeness in corpus design. *Literary and Linguistic Computing* 8: 243–57.

Biber, D. (1995) *Dimensions of Register Variation: a Cross Linguistic Comparison.* Cambridge: Cambridge University Press.

Biber, D. and Finegan, E. (1997) Diachronic relations among speech-based and written registers in English. In T. Nevalainen and L. Kahlas-Tarkka (eds), *To Explain the Present: Studies in the Changing English Language in Honour of Matti Rissanen.* Helsinki: Société Néophilologique, pp. 253–75.

Biber, D., Johansson, S., Leech, G., Conrad, S. and Finegan, E. (1999) *Longman Grammar of Spoken and Written English.* London: Longman.

Brazil, D. (1995) *A Grammar of Speech.* Oxford: Oxford University Press.

Carter, R. and McCarthy, M. (1995) Grammar and the spoken language. *Applied Linguistics* 16(2): 141–58.

Carter, R., Hughes, R. and McCarthy, M. (1995) Discourse context as a predictor of grammatical choice. In D. Graddol and S. Thomas (eds), *Language in a Changing Europe.* Clevedon: BAAL/Multilingual Matters, pp. 47–54.

Chomsky, N. (1987) *Language in a Psychological Setting: Sophia Linguistica 22.* Tokyo: Sophia University.

Clark, H.H. and Clark, E.V. (1977) *Psychology and Language.* New York: Harcourt Brace Jovanovich.

Fries, C.C. (1952) *The Structure of English.* New York: Harcourt, Brace & World.

Greenbaum, S. and Svartvik, J. (1990) The London–Lund Corpus of Spoken English. In J. Svartvik (ed.), *The London–Lund Corpus: Description and Research.* Lund: Lund University Press, pp. 11–17.

Hughes, R. and McCarthy, M. (1998) From sentence to discourse: discourse grammar and English Language Teaching. *TESOL Quarterly* 32(2): 263–87.

McCarthy, M. (1998) *Spoken Language and Applied Linguistics.* Cambridge: Cambridge University Press.

Miller, G.A. (1956) The magical number seven, plus or minus two: some limits on our capacity for processing information. *Psychological Review* 63: 81–97.

Palmer, H.E. (1924) *A Grammar of Spoken English.* Cambridge: Heffer.

Quirk, R. (1960) Towards a description of English usage. *Transactions of the Philological Society* 40–61.

Quirk, R., Greenbaum, S., Leech, G. and Svartvik, J. (1972) *A Grammar of Contemporary English.* London: Longman.

Quirk, R., Greenbaum, S., Leech, G. and Svartvik, J. (1985) *A Comprehensive Grammar of the English Language.* London: Longman.

Sperber, D. and Wilson, D. (1986) *Relevance: Communication and Cognition.* Oxford: Blackwell.

Chapter 4

The construction of purpose in discourse

Theo van Leeuwen

1 Introduction

This chapter does not offer a theory of the purpose(s) of discourse. It does not even take a position on whether discourses are, in some absolute sense, purposeful or not. It is about the discursive *construction* of the purposes of social practices (including discursive practices). It takes the view that social action (again, including discursive action) is not inherently purposeful or, at least, we cannot prove that it is. The same action may in one context be constructed as oriented towards a specific goal, in another as performed, not to achieve a particular purpose, but out of tradition (because it is 'the done thing'), in yet another as performed for the sake of the intrinsic satisfaction it provides (because 'I like doing it'). Even when a given action is constructed as purposeful, different purposes may be ascribed to it in different discursive contexts. An advertiser may see the promotion of goods and services as the purpose of advertising, a left-wing social critic the promulgation of consumerist values, a post-modern cultural theorist the celebration of irony and wit. Who is right? One thing is certain, the construction of purpose is often at the heart of conflicts and disagreements between different discursive positions.

The construction of social action as purposeful and the construction and negotiation of specific purposes for specific social actions are not equally important in every domain of discourse. Where action is governed by tradition, or where affective and aesthetic satisfaction determine what is done and how it is done, the discursive construction of purpose will take a back seat. But where new things are to be done, or where old things are to be done in new ways, purpose will be paramount, for instance in instructional texts, syllabuses, or in strategic planning documents which must foreground the aims and objectives of the actions they propose.

It is the purpose of this chapter (I cannot write without doing the very thing I write about) to describe the resources provided by the English language for the construction, interpretation and negotiation of purposes. In other words, the chapter presents a 'grammar of purpose'. I use the term

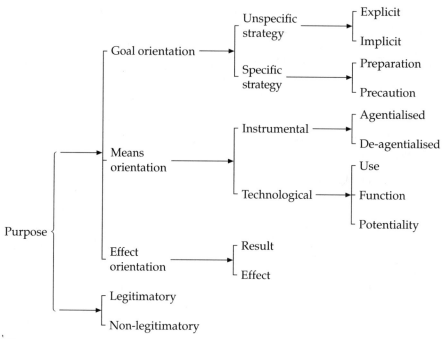

Figure 4.1 Resources for the discursive construction of purpose in English–system network

'grammar' because I will use (lexico-)grammatical criteria to distinguish different kinds of purpose construction, relying to a large extent on Halliday's systemic-functional grammar (1985) and Martin's systemic-functional discourse analysis (1992). However, the first step in my analysis does not rely on grammatical criteria. It consists of identifying all the elements in my corpus (see below) which intuitively seem to express purposes, of whatever kind (strategies, intentions, etc.) and in whatever way. This is then followed by a grammatical sorting of the resulting data, and the final step is a functional-semantic interpretation of the resulting lexico-grammatically defined categories. In other words, the first step is semantic. As such the work discussed in this chapter is part of a larger sociolinguistic project in which I attempt to study language as a means for representing social practices in contextually specific ways and for attaching to these representations elements such as legitimation, purpose, evaluation, and so on. The resulting description is therefore in the first place semantic. It maps a discursive resource. It is possible, therefore, that all or part of the resulting system network (see Figure 4.1) can also be realised in other languages or in other semiotics (or that I have missed out on some categories because I did not include non-verbal material in my corpus). On the other hand, as it stands now, my 'grammar of purpose' represents, not 'how we can think about purpose', 'what discursive resources for thinking about purpose the culture makes available to us at this particular time in history', but 'what thoughts about purpose we can express in *English*' (in this particular culture and at this particular time in history). In the context of semantic networks which were much more oriented towards the interactional resources of language and communication (greeting, parental control, etc.), Halliday (1973: 82–3) said:

> Grammar is about what the speaker CAN SAY, and is the realisation of what he MEANS. Semantics is what the speaker CAN MEAN; and we are looking at this as the realisation of what he DOES.

In this chapter I am concentrating more on the representational resources of language (on what, in earlier work (1993) I called the 'field' rather than the 'genre' of discourse, again following systemic-functional technology). Consequently 'what the speaker does' is here 'recontextualising what people do, how they do it, why they do it, etc.' – that is, the contextually specific representation and interpretation of social practices (one's own or those of others).

The examples are drawn from a corpus of texts I have also used in a number of other publications (van Leeuwen 1993, 1995, 1996). The texts all deal with the same social practice: a key initiation ritual of contemporary society, 'going to school for the first time'. They include story-books for young children, brochures, newspaper and magazine articles directed at parents, and teacher-training textbooks. Most of them continually construct purposes, for schooling generally, and for the specific activities it involves – although there are some interesting exceptions, for instance in the case of certain kinds of children's stories. The corpus also includes some texts by critics of schooling such as Illich and Holt – texts which are concerned neither with the detailed representation of action nor with ascribing purposes to it, but with legitimation, or, more specifically, with the de-legitimation, the critique of the school system.

As I am concerned with exemplifying types of purpose construction, and as purpose construction mostly happens at the level of the clause or clause complex, most of my examples are isolated sentences drawn from across my corpus. But the ultimate aim is, of course, the analysis of texts rather than sentences, and the final section of the chapter attempts to demonstrate one way of using the framework presented here in the analysis of texts.

2 Purpose and legitimation

The discursive construction of purpose is closely related, but not identical, to the discursive construction of legitimation (see, e.g., Verschueren and Blommaert 1992; Rojo and van Dijk 1997; van Leeuwen and Wodak 1999). Like purpose, legitimation is not inherent in action, but discursively constructed, in order to explain why social practices exist, and why they take the forms they do – why, for instance, children must go to school, and why schooling takes places the way it does in our society. This question always lurks in the background, even if it is not explicitly asked, especially, as Berger and Luckmann (1985) have pointed out, in relation to social practices, conventions, rules and laws in whose genesis we have not ourselves played a role, and whose historical *raison d'être* is therefore not part of our own memory.

Elsewhere (van Leeuwen and Wodak 1999) I have proposed a framework for describing modes of legitimation, and the way they are realised in discourse. Legitimation can, for instance, take the form of *authorisation*. The answer to the question 'why' is then, essentially, 'Because I say so', where the 'I' is, in the given context, some kind of authority – a parent, a teacher, an expert, the rules, the law, the Bible. Like other types of legitimation it is associated with specific lexico-grammatical features. It takes the form of either a verbal process with the 'authority' as its subject (*'Experts say . . .'*, *'The rules stipulate . . .'*) or a circumstance of attribution (*'according to Foucault . .'*, *'in line with article 3, paragraph 7 of the Immigration Act . . .'*). Another form of legitimation, I argued, is *purpose legitimation*. Here the answer to the 'why' question is not couched in terms of authority ('because the law says so'), convention ('because everybody does'), tradition ('because that's how it has always been done'), and so on, but in terms of purpose, by saying, for instance, that children have to go to school *'in order to learn to read and write'* or *'to develop their creative, conceptual and motor skills'*.

The question arises, are all purposes also legitimations? And if so, why make 'purpose' a separate category? I think the answer is no: not all purposes are also legitimations. In order to serve as legitimations, an additional feature is required: they must, as Habermas has put it (1976: 22), make 'submerged and oblique reference to moral values':

> Purpose rationalisations embed a submerged and oblique reference to moral values in a frame of instrumentality, to achieve a 'strategic-utilitarian morality'.

Departing from Weber's account of the way modern Western society has made science, morality and art into distinct domains, Habermas characterises the institutions which regulate different kinds of social action in terms of the validity claims or 'kinds of truth' which underlie and legitimate them. Thus 'teleological action' (and this is, of course, the category which most crucially concerns us here) is founded on the principle of success, of 'whether it works or not', i.e. on a rationality of means and ends. 'Conversation' is founded on the criterion of truth, of whether an action truthfully represents states of affairs in the objective world. 'Norm-conformative' action is founded on the principle of right and wrong, on whether an action is morally justified or not, and 'dramaturgical action' (here Habermas leans on Goffman, e.g. 1959) is founded on the principle of honesty, of whether the action is sincere and whether the actor is truthful to his or her feelings. Each of these types of action can be linked to specific social practices and institutions. Norm-conformative action, for instance, dominates in legal/moral institutions (e.g. institutionalised religion). Dramaturgical action dominates in the arts and also in institutions concerned with interpersonal relations and mental health. Teleological action characterises in the first place the domains of science and technology, but also, for instance, business, and, increasingly, politics – in short, every domain in which knowledge is stored principally in the form of technologies and strategies (Habermas 1984: 333).

Concentrating now on 'teleological action', what is meant by 'submerged and oblique reference to moral values', and how is it manifested in discourse? Consider the following examples:

2.1   His mother joins the queue to pay his dinner money to the teacher.

2.2   The reception teachers went to the nursery unit to see their prospective pupils.

2.3   Mary Kate went upstairs after breakfast to have another look at them [i.e. her new school satchel, pinny, etc.].

2.4   Jane's teacher used eye contact and facial expression to establish positive bonds with her.

2.5   The following strategies were employed to make the introduction to PE more smooth.

2.6   The children use specific apparatus and movements to promote muscular co-ordination and agility.

In the first three examples (2.1–2.3), the purposes are realised by a purpose clause with *to* in which the process is a *generalised action*; that is, the actions inside the purpose clauses are the kind of straightforward generalised representations of actions which could serve as labels for whole activity sequences and form what Roland Barthes (1977) called the *nuclei* of activity sequences. The other actions, the more 'micro' actions whose purposefulness is constructed in the text, are purposeful in *relation* to those nuclei, as necessary conditions for them, necessary preparations for them, necessary parts of them, and so on – it would be interesting to work out a precise repertoire for these relations, but that will have to wait for another occasion.

In the second three examples (2.4–2.6), the purposes are also realised by a purpose clause with *to*, but the process is here what, following Habermas, I will call a *moralised action* – a way of referring to a particular action which connotes moral values. Moralised actions are realised by means, not of generalisations, but of abstractions, that is, of expressions which distil, from the actions to which they refer, particular aspects or qualities such as, for instance, 'smoothness' or 'agility'. The expression 'make the transition smooth', in the given context, refers to the teacher's actions on 'the first day', to what the teacher actually does. But it refers to these actions in this peculiar abstract way in order to highlight a quality of them ('smoothness') which can serve to legitimate them. Such qualities are evidently not unique to the actions referred to here. There are many other transitions which can be 'made smooth', many other contexts in which 'positive bonds' can be established, or in which 'muscular co-ordination and agility' can be promoted. They are also *moral* quality, because they trigger intertextual references to the discourses of moral values that underpin them: 'smooth', for instance, connotes a discourse of efficiency, in which action must unfold in an orderly manner, without friction, without hitches, without disturbances. 'Establish positive bonds' intertextually reaches out to discourses of therapeutic values – discourses of personal development, healing, etc. 'Promote muscular co-ordination and agility' invokes discourses of the beautiful and healthy body. Even in these discourses, however, the moral values are rarely made explicit. Their origins and histories remain, as Habermas says, submerged. They are only obliquely referred to, only connoted through the abstract representations of action I have described. They are treated as commonsense and do not make explicit the religious and philosophical traditions from which they ultimately draw their values and on which their legitimatory capacity ultimately rests. This also applies to the idea of purpose itself. Expressions like 'it is purposeful', 'it is useful', 'it is effective' and so on are themselves legitimatory, descendants of philosophical traditions such as utilitarianism and pragmatism, which *explicitly* argued for purposefulness, usefulness and effectiveness as criteria of truth and foundations for ethical behaviour.

3   The grammar of purpose

In this section I will discuss the principal types of purpose which can be realised in English, and the ways in which they are realised. It follows from the preceding section that all of the constructions I will discuss may either be legitimatory (which is grammatically realised by the presence of moralised actions in the purpose construction) or not.

As was already evident in section 2, three elements are necessary for the discursive construction of purposeful action, (a) the *purposeful action*, that is, the action whose purpose is to be constructed (e.g. the action *'using specific apparatus and movements'* in example 2.6); (b) the *purpose*, itself a process, an action or a state (e.g. the action *'promoting muscular co-ordination and agility'* in the same example), and (c) the *purpose link*, the relation of purposefulness between these two (e.g. the non-finite clause with *to*, again in example 2.6). As with other semantic relations, the relation of purposefulness may be explicit or implicit (cf. Martin 1992: 183–4). Explicit relations will be expressed either by some form of conjunction or by a logical process; in this case a 'purpose process' such as *'serves to'*, *'aims to'*, or some kind of metaphorical equivalent. In the case of implicit realisations, the clause expressing the purpose will not be explicitly coded as a purpose clause. Instead of a purpose conjunction there may, for instance, be a temporal conjunction (simultaneity) or an explanatory conjunction. There is, however, an *implicit* purpose conjunction, and it can be demonstrated by inserting a purpose link or by replacing the existing temporal or explanatory link with a purpose link. When this is possible there is an implicit purpose construction; when it is not, there is not. In example 3.1, for instance, it is possible to supply a purpose link. It makes sense to change 3.1 into '*One or two teachers took the new entrants on a tour of the school, to show them where everything was and to introduce them to key figures on the way.*' The same cannot be done with example 3.2. It does not make sense to change that example into '*"Does Mandy Williams live here?", asked the man to raise his peaked cap*':

3.1   One or two teachers took the new entrants on a tour of the school, showing them where everything was and introducing them to key figures on the way.

3.2   'Does Mandy Williams live here?', asked the man raising his peaked cap.

3.1   Goal-oriented action

Some purpose constructions construct purposes as 'in people', as conscious or unconscious motives, aims, intentions, goals, etc. This crucially requires that the agency of the actor of the purposeful action is explicitly realised and that this action is 'activated' (van Leeuwen 1995) by being coded as a finite or non-finite clause. It also requires that the purposeful action and the purpose have the same agent, or, if the purpose is a state, that the person to whom that state is attributed is also the agent of the purposeful action. In other words, the essential meaning of this type of purpose construction can be formulated as '*I do x in order to do (or be, or have) y*'. This can then be realised explicitly, by a purpose clause with '*to*', '*in order to*', '*so as to*', etc. (examples 3.3–3.5) or remain implicit (examples 3.6–3.8).

3.3   Mummy and Mary Kate went upstairs to get dressed.

3.4   Some teachers come in before the term starts to prepare an attractive setting for the children.

3.5   Mothers take their tots to baby clinics to check their health.

3.6   Some head teachers gave talks to parents at local playgroups, giving hints on how best to help the child.

3.7   The children go a few at a time to the class shop and buy a bottle of milk with toy money.

3.8   Your child may respond by spending hours happily entertaining herself drawing, while she develops her visual, creative and motor skills.

Social actors whose actions are *explicitly* constructed as purposeful in this way are discursively empowered as intentional agents – as people who can decide to, and then succeed in, changing the world, whether in minor or major ways, or as people who can set a goal and then determine, autonomously, how to achieve it. *Implicit* realisations retain the agency, but as the intentionality is not explicitly expressed, it can be denied. It remains open to interpretation. It is left to the listener or reader whether to interpret the link between action and purpose as intentional or not.

A specific kind of goal-oriented purpose construction is the *precaution*. Here it is the purpose of the action to *prevent* something from happening or from being done. This is realised by means of a hypotactic clause with *'in case'* or *'because otherwise'*, or with a negative result clause (*'so that . . . not'*).

3.9   'Here are some biscuits to put in your satchel', said Granny, 'in case you feel peckish when you have your mid-morning milk.'

3.10   'That's what we'll call you then. That way we shan't muddle you up with the other Mary.'

Another specific kind of goal-oriented purpose construction is the *preparation*, where it is the purpose of the action to be prepared for something rather than actually to do it. This is realised by clauses with *'ready for'* or *'ready to'*, e.g.

3.11   Mummy had put all her things on the little blue dressing-table, ready for the morning.

3.12   She could see her party dress hanging up, ready to wear when it was time to dress.

Other specific types of goal-oriented purposeful action may exist, although I have not found any in my data. An example would be the subjective coding of purposes, in terms of desire, or other related mental processes (*'I do x because I want to y'*).[1] There were, however, no instances of this in my data.

3.2   Means-oriented action

Purpose constructions may also construct purpose as 'in the action'. In this case the action is represented as a means to an end, and hence objectivated (van Leeuwen 1995) by means of nominalisation, or by using a process noun or metonym. The essential meaning of this type of purpose construction can be glossed as *'I achieve doing (or being, or having) y by x-ing'*, or *'X-ing serves to achieve being (or doing, or having) y'*. The difference between the two cases lies in the presence or absence of human agency ('agentialisation' vs 'de-agentialisation', cf. Figure 4.1). In the first case the purposeful action is coded as a circumstance of means with *'by'*, *'by means of'*, *'through'*, etc. The purposeful action becomes a method, a means to an end, but human agency is preserved:

3.13   The teacher remedied this by assisting him with her shoehorn.

3.14   Children cope with these difficulties by keeping the two worlds apart and never talking about home at school or mentioning school at home.

3.15   The skilful teacher can save the new entrant's face by showing herself to be on his side.

In the second case the instrumental action is lexicalised as, for instance, *'a way'*, *'a mechanism'* *'a means'*, *'a tool'*, etc., in a relational clause where the purposeful action becomes what Halliday (1985: 112–28) calls the Carrier (in the case of an attributive clause) or the Token (in the case of an identifying clause). In this way human agency disappears from view and the purposeful action itself, the 'method', the 'procedure', is constructed as achieving the purpose.

3.16   Formal group time is a powerful mechanism for social control.

3.17   The key to a smooth transition lies in avoiding the shock of anything sudden in the way of sights, sounds or experiences.

3.18   Pairing can be a very successful way of eliminating minor anxieties.

The other category of means-oriented purpose constructions is *technological*. Here the emphasis lies on describing purposes as somehow built into the actions that achieve them. Human agency is again absent, and the purposeful actions are always nominated or referred to by means of a process noun. There are three subcategories, *use*, *function* and *potentiality*.

Use is somewhat of an intermediate category between instrumental and technological action. The purposeful action is represented as using a tool (e.g. *'registration is used to . . .'*) or as being potentially useful with respect to a purpose (registration *'can be used to'*, *'is useful for'*, etc.) – the latter shades into what below we will call 'potentiality'. There is a remnant of agency, as a result of the realisation by a passive with deleted agent. One can always ask 'By whom?', 'Who is this user?'. At the same time the use itself – the goal as well as the means by which it is or can be achieved – have been determined by someone other than the user, and this restricts the extent of the user's agency:

3.19   Registration can also be used to encourage children to respond to their own names and learn each others'.

3.20   Drink time is used for the discussion of news.

3.21   Assembly may be used as an opportunity to celebrate birthdays, to launch appeals, to award praise and blame, and to reiterate school rules.

In the case of *function* the purposeful actions are represented as though they have their purposes built in. This is typically realised by an identifying clause in which the purposeful action is Token and the purpose Value, e.g. *'Assembly* (Token) *is* (identifying process) *a gathering to worship God* (Value)', or in which the purpose postmodifies the purposeful action in a nominal group (as in *'a gathering to worship God'*). In my data this is often (but not exclusively) used to construct the purposes of objects rather than the purposes of actions. But even when it constructs the purpose of an action, that action is, in a sense, constructed as an object by the very use of this construction:

3.22   This is so you won't forget where you are.

3.23   This is to carry all your bits and pieces to school.

3.24   Assembly is a gathering of all or part of the school to worship God.

3.25   She shows her a peg on which to hang her coat.

Rather than as uniquely designed for a given purpose, the purpose of an action may also be constructed in terms of its *potential* for serving certain purposes. This is typically realised by clauses with 'facilitating' processes such as *'allow'*, *'promote'*, *'help'*, *'teach'*, *'facilitate'*, *'build'*, etc., in which the purposeful action is subject and the purpose is object or complement. There is again maximum objectivation of the purposeful action and irretrievable removal of human agency from it.

3.26   This after-school conversation trains your child to memorise a sequence of events.

3.27   This promotes healthy feet and strong arch muscles.

3.28   It helps her to develop her sense of time.

3.3   Effective action

Finally, purpose constructions may emphasise the outcome of actions. In that case purposefulness is looked at from the other end, as it were, as something that turned out to exist in hindsight, rather than as something that could have been fully planned. As a result the people who perform the effective actions are represented as not fully able to be purposeful, not fully in control. They may be able to predict the outcome, but they cannot fully bring it about through their own actions. This requires that there is no identity between the agent of the action whose purpose is to be constructed and the agent of the action which constitutes the purpose. Instead of a goal, as in 3.29, or a means, as in 3.30, the purpose is the *outcome* of an action, as in 3.31 (3.30 and 3.31 are made-up examples).

3.29   Mothers take their tots to the clinic to check their health.

3.30   Mothers check their babies' health by taking them to the clinic.

3.31   Mothers take their babies to the clinic, so that doctors can check their health.

In the case of the *result* (e.g. 3.32), the purposeful action enables or causes the actions of other persons. This is typically realised by result clauses with 'so that', 'that way', etc.

3.32   We'll get there nice and early, so you can find your way about a bit before school starts.

3.33   Your child has to learn to control aggressiveness, so others accept him.

3.34   Left-handed children should sit facing slightly to the right, so that the left arm is properly supported from elbow to wrist.

In the case of the *effect* the purposeful action is itself agent or initiator of the purpose action.

3.35   Sending children away from home at an early age builds character.

3.36   Establishing the same routine going to and from school will make your child feel secure.

3.37   Recognising the symptoms makes them easier to live with.

The distinctions discussed are summarised in Figure 4.1 in a system network.

4   Purpose and power: the grammar of purpose as a tool for critical discourse analysis

In this section I will present an analysis of four of the texts from my 'First Day at School' corpus, to try to demonstrate how the categories introduced in the chapter can be used for the critical analysis of discourse. The first two are children's stories. *Mary Kate and The School Bus* is a children's Penguin book, aimed at a middle-class public, available only in bookshops and carrying a Times Literary Supplement recommendation on its cover. The text is too long to reproduce in its entirety, but 4.1 gives an idea. *Mark and Mandy*, by contrast, is a mass-market product sold in newsagents and at supermarket checkouts, and hence available to a much wider public. The extract in 4.2 gives the flavour. The two books look strikingly different. *Mary Kate* carries only one black-and-white pen drawing every three or four pages. *Mark and Mandy* has at least one and often two colour pictures on every page and a garishly colourful hard cover.

4.1   As soon as Daddy had gone, Mummy and Mary Kate went upstairs to get dressed.
        Mary Kate fastened her shoes herself, just to show Mummy that she could. When she was dressed, she looked very smart – except for her hair, which was all night-wild and anyhow.
        Mummy brushed out the tangles and tied the hair back with a ribbon.
        'There!', said Mummy. 'You'll do.'
        Mary Kate looked at herself in the mirror and thought she didn't look like Mary Kate at all. It was very odd. She didn't even *feel* like Mary Kate this morning.
        'Are we going on the school bus?', she asked, as Mummy helped her into her coat.
        'Not this morning,' Mummy said. 'We'll walk across the field. We've plenty of time. We'll get there nice and early, so you can find your way about a bit before school starts.'
        So they went out the back way. Mummy had to push Jacky back into the kitchen and shut the door quickly, because he wanted to go with them. They could hear him barking as they went down the garden and through the gate into the wood.

4.2   The great day came at last. Mark and Mandy were off to school for the first time. They were both very excited, and, to tell the truth, just a little nervous. Would it be easy? What would it be like? Would the teacher be strict?

Mandy was wearing a new red dress and white blouse, and felt very smart as she stood for Mummy to tie a red bow in her hair. Mark wore a green shirt and dark trousers.

Far too early for they were both so excited they could not wait, they started out, Auntie Barbara pushing Debbie in her pram, and Auntie Margaret holding on to Mandy's and Mark's hands. Smudge followed to the door.

'You'll have to wait until we get back,' said Mark, and Smudge looked very sad. Where could they be going, and why were they carrying satchels?

The two books differ considerably in the way they construct the purpose of the actions of children, teachers and parents. Mary Kate, an only child from a middle-class home, is constantly represented as engaged in intentional goal-oriented action:

4.3   She rubbed it with her handkerchief so as not to leave a mark on the shiny brown leather.

4.4   She fastened her shoes herself, just to show Mummy that she could.

4.5   She stretched the elastic front of one of them to see it spring back into shape.

The same applies to her parents, and to the way they represent their own and Mary Kate's actions in the dialogue:

4.6   Mummy slipped the pinny over Mary Kate's head to see if it fitted her.

4.7   Mummy had put all Mary Kate's things on the little blue dressing-table, ready for the morning.

4.8   'So you are', cried Daddy, 'Well you'd better come and eat a hearty breakfast. You'll need to keep your strength up.'

I analysed two chapters from each book (amounting to approximately 3500 words in the case of *Mary Kate* and 1600 words in the case of *Mark and Mandy*). In *Mark and Mandy* I found only 1 instance of intentional action (on the part of parents), in *Mary Kate* 24 – only two of these contained moralised actions (example 4.8 is one of them). The actions of Mark and Mandy, on the other hand, are not constructed as purposeful, but as the effect of physical states and emotions (4.9–4.12). Mark and Mandy's parents and teachers, similarly, do not construct as purposeful what they ask Mark and Mandy to do: in *Mark and Mandy* things are fated (4.12) or authoritatively imposed (4.13–4.14).

4.9   Mark was so excited he could not wait.

4.10   Mandy was too happy swinging to and fro to stop.

4.11   'Oooh I am tired', she said and sat down.

4.12   Soon autumn would be here and Mark and Mandy would have to start school.

4.13   'No talking', said the teacher, and lessons began.

4.14   Then Mummy stood up, 'Come along, we'll feed the ducks now.'

The other two texts are (a) *Your Child and Success at School*, a heavily illustrated, magazine-format booklet for parents, distributed through newsagents, hence widely available, and (b) *And So To School*, an NFER-Nelson report on a study of the transition from home to school, containing many recommendations for teachers, and distributed only to specialist outlets, hence not easily available to the general public. Examples 4.15 and 4.16 show how these two books represent 'setting off for school in the morning':

4.15   Start the day with a nourishing breakfast eaten in a well-protected uniform, because in the excitement your child may spill things. The family can talk calmly and happily to her about the day ahead. When she is ready with her school-bag complete with lunch box, pencil case, tissues and treasures, set off for school together with plenty of time to spare.

4.16   'Today I'm going to school.' Jane is up early, eager to put on her grey pinafore dress and red jumper. These are the clothes suggested by her head teacher and purchased from a local chain store. Many infant schools now adopt this practice. Her mother makes sure Jane has a substantial breakfast today, and instead of a leisurely look at the paper gets herself ready to take Jane to school.

I analysed the sections from *Your Child and Success at School* which deal specifically with 'The First Day'. They contain a total of about 1700 words. There were only three purpose constructions which represented parents as engaged in goal-oriented action:

4.17   Display your child's school creations to show how much you appreciate them.

4.18   You should start early to avoid unnecessary stress.

4.19   You need to plan practically to ensure this milestone in your child's life passes smoothly and enjoyably.

Children's actions were constructed as goal-oriented only once ('Right-handed children will face slightly to the left, to support the right arm') and the actions of teachers only twice.

More frequent were means-oriented (7 cases, e.g. 4.20–4.22) and, especially, effect-oriented purpose constructions (11 cases, e.g. 4.23–4.25).

4.20   Early school activities are teaching basic mathematical skills such as measurement.

4.21   It helps your child to develop her sense of time.

4.22   Establishing the same routine to and from school will make your child feel secure.

4.23   It is important for you to meet the teacher, so you have some idea of the person your child will be spending time with.

4.24   This teacher welcomes our help with the reading lessons, so that the children can have turns of individual attention.

4.25   Your child has to learn to control aggressiveness, so others accept him.

Such effect-oriented constructions of parents' actions are also very common in articles about 'The First Day' in the family pages of tabloid and local newspapers. The writers seem to assume that parents are, in principle, not convinced of the benefits of schooling. These benefits cannot be intended by them, but only appear as the effect of actions imposed on them by expert advice and reluctantly undertaken. For the same reason the purposes of parental action are almost always 'moralised'. Looked at from the point of view of the parent (and in these texts this is almost exclusively the mother), the handing over of their children to the education system is a sacrifice to be made for the greater good of society. No wonder that legitimation plays such a key role here and that so much emphasis is placed on 'smoothness', on trying to avoid distress on the part of both mothers and children.

The 'First Day' chapter from *And So To School* contains approximately 6500 words. There are 30 goal-oriented purpose constructions, 35 means-oriented purpose constructions and only 2 effect-oriented constructions. Children are often constructed as purposeful actors, but while the purposes of Mary Kate's actions (cleaning her shoes, trying on her clothes to see if they fit, etc.) are constructed as rational, those of the children in *And So To School* are often 'irrational', inappropriate (4.26 and 4.27), and if they are not, they are clearly moralised (e.g. 4.28).

4.26   Rosalie, seeing a brand-new slide, eagerly ran to try it out.

4.27   In order to get it [i.e. encouragement and approval], new children ignored queues and went straight to the teacher.

4.28   The children use specific apparatus and movements to promote muscular coordination.

The actions of the teachers are either goal-oriented (e.g. 4.29 and 4.30) or, more frequently, means-oriented (4.31–4.33):

4.29   The reception teachers went to the nursery unit to see their prospective pupils.

4.30   From time to time Jane's teacher paused to explain personally to her what was going to happen next.

4.31   'Register time' often forms part of a conscious attempt to train children in listening and responding.

4.32   The teacher resolved this by explaining that the other children would be undressing too.

4.33   The embarrassment which can be incurred by an individual in group situations is a potent weapon in the hands of a teacher who wants to shame a child in front of his peers.

As can be seen, the purposes of the teacher's own activities are rarely moralised. They are constructed as practical solutions for the problem of 'ensuring a smooth transition' and keeping order; but they are frequently means-oriented. Teachers are represented as the users of methods and techniques designed by experts, and it is these means, rather than the teachers, which achieve the purpose.

As we have analysed only a few texts, no hard and fast conclusions can be drawn. Nevertheless, some patterns emerge. First, there is a class dimension in all this, a set of differences that relate to the social distribution of these texts. Children are endowed with purposefulness in a text which represents the middle-class home and the middle-class school – and which reaches the middle-class child. In the mass market publication they are represented as either acting on impulse or in response to authoritative commands. This clearly reminds us of Bernstein's work on socialisation and class (e.g. 1971).

But even in the middle-class school, as represented in our examples, the child's purposefulness can become problematic. Not all of the child's own goals are appropriate. Children must learn to act according to the goals of the system. Hence 'moralised' purposes occur often. In the mass-marketed publication, on the other hand, neither children nor adults are represented as engaged in purposeful action. If parental behaviour has the desired out-come, this is the result of following expert advice, not of implementing goals which they have set themselves.

Clearly, the discursive distribution of purposefulness has everything to do with the distribution of power in concrete social practices (here the relations between children, parents and teachers in the context of schooling, and also the relation between educational experts and teachers), and in society generally (the class relations involved): 'Discourse is a place where relations of power are exercised and enacted' (Fairclough 1989: 43).

Note

1. I owe this observation to Ruth Wodak. I would like to take the opportunity to thank her, as well as Malcolm Coulthard, Radan Martinec and Srikant Sarangi for their useful useful comments on an earlier draft.

References

Barthes, R. (1977) Introduction to the structural analysis of narratives. In *Image-Music-Text*. London: Fontana.

Berger, P. and Luckmann, T. (1985) *The Social Construction of Reality*. Harmondsworth: Penguin.

Bernstein, B. (1971) *Class, Codes and Control, Vol. 1: Theoretical Studies towards a Sociology of Language*. London: Routledge.

Fairclough, N. (1989) *Language and Power*. London: Longman.

Goffman, E. (1959) *The Presentation of Self in Everyday Life*. Harmondsworth: Penguin.

Habermas, J. (1976) *Legitimation Crisis*. London: Heinemann.

Habermas, J. (1984) *The Theory of Communicative Action, Vol. 1: Reason and the Rationalization of Society*. Boston: Beacon Press.

Halliday, M.A.K. (1973) *Explorations in the Functions of Language*. London: Longman.

Halliday, M.A.K. (1985) *Introduction to Functional Linguistics*. London: Arnold.

Martin, J.R. (1992) *English Text: System and Structure*. Amsterdam: Benjamins.

Rojo, M.L. and van Dijk, T.A. (1997) 'There was a problem, and it was solved!': legitimating the expulsion of 'illegal' migrants in Spanish parliamentary discourse. *Discourse and Society* 8(4): 523–67.

van Leeuwen, T. (1993) Genre and field in critical discourse analysis. *Discourse and Society* 4(2): 193–225.

van Leeuwen, T. (1995) Representing social action, *Discourse and Society* 6(1): 81–107.

van Leeuwen, T. (1996) The Representation of Social Actors. In C.R. Caldas-Coulthard and M. Coulthard (eds) *Texts and Practices. Readings in Critical Discourse Analysis*. London: Routledge.

van Leeuwen, T. and Wodak, R. (1999) Legitimizing immigration control: a discourse-historical approach. *Discourse Studies* 1(1): 83–119.

Verschueren, J. and Blommaert, J. (1992) The role of language in European nationalist ideologies. *Pragmatics* 2(3): 355–75.

Chapter 5

Contrastive rhetoric and discourse analysis: Who writes what to whom? When? In what circumstances?

Robert B. Kaplan

1 Introduction

The questions posed in the subtitle are complex – much more complex than they appear on the surface – and they in turn raise a host of other questions. Without doubt, some languages have *lacunae*[1] – blank spaces – with respect to functions that occur in other languages. At the syntactic level, the occurrence of blank spaces between languages is readily acknowledged. At the lexical level, the matter may be even more obvious; Sa'Adeddin (1987), for example, points out that the title of James Joyce's short story 'Araby' simply cannot be translated into Arabic. But these examples belie the complexity of the issue. Indeed, if we take as a premise the definition that 'a language is the ideal means for a community of speakers to deal with the phenomenological world in which they live and with each other', the notion of *a blank space* seems perfectly reasonable.[2]

The idea of a 'blank space' is not particularly new. Unfortunately, in many past attempts to approach this matter, the 'blank space' was perceived as a deficit. There is a long history of research in 'error analysis' – analysis of the 'lacks' displayed by second-language learners. Ever since the 'doodles' article – officially known as 'Cultural thought patterns in intercultural education' (Kaplan 1966) – appeared, I have been accused of xenophobia by various scholars, when it was merely my intention to suggest that 'blank spaces' occurred between languages at the rhetorical level as well as at the syntactic and lexical levels (Figure 5.1). In any case, the publication of that article marked the birth of the notion now known as 'Contrastive Rhetoric' [hereinafter CR].[3]

In 1966, when I wrote the 'doodles' article, I was thinking of *rhetoric* in the Aristotelian sense, but I tried to make the notion more transparent for what I thought was my audience; the original article was published in *Language Learning* and was intended not as some grand theoretical pronouncement, but merely as an aid to teachers in moving past listening/ speaking (in the Audio-Lingual Method [ALM]) and on to reading/writing.

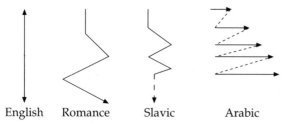

English   Romance   Slavic   Arabic

Figure 5.1   The dominant trends in the rhetoric of several language groups (Kaplan 1996, 1972)

After all, at the time, I was directing a university-based English as a Second Language (ESL) program in the USA, and my colleagues and I were expected, in the span of one academic term, to teach students who had little or no English to write acceptable academic papers. (No one was, at the time, particularly concerned about the advanced speaking and listening skills of those L2 learners.) In Aristotle's sense, then, I was concerned with *ethos*, *pathos*, and *logos*, but mainly with *logos*, since the presumption was that the students with whom we worked were expected to write exposition, not persuasion. It is also necessary to point out that the following discussion is essentially about written language; I use the term *discourse analysis*[4] with some trepidation since it covers a multitude of other sins.

2   The CR model

2.1   The flaws in the CR model

There were serious flaws in the initial articulation of the notion of CR. Those flaws have been frequently and elaborately pointed out by any number of scholars (e.g. Enkvist 1997). The 1966 article contrasted professional writing by native speakers with student writing by second-language learners; it did not control for topic, for genre, or for length. It was ethnocentric because it looked at the writing of speakers of languages other than English from the perspective of English; it did not look at the perception of English or other languages by speakers of languages other than English (although it recommended such research). It was, in fact, based on an admittedly relatively poor research design, but, thirty years later, the question is not 'Were the "doodles" accurate as specified?' Of course, they were not; they perhaps tended to suggest stereotypes. Texts reflecting any of the doodles can and do occur in every language, but it is probable that particular languages have particular organisational preferences.

Whenever I have presented the 'doodles' to audiences made up of speakers of languages other than English, those speakers have pointed out that it is not English that is linear; rather, their languages, they have claimed, were linear, and English represented some other pattern. The real issue, however, is that there are differences between languages in rhetorical preference; and it hardly matters whether one or another is defined as 'linear' or 'circular'. The perception of linearity represents a classic playing out of the emic/etic variable; every speaker *perceives* his/her language as linear and all others as non-linear. The central issue, however, is that every speaker perceives a difference between what happens in his or her language and what happens in other languages. That fact constitutes the central idea of CR.[5]

2.2 History of CR studies

Gradually, over the ensuing thirty odd years, a relatively large number of CR studies has been undertaken in some two dozen languages and language varieties.[6] As a consequence of these studies, the CR notion has evolved to overcome some of its initial flaws and to develop a more robust investigative model. In the initial interest in CR, the attention was primarily focused on languages represented in US foreign student populations in the 1960s and 1970s: Arabic, Chinese, French, Japanese, Korean, Spanish, and a small number of other languages (see, e.g., Kaplan et al. 1983). Work on this set of languages has continued, and other languages have been added.[7]

It is unfortunate that the great majority of the CR studies have involved only a contrast between English and some other language; there are very few studies that explore the relationship between two languages not involving English. (See, e.g., Strother and Ulijn 1991 and Ulijn and Strother 1995 for cross-linguistic studies involving languages other than English.) On the one hand, having English as a common factor in so many of the studies is an advantage; on the other hand, the concentration on English clearly reflects the hegemony of English as well as an unfortunate bias.

2.3 The extension of the CR model

The CR model has, more recently, moved in two different directions, trying in various ways to account for the text generator, the text receiver, the text itself, and the discourse and sociolinguistic environment in which text generation and text reception occur. As Connor notes: '. . . the time has not yet come to dismiss [CR] as a viable theory of second language writing' (1996: 18). On the contrary, Connor (ibid.) suggests that CR has undergone a paradigmatic shift:

> A broader definition that considers cognitive and sociocultural variables of writing in addition to linguistic variables has been substituted for a purely linguistic framework interested in structural analyses of products.

To a certain extent, this suggestion may constitute something of a misunderstanding of the original intent of CR. It was always the case that CR was concerned with cognitive and sociocultural variables as well as linguistic ones. In the time frame in which CR evolved, the only quantifiable aspect of a text readily available for analysis consisted of its linguistic features, and in a world which stressed empirical research, quantifiable features were important; ethnographic studies are of more recent origin. The basic notion that rhetorical structures tend to be language specific implies some consideration of sociocultural variables and – to a lesser extent – cognitive variables (Scollon 1997). CR research, however, has never given credence to the notion that there were significant cognitive differences that could be linked to linguistic and/or cultural differences; the notion was not (and is not) dependent on the strong version of the Sapir–Whorf hypothesis (see, e.g., Penn 1972). It is not the case that linear writing – however attributed – is cognitively superior to non-linear writing, nor is it the case that Aristotelian logic and Galilean systematization are in any sense cognitively superior to any other framing concepts. There is no question that different languages have evolved different solutions to recurring rhetorical problems, but difference does not necessarily implicate a value judgement; solutions to rhetorical problems may be different without being cognitively superior or inferior to other approaches depending on the sociocultural environment in which they are instantiated.

Value judgements emerge as the result of the hegemony of English in certain registers; publishers, editors, journal guidelines, textbooks, and other social artifacts necessitate value judgements which tend to mask the validity even of varieties of English falling outside the mainstream. (See, e.g., Kachru 1992 for an extended discussion of this problem.) The enormous global industry that is the teaching of English as a second or foreign language necessitates value judgements. Indeed, language teachers have been reinterpreting and reinventing the CR model to suit their needs for much of the past thirty years, sometimes without much reference to the CR notion itself.

3   The role of linguistic resources

Writers are, however, bound by the resources of the languages they use. There is a tendency to bring to a second language the resources available in the first, whether or not those resources are actually available in the L2. Writers select and arrange textual material in terms of their '. . . abilities to convey just those analyses . . . of event[s] that are most compatible with the linguistic means provided by their languages . . .' (Berman and Slobin 1994: 12). Berman and Slobin present four versions of the same phenomenological event, interpreted in several different languages to illustrate the point that the resources available to speakers of different languages prompt somewhat different presentations of the event; the examples in Table 5.1 show how different languages encourage variation in the ways in which events are narrated. The examples come from transcripts of children speaking different native languages relating the 'Frog Story' from a set of pictures without words (Berman and Slobin 1994: 11). All of the children in these examples are native speakers of the languages represented.

Table 5.1 Four culturally constrained examples

English
And he starts running. And he tips him off over a cliff into the water. And he lands.

German
Der Hirsch nahm den Jungen auf sein Geweih und schmiß ihm den Abhang hinunter genau ins Wasser.
[The deer took the boy on his antlers and hurled him down from the cliff right into the water.]

Spanish
El ciervo le llevó hasta un sitio, donde debajo había un río. Entonces el ciervo tiró al perro y al niño al río. Y después, cayeron.
[The deer took him until a place, where below there was a river. Then the deer threw the dog and the boy to the river. And then they fell.]

Hebrew
Ve ha'ayil nivhal, ve hu hitxil laruts. Ve hakelets rats axarav, ve hu higia lemacok she mitaxat haya bitsa, ve hu atsar, ve hayeled ve hakelev naflu labitsa beyaxad.
[And the deer was startled, and he began to run. And the dog ran after him, and he reached the cliff that had a swamp underneath, and he stopped, and the boy and the dog fell into the swamp together.]

Berman and Slobin claim that the difference between these excerpts is to some extent determined by the linguistic possibilities inherent in each of the languages. The first two, in English and German, describe the complexity of the fall via a series of adverbial particles and prepositional phrases (*tips off, over a cliff, into the water; schmiß, den Abhang hinunter, ins Wasser*). The verbs *tip* and *schmeißen* [hurl] signify the manner in which the deer causes the fall. The Spanish and Hebrew versions resemble each other but differ from the English and German versions. In Spanish and Hebrew the event is recounted as a series of episodes. First there is a description of location (cliff with river below, place with swamp underneath); then the deer acts and, as a result, the boy and the dog fall. Berman and Slobin (1994: 12) point out that the verbs chosen (*throw, fall, stop*) are '. . . bare descriptions of change of state, with no elaboration of manner . . .'. Furthermore, they write (ibid.):

> These are not random differences between the narrative styles of these . . . children, but rather show their abilities to convey just those analyses of the event that are most compatible with the linguistic means provided by their languages. English and German provide large sets of locative particles that can be combined with verbs of manner, thereby predisposing speakers toward a dense style of encoding motion events . . . . A different style arises in [Spanish and Hebrew], which rely more on simple change-of-state and change-of-location verbs, . . . predisposing speakers towards more extended analyses of motion events.

The order of presentation appears to be culture specific, conditioned by the linguistic resources available in the L1, but also by customary modes of perception.

4   Does the Universal Grammar (UG) model apply to text?

This set of ideas may be considered in opposition to the notion of a Universal Grammar. UG (Chomsky 1981; Cook 1988) constitutes a mentalist theory claiming that all human beings within the normative range have a biological endowment consisting of an 'innate language faculty' which permits children to acquire the grammar of any particular language (or languages in the case of early bilingualism). The language faculty is seen as unrelated to other cognitive abilities, as containing awareness (knowledge?)[8] of abstract principles which organize language, and as also containing an awareness (knowledge?) of the parameters through which those principles are instantiated in any given language(s). Input triggers parameter setting, enabling a learner to discover which parameters must be set for some particular language. The trigger is activated through minimal exposure and requires only positive evidence (rather than the sort of negative evidence that ensues through error correction). Whether the UG model applies to second-language learners is not absolutely understood. If UG does apply to second-language acquisition, the learner must 'reset' the parameters for each language.

Although the UG model dominates in Second Language Acquisition (SLA) studies, it has been challenged, and various alternative models have been suggested; e.g. the competition model, the connectionist model, the emergenist model, the noticing model, etc. Debate rages in the cognitive sciences (including artificial intelligence studies) over the specification of the several models and over the theoretical validity of each.[9] Furthermore, Deacon (1997) and Edelman (1992) have argued, on the basis of their research, respectively, in neurobiology and evolutionary anthropology, that it is simply not feasible from an evolutionary perspective to explain the notion of innate knowledge as posited in UG. (See also Donald 1991.)

There are other problems. The UG model assumes an equation between linguistic theory and grammatical theory and does not recognize that language is only one 'tool set' for construing experience; as Halliday writes: 'language is the essential condition of knowing, the process by which experience *becomes* knowledge' (1993: 94, italics in the original). Thus, language is complemented by the resources of other semiotic systems, all of which have been developed over cultural history, shaping and shaped by the various activities in which they are used. Language is not – cannot be – an isolated system, and grammar cannot be equated with language. As Enkvist (1997: 199) puts it:

> The important point is to realize that the text is the father of the sentence, and that text strategies come before the syntactic formation of individual sentences. Giving a sentence its textual fit, its conformity with the text strategy, is not a cosmetic surface operation polishing the sentence after it is already there. Textual fit is a far more basic requirement, determining the choice of words as well as the syntactic structure of a sentence. To modern text and discourse linguists this is so obvious

that it seems curious that grammarians and teachers of composition have, through the centuries, spent so much time and effort on syntactic phenomena within individual sentences, while overlooking the fundamental questions of text strategy and information flow.

The strong inclination to restrict analysis to morphosyntactic phenomena makes the analysis of text structure virtually impossible since text is not simply the sum of the syntactic structures contained. To focus only on morphosyntactic structure means that pragmatic functions are irrelevant, but text is heavily dependent on pragmatic functions. Morphosyntactic structure involves not merely the recognition of correct syntactic structures; it involves the recognition of the appropriate usage of various correct (and even incorrect) syntactic structures. Additionally, any 'universalist' view overlooks the role of culture, of situation, and of a variety of other important variables. Speakers of two different languages will organize the same reality in slightly different ways.[10] That they should do so seems self-evident, because different languages will provide different resources for organizing text. However, this filtering of text logic through language is largely unconscious; that is, learners of an L2 are not aware of the manner in which their L1 influences the way they organize text logic, nor are they aware of the manner in which an L2 organizes text logic, nor are they aware that there is a difference.

> ... Most of what falls under 'thinking for speaking [or writing in an L2]' is usually inaccessible to meta-awareness .... We probably do not 'notice' the way the L2 does its filtering, ... and we probably have no awareness of the language-specific nature of our own options .... Such knowledge may be very largely 'unanalyzed ...'. In the absence of such awareness, the L2 does not provide loci for (mis)generalization of L1 material .... The blueprint established for the verbal expression of experience continues to function regardless .... Coping with new ways of 'thinking for speaking [or writing] ...' means attending to features of context that are either not relevant or are defined differently in the native language .... (Kellerman 1995: 141)

To put it in a slightly different way, as Mauranen (1993: 1–2) does:

> ... [writers] differ in some of their culturally determined rhetorical practices, and these differences manifest themselves in typical textual features. *The writers seem not to be aware of these textual features, or the underlying rhetorical practices.* This lack of awareness is in part due to the fact that textlinguistic features have not been the concern of traditional language teaching in schools. Sometimes text strategies are taught for the mother tongue, but rarely if ever for foreign languages separately. Such phenomena have therefore not been brought to the attention of [writers] struggling with writing .... Nevertheless, these sometimes subtle differences between writing cultures, often precisely because they are subtle and not commonly observable to the non-linguist, tend to put ... [various] native language [writers] at a rhetorical disadvantage in the eyes of [other language] readers .... This disadvantage is more than a difference in cultural tastes, since it may not only strike readers as lack of rhetorical elegance, but as lack of coherent writing or even [coherent] thinking, which can seriously affect the credibility of non-native writers. (Emphasis added.)

All of this argues for a model which places emphasis on 'noticing', as Schmidt (1990, 1993) has argued.

Towards a revised model

A serious model of text analysis must look beyond the morphosyntactic structure of written discourse. The CR model has moved in two different directions, trying in various ways to account for the text generator, the text receiver, the text itself, and the discourse and sociolinguistic environment in which text generation and text reception occur. The model has been influenced by the evolution of other developments in discourse analysis and in turn has influenced those developments to some extent. In its present configurations, it attempts to take advantage of ideas of:

- the linguistic resources of particular languages,
- reader and writer competence, and
- reader and writer stance towards audience, text and context,
- certain difficulties that the writer introduces (intentionally or unintentionally) into the text,
- the existence of co-text and the differentiation of co-text into culturally constrained genres.

The original 'doodles' erred in attempting to represent cultural rhetorics as unique generalizations that have been perceived as stereotypes; what has been shown subsequently to be significant is not the 'shape' of culturally defined types but rather the reality that linguistic/cultural systems do differ from each other in subtle ways in the development of text – that applied linguists and language teachers must look at discoursal macro-patterns in the light of underlying cultural traditions and not merely in terms of syntactic surface features.

5   Solutions to common discourse problems

It may be useful to look at several variables. First, text does not occur in a vacuum; its existence is conditioned by the cultural and historical context in which it occurs. That cultural and historical context, in any given language, has evolved a number of common solutions to discourse problems – what one might call 'formulae for particular types of solutions', or genres. Speakers of any given language are aware of various genres, largely inculcated through the educational system with the powerful support of canonical literature and the media. Part of 'what everybody knows' in English, for example, is that a sonnet is a poetic form which is not normally used to convey a cooking recipe, and Japanese speakers know that a Haiku is a poetic form different from a sonnet, but also not appropriate for transmitting a cooking

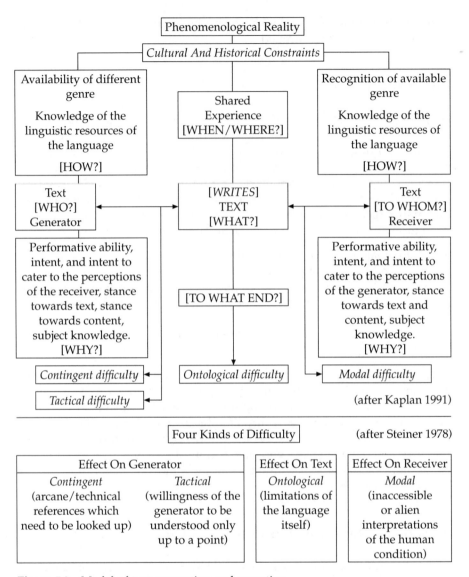

Figure 5.2 summary labels:

Phenomenological Reality

Cultural And Historical Constraints

Availability of different genre

Knowledge of the linguistic resources of the language

[HOW?]

Shared Experience [WHEN/WHERE?]

Recognition of available genre

Knowledge of the linguistic resources of the language

[HOW?]

Text [WHO?] Generator

[WRITES] TEXT [WHAT?]

Text [TO WHOM?] Receiver

Performative ability, intent, and intent to cater to the perceptions of the receiver, stance towards text, stance towards content, subject knowledge. [WHY?]

[TO WHAT END?]

Performative ability, intent, and intent to cater to the perceptions of the generator, stance towards text and content, subject knowledge. [WHY?]

Contingent difficulty   *Ontological difficulty*   *Modal difficulty*

Tactical difficulty

(after Kaplan 1991)

Four Kinds of Difficulty

(after Steiner 1978)

Effect On Generator		Effect On Text	Effect On Receiver
Contingent (arcane/technical references which need to be looked up)	*Tactical* (willingness of the generator to be understood only up to a point)	*Ontological* (limitations of the language itself)	*Modal* (inaccessible or alien interpretations of the human condition)

Figure 5.2 Model of text generation and reception

recipe. Writers choose a genre, perhaps unconsciously, to accomplish a particular communicative function, and readers recognize, again perhaps unconsciously, what the writer's choice of a genre communicates.

5.1 *The question of convention*

Obviously, both reader and writer must have some control of the language conventions; they must be able to produce structures that are neither syntactic mazes nor hopelessly ambiguous, and they must arrange such structures in conventional ways – in English, providing margins all around the page, indenting paragraphs, spelling in more or less recognisable ways, capitalizing appropriate items, hyphenating mainly at the ends of lines and usually between syllables, snugging punctuation up to the most immediate leftmost word, etc. Texts which are not conventional in appearance may be rejected by readers solely on the grounds of the lack of conventional presentation.[11]

5.2   The question of cohesion

Cohesion and coherence across the text is a significant feature of text organization. Halliday and Hasan (1976) undertook to produce a taxonomy of cohesive and coherent features. More recently, Hoey (1991) described a system of text analysis based on the study of lexical cohesion, attention here being focused not on itemizing cohesive features but rather on observing how such features combine and interact to organise text. *Cohesion* may be defined as 'the way certain words or grammatical features of a sentence can connect that sentence to its predecessors (and successors) in a text' (Hoey 1991: 3). *Coherence* is a quality assigned to text by readers as an index of the accuracy of the representation of component features in terms of the phenomenology in which the reader lives. Thus, both coherence and cohesion are culturally constrained, the former because it is to some extent at least a phenomenon of a particular language, the latter because it can only be described in terms of the reader's perceptions of the world.

Both writer and reader need to enter into a compact of intent; the writer must estimate and attempt to meet what he or she believes to be readers' expectations, and the reader must estimate and attempt to meet what he or she believes to be the writer's intent. When the compact is violated, readers will reject the text. The writer needs to make implicit his or her stance towards the audience (including the appropriate gender assumptions[12]), stance towards the text (entitlement to write), and stance towards the information contained therein (authority), and those several stances must be acceptable to the reader; that is, they must be apparent, or the writer needs to 'sell' his or her knowledge and authority. The writer needs to show his or her control of the knowledge encoded in the text; the reader presumably seeks that knowledge and, if it is apparent that the writer doesn't possess sufficient knowledge, the reader will reject the text.

5.3   Four kinds of difficulty

The writer may, intentionally or unintentionally, introduce difficulties into the text, by choosing to use arcane or technical vocabulary (contingent difficulty), or by allowing the text to be understood only up to a point (tactical difficulty). The reader may find the writer's representation of the human condition to be inaccessible or alien (modal difficulty). Or the writer may undertake to bend the language itself out of its conventional shape (ontological difficulty).[13]

Finally, both writer and reader must recognise that meaning does not reside in the text itself; rather, both must understand that they are engaged in a negotiation to make meaning – a negotiation in which the text is merely the means to that end. The choices that the writer makes establish the conditions under which the negotiation occurs, but the willingness of the reader to participate is critical to the making of meaning. In sum, the writer may create an amazing text, but if no one (other than the writer) ever reads it, can that text be said to exist?

6   A set of questions

Thus the questions posed in the subtitle of this article –

- Who writes what?
- To whom?
- When?
- In what circumstances?

– constitute important questions which must be addressed to understand how texts work, how a text is different from the sentences which compose it, and what may be involved in teaching writing. The L2 writer is faced with five terrible questions:

- What may be discussed?
- Who has the authority to write?
- What form may the writing take?
- What constitutes evidence?
- How can evidence be convincingly arranged?

These questions can only be answered through an address to cultural constraints. Topics are culturally constrained; it is inappropriate to invite L2 writers to address certain questions, because those questions may not be addressed or may not constitute questions at all in the L1; for example, the US press is full of political discussion of abortion, but for some cultures abortion is a medical issue, for others a religious issue, not a political one.

6.1   The question of authority

Not everyone has the authority to undertake writing. That authority may reside in age, or fame, or gender, or great wisdom (see, e.g., Yoshikawa 1978 for Japanese). There is also a connection between the authority of the writer and the genre he chooses to carry his message.

... [G]enre stability is partially maintained by the *'experts' in any disciplinary discourse community*,[14] thereby contributing to the community's structuration process. The relatively fully developed nature of the experts' disciplinary selves exerts influence on what can be said and how, thus contributing to the stability and reproduction of certain systems. These experts are people who, through their publications and research have reached wide audiences, whose opinions and views serve as authority sources, who have produced some of the key touchstones of the community; Heath's and Och's work on language socialization ... , Labov's analysis of narrative, Swales' work on genre, Tannen's work in discourse analysis, among others .... Kaplan's (1966) controversial 'doodles' article would not have fueled as much research in contrastive rhetoric if he had written it in the form of a memo, for instance. For one thing, *Language Learning* would not have accepted it for publication. (Ramanathan and Kaplan, in preparation)

However, the 'authority' of any of these authors is confined to their particular discourse community; it may not be recognized in an alternative discourse community in the same language (e.g., Kaplan's 'doodles' have no weight in the chemistry discourse community). Certainly, if the weight of authority varies across discourse communities in the same language, it will also vary across language communities.

6.2 The question of evidence

The validity of evidence is critical; some Asian writers, for example, may invoke traditional texts as evidence, while some western writers may be more inclined to rely on empirical evidence. Empirical research was essentially invented by Robert Boyle and his colleagues in the early Royal Society of London and in the Society's *Philosophical Transactions*, in the seventeenth century. In his *Proemial Essay*, Boyle wrote:

[I]n almost every one of the following [experimental] essays I ... speak so doubtingly, and use so often, *perhaps, it seems, it is not improbable,* and such other expressions as argue a diffidence of the truth of the opinions I incline to, and that I should be so shy of laying down principles, and sometimes of so much as venturing explications. (Cited in Atkinson 1999: 103)

But it is not only for the invention of the research article that Boyle is remembered; he and his colleagues in the Royal Society created the overriding code of the gentleman in science – a code which persisted into the twentieth century. The Royal Society was the first '... *public institution for the pursuit of scientific research* ...' (Atkinson 1999: 16; italics in the original). That the rules established more than 300 years ago have persisted into the present is demonstrated in much of the current genre research – research that itself '... is carried out and codified largely through generic forms of writing: Lab reports, working papers, reviews, grant proposals, technical reports, conference papers, journal articles, monographs, and so forth' (Berkenkotter and Huckin 1993: 476). CR takes the position that each of these genres, and many other conventionally used in the West, define the nature of evidence acceptable in the discourse communities using these genres. But it is important to note that the genres listed by Berkenkotter and Huckin are genres common to English (and Western) scientific and technical discourse communities. Discourse communities in a language other than English (LOTE) define evidence in different ways. Li, writing about writing in China, repeatedly points out the relative unimportance of data: in China over long historical time, '[n]atural science, an imported subject, . . . was looked down upon as a bunch of "trivial tricks"' . . . (1996: 3); '. . . [T]o use "definite, specific, concrete language" is one maxim that is followed with almost religious exactitude by most American [writing] teachers' (p. 119); but '[t]he preference for multitudinous specifics is . . . at odds with a Chinese literary tradition that prefers a densely selective and suggestive . . . style . . .' (p. 120). There is other evidence with respect to the nature of evidence in linguistic systems more or less distant from the Western tradition. It is important to note that the Western tradition is not necessarily 'right'; only that traditions defining the nature of evidence vary cross-culturally.

6.3 The question of arrangement

What constitutes the best arrangement of text is a complex question; editors frequently complain that a particular text is sufficient but not appropriate in terms of its presentation. Texts become the vehicles through which a discourse community's problems get addressed and its goals resolved; as Kamberelis (1995: 122) points out, '. . . [texts] are constructed for specific purposes by speakers and writers, and they always embody sets of generic conventions . . .'. The generic conventions specifically address the matter of arrangement. Commonly, there is a logical principle which defines the order of arrangement – a logical principle often derived, in the West, from Aristotelian logic and Galilean systematization. Articles written by speakers of other languages are regularly rejected by technical journal editors because the texts do not 'hang together' but rather seem to ramble aimlessly across the textual argument.[15] CR takes the position that the order of arrangement is a culturally-coded phenomenon. Again, there is no suggestion that the order implicit in Aristotelian logic and/or Galilean systematization is the best possible order; the point is that there are cross-cultural differences which must be recognized and attended to, not only in translation but in the teaching of writing across cultures.

7 The end of the affair

In conclusion, writing is not a matter of learning some set of morphosyntactic rules; rather, it is a complex multidimensional enterprise. It is not enough to look only at process (the actions through which a text is generated); after all, the product – the text – is what will be read (Kaplan 1988). While convention plays a role, the mere satisfaction of conventional rules is necessary but not sufficient. Part of what has been suggested here moves clearly into the realm of pragmatics, but that too is not in itself sufficient. Certainly, a knowledge of the subject is important, but in the absence of the recognition of the negotiation between writer and reader and the multiple variables involved in that negotiation, writing probably cannot be learned in the L1, and certainly not in the L2.

Notes

1. The concept of *lacunae* was developed primarily by J.A. Sorokin within the framework of Russian ethnopsycholinguistics. Ertelt-Vieth (1990) introduced the *lacuna* model to German intercultural studies, developing it in the direction of 'empirically, contrastively, and semiotically oriented cultural studies' ['*Beitrag zu einer empirisch, kontrastiv und semiotisch ausgerichteten Landeswissenschaft*'], as suggested in the subtitle of her study.
2. While this discussion hints at the problem of intertranslatability, that is not the subject of this essay. Still, while Contrastive Rhetoric has had an appeal to language teachers, it has also had an appeal to translators. This is not to suggest that the issues of intertranslatability are equivalent to the issues of second or foreign language teaching. At the same time, both language teaching and translation implicate the structure of text.
3. The birth of CR, at least in the United States; it would be presumptuous to suggest that the idea is totally unique (see, e.g., Enkvist 1997).
4. It is not the case that discourse analysis is needs-driven; it is, however, true that CR developed out of a teaching need. It has, over time, diverged substantially from that initial motivation.
5. In fact, I would still contend that English is more linear than many other languages; that is, English does not permit the intrusion of large amounts of tangential material into a text.
6. Specifically, Arabic (Hatim 1991; Ostler 1987; Sa'Adeddin 1989), Australian Aboriginal languages/English (Eggington 1990), 'Chicano' Spanish/English (Montaño-Harmon 1988, 1991), Chichewa (Chimombo 1988), Chinese [Standard Written Chinese] (Bloch 1989; Campbell 1989; Cheng 1985; Dunkleblau 1990; Scollon 1991; Tsao 1983), Finnish (Mauranen 1993), French, Georgian, German (Clyne 1987; Skyum-Nielsen and Schröder 1994), Hebrew (Folman and Connor 1992; Folman and Sarig 1990), Hindi (Kachru 1983), Japanese (Hinds 1987, 1990; Neustupný 1997), Korean (Chang 1983), Marathi (Pandharipanda 1983), Native American Languages/English (Leap 1983), Portuguese (Dantas-Whitney and Grabe 1992), Romanian (Manoliu-Manea 1995), Russian, Spanish (Mexican, Puerto Rican, etc.) (Lux 1991; Lux and Grabe 1991; Kamhi-Stein 1995; Ostler 1992; Reid 1988; Reppen and Grabe 1993), Thai (Bickner and Peyasantiwong 1988; Indrasutra 1988), Turkish (Enginarlar 1990; Oktar 1991), Urdu (Baumgardner 1987, 1992), Vietnamese (Soter 1988). There is some work involving several languages: e.g. English, French and Arabic (Daoud 1991), some of this work in particular registers/genres – e.g. business text in English and Japanese (Connor 1989; Oi and Sato 1990), conference abstracts in Chinese (Cantor 1994) – and there is

some work on particular grammatical categories; e.g. epistemic modals in Chicano English (Youmans 1995). Some work has been directed specifically to ESL teaching (Ferris 1991, 1992, 1993, 1994a, 1994b; Ferris and Hedgcock 1998) or to language assessment (Weasenforth 1995). Additionally an 'eclectic philosophy of language' based on CR and rhetorical theory has been developed (Kowal 1994). Biber (1988, 1992, 1995) introduced a multidimensional model of analysis employing complex computer-based techniques, and that model has been employed by some of the researchers enumerated above.

7. For additional discussion, see Ch. 7, 'Writing across cultures: Contrastive rhetoric', pp. 176–201, in Grabe and Kaplan (1996); see also Leki (1991). Additionally, E. Ventola has recently (October 1998) convened a symposium on 'Academic English – Research in the field of academic writing in Germany and elsewhere' in Halle; the papers from that symposium may be published in the future.

8. 'Knowledge' is very difficult to define, and the demarcation between 'awareness' and 'knowledge' seems imprecise. It is not my intent to suggest that the concepts are identical.

9. It would be inappropriate in this article to summarise each of the models; excellent reviews can be found in Elman et al. (1996), in Grabe et al. (1999), in Kasper (1996), and in the new journal *Bilingualism: Language and Cognition,* published by Cambridge University Press as of 1998.

10. Consider the description of any given open field by a farmer, a hydrology engineer, and a military strategist, even when all three are speakers of the same language.

11. For example, in her discussion of Dutch text, Burrough-Boenisch, a technical editor, writes: 'It's possible to identify a page of English text that has gone Dutch, just by looking at it. This is because in texts written by Dutch authors, paragraphs are not always stylistically . . . what they ought to be. The most striking difference is the mannerism of presenting a paragraph as an assemblage of subparagraphs, each of which is indicated by starting a new line' (1998: 12).

12. Even casual observation suggests, for example, that contemporary romance novels tend to be attributed to authors with feminine names (whether or not, in fact, they are females).

13. Writers of nonsense verse, like Lewis Carroll, or experimentalists, like e e cummings, have tried, with varying degrees of success, to bend the language out of its conventional shape.

14. This is in fact the sixth criterion in Swales' (1990) list of factors that define discourse communities.

15. Personal communication, Pompeya Falcón, an Argentinian technical translator. It is in fact the case that the great bulk of scientific and technical journals are now published in English regardless of the polity in which they are originated or the language(s) spoken in that polity. The desirability of such a practice is not here under discussion (see Kaplan, in preparation).

References

Atkinson, D. (1999) *Scientific Discourse in Sociohistorical Context: The Philosophical Transactions of the Royal Society of London, 1675–1975.* Mahwah, NJ: Lawrence Erlbaum.

Baumgardner, R. (1987) Utilizing Pakistani newspaper English to teach grammar. *World Englishes.* 6, 241–252.

Baumgardner, R. (1992) 'To Shariat or not to Shariat?' Bilingual functional shifts in Pakistani English. *World Englishes.* 11, 129–140.

Berkenkotter, C. and T. Huckin (1993) Rethinking genre from a sociocognitive perspective. *Written Communication.* 10(4), 475–509.

Berman, R. and D. Slobin (eds) (1994) *Relating Events in Narrative: A Crosslinguistic Developmental Study.* Hillsdale, NJ: Lawrence Erlbaum.

Biber, D. (1988) *Variation across Speech and Writing.* Cambridge: Cambridge University Press.

Biber, D. (1992) On the complexity of discourse complexity: A multidimensional analysis. *Discourse Processes.* 15, 133–163.

Biber, D. (1995) *Cross-linguistic Patterns of Register Variation: A Multi-dimensional Comparison of English, Tuvaluan, Korean, and Somali.* Oxford: Oxford University Press.

Bickner, R. and P. Peyasantiwong (1988) Cultural variation in reflective writing. In A. Purves (ed.) *Writing across Languages and Cultures.* Newbury Park, CA: Sage, 160–174.

Bloch, J. (1989) Toward a theory of contrastive rhetoric: The relationship between English and Chinese. Paper presented at the Pennsylvania State Conference on Rhetoric and Composition. July.

Burrough-Boenisch, J. (1998) *Righting English that's gone Dutch.* Antwerp: Standaard Uitgeverij.

Campbell, K. (1989) Structural patterns in Chinese and English persuasive discourse. Paper presented at the Pennsylvania State Conference on Rhetoric and Composition. July.

Cantor, S. (1994) Writer involvement in abstract writing: An analysis of theme in English and Chinese abstracts. Los Angeles: Department of Linguistics, University of Southern California. M.A. Screening paper.

Chang, S.-J. (1983) English and Korean. In R.B. Kaplan et al. (eds) *Annual Review of Applied Linguistics, 3.* Rowley, MA: Newbury House, 85–98.

Cheng, P. (1985) An analysis of contrastive rhetoric: English and Chinese expository prose, pedagogical implications, and strategies for the ESL teacher in a ninth grade curriculum. University Park, PA: The Pennsylvania State University. Ph.D. Diss.

Chimombo, M. (1988) Readability of subject texts: Implications for ESL teaching in Africa. Paper presented at the Annual TESOL Conference, Chicago. March.

Chomsky, N. (1981) Principles and parameters in syntactic theory. In N. Hornstein and D. Lightfoot (eds) *Explanation in Linguistics: The Logical Problem of Language Acquisition.* London: Longman.

Clyne, M.G. (1987) Cultural differences in the organization of academic texts: English and German. *Journal of Pragmatics.* 11(2), 211–247.

Connor, U. (1989) A contrastive study of persuasive business correspondence: American and Japanese. In S.J. Bruno (ed.) *Global Implications for Business Communications; Theory, Technology, and Practice.* Houston, TX: School of Business and Public Administration, University of Houston – Clear Lake. [*Proceedings of the 53rd National and 15th International Convention of Associations of Business Communication.*]

Connor, U. (1996) *Contrastive Rhetoric: Cross-cultural Aspects of Second-language Writing.* New York: Cambridge University Press.

Cook, V. (1988) *Chomsky's Universal Grammar: An Introduction.* Oxford: Basil Blackwell.

Dantas-Whitney, M. and W. Grabe (1992) A comparison of Portuguese and English newspaper editorials. Flagstaff, AZ: Northern Arizona University.

Daoud, M. (1991) The process of EST discourse: Arabic and French native speakers' recognition of rhetorical relationships in engineering texts. Los Angeles: University of California. Ph.D. Diss.

Deacon, T.W. (1997) *The Symbolic Species: The Co-evolution of Language and the Brain.* New York: Norton.

Donald, M. (1991) *Origins of the Modern Mind: Three Stages in the Evolution of Culture and Cognition.* Cambridge, MA: Harvard University Press.

Dunkleblau, H.S. (1990) A contrastive study of the organizational structure and stylistic elements of Chinese and English expository texts by Chinese high school students. (Unpublished paper.)

Edelman, G. (1992) *Bright Air, Brilliant Fire.* New York: Basic Books.

Eggington, W.G. (1990) Contrastive analysis of Aboriginal English prose. In W. Walton and W. Eggington (eds) *Language: Maintenance, Power and Education in Australian Aboriginal Contexts.* Darwin: Northern Territory University Press: 151–159.

Elman, J.L., E. Bates, M. Johnson, A. Karmiloff-Smith, D. Parisi, and K. Plenkett (1996) *Rethinking Innateness: A Connectionist Perspective on Development.* Cambridge, MA: A Bradford Book.

Enginarlar, H. (1990) A contrastive analysis of writing in Turkish and English of Turkish high school students. Turkey: Hacettepe University. Ph.D. Diss.

Enkvist, N.E. (1997) Why we need contrastive rhetoric. *Altern*ation. 4(1): 188–206.

Ertelt-Vieth, A. (1990) *Kulturvergleichende Analyse von Verhalten, Sprache und Bedeutungen im Moskauer Alltag. Beitrag zu einer empirisch, kontrastiv und semiotisch ausgerichteten Landeswissenschaft.* [*Beiträge zur Slavistik,* Vol. 11.] Frankfurt am Main.

Ferris, D. (1991) Syntactic and lexical characteristics of ESL student writing: A multi-dimensional study. Los Angeles: University of Southern California. Ph.D. Diss.

Ferris, D. (1992) Cross-cultural variation in ESL students' responses to an essay prompt. Sacramento, CA: California State University.

Ferris, D. (1993) The design of an automatic analysis program for L2 text research: Necessity and feasibility. *Journal of Second Language Writing.* 2(2): 119–129.

Ferris, D. (1994a) Lexical and syntactic features of ESL writing by students at different levels of proficiency. *TESOL Quarterly.* 28(2): 414–420.

Ferris, D. (1994b) Rhetorical strategies in student persuasive writing: Differences between native and non-native English speakers. *Research in the Teaching of English.* 28(1): 45–65.

Ferris, D. and J.S. Hedgcock (1998) *Teaching ESL Composition: Purpose, Process, and Practice.* Mahwah, NJ: Lawrence Erlbaum.

Folman, S. and U. Connor (1992) Intercultural rhetorical differences in composing a research paper. Paper presented at the International Teachers of English to Speakers of Other Languages Conference, Vancouver, BC. March.

Folman, S. and G. Sarig (1990) Intercultural rhetorical differences in meaning construction. *Communication and Cognition.* 23(1): 45–92.

Grabe, W. and R.B. Kaplan (1996) *Theory and Practice of Writing: An Applied Linguistic Perspective.* London: Longman.

Grabe, W. et al. (eds) (1999) *Annual Review of Applied Linguistics, 19.* New York: Cambridge University Press.

Halliday, M.A.K. (1993) Towards a language-based theory of learning. *Linguistics and Education.* 5: 93–116.

Halliday, M.A.K. and R. Hasan (1976) *Cohesion in English.* London: Longman.

Hatim, B. (1991) The pragmatics of argumentation in Arabic: The rise and fall of a text type. *TEXT.* 11: 189–199.

Hinds, J. (1987) Reader versus writer responsibility. In U. Connor and R.B. Kaplan (eds) *Writing across Languages: Analysis of L2 text.* Reading, MA: Addison-Wesley: 141–152.

Hinds, J. (1990) Inductive, deductive, quasi-inductive: Expository writing in Japanese, Korean, Chinese and Thai. In Connor, U. and A. Johns (eds) *Coherence in Writing: Research and Pedagogical Perspectives.* Alexandria, VA: TESOL.

Hoey, M. (1991) *Patterns of Lexis in Text.* Oxford: Oxford University Press.

Indrasutra, C. (1988) Narrative styles in the writing of Thai and American students. In A. Purves (ed.) *Writing across Languages and Cultures.* Newbury Park, CA: Sage: 206–226.

Kachru, B.B. (ed.) (1992) *The Other Tongue: English across Cultures.* 2nd edn. Urban, IL: University of Illinois Press.

Kachru, Y. (1983) English and Hindi. In R.B. Kaplan et al. (eds) *Annual Review of Applied Linguistics,* vol. 3. Rowley, MA: Newbury House: 78–84.

Kamberelis, G. (1995) Genre as institutionally informed social practice. *Journal of Contemporary Legal Issues.* 6: 115–170.

Kamhi-Stein, L. (1995) The effect of strategy instruction on the summarization strategies of native speakers of Spanish in university-level general education courses. Los Angeles, CA: University of Southern California. Ph.D. Diss.

Kaplan, R.B. (1966) Cultural thought patterns in intercultural education. *Language Learning.* 16: 1–20.

Kaplan, R.B. (1972) *The Anatomy of Rhetoric: Prolegomena to a Functional Theory of Rhetoric.* Philadelphia: The Center for Curriculum Development.

Kaplan, R.B. (1988) Process vs. product: Problem or strawman? *Lenguas Modernas.* 15: 35–44.

Kaplan, R.B. (1991) On applied linguistics and discourse analysis. In W. Grabe et al. (eds) *Annual Review of Applied Linguistics,* II. New York: Cambridge University Press, 199–204.

Kaplan, R.B. (in preparation). English – the Accidental Language of Science? In U. Ammon (ed.) *Effects of the Dominance of English as a Language of Science on the non-English Language Communities.* Berlin: Mouton de Gruyter.

Kaplan, R.B. et al. (eds) (1983) *Annual Review of Applied Linguistics, 3.* Rowley, MA: Newbury House.

Kasper, G. (ed.) (1996) *The Development of Pragmatic Competence.* [Special issue of *Studies in Second Language Acquisition.* 18(2).]

Kellerman, E. (1995) Crosslinguistic influence: Transfer to nowhere. In W. Grabe et al. (eds) *Annual Review of Applied Linguistics,* vol. 15. New York: Cambridge University Press: 125–150.

Kowal, K. (1994) Contrastive rhetoric and rhetorical theory: Some prolegomena to an eclectic philosophy of language. Paper presented at the CCCC Conference. Chicago. March.

Leap, W.L. (1983) English and Native American languages. In R.B. Kaplan et al. (eds) *Annual Review of Applied Linguistics, 3.* Rowley, MA: Newbury House: 24–37.

Leki, I. (1991) Twenty-five years of contrastive rhetoric: The state of the Art. *TESOL Quarterly.* 25(1): 123–143.

Li Xiao-ming (1996) *'Good Writing' in Cross-cultural Context.* Albany, NY: State University of New York Press.

Lux, P. (1991) Discourse styles of Anglo and Latin American college student writers. Tempe, AZ: Arizona State University. Ph.D. Diss.

Lux, P. and W. Grabe (1991) Multivariate approaches to contrastive rhetoric. *Lenguas Modernas.* 18: 133–160.

Manoliu-Manea, M. (1995) *Discourse and Pragmatic Constraints on Grammatical Choices: A Grammar of Surprises.* Amsterdam: Elsevier Science.

Mauranen, A. (1993) *Cultural Differences in Academic Rhetoric.* Frankfurt am Main: Peter Lang. [Scandinavian University Studies in the Humanities and Social Sciences, Vol. 4.]

Montaño-Harmon, M. (1988) Discourse features in the compositions of Mexican, English as a second language, Mexican-American/Chicano and Anglo high school students: Considerations for the formulation of educational policies. Los Angeles, CA: University of Southern California. Ph.D. Diss.

Montaño-Harmon, M. (1991) Discourse features of written Mexican Spanish: Current research in contrastive rhetoric and its implications. *Hispania.* 74: 417–425.

Neustupný, J.V. (1997) Teaching communication or teaching interaction? *Chiba University Journal.* November 1997: 1–13.

Oi, K. and T. Sato (1990) Cross-cultural rhetorical differences in letter writing: Refusal letter and application letter. *Daigaku eigo kyoiku gakukai*: 117–136.

Oktar, L. (1991) A contrastive analysis of specific rhetorical relations in English and Turkish expository paragraph writing. Turkey: Ege University. Ph.D. Diss.

Ostler, S.E. (1987) English in parallels: A comparison of English and Arabic prose. In U. Connor and R.B. Kaplan (eds) *Writing across Languages: Analysis of L2 text.* Reading, MA: Addison-Wesley: 169–185.

Ostler, S.E. (1992) Cultural Sensitivities: Teaching Spanish Speakers to Write in English. Bowling Green, OH: Bowling Green University.

Pandharipanda, R. (1983) English and Marathi. In R.B. Kaplan et al. (eds) *Annual Review of Applied Linguistics, 3.* Rowley, MA: Newbury House: 118–136.

Penn, J.M. (1972) *Linguistic Relativity versus Innate Ideas: The origin of the Sapir-Whorf Hypothesis in German Thought.* The Hague: Mouton. [Janua Linguarum, Series minor, 120.]

Ramanathan, V. and R.B. Kaplan (in preparation). Genres, authors, discourse communities: Theory and application for L2 teacher-training. [A version of this paper was presented at the TESOL Conference, Seattle, 1998.]

Reid, J. (1988) Quantitative differences in English prose written by Arabic, Chinese, Spanish, and English students. Ft. Collins, CO: Colorado State University. Ph.D. Diss.

Reppen, R. and W. Grabe (1993) Spanish transfer effects in the English writing of elementary school students. *Lenguas Modernas.* 20: 113–128.

Sa'Adeddin, M.A. (1987) Target world experiential matching: The Arabic–English translating case. *Quinquireme.* 10(2): 137–164. [University of Bath.]

Sa'Adeddin, M.A. (1989) Text development and Arabic–English negative interference. *Applied Linguistics.* 10: 36–51.

Schmidt, R. (1990) The role of consciousness in second language fluency. *Applied Linguistics.* 11: 129–156.

Schmidt, R. (1993) Awareness and second language acquisition. In W. Grabe et al. (eds) *Annual Review of Applied Linguistics, 13.* New York: Cambridge University Press: 206–226.

Scollon, R. (1991) Eight legs and one elbow: Stance and structure in Chinese English compositions. Paper presented at the International Reading Association Second North American Conference on Adult and Adolescent Literacy. Banff. March.

Scollon, R. (1997) Contrastive rhetoric, contrastive poetics, or perhaps something else? *TESOL Quarterly.* 31(2): 352–358.

Skyum-Nielsen, P. and H. Schröder (eds) (1994) *Rhetoric and Stylistics Today.* Frankfurt am Main: Peter Lang.

Soter, A. (1988) The second language learner and cultural transfer in narration. In A. Purves (ed.) *Writing across Languages and Cultures.* Newbury Park, CA: Sage: 378–388.

Steiner, G. (1978) On difficulty. *On Difficulty and other Essays.* New York: Oxford University Press: 18–47.

Strother, J.B. and J.M. Ulijn (1991) The ties that bind readability to writing research: Who writes the most texts? In C. Harrison and E. Ashworth (eds) *Celebrating Literacy: Defending Literacy.* Oxford: Basil Blackwell.

Swales, J. (1990) *Genre Analysis: English in Academic and Research Settings.* Cambridge: Cambridge University Press.

Tsao, F.-F. (1983) Linguistics and writing in particular languages: English and Chinese. In R.B. Kaplan et al. (eds) *Annual Review of Applied Linguistics, 3.* Rowley, MA: Newbury House: 99–117.

Ulijn, J.M. and J.B. Strother (1995) *Communicating in Business and Technology: From Psycholinguistic Theory to International Practice.* Frankfurt am Main: Peter Lang.

Weasenforth, D. (1995) Rhetorical abstraction as a facet of expected response: A structural equation modeling analysis. Los Angeles: University of Southern California. Ph.D. Diss.

Wijst, van der, P. and J.M. Ulijn (1995) Politeness in French/Dutch negotiations: The linguistic realization of politeness strategies. In K. Ehlich and J. Wagner (eds) *The Discourse of Business Negotiations.* Berlin: Monton de Gruyter: 313–348.

Yoshikawa, M. (1978) Some Japanese and American cultural characteristics. In M.H. Prosser (ed.) *The Cultural Dialogue: An Introduction to Intercultural Communication.* Boston: Houghton Mifflin: 220–230.

Youmans, M. (1995) Communicative rights and responsibilities in an east Los Angeles barrio: An analysis of epistemic modal use. Los Angeles, CA: University of Southern California. Ph.D. Diss.

Chapter 6

Professional gatekeeping in intercultural encounters

Celia Roberts

1 'Gatekeeping' and diversity

The notion of gatekeeping is one that anybody living in a bureaucratic society can relate to. We have all had the experience of being checked through some 'gate', either an actual door or turnstile or through the surveillance procedures at reception. There are two aspects to this process – the physical and social passage from outside to inside the institution and the process of being assessed and let in (or not). The metaphor of passing through gates or doors is, of course, a common one in western literature. Gerard de Nerval wrote of passing into the world of dreams as: '. . . a second life. I have never been able to pass through those ivory gates that lead to the invisible world without a shudder.' Huxley also wrote of his experience of LSD with the title 'Doors of Perception'. More generally, within anthropological literature, rites of passage have been studied with the notion of a liminal/liminoid time and space in which success in some trial or assessment confers on the individual a new status. The recent discourses of social equality represent barriers to upward mobility not so much in terms of 'invisible gates' but 'glass ceilings'. However, the underlying metaphor is the same.

Institutional gatekeeping interviews are a highly ritualised example of this liminoid space. The careful configuration of furniture, the conventionalised routines and the standards of appropriateness and politeness reflect and help to constitute the ritual, but also to mask the purpose of the encounter. The function of the gatekeeping event is to assess and decide on the relative merit of an individual's case and on the basis of this decision to allow access (or not) to scarce resources. The role of the gatekeepers in surveillance and as guardians of these resources, and the consequent impact on equality of opportunity and social justice, has turned encounters with them into strategic research sites for sociolinguists and anthropologists.

The use of the term 'gatekeeping' was introduced into studies of interaction and discourse by Erickson (1975) in his seminal paper on educational counselling interviews and further developed in his monograph on these interviews (Erickson and Shultz 1982). Subsequently, studies of gatekeeping

102

interviews have ranged from routine encounters with bureaucratic officials to the full panoply of extended job interviews (Gumperz 1982a, 1982b, 1992a).[1] However different the setting or specific purpose, they all show how crucial such encounters are to life chances despite their often *apparently* fleeting and low-key contribution to individuals' social and material success. They demonstrate how the processes of assessing and decision making on the basis of talk are essential to the guarding of resources, which are both scarce and made scarce by the ruling elite.

This chapter focuses on an explicit form of gatekeeping interview: the peer assessment of general practitioners (GPs) to select members for the Royal College of General Practitioners (RCGP).[2] Peer assessment produces particular tensions which have something in common with Erickson and Shultz's counselling interviews. As with the counsellors, there is a role conflict. But here the conflict is between the GPs as examiners on the one hand, and their 'co-membership' (Erickson and Shultz 1982: 17) with the GP candidates on the other. The people they are assessing are 'one of us' and yet they must discriminate (in the testing sense) between those worthy of being selected and those who are not.

Such tensions throw into relief the perennial problem of how candidates can be 'objectively' assessed in face-to-face encounters. Weber's arguments for efficient, objective and rational forms of work control have cast a long shadow on the selection processes in employment. As formal encounters with publicly available criteria and modes of conduct, they were seen as objective, unbiased procedures which would be both fair and efficient (Mehan 1984). The 'objective' procedures were, in part, designed to cater for the ethnically and linguistically diverse societies which were increasingly the norm in urban environments. Yet it was this very diversity which was to shed light on the gatekeeping process and prove that the 'fair' and 'objective' test was a chimera:

> (G)atekeeping encounters are not a neutral and 'objective' meritocratic sorting process. On the contrary, our analysis suggests that the game is rigged, albeit not deliberately, in favour of those individuals whose communication style and social background are most similar to those of the interviewer with whom they talk.
>
> (Erickson and Shultz 1982: 193)

Similarly, the RCGP exam board found that, despite their best efforts (Wakeford et al. 1995) minority ethnic candidates who had been trained abroad were consistently assessed less positively than their white and ethnic minority counterparts who had been trained in Britain. The interview game is 'rigged' because it is a social encounter which depends upon some kind of social relationship being formed. This, in turn, relies on conversational involvement, what Goffman (1956) calls 'engrossment', in jointly producing the gatekeeping event. Assessments of candidates are embedded in and arise out of these interactional productions. Where the grounds for such involvement are not shared, the conditions exist for biased and potentially discriminatory judgements.

So the key issue is how different communicative practices become the grounds for social evaluation. This means understanding the ways in which such interviews are socially and culturally organised, how such organisation produces interpretations of meaning and intent and how, in turn, these interpretations become judgements and then decisions which feed into the social facts of institutional discrimination and the wider ideological formations around race and ethnicity. In other words, there is a linguistic and cultural dimension to discrimination.

In this chapter I want to re-analyse some data from the RCGP examinations already discussed in Roberts and Sarangi (1999) to bring out this linguistic and cultural dimension, showing how a fine-grained analysis of the data illuminates the ways in which cultural processes feed into interaction and the consequent social evaluations of certain groups of minority ethnic candidates.

2 Ethnography of communication and contextualisation

The social and linguistic theories which have developed out of the analysis of gatekeeping encounters, and have been used to shed light on them, derive from a fundamental interest in linguistic and cultural diversity in stratified multilingual urban settings. This work, which is relatively eclectic both in its theories and methods, represents some of the most substantial studies in interactional sociolinguistics (IS) and micro-ethnography. Here, macro issues to do with inequality, institutionalisation, urbanisation and discrimination and sociological notions of ethnicity, social identity, networks and gatekeeping are linked to micro issues of discourse coherence, sequential organisation of conversations, the integration of verbal and non-verbal behaviour and pragmatic concepts of, for example, face and frame. The theoretical and moral concerns of these studies are well summed up in Levinson's comments on Gumperz's work:

> . . . it is the large-scale sociological effects of multitudes of small-scale interactions that still partially fuels his preoccupations with conversation, most evident perhaps in his concern with the plight of the individual caught up in these large-scale forces. (Levinson 1997: 24)

In this quote are a number of the themes which run through these studies: the relationship between determining social forces and discourses on the one hand and the scope for individual agency on the other; the focus on interaction as a level of analysis in its own right – drawing on Goffman's 'interaction order' and the fine-grained detail of conversation analysis – and the concern with the whole social being in interaction and not just the mechanisms and strategies of conversation. Two key areas, the ethnography of communication and notions of context and contextualisation, are central to this linkage of macro- and micro-processes in gatekeeping encounters.

The ethnography of communication (Hymes 1964; Gumperz and Hymes 1972; Bauman and Sherzer 1974) provides a crucial insight into how events are culturally and interactionally produced. Firstly, the idea of the event as a unit of analysis meant that speech could be interpreted with reference to the whole encounter and not just to what individual utterances meant. Secondly, the notion of the event as a formal, 'partially bounded setting' (Goffman 1961; Erickson and Shultz 1982) coincides precisely with the gatekeeping interview and foregrounds it as a significant unit of analysis and not just some routine and analytically ill-defined institutional procedure. Thirdly, it draws ethnography into linguistic analysis and so requires the analyst to use the participants' or members' own processes of inferencing in coming to an understanding of what is going on. In both interactional sociolinguistics and micro-ethnography, a more general ethnography is part of the analytic focus whether it is to establish 'the communicative ecology' (Gumperz 1999) within which the interaction to be studied is set or to know more about the life histories, social networks and institutional culture in a broader sense (Erickson 1986). Fourthly, it extends the notion of context in interaction to include non-verbal, spatial and temporal aspects of the situation and, finally, it focuses on the idea of language as social action, as performance. This is not in the narrow sense of speech acts but as social acts in which people do things to each other, moment by moment in the act of conveying intent and interpreting the other's intent.

For example, a South Asian candidate in a selection interview who does not respond immediately to the question: 'How's your maths?' finds that he has been rated as poor at maths by the interviewer and is not selected for the training course (Roberts and Sayers 1987). It is only possible to understand how a moment of silence after a question could have such disastrous results if this brief exchange is seen to be framed by selection interviewing presuppositions in which silence is interpreted as an admission of weakness.

So, the ethnography of communication created a new agenda in which institutional activities such as gatekeeping interviews could be analysed as culturally framed activities. Once our analytic gaze shifts to the cultural framing of these events, then issues of intercultural communication come to the fore. In particular, the central role of context and contextualisation in creating (or not) the grounds for shared understanding takes us to Gumperz's work.

The idea that it is impossible for speakers to make sense of each other without a context is, of course, not new; but as well as extending the scope of what counts as context, drawing on the ethnography of communication, Jenny Cook-Gumperz and John Gumperz's notion of 'contextualisaton' (1976) developed the idea that utterances create their own contexts. Bateson's earlier work on metacommunication had already introduced the idea of language and interaction as context-creating (1956) but the crucial insight of 'contextualisaton' was that linguistic and paralinguistic signs invoke contexts which shape the interaction moment by moment in the very act of being shaped by it. The active verb-like nuances of 'contextualisaton' emphasise that it is not some static given but rather what is accomplished *as* people make sense to each other and *because* they make sense to each other. Auer and di Luzio (1992: 4) sees contextualisaton as comprising:

> . . . all activities by participants which make relevant, maintain, revise, cancel . . . any aspect of context which, in turn, is responsible for the interpretation of an utterance in its particular locus of occurrence.

Auer makes the important point that contextualisation is not only about framing the activity in which participants are involved, or what the topic is, but is also about participants' roles and participant structure, social relationships, the mood or 'key' of the activity or the moment and what counts as part of the 'focused interaction'. Contextualisation works, therefore, to give a feel for the game. The framing work of contextualisation shows Gumperz's debt to Goffman's notions of frame and footing (1974) but he extends Goffman's sociological insights by showing how language and the fine details of interaction enter into the framing process. He has also been influenced by Garfinkel's notion of inferential processes (1967). However, as Gumperz suggests (1997), Garfinkel never addressed how inferences are made and it was necessary, therefore, to look at the specifics of interaction to understand the ways in which contextualising work allows participants to make and draw inferences.

Contextualisation, therefore, is crucial to social involvement and links detailed linguistic understanding to cultural knowledge through the ideas of framing and inferencing. As such, it provides a central tool for understanding intercultural encounters through Gumperz's notion of 'contextualisation cues'.

3 Contextualisation cues and cultural difference

'Contextualisation cues' (Gumperz 1982a, 1992a, 1992b, 1996) offer a theory and a method for understanding conversational inference by looking at the detailed signalling of messages and 'metamessages' in interaction. These cues are surface features of a message which function metapragmatically in that they cue:

> . . what is to be expected in the exchange, what should be lexically expressed, what can be conveyed only indirectly, how moves are to be positioned in an exchange, what interpersonal relations are involved and what rights to speaking apply. (Gumperz 1996: 396–7)

So, they act as prompts and guides to the many hidden processes in interaction which make participants feel they 'can get along together', 'have things in common', 'understand each other'. This awareness or implicit knowledge of pragmatics is, as Gumperz asserts, important both to survive in a bureaucratic world and also to learn from your own misunderstandings

(Gumperz 1997). Differences in contextualisation cues are problematic when participants have been socialised into using them in different ways or bring different means to contextualising their contributions influenced by early socialisation in other languages. Even when participants share other communicative practices, as in the RCGP data, differences are highlighted by the nature of the gatekeeping interview.

The way contextualisation cues work is illustrated in a small segment of the RCGP data[3] in which two white examiners are questioning, in turn, a minority ethnic candidate. The candidate is presented with a hypothetical scenario about a young boy who could possibly have been infected with the AIDS virus from a syringe on the beach which pricked his heel. The aim of the question is to assess the candidate's 'problem-solving' skills when faced with a distraught mother who wants to know how anything drastic can be prevented. The segment begins some 18 turns into the interview with the question of how the mother can be reassured still unanswered:

1.   **SO** it's really to get history
                                /

2.   and to know MORE about her <u>con</u> <cerns>
                                    ↑
                                                  ≪E. nods≫

3.   <as part of (- -)>
          ↓   /
          ≪p≫

4. E: <ye : s.>
           /\/
           ≪len≫

5. C: ag<u>ain</u> = =

6. E: = = so shes immed (--) <its **AIDS** (-)
                            ≪Moves head to the right≫

7.   whats on her mi : nd.>
                     _
      <shifts gaze down to the paper on his desk>

8. C: AIDS <on her mind ok (2)>
          ↑   ≪p≫ _

9.   sorry (-) <you want me to see>
          ≪h≫

I will concentrate on lines 1 to 6. In line 1, '**SO** it's really to get history', the candidate appears to be closing this part of his answer. The formulaic and strongly accented 'so' with the emphatic 'really' suggest a kind of summing up. However at line 3, C pauses and does not complete. E, at line 6, follows up a slow and strongly contoured 'yes' (line 4) with an attempt to refocus C on the task of how to advise the mother on the HIV/AIDS question. The latching on to line 5 and the accented '**AIDS**' are used by the examiner as steering cues. Bearing in mind that this is a peer assessment, E may rely particularly heavily on contextualisation cues in order to convey his intent rather than bring out in the open, so to speak, that he is not getting a preferred answer.

So, in this short extract, we see a number of examples of typical contextualisation cues as defined by Gumperz (1982a): prosodic and paralinguistic features and formulaic expressions such as opening or closing phenomena (in this case apparently closing a topic). Another type of contextualisation cue, code or style switching, appears a little later in this sequence. Here the examiner switches to a slightly higher pitch and more breathy voice to cue that he has become 'the mother' in order to role play the hypothetical scene since he has failed by other means to elicit from the candidate exactly how he would advise the boy's mother.

We can also see how these cues function at three levels (Gumperz 1992a: 232–3):

1. The perceptual plane in which speech is chunked into manageable units and assessed for coherence and relevance. For example, in line 6 C has to process the false start made by the examiner and switch his attention to the thematic focus E. gives to 'AIDS'.
2. The level of communicative intent in the sense of what is going on right now. Here C needs to be able to make sense of the latching at line 6, as well as the metamessage given off by the accent on 'AIDS'. Both seem to be cueing some kind of request for repair work on the part of C. Similarly, E interprets C's utterance at line 1 as a summing up and closing.
3. At the level at which more general framing work is going on, in which the candidate is expected to give an institutionally appropriate response according to the oral examination criteria to produce a coherent and consistent response.

So both sides bring interpretive resources to manage the particular and local work that must be done to process the stream of talk as it happens and make a situated assessment of intent. The problem is, as line 9 indicates, they do not seem to share the same intepretive conventions. We can therefore see how this level of analysis brings out the intercultural dimension which a more general level of analysis would overlook.

Any aspect of language can function as a contextualisation cue, but the focus on the particular features just listed is to emphasise the point that these cues function as 'pure indexicals' (Silverstein 1992); that is to say, unlike lexis and grammar which communicate through well-known rules, contextualisation cues 'communicate by virtue of direct conventional associations between signs and context, established or transmitted through previous communicative experience' (Gumperz 1997: 8). This means that they cannot be assigned stable, core lexical meanings. For example, a shift in register pitch or a change in tempo do not mean anything in themselves – they function relationally (Gumperz 1992b). It is in relation to other features of the interaction, which may be more stable, that contextualisation cues guide or channel relevant meaning. So, for example, the 'yes' in line 4 takes on a specific meaning because of the prosodic and paralinguistic features – the rise, fall, rise with a decrease in tempo and stretched vowel – with which it is uttered. And the social import of this 'yes' depends, of course, upon the extent to which there are shared conventions for making inferences, which, in turn, depend upon social and cultural experience.

4   Contextualisation cues and micro-ethnography

So far, we have looked at the fine-grained detail of linguistic analysis, but in order to conceptualise how culturally-based mismatches in contextualisation cues lead to negative social evaluations we also need an intermediate level of contextual analysis. This returns us to Erickson's work. Here, context is an environment in which identities, roles and status are played out through the social and cultural organisation of interaction. The fine-grained detail of what Erickson (1985) calls the 'local micro-culture', particularly the rhythmic co-ordination of verbal and non-verbal features, is crucial but it serves to build up concepts around: on the one hand, organisational features such as 'participant structures' and 'holding the floor', and on the other hand, participant identity such as 'co-membership' and 'performed social identity'. Erickson and Shultz (1982) show that the social identity that is made relevant to the counsellor depends upon the quality of the student's interactional performance and the extent to which counsellor and students found they were, in some ways, members of the same group or community (in terms of, for example, being supporters of the same football club or even just having some acquaintances in common). The solidarity that this invoked, combined with interactional aspects such as stable rhythmic organisation of the interview, were over-riding factors in relatively successful outcomes for some students. The converse was also true, and lack of 'co-membership' and uncomfortable moments arising out of conversational arhythmia led to less helpful and optimistic advice for students.

Erickson also uses the concept of frame (Goffman 1974) at a more general level. For Gumperz, frames are retrieved through contextualisation cues in order to channel the interpretive process. In Erickson's work and in other micro-ethnographic studies, 'frame' is interpreted again at an intermediate level, as focus of attention (Erickson and Shultz 1982: 14–15). It acts as a boundary between the encounter and the everyday world outside, putting a particular attribute of attentional focus in the foreground. So framing becomes a key way of constructing social identity:

> A wide range of attributes of status of the student and counsellor is available to be drawn within the frame of the encounter for attention, in the construction of social identity for particular purposes in the moment at hand. (Ibid.: 15)

If we return to the RCGP data we can begin to see how interactional sociolinguistics (IS) and micro-ethnographic studies together can give insights into the processes of social evaluation in this particular type of oral assessment, and indeed gatekeeping interviews more generally. In particular, we can see how contextualised cues frame moments in the encounter which are interpreted differently by examiner and candidate, how such misinterpretations turn these moments into uncomfortable ones and how these affect the performed social identity of the candidate by drawing on wider frames of the candidate's status. We can also see how the social evaluation of candidates is fixed through the reporting on them after the assessment and how indirect and subtle the process of discrimination can be. The small segment from the exam is now put in the larger context of the first 34 lines of the 'problem-solving' question sequence:

01 E: [. . .] a mother bringing up five year old child and she is obviously very uptight (--) erm and anxious (-) the reason being they were in benidorm and they've just come back the day before seeing you (---) and when the son was on the beach er in benidorm he got a needle stick injury (-) syringe and needle (--) in the sand (--) er two days ago

02 C: two days ago = =

03 E: = = hmm so erm (1.5) she is really wanting you to tell her how anything drastic can be prevented (1) from this injury (-) she's got ideas obviously about erm (1) aids because this was hm (-) er (-) presumably from a person who is injecting

04 C: ok (-) well it depends if I know the patient well it will be easy for me to establish rapport first and maybe with her child who is coming and both of them (   )

05 E: hm mhm

06 C: if it is not I'll start from the beginning (-) so establish rapport first

07 E: hm mhm

08 C: and (--) get to the problem and ask more about the details of the history (---) what was the needle like (-) was it = =

09 E: = = yeah

10 C: = syringe =

11 E: = syringe = attached to it (--)

12 C: = was there blood on it =

13 E: = it looked a little =

14 C: what did she do immediately after (--) did she squeeze it (-) did = she =

15 E: = right = it was washed and cleaned = =

16 C: = = and is she sure that the babys (-) sorry her = child =

17 E: = five year = old

18 C: sorry (--) the child er has pricked himself or was just he was playing that (--) did she see any blood

19 E: it was actually his heel (-) he was (-) he didnt pick it up or anything

20 C: yeah and just about details (--) the area is well known for drug addicts does she know any (--) is she concerned about hiv etc (-) why are you concerned about it (--) maybe she will say to me oh the incident of hiv in this area is ten per cent and so on (---)

SO it's really to get history
/

and to know MORE about her con<cerns>
↑

                                ≪E. nods≫

<as part of (--)>
↓   /

≪p≫

21 E: <ye : s>
         /\/
        ≪len≫

22 C: again = =

23 E: = = so shes immed (--) <its **AIDS** (-)
                         ≪Moves head to the right≫
    whats on her mi : nd.>
            _

    <shifts gaze down to the paper on his desk>

24 C: AIDS <on her mind ok (2)>
      ↑   ≪p≫ _
    sorry (-) <you want me to see
          ≪h≫
    how I go through the = consultation> =
                      /

25 E: = communicating = with her now about this . . what are you going to say to
    her now . . in the context of this alarm = =

26 C: = = ok well (--) well my aim will be just to reassure her then take active
    steps (--) to reassure I must establish rapport with her = and =

27 E: = youve = done that
    <smiles and moves hand forward>

28 C: ok (--) again to get to the (--) her concerns (--) is it anything else she is
    concerned about (--) anything going around that (2) = ( ) =

29 E: = she wants to = know what -- what you are going to do because

30 C: what I am going to do

21 E: yes

32 C: ok (--) first of all explain to her that erm its just a needle stick injury and I
    say it's a needle and no blood attached to it and the chance of this happen-
    ing is extremely extremely rare

33 E: in terms of what happening (--) the

34 C: eh catching = hiv =

35 E: = causing = aids mhm hm

36 C: but of course there are other concerns like hepatitis b and a and c . . .

Thirty out of the 84 turns in this question are spent trying to negotiate a
shared frame. On the one hand, there is the professional frame which concerns
the actual advice the GP would give and on the other hand there is what we
have called the institutional frame (Roberts and Sarangi 1999) in which the
candidate is expected to use hypothetical cases to talk in a more abstract
and analytic way. The interrelationship of these two modes of talk, the

institutional and the professional, is problematic for many RCGP candidates as we discuss (op. cit.), but what a detailed analysis of the data shows is that, for candidates who do not share the same communicative conventions as the examiner, the difficulty is finding shared grounds for negotiating the frames.

The candidate (C) starts to answer by using a well-known model of communications in which the GP is first expected to establish rapport and take details of the history. In following this model, he introduces details of the hypothetical case which involves him in negotiating the 'facts' with the examiner (E). This negotiation is foregrounded and the actual advice C would give becomes backgrounded. The degree of latching and overlapping in this sequence suggests that the examiner wants to press on with the business of how the candidate will tackle advice on AIDS. In other words, he wants to get a 'markable' response from the candidate as examiners are instructed to do in their examiner training. At turn 18 C shifts to this topic but instead of detailing what advice he would give the mother, he sums up 'so it's really to get history and to know more about her concerns as part of' and he then pauses. At this point, turns 20 to 32, there is marked arhythmia and a number of other perturbations which produce quite a rocky ride for the participants. These interactional differences coincide with difficulties in understanding the other's contextualisation work – in particular prosodic features and I shall look again in more detail at lines 20 to 24 (see above – this segment was used to exemplify contextualisation cues) to illustrate these in the light of this wider context.

C's summing up in utterance 20, as I have suggested, appears to give off two different messages which are indicated both lexically and prosodically. He uses the discourse marker 'so' and the emphatic 'really' together with the more abstract 'her concerns' to suggest closure. Prosodically, the accent on 'so' would also suggest a rounding off. He seems to be in the 'frame': 'I am demonstrating to you my knowledge of the communications model widely used when giving advice to patients'. However, lexically, he appears to be in mid-sentence with 'part of' at the end of utterance 20 but then he pauses for nearly a second. Prosodically, the shift to a higher register at 'more' and the mid-rise on 'of' would suggest that there is more coming, possibly more detailed advice. E's 'yes' at 21 may be an interruption or a gap filler. (It is difficult to interpret C's 'again' at line 22 as coherent with his last few words and so acting as a continuation of his theme.) What does seem clear from E's 'yes' is that he is signalling dissatisfaction with C's answer and possibly with the mixed messages that C is giving off that he is both closing and continuing his response. C's 'again' at mid-level pitch seems ambiguous both lexically and prosodically and E latches his next turn onto it with an attempt to focus the candidate on the issue of giving specific advice about AIDS. This is done by the accenting of AIDS and the steep intonational fall and lengthening of the vowel on 'mind'. The cue here seems to be calling up a professional consultation frame: 'What would you actually say to the mother?' At utterance 24, C virtually echoes E's line and then pauses for two seconds, apologises and then shifts to a higher register on 'you want me to see how I go through the consultation'. The echo and then pause, suggest that C has not picked up on E's contextualising work to get him into consultation mode. At line 24, C appears to infer from E that he has not yet given an acceptable answer and metacommunicates about what this exchange is about but, as the subsequent lines indicate, he has not made the inferences that E expected. Instead he goes back to the communication model which he started with.

E's reliance on contouring, accenting and pitch movements to contextualise his perspective on C's response and attempt to move the encounter on are, of course, indirect cues which rely on shared prosodic conventions. E, in turn, appears to have difficulty in interpreting C's contextualisation cues. C's identity as a successful candidate may be further at risk because in metacommunicating about what he must now do, he is bringing the problem to the surface and such metacommunication often indexes interactional discomfort (Gumperz 1992a; Roberts et al. 1992). As I have suggested, this is also indexed by arhythmia – the lack of rhythmic co-ordination between participants. Throughout this question and answer session, there is a high incidence of interruption, overlap and latching which contrasts with pauses at critical moments and contributes to negative evaluative outcomes. The mismatch in frames means that the examiner is attending to the problem of how to get C back on track rather than assessing the adequacy of his answer. C's 'performed social identity' at this point must, at least in part, be constituted by these interactional difficulties.

After this moment of hiatus, E and C seem to go through the same routine, with C again describing the procedures he would follow: establish rapport and ask about her concerns. This time, E is slightly more direct in attempting to elicit a preferred response when at utterance 29 he says: 'she wants to know what you are going to do because'. Finally, at utterance 32, C seems to be addressing the question of how he would advise the mother.

5   Processes of social evaluation

This segment is one of a number of difficult moments in the interview despite the fact that the examiners do not query C's medical knowledge and he presents himself positively as a highly qualified person with compassion and enthusiasm (his own words). In addition, his grammar and lexis and some of his prosodic and paralinguistic features are similar to those of the examiner and there was no question of his responses being unintelligible because of accent or syntax. Nevertheless, of the five assessors (four examiners and the examinations consultant), only one assessed him positively. It is difficult to account for the negative assessments of these four other than through the interactional discomfort and failures to share interpretive conventions. So, it is in the negotiation of shared frames and in the attempts at repair that the difficulties emerge. And the analysis of this particular gatekeeping encounter illustrates this crucial point: the gap between cues and their interpretation is not about understanding what utterances mean but is about being able to agree (implicitly) on the grounds for negotiating meaning, conversational involvement and repair as the interaction ebbs and flows.

How do these small moments of frame mismatch and interactional discomfort lead to the 'clinical labelling' of individuals which determines their possibility of access to scarce resources? (Erickson 1985; Mehan 1983). Judgements about candidates' or clients' suitability and worth depend upon the way in which they are categorised or classified by gatekeepers. At the heart of this classification is the idea of exclusion/inclusion (Herzfeld 1992) as individuals are ascribed a certain identity built up from labels such as 'motivated', 'wouldn't fit in', 'unreasonable' and so on. This identity ascription is the product of immediate and local inferences from the ongoing interaction which are linked to an intermediate level of judgements about performance and attributes which are asserted and recorded by the examiners.

The slippage from local inferences to negative recording arise out of two interrelated features of contextualisation cues and rhythmic co-ordination. The first relates to the fact that these cues and co-ordinating features are not subject to conscious control or awareness. So their function in channelling meaning, signalling coherence, marking speaker orientation, establishing interactional comfort and more generally guiding social relationships and the emotional climate of the encounter go largely unnoticed by participants. And yet their very multi-functionality makes them powerful, but largely hidden, means of making inferences about the quality and adequacy of clients' and candidates' talk in gatekeeping interviews.

As well as being unnoticed, contextualisation cues are suggestive rather than assertive. Levinson (1997: 27) describes them as being 'like a knot in a handkerchief, where the content of the memo is inferentially determined. Thus the "cue" cannot be said to encode or directly invoke the interpretive background, it's simply a nudge to the inferential process.'

The implications of these features of contextualisation cues are dire for any-one on the supplicant side of the gate-keeping process if they do not share the same grounds for making inferences. Firstly, since they are unnoticed, any misunderstandings or uncomfortable moments are not attributed to them but to faults in personality and competence. This may be true in any encounter but, of course, in gatekeeping it can lead to social exclusion since small interactional differences can have large outcomes. Secondly, the 'large dose of inferential reconstruction' (Levinson 1997) required to contextualise appropriately – the suggestiveness but no more of these cues – provides plenty of space for the wrong inferences to be made where participants do not share interpretive traditions. It is the very taken for granted quality of the inferential process which allows gatekeepers to be so assertive in their judgements when paradoxically these are at least in part based on cues which are only suggestive. It is in the slippage from doing the interactional business to reporting on it that the candidate or client's performed social identity is transformed into some more permanent identity as a 'good' or 'poor' GP.

The tensions and complexities built into the examination make it all the more likely that judgements will be based on some general classification of performed social identity despite the exhortation to examiners not to make 'unidimensional global judgements'. The extent to which the candidate is 'one of us' seems to depend less on their rational and knowledgeable display of medical practice and more on the extent to which they can negotiate the grounds for agreeing on the activity or frame. In other words, where candidates did less well it was where they were 'not adequately social – not adequately reciprocal and complementary' (Erickson and Shultz 1982: 192). So, 'co-membership', even more strongly than Erickson and Shultz suggest, depends upon shared communicative conventions. Indeed, the formal procedures of the exam and the fact that it is peer assessment makes the quality of the interaction and the sharing of communicative practices even more significant than in counselling interviews.

6   Critiquing the 'cultural difference' approach

IS and micro-ethnography bring out the intercultural dimension of gatekeeping interviews by highlighting the small and unnoticed ways in which the grounds for mutual negotiation of meaning are not shared. But it would be quite wrong to see such approaches as a simple reading off of general cultural differences in interaction. The picture is much more complex and subtle, as Gumperz argues. Shared inferential practices are not the result of simply belonging to a particular ethnic group or community but are the result of participation in similar 'networks of relationships' which socialise individuals into similar communicative practices:

> It is long-term exposure to similar communicative experience in institutionalised networks of relationships and not language or community membership as such that lies at the root of shared culture and shared inferential practices.
>
> (Gumperz 1997: 15)

So, for example, the candidates for the RCGP examinations share many communicative experiences as part of their training and work as doctors. In one sense, they have a clear professional identity and simply could not function or manage the oral exams at all if they did not share many of the inferential processes about doctoring assumed by the examiners. In other ways, they do not necessarily share 'networks of relationships' if they have been trained overseas and live and work in areas where there are family, friends, patients and colleagues from similar linguistic and ethnic backgrounds.

To this extent, the GP candidates from minority ethnic groups are similar to many other groups who have settled in a new country as adults or who live in what are still relatively homogeneous communities or neighbourhoods. For them, the metapragmatic and discursive conventions of their first or heritage language continue to influence their communicative style. Recent studies of linguistic relativity, however, have shown that the different semiotic modes of communicating in a particular language – grammatical, lexical, prosodic, paralinguistic and non-verbal – do not contrast systematically with another language (Gumperz and Levinson 1996). It has been shown that the relationship between prosody and syntax in conveying, for example, emphasis, speaker orientation, given/new information differs systematically between Hindi and English in some respects but not in others (Gumperz 1982a).

The upshot is that a number of largely automatic aspects of speaker involvement and discourse coherence from the languages of minority groups continue to influence their use of the majority language despite extensive and long-term experience in new communicative networks. This does not mean, for example, that in any global way a Chinese or Hindi or Spanish speaker of English will always display certain styles of communicating influenced by all the features of that language which contrast with English.[4] Small and subtle ways of contextualising contributions and managing conversational involvement may remain long after grammar, lexis and other communicative conventions have changed, as the data above illustrate.

I would argue, therefore, that the allegations against IS and micro-ethnography for reifying cultural differences are misleading. Indeed, these studies tend to support the 'new ethnicities' literature which argues against the idea of ethnic and cultural groups as having fixed and essential characteristics (Hall 1992), and, like this literature, they show that identities are constructed out of communicative practice (Lave and Wenger 1991; Hanks 1996; Rampton 1995 and in press). The gatekeeping studies demonstrate that, in the charged environment of the oral examination or interview, subtle and largely unnoticed differences in contextualisation and co-ordination, which were learnt in previous communicative experiences, become the justification for negative social evaluation.

7 Conclusion

These studies suggest, therefore, that ethnic identity may in some ways be automatically conveyed. There is no overall contrastive style which assigns an ethnic identity to a candidate or client but there may be features of communicative style which remain long after others have changed. The gatekeeping interview will make some of these features particularly salient.

In looking at gatekeeping and sociolinguistic theories of communication reflexively – i.e. seeing how each sheds light on the other – I have argued that micro-interactional processes feed into the process of classification and so social evaluation and exclusion. Differences and discomfort arise from the fine-grained contextualising work of oral assessment, but have great consequences in contributing to the social identity of groups in ethnically stratified societies. The more ambiguous and held in tension is the gatekeeping – and the peer assessment of GPs is a good example of this – the more indirect are the means of negotiating a shared understanding and the more difficult it is to reach a fair decision. The small and subtle differences in those aspects of interaction which are most hidden from conscious awareness are paradoxically the ones that may be most powerful in making judgements about speaker perspective, competence and social relationships. It is these judgements in gatekeeping interviews which can produce the small tragedies of everyday life and, cumulatively, contribute to institutional exclusions and travesties of social justice.

4.1 Transcription

This is based on the GAT system developed at Konstanz and Potsdam Universities (Selting, M, Auer, P, Barden, B, Bergmann, J Couper-Kuhlen, E, Günthner, S, Meier, C, Quasthoff, U, Schoblinski, P and Uhmann, S (1998): Gesprächsanalytisches Transkriptionsystem. *Linguistische Berichte 173: 91–122*).

= overlapping talk
= = latching
(.) micro pause
(-), (- -), (- - -) brief, mid, longer pauses of about 0.25 up to 1 second.
(2), (3) estimated pause of more than one second
:, ::, ::: segmental lengthening according to duration
- truncation
ac**CENT** strong, primary accent
ac**CENT** weaker secondary accent

Pitch at end of turn transition unit
? rising to high
– level

Conspicuous pitch jumps
↑ to higher pitch
↓ to lower pitch

Changed register
≪l≫ low register
≪h≫ high register

Pitch accent movements
\ falling to mid
_ falling to low
/ rising to mid
/\ rising–falling
/\/ rising-falling-rising

117

Changes in loudness and speech rate
≪f≫ loud
≪p≫ soft
≪len≫ slow

Other conventions
< > non-lexical phenomena which occurs between lexical stretches
≪ ≫ non-lexical phenomenon which overlays lexical stretch
( ) unclear words

Notes

1. Other studies of discourse which focus on the assessment and selection interviews include Adelswärd (1988), Auer (in press), Kern (1998), Kern and Birkner (in press), Gumperz, Jupp and Roberts (1979), Roberts (1985) and Sarangi (1994).
2. The data in this chapter was collected as part of a project carried out by Srikant Sarangi and myself for the Royal College of General Practitioners in 1997. The aim of the project was to identify ways in which the oral assessment examination for membership of the college might be unwittingly discriminating against candidates from minority groups who had been trained overseas. I am very grateful to the RCGP for allowing this data to be used.
3. The RCGP oral examination consists of two half-hour interviews during which the candidate is asked six questions by two examiners. Marks are awarded for each question and a total mark is then given. The final mark is the aggregate of the four examiners' marks.
4. Erickson's case study of an Italian American speaker suggests that his interpretation of listening behaviour by the interviewer created uncomfortable moments because one, but perhaps only one, aspect of his communicative style was influenced by the Italian neighbourhood where he grew up, despite the fact that both he and his parents were born in the USA (Erickson 1985).

References

Adelswärd, V. (1988) 'Styles of success. On impression management as collaborative action in job interviews'. Linköping Studies in Arts and Sciences, Linköping University, Sweden.

Auer, P. (1998) 'Introduction: John Gumperz's approach to contextualisation'. In P. Auer and A. di Luzio (eds), 1–39.

Auer, P. (1998) 'Learning how to play the game: An investigation of role-played job interviews in East Germany'. *Text* 18/1, 7–38.

Auer, P. and di Luzio, A. (eds) (1992) *The Contextualisation of Language.* Amsterdam: Benjamins.

Bateson, G. (1956) 'The message "This is play" '. In Schaffner, B. (ed.) *Group Processes.* New York: Josiah Macey Foundation, 145–242.

Bauman, R. and Sherzer, J. (1974) *Explorations in the Ethnography of Speaking.* Cambridge: Cambridge University Press.

Cook-Gumperz, J. and Gumperz, J. (1976) 'Context in children's speech'. In *Papers on Language and Context.* Working Paper no. 46. Language Behaviour Research Laboratory: Berkeley.

Duranti, A. and Goodwin, C. (eds) (1992) *Rethinking Context: Language as an Interactive Phenomenon.* Cambridge: Cambridge University Press.

Eerdmans, S., Previgagno, C. and Thibault, P. (eds) (1997) *Discussing Communication Analysis 1: John Gumperz.* Lausanne: Beta Press.

Erickson, F. (1975) 'Gatekeeping and the melting pot: Interaction in counselling encounters'. *Harvard Educational Review*, 45/1, 44–70.

Erickson, F. (1985) 'Listening and speaking'. Paper presented at Georgetown University Round Table on Linguistics, Washington, DC, 29 June.

Erickson, F. (1986) 'Qualitative methods in research in teaching'. In M.C. Wittrock (ed.) *Handbook of Research on Teaching* (3rd edition). New York: Macmillan, 119–161.

Erickson, F. and Shultz, J. (1982) *The Counsellor as Gatekeeper: Social Interaction in Interviews.* New York: Academic Press.

Garfinkel, H. (1967) *Studies in Ethnomethodology.* New York: Prentice Hall.

Goffman, E. (1956) 'Embarrassment and social organisation'. *American Journal of Sociology*, 62, 264–74.

Goffman, E. (1961) *Encounters: Two Studies in the Sociology of Interaction.* Indianapolis: Bobbs-Merrill.

Goffman, E. (1974) *Frame Analysis: An Essay on the Organisation of Experience.* New York: Harper Row.

Gumperz, J. (1982a) *Discourse Strategies.* Cambridge: Cambridge University Press.

Gumperz, J. (ed.) (1982b) *Language and Social Identity.* Cambridge: Cambridge University Press.

Gumperz, J. (1992a) 'Contextualisation and understanding'. In A. Duranti and C. Goodwin (eds), 229–252.

Gumperz, J. (1992b) 'Contextualisation revisited'. In P. Auer and A. di Luzio (eds), 39–54.

Gumperz, J. (1996) 'The linguistic and cultural relativity of conversational inference'. In G. Gumperz and S. Levinson (eds), 374–406.

Gumperz, J. (1997) 'A discussion with John J. Gumperz'. In Eerdmans et al. (eds), 6–23.

Gumperz, J. (1999) 'On interactional sociolinguistic method'. In S. Sarangi and C. Roberts (eds), 453–472.

Gumperz, J. and Hymes, D. (eds) (1972) *Directions in Sociolinguistics: The Ethnography of Communication.* New York: Holt, Rinehart & Winston.

Gumperz, J. and Levinson, S. (eds) (1996) *Rethinking Linguistic Relativity.* Cambridge: Cambridge University Press.

Gumperz, J., Jupp, T. and Roberts, C. (1979) *Crosstalk.* National Centre for Industrial Language Training, Southall.

Hall, S. (1992) 'The question of cultural identity'. In S. Hall, D. Held and T. McGrew (eds) *Modernity and its Futures.* Cambridge: Polity Press, 274–316.

Hanks, W. (1996) *Language and Communicative Practices.* Boulder Colorado: Westview Press.

Herzfeld, M. (1992) *The Social Production of Indifference: Exploring the Symbolic Roots of Western Bureaucracy.* New York: Berg.

Hymes, D. (1964) *Language in Culture and Society.* New York: Harper Row.

Kern, F. (1998) 'Symptom/Symbol/Handicap. Language and cultural difference in Germany'. Paper presented at the Winter Workshop, London, January, 1998.

Kern, F. and Bickner, B. (in press) 'Frictional encounters. German-German communication in job interviews'. To appear in *Monash Linguistic Papers*.

Lave, J. and Wenger, E. (1991) *Situated Learning: Legitimate Peripheral Participation*. Cambridge: Cambridge University Press.

Levinson, S. (1997) 'Contextualising contextualisation cues'. In Eerdmans et al. (eds), 24–30.

Mehan, H. (1983) 'The role of language and the language of role in institutional decision making'. *Language in Society* 12, 187–211.

Mehan, H. (1984) 'Institutional decision making'. In B. Rogoff and J. Lave (eds) *Everyday Cognition: Its Development in Social Context*. Cambridge, MA: Harvard University Press, 41–66.

Rampton, B. (1995) *Crossing: Language and Ethnicity Among Adolescents*. London: Longman.

Rampton, B. (in press) 'Speech community'. To appear in the *Handbook of Pragmatics*.

Roberts, C. (1985) *The Interview Game*. Broadcast by BBC between 5 and 19 January 1986.

Roberts, C. and Sarangi, S. (1999) 'Hybridity in gatekeeping discourse: Issues of practical relevance for the researcher'. In Sarangi and Roberts (eds), 473–504.

Roberts, C. and Sayers, P. (1987) 'Keeping the gate: How judgements are made in interethnic interviews'. In K. Knapp, W. Enninger and A. Knapp-Potthof (eds) *Analysing Intercultural Communication*. Berlin: Mouton de Gruyter, 111–135.

Roberts, C., Garnett, C., Kapoor, S. and Sarangi, S. (1992) *Quality in Teaching and Learning: Four Multi-cultural Classrooms in Further Education*. Sheffield: Department of Employment.

Sarangi, S. (1994) 'Accounting for mismatches in intercultural selection interviews. *Multilingua* 13–1/2, 163–194. *Cross-cultural Communication in the Professions*. Special issue edited by A. Pauwels.

Sarangi, S. and Roberts, C. (eds) (1999) *Talk, Work and Institutional Order: Discourse in Medical, Mediation and Management Settings*. Berlin: Mouton de Gruyter.

Selting, M., Auer, P., Barden, B., Bergmann, J., Couper-Kuhlen, E., Günthner, S., Meier, C., Quasthoff, U., Schoblinski, P. and Uhmann, S. (1998) 'Gesprächsanalytisches Transkriptionsystem'. *Linguistische Berichte* 173, 91–122.

Silverstein, M. (1992) 'The indeterminacy of contextualisation: When is enough enough?' In P. Auer and A. di Luzio (eds), 55–76.

Wakeford, R., Southgate, L. and Wass, V. (1995) 'Improving oral examinations: Selecting, training and monitoring examiners for the MRCGP'. *British Medical Journal* 311, 931–935.

Chapter 7

Becoming a group: face and sociability in moderated discussions

Greg Myers

1 Introduction

Why do people talk to one another in groups? Some pragmatic models assume that the social world consists of individuals who interact to maximise gain and minimise losses of some sort, making careful calculations of which strategy to employ. But this model of fraught encounters between vulnerable, isolated individuals leaves out a crucial fact about language: it's fun to talk, to be with other people, to socialise just for the sake of sociability. The broader purpose of this chapter is to explore the ways in which the structures of a conversation can show the pleasure that people take in talking in a group, even when they have to do it.

In exploring these structures, I will draw on work by two social theorists that could help redress the individualist bias of so much discourse analysis. The German sociologist Georg Simmel developed the concept of 'sociability' in a classic paper (first published in 1917, translated in 1950). He used the concept as part of a larger project of defining the proper terrain of sociology, as apart from political economy and philosophy; his speculations on the basic components of social life led to fascinating essays on such issues as the life of a couple, the effects of size of groups, and the figure of the stranger. For Simmel, sociability is a form of social interaction pursued for its own sake, apart from anything participants have to gain from it. It is 'the play-form of sociation', as card-playing would be a play-form of business, and games a play-form of conflict. The focus on language play has been taken up by anthropologists and linguists (e.g. Labov 1972; Goodwin 1985; Rampton 1995; Crystal 1998), but it is a focus that tends to be overlooked in discourse analysis (see Cook forthcoming).

I would also like to look again at the approach to politeness developed in Erving Goffman's classic essay 'On face-work' (first published 1955, republished in Goffman 1967). Goffman's essay is also part of a larger project, which in his 'Preface' (1967) he puts in its most reductive form: 'What minimal model of the actor is needed if we are to wind him up, stick him in amongst his fellows, and have an orderly traffic of behavior emerge?'

(1967: 3). In developing this model, he focused on how people could maintain order in an interaction, how they defined what sort of interaction was going on and what roles were taken by each participant (see also Goffman 1963). For my purposes, we need to disentangle this exploratory outline from its later elaborations in linguistic politeness theory, and recover Goffman's original emphasis on the self as a 'line' played in an ongoing interaction.

One strength of Goffman's reductive approach is that it provides a heuristic for more detailed linguistic work – for instance, that in which Penelope Brown and Stephen Levinson (1978/1987) compare different realisations of Face Threatening Acts in three different languages, and classify a wide range of linguistic features employed to mitigate them. The Brown and Levinson classification has been the basis of much of the linguistic work on politeness since then.[1] But like any useful model, it has its blind spots (see also Sarangi and Slembrouck 1997; Coupland et al. 1988). One is that analysts tend to reify linguistic devices listed by Brown and Levinson (e.g. modals, questions, impersonal construction, irony, forms of address) apart from their immediate situation in a sequence of turns. We will see in my analysis of two groups that we need to look at more extended sequences of interaction (as Goffman himself suggested in discussing the preservation of face in a four-part *interchange* over several turns, rather than one). Another blind spot is that analysts tend to analyse these features apart from participants' interpretations. Of course this is an issue in all discourse analysis, but it is particularly crucial in understanding how hearers might respond to devices that are admittedly conventionalised. So we need to look at speakers' responses, as indicating how they take each turn. A third blind spot is the one with which I began, the lack of a motivation for interaction. The emphasis on form rather than aim is pointed out by Goffman himself (1967: 12):

> Ordinarily, maintenance of face is a condition of interaction, not its objective . . . . To study face-saving is to study the traffic rules of social interaction; one learns about the code the person adheres to in his movement across the paths and designs of others, but not where he is going, or why he wants to get there.

To find an alternative to the strategic self, I would like to go back to the essay 'on face-work' and emphasise aspects that have not been picked up by later work on politeness. Goffman (1967: 31) notes an ambivalence in his definition:

> So far I have implicitly been using a double definition of self: the self as an image pieced together from the expressive implications of the flow of events in an undertaking; and the self as a kind of player in a ritual game who copes honorably or dishonorably, diplomatically or undiplomatically, with judgemental contingencies of the situation.

The first of these definitions of self, as an image mutually constructed over the course of a specific interaction, Goffman associates with the term *line*: 'a pattern of verbal and nonverbal acts by which [a person] expresses his view of the situation and through this his evaluation of the participants, particularly himself. Regardless of whether a person intends to take a line, he will find that he has done so in effect' (1967: 5). This work of interactive, ongoing, unintentional construction gets lost in later linguistic studies. Brown and Levinson and later analysts have focused on the second of these definitions, on self as strategist, and on *face*: 'the positive social value a person effectively claims for himself by the line others assume he has taken during a particular contact' (1967: 5). Attention only to face narrows the focus from the whole, ongoing interaction, to the features of a particular turn, as part of a process of the speaker and hearer processing meanings. In going back to the idea of a *line*, I am trying to link Goffman's framework to the approach of Conversation Analysis, which starts with sequential analysis of instances of talk, rather than with a 'minimal model of the actor'.[2]

Simmel's aim in his essay on 'sociability' parallels Goffman's in his essay on 'face-work', in that Simmel too was interested in the general and convergent forms of social interaction, rather than the specific and various content: what it means to associate with other people, apart from the pursuit of money or status or sex or power or self-esteem. But where Goffman brackets off the practical, personal objectives of interaction as being outside of his current study, Simmel proposes that there is a kind of interaction that has no such objectives – interaction for its own sake. 'This does not imply that the content of sociable conversation is indifferent. On the contrary, it must be interesting, fascinating, even important. But it may not become the purpose of the conversation, which must never be after an objective result . . .' (1950: 52). I would argue that a category of sociability is crucial to an understanding of why people talk. Simmel's emphasis on sociability for its own sake was taken up by Deborah Schiffrin (1984); she wanted to explain how the arguments between the people she was interviewing for her sociolinguistic project – couples or close friends – might indicate solidarity rather than conflict. Apart from Schiffrin's work, the idea of sociability has not been widely used in linguistics, perhaps because it requires us to go beyond the strategic self that is assumed in most linguistic approaches.

Simmel (1950: 51) gives a lively description of how groups emerge and shift, again distinguishing the contents of most conversations from the play of talk for its own sake:

> In a purely sociable conversation, the topic is merely an indispensable medium through which the lively interchange of speech itself unfolds its attractions. All the forms in which this exchange is realized – quarrel, appeal to norms recognized by both parties, pacification by compromise or by discovery of common convictions, grateful acceptance of the new, and covering up of everything on which no understanding can be hoped for – all these forms usually are in the service of the countless contents and purposes of human life. But here, they derive their significance from themselves, from the fascinating play of relations which they create among participants, joining and loosening, winning and succumbing, giving and taking.

Following Simmel, I will look at the play of relations among participants as a group forms itself, rather than at their strategies and purposes as individuals. Despite his insightful list of what one might find in such discussions, he does not develop his point in analytical detail. I will link his basic observation to conversational features: topic shifting, agreement, collaborative construction of utterances, echoing, and generic narratives.

2 Focus groups

I will analyse two passages from transcripts of group discussions, and will argue that a consequence of attention to Simmel and Goffman is greater attention to the group as an emerging entity, and to the development of talk through stages as a group is defined. The dynamics of group discussions are of interest in a wide range of settings: in university seminars, counselling groups (Sacks 1992), community organisations (Labov 1972), consciousness-raising groups (Coates 1996), business meetings (Boden 1994), or management training. Much of the linguistic interest in group discussions has focused on power differentials and differences in style that result in different access to the group; thus much of the important work has been done around language and gender (e.g. Tannen 1993; Coates 1996). While granting these issues of differences within a group, it can also be useful to look at how a group that has no history or institutional necessity becomes a group.

My examples are drawn from focus groups, which may seem an odd choice of material with which to explore sociability. A focus group is a discussion held to gather data about attitudes (for instance, in social science, marketing or public opinion research), usually with six to ten participants, and a moderator following a predetermined topic guide.[3] So the participants are generally strangers, recruited from social categories that might be relevant to the question under study. The answer to my question of why they talk seems simple – we pay them a fee and give them drinks. This, however, does not answer the questions of why they talk *to each other*; a focus group, like a bad university seminar, can easily break down into a series of dyadic conversations between the leader and the participants. Focus groups are not groups at the beginning; the participants do not share, or recognise each other as sharing, common experiences or goals or identities. In most cases they did not know each other before the researchers brought them together, and they have to find out for themselves whether they have anything in common that they can recognise. The moderator usually intervenes if their discussions wander from the topic guide, so they don't control topics. It is all the more surprising therefore that, in nearly every case, they have a breakthrough into the kind of sociable discussion for its own sake that Simmel describes.

I chose my data from focus groups in northwest England for a study of 'Global Citizenship and the Environment'.[4] The opening half hour or so of each of these groups was devoted to local communities and everyday activities of the participants, and in these sections most of the interaction consists of questions from the moderator and responses from individual participants. At some point in the discussion, however, and at the same point in the topic guide for almost every group, participants start to address each other ('Do you never think, Margaret, when you see that . . .'), chime in agreement ('More like Mediterranean style, isn't it'), challenge ('but surely the bottom line must be . . .'), formulate the comments of others, comment on the discussion, and in general treat each other as co-present participants in ongoing interaction, rather than as witnesses to individual responses. I chose the first passage involving ten or more turns without the substantial intervention of the moderator, with at least four of the eight participants speaking.[5] I will consider here two of these passages from focus group transcripts, one that shows especially the development of topics as a collaborative activity, and the other that illustrates an emergence of conversational patterns (collaborating, echoing, generic narratives) that define the group as a group.

3   Topics and agreement

It may seem obvious that a given group of people is more likely to talk about some topics than others, but this observation is not as simple as it seems; for instance, the proverbial standby of British conversation, small talk about the weather, is essential for everyday phatic exchanges, but unlikely to be a topic for extended and intense participation (the only way in which the weather is too dry). Harvey Sacks discussed conversation topics in analysing the structural significance of a turn in which members of a counselling group for joyriders jointly tell a newcomer joining the group,

Joe:	We were in an automobile discussion
Henry:	discussing the psychological motives for
Mel:	drag racing in the streets. (Sacks 1992: I, 175 and II, 72)

Sacks makes several points. First, this way of putting it presents the topic as having a name recognisable to this group: it is 'an automobile discussion'. Second, the topic defines the group, telling the newcomer what kind of group it is and whether he will or will not fit in. Sacks makes this point by noting that the social worker who leads the group could not say 'we were in an automobile discussion' or 'they were in an automobile discussion' with the same import; he would be calling them back to the specified topic of the group, rather than using it to define the group as the boys do (1992: II, 82). Third, an 'automobile discussion' is, for these boys, an 'infinite topic', not just a topic that a given group likes to talk about, but one that has no necessary resolution, no point at which all that can be said has been said. Sacks compares their talk about cars to the talk of the Nuer about cattle, in Evans-Pritchard's account; other groups might find infinite topics in their own ailments, their children's schools, football league tables, or the ratings of UK Linguistics departments in the Research Assessment Exercise.

An example shows how a topic can take different courses as participants develop different lines. At this point, about forty minutes into a two-hour discussion, we have just shown a clip of four television commercials (for Norwich Union insurance, Coke, the International Red Cross Land-mines Appeal, and recruitment for the Special Constabulary) and asked about similarities or differences between the appeals they make. The extended exchange from the Small Business Owners group (middle-aged men in a medium-sized city) begins with the moderator formulating an earlier exchange about the difficulty of telling what each ad was advertising, and continues with a discussion of whether the ads are linked to branding and whether branding affects their own purchasing decisions.

3.1 Small Business Owners 1: 30[6]

I

(1)	Mod	so the connection the connection between the Volkswagen one you're talking about and the Coke one . is that you watch large sections of the ad . without knowing what /this could possibly be for
(2)	P1	/you watch it to see the ending don't you
(3)	M1	if you've not seen it before
(4)	Mod	yeah yeah so it intrigues you/
(5)	P2	/that's right/
(6)	Mod	/in that way . and it doesn't . in this case the imagery at the end doesn't have to connect with the product
(7)	A1	it could have been anything in that fridge couldn't it . you'd still probably you'd have watched that =
(8)	P1	= you'd have watched it to see what what was coming up
(9)	Mod	mmm
(10)	P1	but surely again I mean I'm not harping back on the Coke one . when you see the first few seconds of it . you think Coke straight away [laughs]
(11)	Mod	mmm
(12)	P1	you know but if you see it /
(13)	A1	/ that's because you've seen it before
(14)	P2	is that because you've seen/ it before . yeah
(15)	P1	/yeah but if you see a picture you've seen the the man on the bridge before but would you see Constabulary /
(16)	A1	/ no . no no
(17)	P1	as soon as you see the man on the bridge?
(18)	A1	no I have to be frank

II

(19)	J1	but surely the bottom line must be . when you consider how much it's costing them to put that image on your television . the bottom line must be selling Volkswagen cars . or selling Coke . or whatever

(20)	P1	yeah but it's got
(21)	J1	is it is it . as far as we're concerned is it working . it's not to me cause I don't buy a Volkswagen and / I don't drink Coke.
(22)	A1	/ it might . it might not work now but it may work . later if that's / in your head.
(23)	P1	/ no but how many people will it <u>will</u> it relate to
(24)	J1	yeah well I don't know yeah
(25)	P1	you know
(26)	J1	I mean . do you <u>buy</u> things you see advertised on television . do <u>you</u> buy things /yourself
(27)	P1	/<u>I</u> don't personally / no [I only buy the one]
(28)	J1	/ well I don't . I don't . cause I think if they can if they can <u>ad</u>vertise on television they must be making a <u>hell</u> of a lot of money out of you
(29)		[laughter]
(30)	J1	or they wouldn't want to <u>know</u> it.

III

(31)	A1	but what happens if you've got a choice . there's two products and one's (2.0) but you've seen one on the telly so you you know that they are both <u>roughly</u> the same . and I tend to th– well I go for the one that I don't know/ [perhaps I'm being unconsciously]
(32)	J2	/ it goes back <u>really</u> to what. [P1]'s been saying
(33)	A1	yeah
(34)	J2	if you . you don't drink Coke but if there's two there you'd go for / [ ]
(35)	P1	/ if you went for something I mean . I drink very little I've got a [cider shandy . which you've never heard of] but . do you drink at all?
(36)	A1	yeah
(37)	P1	what would you go for, would you go and . if <u>I</u> went I might go and ask for a pint of <u>bit</u>ter cause I wouldn't know one bitter from another
(38)	A1	well
(39)	P1	you'd go in and ask for a spe<u>cif</u>ic bitter
(40)	A1	yeah yeah I do tend to
(41)	P1	you know what I mean . I would be none the wiser . now
(42)	A1	so that's helping you to make your mind up the adverts
(43)	P1	yeah, if they kept putting say Tetley Tetley Tetley all the time
(44)	A1	which they <u>did</u> didn't they
(45)	P1	yeah if I went there now I might say have you got a pint of <u>Tet</u>ley's please
(46)	A1	yeah
(47)	P1	not that I know that it is any different from any other
(48)	A1	yeah
(49)	P1	like Coke I don't know if that's any different from any other . but if I am picking up a bottle, that's what I'll pick up
(50)	A1	yeah yeah
(51)	Mod	mm . can I go back to one particular of these ads ...

What counts as the current topic here is constantly negotiated (Myers 1998; Malone 1997), but the topic is not wandering in any uncontrolled way. The larger interaction can be divided into three episodes (marked by roman numerals), each of which shows different devices for marking the current topic, defining the currently available lines, and acknowledging the group as a group. We might see them, schematically, as three *buts*. We can see, over the course of these three episodes, how the moderator withdraws, the interaction between participants shifts, and the topic develops.

In episode I, the discussion moves from interactions between the moderator and individual participants to interactions between participants. The moderator begins by formulating what was said earlier (turn 1), and he is overlapped by three participants (2, 3, 5), all confirming the formulation. A1 presents a formulation of this formulation ('it could have been anything in that fridge couldn't it'), with the tag question offering the possibility of general agreement (7). P1 at first seems to be agreeing (as is characteristic of second assessments), latching onto, echoing and apparently addressing A1 (8). A closer look, though, shows that it is the moderator who is giving continuers here, so P1 must be suggesting, perhaps by gaze or body orientation, that the remarks are still addressed to him. Even if the moderator is still participating as an active listener, the group is already emerging, in the way P2 refers to previous talk. Where A1 and P2 break in, P2's question echoes A1's statement (13–14). P1 phrases his question in response (15) as addressed to A1, not to a generalised *you*, and here it is A1, not the moderator, who offers the audible continuers (16). The episode ends with A1's concession (18), and we know that there is some sense of resolution here for the participants, because J1 can come in.

Episode II begins with another *but*, turning the topic from recognition of these ads to advertising effects in general. J1 refers to 'the bottom line' as a possible resolution of the difference between P1 and A1, and refers back to the moderator's statement of the topic ('selling Volkswagen cars or selling Coke or whatever') (19). He also refers to the group as an entity with its own particular experience, 'as far as we're concerned' (21). A1 and P1 begin objections (22, 23), but J1 turns the question back to them, with his shift of emphasis from a generic *you* to the specific *you* of the group members: 'do *you* buy things yourself' (26). The episode ends with J1 restating what he'd said at the beginning, in stronger terms, to laughter this time (30). It's the same topic, but now they are seeing it in different terms, in terms of its relation to their purchasing in particular. Again the resolution provides the basis for someone else shifting the topic.

Episode III begins with A1 raising another *but*, moving on from J1's proposed resolution in terms of their shared experience (31). J2 refers to what P1 had said earlier; the group has developed a memory for the positions of its participants. P1 takes this up by asking A1 a question, as in (15), but here a question about his own practices (whether he drinks) not his views (25). P1 then develops a series of contrasts; as J1 stressed the shared experience of the group (28), P1 stresses the different kinds of experience between him and A1:

> what would you go for / if I went I might go (37)
> you'd ask for a specific bitter / I'd be none the wiser (39–41)

Here the closure comes when A1 picks up P1's hypothetical example (44), and P1 relates this example (bitter) back to his previous example (Coke). Again the episode ends only when participants signal some limited agreement, and it is at this point that the moderator comes back in (see Myers 1998).

The topic shifts over the three episodes as the participants work out ways of disagreeing, agreeing again, and opening up new possibilities of disagreement, in a rhythm of hypothetical (if) and adversative (but) statements. They develop the topic independently of the moderator, who has to seize back control abruptly. The patterns seen here – questions, overlapping, echoing, and references to previous talk – are seen in the passages of wider discussion in almost all these groups. Participants also refer implicitly to the group, and the assumed similarities and differences between its members.

This acute awareness of what it is to be grouped, along with their own shared identity as 'small business owners', may affect the various attitudes of the participants: P1's delight in recognition of a successful sales job (10) shared with other people whose job is selling; A1's opposition to the mass marketing of products (compared to their small local shops) (7); and J1's doubts based on his (and their) own everyday experiences as a consumer (19, 28), as set against the assumptions of big corporations. They are not each trying to get their own way; they are taking pleasure in the interplay. Each of these attitudes is not just expressed, but enacted in a line, 'a pattern of verbal and nonverbal acts by which [a person] expresses his view of the situation and through this his evaluation of the participants, particularly himself'. The situation is to be one in which one contributes if one possibly can, builds on contributions of others, disagrees if possible, concedes when necessary, and always closes with a kind of agreement. The preferred selves enacted here are two-sided: sceptical and individual, but willing to offer themselves as examples of the typical.

4   Sociable argument

One group, which we called the 'New Europeans', consisted of men and women in their twenties who were in Britain for university, training, or jobs. Unlike the Small Business Owners, this group of people from Germany, Italy, Spain, and Greece would not usually consider themselves as a group sharing characteristics; only in the eyes of native xenophobes are 'foreigners' all one category. But they could discover which aspects of their experience they share. They also differ from other groups in their complex relation to the moderator. The Small Business Owners could include the moderator in their generalisations about responses to advertising, though they might exclude him when speaking of their business experiences. When the New Europeans talk to each other about the UK, the moderator and the project are overhearers from the UK (although in this case the moderator stressed that he was second-generation Polish). These two factors, their diversity and their difference, mean that they became a group in rather different ways from the Small Business Owners, both testing out each other for shared experiences, and orienting to an overhearing audience.

The response that sets them off on their first extended discussion is when one participant, a German who works in the local university student union, talks about moving to Spain.

4.1 New Europeans 1: 12

(1) Mod   so where would you go on to . within England . or elsewhere in Europe?

(2) S   no . I am going to Spain after [right] when I've finished [right] in May I'm going to move to Spain [right] to start working in Spain [Mod (laughs) yeah] (1.0) because I just . you know, for me Spain has got something, I don't know, I love the mentality [yeah:] the way of life . which is

(3) N   more like a Mediterranean / style isn't it

(4) S   / yeah   it's just great yeah . I love it.

(5) T   well yes. I think that's that's the point . here in England is more . routine . you know

(6) S   yes yes

(7) T   more routine like . home to work and then work to home

(8) S   like a

(9) T   like this . you know . and then you are restricted also to . to a time . you know . like [mm mm] you cannot have a drink after 11 . or 10 o'clock there's no one in the street [mm] . whereas in . big cities, maybe London or . Spain and all that . it's like 2 or 3 o'clock in the morning [mm] and you see families with kids [mm mm] you know [mm] and nobody cause any trouble [mm] unless you ask for it [Mod (laughs)] and everybody's happy and goes around [yes yeah] and that's it

(10) Mod   yeah it's more

(11) T   so it's more. you can socialise more no . and you don't feel as . you know as [mm] nothing to do or nowhere . nowhere to go no? [mm] so where shall where do I go . where could I go no? [mm] so well   . it's either a club [mm] or nothing else [mm] because there's no / nowhere else to choose

(12) N   / yeah, but that's not all that's not everywhere in England I mean

(13) ?   yeah

(14) N   you can go to London and it's like [in Spain for instance] you can stay out until like 3 or 4 o'clock in the morning so don't . we shouldn't criticise the whole thing because of Preston . I mean fair enough Preston

(15)	?	is just <u>P</u>reston but if you go to other places you can still have <u>life</u> there . I mean . I've been here so many years and . still don't like that idea that when you get into the mood of having fun and enjoying yourself ( )

(16)   N   you just have to go home but if you go to London that's not the sa:me [yea:h] I mean we shouldn't <u>criti</u>cise it =

(17)   T   = but you can go to London and it'll be the same. either you go clubbing . or where else you go? (1.0)

(18)   N   well yeah . / I mean I don't know

(19)   T   / And if I don't like clubbing . where should I go?

(20)   S   yeah that's a common–

(21)   N   yeah but London has become so international . I mean there are so many different men- ./ in quotation marks men<u>tali</u>ties shall we say

(22)   T   / yeah   yeah but at the end of the day . at the end of the day . the <u>rules</u> that are here for dri:nks and ( ) licenses and all that .they're in London / they're the same

(23)   N   / yea but it's not as strict everywhere .   in in the <u>North</u> right . is really strict laws . fair enough and I agree with that because its just differ- ent pe- . if you think about it on the map there's just . two different . categories of people . I mean things are different aren't they . I mean the population of <u>Pre</u>ston can't be compared to the population in <u>Lon</u>don . so its bound to be like . different laws and different / kind of

(24)   T   /well they're but they're

(25)   C   yeah but they are trying to fight the alco<u>hol</u>ism as well which is quite a [mm] big problems over here . and they give you so many hours to drink . so what do you do =

(26)   N   = well yeah but =

(27)   C   = you go there and you stuff your face with as many pints as you *like* [laughter] and if you drink three pints. in three hours then . I don't think they give you the big harms . but if you go into the pub and you go . like that with three pints one the other one [yeah] after the <u>third</u> one . pfft . you go

(28)   N   but that can happen anywhere

(29)   Mod um

The moderator is central at the beginning of this passage, where his continuers are still audible, and he begins to cut in again at the end. In between, he seems to be absent. But the discussion is concerned with attitudes towards the English, and the participants show their awareness of English listeners. The topic involves a complex interplay of two kinds of contrast: Preston vs London (14, 23) (showing that England is not all the same) and English 'mentality' (2) vs 'Mediterranean style' (3) (implying that England is all the same). T appeals (9, 11) to an experience of English life, an awareness of alternatives, that they share as foreigners (even including S, the non-Mediterranean one among them). Thus to reject his line is to reject an identification with the group. N's argument for the difference between Preston and London implies that they should, as non-English people living in England, present favourable aspects in a public discussion: 'I mean we shouldn't criticise it' (16). Thus to reject her line is to reject a view of what is allowable in interaction. As with the Small Business Owners, the line taken is not just a matter of opinion, but of orientation to the interaction, the group, and one's self presentation.

In this group, all participants maintain their line, without any attempt at resolution of contradictions, through a remarkably long string of dispreferred second assessments (Pomerantz 1984). That is, speakers normally express agreement with expressions of opinion in the previous turn, or preface their disagreement with a concession, weakening, or hesitation:

T   . . . either you go clubbing . or where else you go? (1.0)
N   well yeah . I mean I don't know (turns 20–21)

In this group, most often, a new speaker begins with some form of *yeah but*, briefly conceding agreement before going on to present some contrary assessment (12, 17, 21, 22, 24, 25). N and T largely repeat themselves, until C tries to move the topic on (in turn 25) from the limited hours and places for social life to alcoholism as a problem. The exchange, when read as a transcript, has a ping-pong effect. But the participants do not seem to perceive this exchange as confrontational; they don't back off and seek consensus, or joke, or fall silent, or change the subject, as groups do when someone feels it has gone too far. A sense of confrontation is avoided because the participants relate their contributions to the group using collaborative construction, echoes, formulations, and hypothetical stories.

One indication of the sense participants have of the group is the way N can complete S's sentence:

S   I love the mentality [yeah:] the way of life . which is
N   more like a Mediter<u>ra</u>nean / style isn't it
S   / yeah it's just great (turns 2–4)

This kind of *collaborative construction* is a phenomenon Sacks (1992) discussed, in analysing the example given earlier in this paper (see also Lerner 1991; Coates 1996). Here it marks a strong kind of agreement that can come even before the completion of the turn, and S acknowledges it as supportive instead of treating it as an interruption (4). But as the passage develops into disagreement, the links between turns become more complex. Many turns *sum up*, *echo* or *formulate* the previous one. Almost every speaker uses a pronoun to stand for the previous speaker's statement, guaranteeing the relevance of their contribution ('that's the point' (5), 'that's not all' (12), and so on). Or they repeat phrases from the previous turn: 'that's not the sa:me' 16) / 'it'll be the same' (17). So a clear pattern emerges that, when disagreeing or changing topic, speakers first orient to the immediately previous turn.

Participants typically justify their claims with *generic narratives* involving a generalised second person *you*, narratives that gain their force from the recognition by other participants that this is, indeed, what typically happens:

you cannot have a drink after 11 or 10 o'clock there's no one in the street (9)

you can go to London and . . . you can stay out until like 3 or 4 o'clock in the morning (14)

Each of these narratives is offered as what happens repeatedly and generally, to be picked up and affirmed by others in the group (on the use of reported speech in such narratives, see Myers 1999b). These appeals work (they are never questioned) not because they are powerful evidence, but because they rely on the sense that the group shares something – in this case, their status as observers of the English.

All these features – collaborative construction, echoes, generic narratives – suggest that the participants are relating their turn to the group, acknowledging previous turns and predicting possible responses. They develop their different lines in relation to each other; for instance T, who had first contrasted Preston with 'big cities . maybe London or . Spain' moves into maintaining that London too is restricted. What might seem (on the transcript page) to be tension in the ping-pong argument comes across for participants as an experience of sociability with a group of people with whom they might previously have found little in common. The running conversation is so strong that (after this excerpt) the moderator finds it difficult to regain control and move on to the next issue on the topic guide.

5 Conclusion

At the end of the first session of each of these groups, participants are asked to discuss the meanings of some key words they used earlier in the session. For the New Europeans, the word 'community' evokes comments about their home communities and their host community in Preston, and also a broader sense 'So I think that all the world is now a community'. But one participant, unprompted, says 'You know, we called ourselves a community'. The participants start as just a group of people from various countries brought together for research, but take on some of the collective identity we might associate with much more established and deeply felt groups, where members share history, aims, or daily experiences. In looking at how groups develop, we have come back to the issue of *identity* that has been central in discourse analysis in recent years:

> Identity thus not only resists easy definition but is itself a crucial site, and one which houses a multitude of critical moments whose characteristics are that it is just in such moments that the definitions are being proposed, struggled with and over, resisted and collaboratively negotiated. (Candlin 1997)

But here we see that the identity is not defined against the group, or in terms of some pre-existing social group, but arises as part of its temporary social community.

Facilitators of focus groups, like other people who conduct discussions professionally, are often surprised by just how strong the sense of group identity can be, on such a flimsy basis. I would argue that the key is in the way these people have talked, in a kind of safe space in which the usual forms of behaviour to strangers are temporarily suspended. In this safe space, they each develop lines, as the person who won't be manipulated, or who won't criticise a host country, or who sees through the beer ads, and others work around these lines, developing them. Simmel (1950: 54) suggests that this sort of sociability is a kind of ideal:

> The ways in which groups form and split up and in which conversations, called forth by mere impulse and occasion, begin, deepen, loosen, and terminate at a social gathering, give a miniature picture of the societal ideal which might be called the freedom to be tied down.

Goffman's view of lines (entered into and then inescapable) and face (personal investments always threatened) suggest a tragic, or at least very uncomfortable, view of conversation. For Simmel, the 'freedom to be tied down' is the one social engagement entered into freely and fully, if only temporarily.

It is interesting that many of these discussions take off, as in the Small Business Owners example, just where they discuss ads. There are several possible reasons why this may have offered an opening that was lacking in earlier sections on the participants' communities and regular activities. All the participants had immediate, shared, and equal experience of the commercials (the kind of common reference one would have in the ideal literature seminar, in which all the students had actually read the set text the night before). But it may also be because ads in general, and these ads in particular, always raise questions about just what group one is in. Each ad carries an implicit target audience (Myers 1999a), and one cringes as one is addressed as a father, or as a teenage girl, but one feels the interpellation. The participants are very careful how they identify with or disassociate themselves from these implied identities. And they are especially careful because the same identity is being offered to the rest of the group present – a group already typed in some way (Corporate Professionals, New Europeans, Active Retired) by the focus group research itself. They engage with this actually present group in the course of disengaging themselves from the target audience.

Attention to Goffman's *lines* leads us to focus on selves as entities emerging over the course of interaction. Attention to Simmel's *sociability* leads us to focus on the element of play, even in fairly constrained talk among strangers, and a pleasure that comes just from being in a group, for its own sake and apart from individual aims and strategies. This has practical implications for discourse analysis; we need to look at longer interchanges, rather than individual turns, to look at utterances in context, rather than counts of linguistic features, and to look at participants' responses, rather than our own. It also has wider implications for the way we think about social structure, as suggested in a quotation from Simmel (1950: 50) that could also serve as a guide to Goffman:

> The more profound, double sense of 'social game' is that not only the game is played in society (as its external medium) but that, with its help, people actually 'play' 'society'.

From this perspective, talk in focus groups is not just an artificial version of talk in the real world, but a chance to explore how society emerges.

Notes

1. Besides Brown and Levinson (1978/1987), classic work includes Brown and Gilman (1960), Leech (1983), and Thomas (1995). My own work applies this model to writing, not talk; see for instance Myers (1989).
2. For a brief critique of Goffman from a conversation analytic perspective, see Hutchby and Wooffitt (1998: 27–9). For a more extended and sympathetic treatment of Goffman and conversation analysis, see Malone (1997).
3. On focus groups, see the handbook Morgan and Krueger (1998), the collection of critical studies in Barbour and Kitzinger (1999), and for linguistic studies Myers (1998, 1999b, forthcoming), Myers and Macnaghten (1999), and Puchta and Potter (1999).
4. This research was made possible by a grant from the UK Economic and Social Research Council, R000236768, 'Global Citizenship and the Environment'. My thanks to my colleagues on this project, Bronislaw Szerszynski, Mark Toogood, and John Urry.
5. This application of these criteria for the group taking off is complicated by transcription conventions. Discussions were originally transcribed with no indication of back-channel continuers from the moderator, so he sometimes seems to be out of the discussion for long periods. As we will see, when they were retranscribed with more of the detail of interaction, the moderator's continued participation in these interactions was more apparent.
6. Transcription conventions: / indicates beginning of overlap with line above or below; = links two turns with no pause between them; . short pause; (2) pauses over one second; underline – stressed syllable; (uncertain transcription); [laughter] transcription of non-verbal features. Back-channel utterances of the moderator are included within turns in brackets, [yeah].

References

Barbour, R. and Kitzinger, J. (eds) (1999) *Developing Focus Group Research: Politics, Theory, and Practice*. London: Sage.

Boden, D. (1994) *The Business of Talk: Organizations in Action*. Cambridge: Polity.

Brown, P. and Levinson, S. (1978/1987) *Politeness* (revised edition). Cambridge: Cambridge University Press.

Brown, R. and Gilman, A. (1960) 'The pronouns of power and solidarity'. In T. Sebeok, (ed.) *Style in Language*. New York: Wiley, 253–276.

Candlin, C. (1997) 'Preface'. In B.-L. Gunnarsson, P. Linell and B. Nordberg (eds) *The Construction of Professional Discourse*. London: Longman, viii–xiv.

Coates, J. (1996) *Women Talk: Conversation Between Women Friends*. Oxford: Blackwell.

Cook, G. (forthcoming) *Language Play, Language Learning*.

Coupland, N., Grainger, K. and Coupland, J. (1988) 'Politeness in context: intergenerational issues'. *Language in Society* 17, 253–262.

Crystal, D. (1998) *Language Play*. London: Penguin.

Goffman, E. (1963) *Behavior in Public Places*. New York: The Free Press.

Goffman, E. (1967) 'On face-work: An analysis of ritual elements in social interaction' (originally published 1955). In *Interaction Ritual*. New York: Anchor Books, 5–45.

Goodwin, M. (1985) 'The serious side of jump rope: conversational practices and social organisation in the frame of play'. *Journal of American Folklore* 98(389), 315–330.

Hutchby, I. and Wooffitt, R. (1998) *Conversation Analysis: The Study of Talk in Interaction*. Cambridge: Polity.

Labov, W. (1972) *Language in the Inner City*. Oxford: Blackwell.

Leech, G. (1983) *Principles of Pragmatics*. London: Longman.

Lerner, G. (1991) 'On the syntax of sentences-in-progress'. *Language in Society* 20, 441–458.

Malone, M.J. (1997) *Worlds of Talk*. Cambridge: Polity.

Morgan, D. and Krueger, R. (1998) *The Focus Group Kit* (6 vols). Thousand Oaks: Sage.

Myers, G. (1989) 'The pragmatics of politeness in scientific articles'. *Applied Linguistics* 10, 1–35.

Myers, G. (1998) 'Displaying opinions: Topics and disagreement in focus groups'. *Language in Society* 27, 85–111.

Myers, G. (1999a) *Ad Worlds*. London: Arnold.

Myers, G. (1999b) 'Functions of reported speech in group discussions'. *Applied Linguistics* 20/3, 376–401.

Myers, G. (forthcoming) 'Analyzing talk in social science research data'. In M. Bauer (ed.) *Qualitative Research Methods*. London: Sage.

Myers, G. and Macnaghten, P. (1999) 'Can focus group discussions be analyzed as talk?' In R. Barbour and J. Kitzinger (eds) *Developing Focus Group Research: Politics, Theory, and Practice*. London, Sage: 173–185.

Pomerantz, A. (1984) 'Agreeing and disagreeing with assessments: Some features of preferred/dispreferred turn shapes'. In J.M. Atkinson and J. Heritage (eds) *Structures of Social Action: Studies in Conversation Analysis*. Cambridge, Cambridge University Press, 57–101.

Puchta, C. and Potter, J. (1999) 'Asking elaborate questions: Focus groups and the management of spontaneity'. *Journal of Sociolinguistics* 3(3), 314–335.

Rampton, B. (1995) *Crossing: Language and Ethnicity Among Adolescents*. London: Longman.

Sacks, H. (1992) *Lectures on Conversation*. Oxford: Blackwell.

Sarangi, S. and Slembrouck, S. (1997) 'Confrontational asymmetries in institutional discourse: A sociopragmatic view of information exchange and face management'. In J. Blommaert and C. Bulcaen (eds) *Political Linguistics*. Amsterdam: John Benjamins: 255–275.

Schiffrin, D. (1984) 'Jewish argument as sociability'. *Language in Society* 13, 311–335.

Schiffrin, D. (1993) ' "Speaking for another" in sociolinguistic interviews: Alignments, identities, frames'. In D. Tannen (ed.) *Framing in Discourse*. Oxford: Oxford University Press, 231–258.

Schiffrin, D. (1996) 'Narrative as self-portrait: Sociolinguistic constructions of identity'. *Language in Society* 25, 167–203.

Simmel, G. (1950) 'Sociability: An example of pure, or formal, sociology' (originally published in 1917). In K.H. Wolff (ed.) *The Sociology of Georg Simmel*. New York: The Free Press, 40–57.

Tannen, D. (ed.) (1993) *Gender and Conversational Interaction*. Cambridge: Cambridge University Press.

Thomas, J. (1995) *Meaning in Interaction*. London: Longman.

Chapter 8

Methodological interdiscursivity: an ethnographic understanding of unfinalisability

Ron Scollon

If we start with a concrete bit of field data,[1] what Atkinson (1990) has called the 'ethnographic exemplar', we could use the photograph of an electronics shop in the Mongkok area of Hong Kong (Figure 8.1). The photograph was taken in the summer of 1997, a few weeks after the ceremonies centring on midnight of 30 June, when Hong Kong returned to Chinese sovereignty after some century and a half of British rule.

Several discourses can be read in this photograph. At the centre is a shop selling small electronic goods – pagers, cell phones, walkmans and the like

Figure 8.1   A street in Mongkok, Hong Kong

on Sai Yeung Choi Street in Hong Kong's Mongkok, a district well known for the electronics stores found there. The upper portion of the sign says,

特区 电 讯
TE QU DIAN XUN

('SAR Telecommunications')

Below that in the smaller typeface we read,

手提电话维修服务

('Hand-held telephones (cellphones), repair services')

With little difficulty we read off the discourse of the sale of electronic goods within a globalising world economy. This reading could be developed by contrasting this photograph with another one in the ethnographer's archive of an electronic goods store in the Washington, DC, area of the USA. Most immediately one sees size as a significant dimension of contrast. Here in one photo we have two competing small stores which together would not fully occupy the space of the entrance to the American outlet store; we read small entrepreneurship against massive, nationwide franchised retailing.

The photograph supports other, geographical readings (Pierce 1996) having to do with Mongkok's reputation for being the world's most densely populated urban district. For those with the ability to do so, the 'FREE TALK' sign above the shop sign signals a large, commercial English language school. The street sign, Sai Yeung Choi Street, embeds Cantonese language through the use of the romanisation of the Chinese characters. The name, Sai Yeung Choi, more deeply embeds 'Portuguese' (Sai Yeung – an old name for Portugal; now also meaning 'foreign') as a modifier of a vegetable, 'choi', to produce 'watercress' – a vegetable once grown in this region of Hong Kong.

The discourses of the transition of political sovereignty are legible here in the use of the term (*te qu*, 'SAR'). 'SAR' is an acronym for 'Special Administrative Region', the Chinese designation of the special political structure through which Hong Kong began to be administered following the change in sovereignty on 1 July. As this was not a possible designation of Hong Kong before that date, we read SAR in the naming of the shop as dated after the political change in contrast with the shop next door where the company is named 'Hong Kong Electronics'. This positioning of the two neighbouring shops in two differing political discourses is further played out in the use of two languages. Chinese and English are seen in the older, colonial store; on the other, in the post-SAR store we see hanyu pinyin romanisation to pedagogise reading of the Chinese characters as to be pronounced in Mandarin, not Cantonese (Scollon and Scollon 1998). Thus the store on our left asserts a bi-dialectal polarity with the centre in Beijing while the store on the right asserts the traditional colonial positioning of English above Chinese (Cantonese is presumed) which parallels the road sign just above.

One further set of discourses in a dialectical position here is what Gu (1996) has called the 'discourse of revolution' and the 'discourse of reform' in contemporary China. As part of the revolutionising of China initiated with the new government in 1949 was the revision of the traditional Chinese writing system. What is written here as:

特 区 电 　 讯
TE QU DIAN XUN

手提电话维修服务

would be written in the traditional writing system as:

特區電訊

手提電話維修服務

While the move to simplify writing pre-dated the current communist government, it was under this revolutionary government that the new, simplified forms of writing Chinese were adopted in several waves of changes. Chinese in Taiwan, Hong Kong, and overseas on the whole, with the notable exception of Singapore, continued to use the traditional writing of characters and thus there opened up for Chinese a dialectic of positioning in the choice of writing systems. The new sign on the left has adopted the simplified, Mainland Chinese writing system while the sign on the right, the street sign and all of the other writing here are in the traditional writing system. These differences, though somewhat slight in this case, signal to any reader of Chinese alignment with either the goals and policies of the Mainland government or, to some degree, opposition to that government.

1   Reading public discourses

My reading of these electronic shop signs appropriates from several analytical discourses of reading. The reading of public discourses is central to several contemporary analytical discourses. Early readers, of course, have been Roland Barthes and the other semioticians who began to call our attention to the rising significance of popular culture in defining the archives of much of our common day-to-day discourse.

Communication studies (Morley 1980, 1990; Morley and Silverstone 1991; Livingstone 1992; Press 1992; and Ang 1996) have turned our attention to the importance of the reader of the texts of the mass media while arguing that the long perceived boundary between public display and the living room is rapidly being elided. Developing in tandem with cultural studies and finding inspiration in the decoding of Hall (1980), these studies have focused on the active interpretive work of the reader or audience of contemporary media products.

A motivating question in much of this research is: how may publicly available forms of discourse (signs, advertising posters, announcements, road and building identifications) be read as indicators of the discursive positioning of implied reader/viewers? That is, how does literate and semiotic design – from the choice of code to the choice of layout, typography, accompanying images, and even placement in physical space – reflect the broader sociocultural processes of the societies in which these semiotic spaces occur?

The geographer Pierce (1996), for example, in a study of Belfast neighbourhoods, showed that the sociopolitical structure of the neighbourhoods was reflected in the entire range of public literate displays including street names, store names and displays, and graffiti. He argued that as one walked the street crossing from Protestant to Catholic areas, this boundary was clearly reflected in the words written on the landscape, and thus Pierce argues for studies of geolinguistics. As Ley and Cybriwsky (1974) put it, 'Graffiti are a visible manifestation of a group's social space' (p. 505).

'Whether language is carved in stone or scratched with chalk, its message is influenced by its form. Material forms are also connected to a specific moment in history' (Drucker 1984: 8). Names in English such as 'NO D-LAY KLEENERS', according to Drucker, reflect specific times and places. Concerning information and identification, Drucker (1984: 9–10) writes:

> Street names, plant markers in a botanical garden and the sign on the bank that gives the time. How neutral are these? Each helps us identify and remember something, whether it is a place, a plant, or our progress in the daily routine. In street names this identification is tied to possession, maintenance, business, and civic order. The name of the street reminds us that some political body supervises the existence of the street, that it has a legal as well as functional existence. The plant markers help justify the existence of the park.

Perhaps nowhere more than in Chinese is the written form, the literate design, of public spaces the central aspect of its meaning. Tuan (1991), for example, quotes from the very popular *Story of the Stone*:

> Chia Cheng reflected for a while, then said, 'The inscriptions *do* present a problem. By rights, we should ask the Imperial Consort to do us the honour of composing them, but she can hardly do this without having seen the place. On the other hand, if we leave the chief sights and pavilions without a single name or couplet until her visit, the garden, however lovely with its flowers and willows, rocks and streams, cannot fully reveal its charm.' (Tsao Hsueh-Chin and Kao Hgo 1978: 226)

He then notes that 'the physical features of the garden are all very well, but they will seem unfinished and lacking in poetry unless the written word comes to their aid' Tuan (1991: 691). Kraus's (1991) study of the role of calligraphy in the display and, in fact, production of political power in China simultaneously ratifies that this interest in reading the discourses in public is an active aspect of contemporary Chinese life and brings such analyses of reading into play in the discourses of political science.

From Bourdieu's interest in photography (1990) to the new critical semiotics of Kress and van Leeuwen (1996) we find again the centrality of the reading of public images from advertising hoardings to the design of public spaces and works of art. Increasingly, sociology and critical discourse analysis (Fairclough 1992) are encompassing reading practices within the domain of the social practices needing to be explicated in coming to understand the workings of power in contemporary social life.

The study of public discourse in contemporary life now forms an interdisciplinary network of interdiscursivity from which our ethnographic work has drawn. This has included the geography of Pierce, Drucker, Ley and Cybriwsky, the sociology of Bourdieu, the mass communication research of Morley, Livingstone, and Ang and the cultural studies of Hall. Political scientists such as Kraus, together with sinologists such as Tuan, have met in our analyses with the critical discourse-semiotics of Fairclough, Kress, and van Leeuwen. As Goodwin (1994) has argued, the work of the analyst himself or herself we now see to be a form of reading which, like all reading, is a work of construction from within, a moment of the interdiscursive play of multiple histories of professional training and positioned motives.

2   An unfinalisable regression

Ethnography is an impossible task if by ethnography we mean any finalised, finished, or putatively complete description of a human society. Using this ethnographic exemplar drawn from an extended and, of course, not yet completed study of the discourses of the political transition in Hong Kong, I argue that the contribution that ethnography has to make to discourse analysis, especially to critical discourse analysis, lies precisely in the unfinalisability of ethnography. Ethnography, I will argue, is unfinalisable because it is fundamentally dialogical. It is dialogical in the ordinary academic sense that it consists of an ongoing discourse of academic researchers with a common interest. But more importantly, I would argue, following Mannheim and Tedlock (1995), Rodseth (1998) and others, ethnography is unfinalisable because an ethnographer does not wish to have the final word. The position of the ethnographer in a discourse analysis is that it is essential to engage in a dialogue not just with other academics about the subjects of our study, but we must also engage in a dialogue with the subjects of our study, and consequently we choose to vacate the privileged position claimed by finalisability. We reject a privileged claim to omniscience.

3   Bakhtin's unfinalisability

I use Bakhtin as a dialogical point of departure for the idea of methodological interdiscursivity. While his ideas of finalisability and, consequently of unfinalisability are quite typically never stabilised in any particular work (Morson and Emerson 1997; Holquist 1997) I have been interested in his speech genres essay (Bakhtin 1986). Finalisability, for Bakhtin, as for the ethnomethodologists following two decades later, was 'the inner side of the change of speech subjects' (1986: 76). The central question is: How do the participants know when it is another's turn to speak. The analytical question is: How is the possibility of response enabled? One aspect of this is, according to Bakhtin, that 'we embrace, understand, and sense the speaker's *speech plan* or *speech will*' (1986: 77). Bakhtin elaborates this by saying that 'We imagine to ourselves what the speaker *wishes* to say'. Bakhtin, Bateson (1972), and Gumperz (1977, 1992) would all argue, of course, that we can never determine that this *speech plan* or *speech will* is, in fact, what the speaker intends. It is always and irresolvably an inference drawn by the hearer upon which the hearer builds the subsequent dialogic response. Thus, while a response is enabled, it is not a specific, particular, or predictable response which is enabled. What is crucial is the inferential processes involved in this dialogicality.

The finalisation of utterance, the enabling condition for dialogue, is undermined at every point by the polyvocality of utterance also elucidated by Bakhtin (1981). When utterance is shot through and through by intertextuality and polyvocality, what becomes of the semantic and referential exhaustiveness of Bakhtin's conditions for dialogue? When recognising the hybrid interdiscursivity of utterance where do we find the clarity of generic closure upon which to build response? In a Bakhtinian world of polyvocality, double-voicedness, intertextuality, and interdiscursivity, where is the equally Bakhtinian finalisation of utterance which enables dialogic response?

In the work I report here, it is out of these paradoxes that the resolute unfinalisability of which Bakhtin wrote (Holquist 1997), and of all utterance, arises. Our dialogic engagement with the lifeworlds of our analysis, our turns at utterance as researchers, are ambiguously enabled because we do not approach semantic/representative exhaustiveness, our inferences about the speaker's *will* or *plan* are tenuous in the extreme, the genres in which we perform are undergoing ever-increasing speeds of change, and the rhythms of our turns of utterance – the research proposals, study protocols, final reports and academic papers – are entirely out of phase with the phenomena we study – the discourses of daily life.

4 Methodological interdiscursivity

The phenomenon we undertook to study was the many, polymorphous, and interacting discourses of the change in political sovereignty in Hong Kong during the period beginning in 1993 and running through to the present. Our central concern in these studies was phrased in most cases as a pedagogical one. To put it in just a few words, we wanted to know how

City University of Hong Kong students learn to write academic prose. To elaborate somewhat on this statement, we wanted to know what are the sources of intertextuality and interdiscursivity and what are the practices of appropriation which together form the writing they do on academically constrained tasks. Most casually we could say we wanted to ask: Why do they write the way they write?

This series of studies took us through a large number of partially intersecting discourses (Gee 1996) or social languages (Bakhtin 1981, 1984), including university classwork assignments, international, Hong Kong, and Chinese (PRC as well as Taiwan) journalistic discourses – the only partly corresponding national political discourses of China, Britain, the USA, and Hong Kong – and global entertainment, fashion, and popular culture discourses. Within the academic domain, these studies also took us through the discourses of discourse analysis (critical and otherwise), genre analysis, political science, cultural studies, and TESL (Teaching English as a Second Language) as well as ESP (English for Specific Purposes). As these students were preparing for work in the rapidly globalising service workplaces of Hong Kong, we also found ourselves moving through Hong Kong, Chinese, and international discourses of government and business.

It was, perhaps, inevitable that we took on a research strategy of methodological interdiscursivity to do this work. Elsewhere (Scollon 1998a) I have used this term to refer to the interpenetration of two rather broad but separate communities of practice – an academic research community and the community of university students in Hong Kong who were the population about which we wanted to learn. Here I would like to expand on three ways in which the term 'methodological interdiscursivity' might reflect the interpenetration of the social languages (Bakhtin, Gee) of discourse analysis and the social languages of the communities we study.

1. We focus on cases of interdiscursivity.
2. Our method itself is interdiscursive.
3. We seek interdiscursivity between method and phenomenon.

4.1 Cases of interdiscursivity

There has been a tendency in social scientific research to seek the purest cases for analysis. Roseberry (1998), for example, reflects on his initial work in the field, and states that if there was a study of a village in New Guinea or South America, and there was a nearby mine at which a number of the villagers worked, that study would 'air-brush' out the participation in the global economy of those villagers. It would describe the village in classical terms of kinship networks, patterns of exchanges with neighbouring equally pure villages, and the like. Now, he argues, a study of the same village would be more likely to place the lifeworld of that village into a globalising world economy, perhaps even to the extent of 'air-brushing' out village exchange practices and kinship networks. Billig (1995) has argued that the practice in sociology, anthropology, and linguistics of isolating and analysing bounded social groups is one of the ways in which what he calls *banal nationalism* is produced in the practices of social science.

One meaning of methodological interdiscursivity, then, is to direct the focus of the research not towards the putative centres of clearly imagined groups (Anderson 1991) but to focus on boundaries and intersections. What is of interest in this sort of work is the social and discursive production of boundaries.

In our studies of student writing in Hong Kong we sought to find and elicit situations in which students would be encouraged to appropriate from the public discourses of the historical-political transition (Scollon et al. 1998). It was just in the interdiscursivity between these journalistic and governmental discourses of public discourse and the academic discourses of their writing in the university that we hoped to see at work the practices of intertextuality that were also operating elsewhere in their writing, where the public sources would be likely to not be so clearly delineated.

4.2   Method is interdiscursive

A discourse analysis which focuses on texts or discourses which are highly interdiscursive might itself remain methodologically hermetic. In seeking to produce methodological interdiscursivity in our data construction we have been concerned to bring together three forms of analysis which have sometimes not kept company. We have appropriated, from critical theory and analysis, strategies for the selection, analysis, and explication of texts. Concurrent with this we have conducted extended ethnographies within the communities in which those texts are grounded as mediational means (Wertsch 1991, 1998) for appropriation. We have also conducted quantitative surveys within those communities as a way of linking sociopolitical analysis of texts with concrete uses of those texts.

4.3   Interdiscursivity between method and phenomenon

The third sort of methodological interdiscursivity is that between method and the phenomenon itself. That is, one engages directly in dialogues between the researchers and the community of practice under examination. In our case we were interested in learning about the writing practices of university students. The form of interdiscursivity we wanted to produce, then, was not just to talk with them about their writing, but also talk to them about our research project. We wanted to engage them in the process of researching their writing. The most direct form of this was to have university students work on our projects as not just low-level research assistants but as active participants in the formulation and study of the problems we were trying to address.

5 The production of an ethnographic exemplar

Our research (Scollon and Scollon 1997, Scollon 1999, Scollon et al. 1998; Scollon 1998a) was motivated by two intersecting interests:

(1) to understand the sources of text and discourse that were being appropriated by our university students in their academic writing and
(2) to develop an analysis of the multiple discourses of change taking place with the political sovereignty over Hong Kong from the British to the Chinese government, particularly as this would affect the discursive construction of identity for young people of Hong Kong.

In these studies we were interested in following the work of Wertsch and others (Ahonen 1997; Penuel and Wertsch 1995 and in press; Tulviste 1994; Tulviste and Wertsch 1994; Wertsch 1997, and to appear) who had studied the role of narratives in the change of sociopolitical identity in Estonia, East Germany, and Russia after the collapse of the Soviet Union.

Like Wertsch and his colleagues we engaged in extended interactions with our researcher-students. We went beyond those analyses, however, and while we conducted our own analyses of the public discourses of change and our own ethnographic studies of these changes, we asked our students to design and carry out studies of the discourses within their own communities. In doing this we used at least the three types of methodological interdiscursivity described above. First, we focused on the boundaries between university and community, between academic genres and those of the public discourses of entertainment, between students as subjects and students as researchers, between participation and observation, and between the historical discourses of colonialism in pre-1997 Hong Kong and of reunification with China thereafter. Secondly, we played off quantitative and qualitative methodologies, critical analyses of text and focus-group interpretations, ethnographic observations and questionnaire survey answers. Thirdly, we engaged ourselves as researchers with the community of study, our students and their home communities. We not only studied their homes and social groups, but we also asked them to study ours.

We organised these projects around two types of questions:

1. *Member-focused questions*: What media sources do university students use/read/view, and when, where, and how do they do this?
2. *Issue-focused questions*: How broadly distributed is a 'signficant issue' and how does such an issue enter into the population under study?

Writing tasks
As part of this research we asked students to perform various writing tasks in the classes we were teaching them. These were done at the beginning, through the research I discuss here, and after we had concluded the bulk of

these projects. Early in this work we found that there were high levels of intertextuality with the broad public discourses of the political transition in their student writing (Scollon et al. 1998, 1999).

Hong Kong is among the world's busiest public discourses with 2.8 million newspaper copies daily in a population of 6 million people (Scollon 1998b). Of these papers, 28 are general dailies, 26 Chinese and 2 English. In addition, there are another 13 special entertainment dailies such as racing papers. Overall, when we count both locally produced and imported papers and magazines, there are 67 daily newspapers and 608 periodicals available on the news-stands of Hong Kong.

The readership survey
Yung (1996) conducted a readership survey as a means of sorting this plethora of sources. She conducted questionnaire surveys of students to quantitatively establish the frequency of use of key sources, then conducted 'through-the-book' focus group sessions as well as journal studies to develop an understanding of how students were using the sources we had identified. From this we were able to determine that, of this plethora of sources, relatively few were used to any signficant extent by our Hong Kong students.

The pager survey
Now that we knew *which* printed sources our students actually read, we needed to know when, where, and how they used these sources as well as any other sources they used, such as television news and infotainment and entertainment shows. Again, the problem was to narrow our focus to significant media use, not to produce a society-wide survey of potential sources. We recruited and trained a group of student-researchers to assist in this ethnography. The problem as we saw it was to resolve the paradox of participant-observation; as senior academics, some of whom were expatriates, we could not meaningfully follow university students whose activities take them on complex routes through one of the world's most complex and crowded urban environments.

The solution they proposed was to use their ubiquitous pagers. A team of student-researchers randomly paged a relatively narrow group of university students over the course of 7 days. At each page the student was to write down in a notebook where he or she was and with whom, what media were present at that moment, and how were they being used. These journals were collected at the end of the week and analysed to produce summary statements of the most salient places, situations, participant structures, and media used. These results, which we felt to be highly valid, were then used in interviews and focus groups to broaden the reliability across the population of university students. We found that students spent most of their time in four sites: the university, their homes, small Chinese fast-food restaurants, and public transportation.

The scene survey

While we were able to observe student practice in the university and, to some extent, in the restaurants and on public transportation, we were concerned about how to observe life when a family lives together in a 400 square foot living space. Our student-researchers argued that the best way to do the scene surveys was for them to study their own living and social spaces as part of their daily lives. Comparatively, we also asked them to study the living spaces of expatriate lecturer/researchers and we also took a field trip to China so that they could make comparisons with Chinese university students.

These results cross-checked with the readership survey and the pager survey which had found a strong preference for small-format media sources, magazines over newspapers, and for short, salient texts and images within those sources. We further learned that our students were virtually never alone in the course of a week (which included 4 university days and 3 weekend/holidays), and that no medium was ever used in isolation from other media. That is, media use was what we described as polyfocal. They watched television *while* reading magazines; they chatted about entertainment magazines *while* they did their coursework; they played music and video CDs on their computers *while* they wrote their term papers and sent e-mail messages to their friends.

These studies focused our view on just those media our students paid attention to, as well as the typical circumstances in which they used these media. It was clear that they paid very little attention to, or had very little knowledge of, the sources of public discourse which are most centrally studied in critical studies of broad questions of political ideology. Our studies suggested that, for a study of the conflicting discourses of political transition for our students, it would be more fruitful to study comic books, small-format magazines, television commercials, fashion advertisements, and infotainment television programmes than the politically focused stories, features, and editorials of *Ming Pao* or the *South China Morning Post*.

From another point of view, however, we still did not know how the discourses of major news and political events penetrated into the daily discourse of our university students, if not from the traditional news sources. Indeed, we did not know, for any part of the population, how an 'event' becomes translated, through the discourses of the mass media, into something people talk about in common conversation, much less how these discourses are appropriated intertextually in student writing.

The event survey

We conducted two types of studies: the first was to collect and analyse the public discourses available for a particular time period to map out the central issues from our own analytical perspective, and the second was to conduct a survey to see if we could come to an understanding of what issues were selected, by whom they were selected, and from what sources.

The first of these studies was simply to collect printed and broadcast media (including radio and television) samples for two continuous weeks in March 1996. As it happened, during those two weeks China tested missiles in the Taiwan Strait and thus produced a highly salient media event for us to analyse. Our readership and pager studies had told us which media to focus upon. Thus during these two weeks we collected all news broadcasts as well as the infotainment shows in these media, both morning and evening, and all of the relevant newspapers and magazines.

At the same time each day for two weeks we surveyed four populations: (1) City University students; (2) Non-City University students; (3) City University non-students, faculty members and staff; and (4) out-of-school adults not associated with City University. We asked them in these surveys to tell us the major topics of discussion that were going on in the media, how they came to know about them, and the sources they used to find out about the topics.

In this survey it developed that two tragic murder stories were more useful for our analysis of the pathways by which the public discourses were flowing into our student population than the very salient Taiwan Missile crisis story. In Dunblane, Scotland, there was the murder of a group of school children and during the same period in Fanling, Hong Kong, there was the murder of a young girl. These stories pushed into the mass media and then, by word of mouth, into the daily discourses about 'what is going on' among our students, and for several days these issues pushed aside any talk of the broader crisis story. From this survey we learned that students got their stories first from friends or from television and then read magazines and newspapers as well as watched the infotainment shows to get further details.

5.1   Follow-up projects

These broad event surveys were then followed up with full coverage of the two weeks prior to and following the change of government on 1 July 1997 and then again the year following with one week prior and one week following the anniversary of the event.

In this series of projects we used ethnographic participant-observation to develop a focus on the significant points at which our students were appropriating the discourses of political transition. The writing tasks told us that they were appropriating in some way from these discourses. The pager survey and the readership survey played off close ethnographic study, interviews, and focus groups against quantitative survey data to get a picture of what sources students were using in making these appropriations. The event survey told us that what we thought were the main sources of public discourse – i.e. the Taiwan Missile crisis, the two murders, or the political transition – were not the main sources for our students, but television infotainment, entertainment shows, and word of mouth were the real mediators of this intertextuality.

149

As part of this methodological interdiscursivity we had engaged dialogic-ally with our students in the production of this research. Ultimately, they began to redefine our understanding not only of our research questions but also of where to focus our attention in doing this research. They took over the cameras used in the focus groups and began to document directly in the streets what they saw as the semiotic carriers of the discourses of transi-tion. While we focused on the construction of the new convention centre where the handover ceremony was to take place, our students were taking pictures of the new Tsingyi Bridge. While we were reading what Governor Patten was saying and how Tung Chee Hwa was selected, they were listen-ing to standup comedians and watching the 16th Annual Hong Kong Film Awards show with its theme, 'This is how we all grew up' (Yung 1998). A group of student-researchers brought back a photo of the electronics shop in Mongkok as an example of the changing discursive climate of Hong Kong.

5.2   Whose interdiscursivities?

It is this latter point which we have found crucial to the ongoing construc-tion of our discourses of transition. When we arrived at the convergence of our attention on this photograph, and others like them, we then wanted to know the extent to which we could rely on our own interpretation of the readings I have suggested in my opening analysis of the exemplar. In the contrast of simplified and traditional writing, for example, I see the interdis-cursivity between the discourse of revolution and the discourse of reform, between the discourse of colonial Hong Kong and post-unification China. Our student-ethnographers also saw this interdiscursivity, but couched it, not as politically motivated but rather pragmatically as a simple commercial attention-getter.

We took a collection of photographs of signs in which we found contrasts of this kind between the old and the new, between revolution and reform. When these photographs were discussed in focus groups in Kunming, Guangzhou, and Hong Kong (Scollon and Pan 1997; Pan 1998) we found that the readings of these interdiscursivities varied across generational groups. Older participants in the focus groups saw the differences to be aesthetic. Traditional writing was more beautiful, simplified writing more ugly. They positioned this interdiscursivity on an aesthetic plane. A younger group of people positioned the differences as political. They pointed to the legal requirement to use simplified writing in China, the role of this writing in increasing literacy, or, in Hong Kong, to the potential for the Mainland government to introduce the use of simplified writing to enforce a kind of post-reunification patriotism. Finally, the youngest group positioned this interdiscursivity pragmatically. They argued that it was a matter of business – just a way to attract people for the purpose of sales. The question of whose point of view to take in this is ultimately unfinalisable.

6   The next turn in the dialogue

The photograph of an electronics shop in Mongkok, Hong Kong, is a polyvocal utterance produced shortly after the return of Hong Kong to Chinese political sovereignty. The analysis we have tried to develop about this photograph, and the many others like it, provides a study in the unfinalisability of which Bakhtin wrote. Rather than approaching referential and semantic exhaustiveness, our analysis moves into ever-widening circles of possibilities of interpretation. If we try to set up an interpretation of what Bakhtin called the *speech plan* of the utterer, it becomes clear that that can only be done in reference to specific and concretely located communities. In this case different age groups or people in different regions produced different interpretations of the intentions of the producers of the electronics shop sign. If we hope for stability of generic form, again we are frustrated by the two signs side by side, each of which serves to destabilise an interpretation which might be made of the other.

The argument I have tried to develop here through this rather simple example is that truth in our research into these discourses of transition lies in the dialogues themselves, not in any finalised and falsely omniscient statement of what these discourses might mean outside of the discourses within which we are analysing them. From this point of view, methodological interdiscursivity is not a resource through which we can bring resolution to the complexities and polyvocalities of discourse analysis. On the contrary, methodological interdiscursivity is the means by which we come to engage directly in the discourses we study.

Note

1. The research on which this study is based has been supported by several research grants which include City University Strategic Research Grant, 'Discourses of Transition: Authoritative History in the Making', Ron Scollon (PI) with David Li, Wai King Tsang, Vicki Yung, Rodney Jones (AI). I wish to thank my colleagues in the Public Discourse Research Group at City University of Hong Kong for insightful critical discussion of the research discussed here.

References

Ahonen, Sirkka (1997) A transformation of history: The official representations of history in East Germany and Estonia, 1986–1991. *Culture and Psychology* 3(1), 41–62.
Anderson, Benedict (1991) *Imagined Communities.* London: Verso.
Ang, Ien (1996) *Living Room Wars: Rethinking Media Audiences for a Postmodern World.* London: Routledge.
Atkinson, Paul (1990) *The Ethnographic Imagination: Textual Constructions of Reality.* London: Routledge.

151

Bakhtin, M.M. (1981) (Originally published in 1934–5). *The Dialogic Imagination*. Austin: University of Texas Press.

Bakhtin, M.M. (1984) (Originally published in 1929). *Problems of Dostoevsky's Poetics*. (Caryl Emerson ed. and tr.) Minneapolis: University of Minnesota Press.

Bakhtin, M.M. (1986) (Originally published in 1952). *Speech Genres and Other Late Essays*. Austin: University of Texas Press.

Bateson, Gregory (1972) *Steps to an Ecology of Mind*. New York: Ballantine.

Billig, Michael (1995) *Banal Nationalism*. London: Sage.

Bourdieu, Pierre (1990) *Photography: A Middle-brow Art*. Cambridge: Polity Press.

Drucker, Johanna (1984) Language in the landscape. *Landscape* 28(1), 7–13.

Erickson, Frederick (1980) Timing and context in everyday discourse: Implications for the study of referential and social meaning. *Sociolinguistic Working Paper Number 67*. Austin, Texas: Southwest Educational Development Laboratory.

Fairclough, Norman (1992) *Discourse and Social Change*. Cambridge: Polity Press.

Gee, James Paul (1996) *Social Linguistics and Literacies: Ideology in Discourses* (Second edition). Bristol, PA: Taylor & Francis Inc.

Gee, James Paul (Forthcoming) *Introduction to Discourse Analysis*. London: Routledge.

Goodwin, Charles (1994) Professional vision. *American Anthropologist* 96(3), 606–633.

Gu, Yueguo (1996) The changing modes of discourse in a changing China. Plenary address, 1996 International Conference on Knowledge and Discourse, Hong Kong. Beijing Foreign Studies University: unpublished manuscript.

Gumperz, John (1977) Sociocultural knowledge in conversational inference. In M. Saville-Troike (ed.), *28th Annual Round Table Monograph Series on Language and Linguistics*. Washington, DC: Georgetown University Press, 191–212.

Gumperz, John (1992) Contextualization and understanding. In A. Duranti and C. Goodwin (eds) *Rethinking Context*. Cambridge: Cambridge University Press: 229–252.

Hall, Stuart (1980) Encoding/decoding. In S. Hall, D. Hobson, A. Lowe, and P. Willis (eds) *Culture, Media, Language: Working papers in Cultural Studies 1972–1979*. London: Hutchinson, 128–138.

Holquist, Michael (1997) Bakhtin and beautiful science: The paradox of cultural relativity revisited. In Michael Macovski (ed.) *Dialogue and Critical Discourse*. Oxford: Oxford University Press, 215–236.

Kraus, Richard Curt (1991) *Brushes with power: Modern Politics and the Chinese Art of Calligraphy*. Berkeley: University of Calfornia Press.

Kress, Gunther and Theo van Leeuwen (1996) *Reading images: The grammar of visual design*.

Ley, David and Roman Cybriwsky (1974) Urban graffiti as territorial markers. *Annals of the Association of American Geographers* 64(4), 491–505.

Livingstone, Sonia M. (1992) The resourceful reader: Interpreting television characters and narratives. *Communication Yearbook* 15, 58–90.

Mannheim, Bruce and Dennis Tedlock (1995) *The Dialogic Emergence of Culture*. Urbana and Chicago: University of Illinois Press.

Moores, Shaun (1993) *Interpreting Audiences: The Ethnography of Media Consumption*. Newbury Park, California: Sage Publications Inc.

Morley, David (1980) *The 'Nationwide' Audience: Structure and Decoding*. London: British Film Institute.

Morley, David (1990) The construction of everyday life: Political communication and domestic media. In D.L. Swanson and D.D. Nimmo (eds) *New Directions in Political Communication*. London: Sage, 123–146.

Morley, David and Roger Silverstone (1991) Communication and context: ethnographic perspectives on the media audience. In Klaus Bruhn Jensen and Nicholas W. Jankowski (eds) *A Handbook of Qualitative Methodologies for Mass Communication Research*. London: Routledge, 149–162.

Morson, Gary Saul with Caryl Emerson (1997) Extracts from a Heteroglossary. In Michael Macovski (ed.) *Dialogue and Critical Discourse*. Oxford: Oxford University Press, 256–272.

Pan, Yuling (1998) Public literate design and ideological shift: A case study of Mainland China and Hong Kong. Paper presented at the 6th International Conference on Pragmatics, Reims, France, 19–24 July 1998.

Penuel, William R. and James V. Wertsch (1995) Dynamics of negation in the identity politics of cultural other and cultural self. *Culture and Psychology* 1, 343–359.

Penuel, William R. and James V. Wertsch (In press) Historical representation as mediated action: Tools for an unofficial or official history? In M. Carretero and J.F. Voss (eds) *Learning and Instruction in History*. Hillsdale, NJ: Erlbaum.

Pierce, Robert M. (1996) Geographers and linguists; sharing a perspective on discourse. Paper presented at the Annual Meetings of the AAAL, Chicago, 25 March 1996.

Press, Andrea L. (1992) The active viewer and the problem of interpretation: reconciling traditional and critical research. *Communication Yearbook* 15, 91–106.

Rodseth, Lars (1998) Distributive models of culture: A Sapirian alternative to essentialism. *American Anthropologist* 100(1), 55–69.

Roseberry, William (1998) Perspectives on globalization, past and present. Paper presented in the session 'Debating "globalization": Anthropology, history, and Marxism' at the 97th meeting of the American Anthropological Association, Philadelphia, 5 December 1998.

Sachs, Harvey, Emanuel Schegloff, and Gail Jefferson (1977) A simplest systematics for the organization of turn taking for conversation. *Language* 50(4), 696–735.

Scollon, Ron (1981) The rhythmic integration of ordinary talk. In Deborah Tannen (ed.) *Georgetown University Roundtable on Languages and Linguistics 1981*. Washington, D.C.: Georgetown University Press.

Scollon, Ron (1998a) *Mediated discourse as Social Interaction: A Study of News Discourse*. London and New York: Longman.

Scollon, Ron (1999) Official and unofficial discourses of national identity: Questions raised by the case of contemporary Hong Kong. In Ruth Wodak and Christoph Ludwig (eds) *Challenges in a Changing World. Issues in Critical Discourse Analysis*. Vienna: Passangen Verlag, 23–35.

Scollon, Ron (1998b) Hong Kong language in context: The discourse of Ch'u. In M.C. Pennington (ed.) *Language in Hong Kong at Century's End*. Hong Kong: Hong Kong University Press, 277–281.

Scollon, Ron and Suzanne Wong Scollon (1997) Political, Personal, and Commercial Discourses of National Sovereignty: Hong Kong becomes China. In Marju Lauristin (ed.) *Intercultural Communication and Changing National Identities*. Tartu: Tartu University Press, 49–71.

Scollon, Ron and Suzanne Wong Scollon (1998) Literate design in the discourses of revolution, reform, and transition: Hong Kong and China. *Written Language and Literacy* 1(1), 1–39.

Scollon, Ron, Wai King Tsang, David Li, Vicki Yung, and Rodney Jones (1998) Voice, appropriation, and discourse representation in a student writing task. *Linguistics and Education* 9(3), 227–250.

Scollon, Ron, Vijay Bhatia, David Li, Vicki Yung (1999) Blurred genres and fuzzy identities in Hong Kong public discourse: Foundational ethnographic issues. *Applied Linguistics* 20(1), 22–43.

Scollon, Suzanne and Yuling Pan (1997) Generational and regional readings of the literate face of China. Paper presented at the Second Symposium on Intercultural Communication, Beijing Foreign Studies University, 10–15 October 1997.

Tsao Hsuen-Chin and Kao Hgo (1978) *A Dream of Red Mansions.* Tr. Yang Hsien-Yi and Gladys Yang. Beijing: Foreign Languages Press.

Tuan, Yi Fu (1991) Language and the making of place: A narrative-descriptive approach. *Annals of the Association of American Geographers* 81(4), 684–696.

Tulviste, Peeter (1994) History taught at school versus history discovered at home: The case of Estonia. *European Journal of Psychology of Education*, IX(1), 121–126.

Tulviste, Peeter and James V. Wertsch (1994) Official and unofficial histories: The case of Estonia. *Journal of Narrative and Life History* 4(4), 311–329.

Wertsch, James V. (1991) *Voices of the Mind: A Sociocultural Approach to Mediated Action.* Cambridge, Mass.: Harvard University Press.

Wertsch, James V. (1997) Narrative tools of history and identity. *Culture and Psychology* 3(1), 5–20.

Wertsch, James V. (1998) *Mind as Action.* New York: Oxford University Press.

Wertsch, James V. (To appear) *Revising Russian History.* Written Communication.

Yung, Vicki (1996) A readership study of tertiary students in Hong Kong. International conference on communication and culture: China and the world entering the 21st century, Peking University, 15 August 1996.

Yung, Vicki (1997) The discourse of popular culture among tertiary students in Hong Kong. Paper presented at the LACUS Forum (Linguistic Association of Canada and the United States) York University, Toronto, 29 July–2 August 1997.

Yung, Vicki (1998) The global construction of the entertainer: Globalization and localization of film awards shows. Paper presented in the session on globalism in Hong Kong Public Discourse: Postmodern ideology and local resistance at the Annual Meeting of the American Anthropological Association, Philadelphia, 2–6 December 1998.

Chapter 9

Critical practices: on representation and the interpretation of text

Henry Widdowson

What I want to do in this chapter is to consider what it means to be critical in response to a text. The term *critical* itself is associated with what would appear to be two rather different approaches to textual interpretation: literary criticism on the one hand, and critical linguistics on the other. In the former, the critical response is typically related to *appreciation*: the apprehension of aesthetic effect in texts identified as literary. In the latter, it is related to *analysis* and the uncovering of covert ideological intent in texts in general. There is no reason, however, why literary appreciation should not be consistent with linguistic analysis, and it is precisely the bringing of these two into close and meaningful conjunction that defines the purpose of stylistics. This is what I sought to show in my book *Stylistics and the Teaching of Literature* (Widdowson 1975).[1] In this book I try to demonstrate how literature can be conceived of as discourse, and how one might infer literary effects from linguistic features and so provide a textual warrant for interpretation. What I was engaged in resembled the practical criticism of literary tradition in its general aesthetic purpose (see Cox and Dyson 1963, 1965), but brought more precise linguistic analysis to bear in the process. The book was, in this sense, an excursion into critical discourse analysis.

Not, of course, as that term is currently understood, for critical discourse analysis (henceforth CDA) is the practice of revealing the underlying ideological bias and exposing the covert exercise of power in all texts. It is committed to a quite explicit political cause. As the preface to a recent collection puts it:

> Critical Discourse Analysis is essentially political in intent with its practitioners acting upon the world in order to transform it and thereby help create a world where people are not discriminated against because of sex, creed, age or social class. (Caldas-Coulthard and Coulthard 1996: xi)

This is quite an agenda, and certainly well beyond the modest aims of my own efforts at critical analysis. I had no such commitment to a cause: my purpose was not to expose, but to explain; not to discover devious intent, but to try to work out what it was in texts that gave rise to certain interpretations.

155

Furthermore, I restricted my attention to literary texts. My practical criticism was a far cry from critical practice as defined by CDA. All of which might be said to reveal a certain liberal naïveté, or worse, a connivance in the concealment of truth. I was not being critical in the currently accepted sense. Indeed, from a CDA point view, I was not really doing discourse analysis at all, for discourse can only mean a set of socially constructed values in which ideology is inevitably implicated. Not only that, but it would seem that the title of my book is a misnomer; I was not really doing stylistics either, as Carter and Simpson (1989: 8) concur with Deirdre Burton that '. . . no analysis can be anything other than ideologically committed. Stylistic analysis is a political activity'.

My work on stylistics was further invalidated by its exclusive concentration on literary texts, and, to make matters worse, by being predicated on the assumption that there is such a thing as literature at all. The orthodox CDA position is that there is no basis for distinguishing one literary text from any other, and therefore there is no such thing as literary criticism: all criticism is linguistic (Fowler 1986). Such an idea is not (as one might suppose) restricted to linguists, as Eagleton (1983: 205) expresses much the same view:

> My own view is that it is most useful to see 'literature' as a name which people give from time to time for different reasons to certain kinds of writing within a whole field of what Michel Foucault has called 'discursive practices', and that if anything is to be an object of study it is this whole field of practices rather than just those sometimes obscurely labelled 'literature'.

So it would seem that CDA has so defined the field that any discourse analysis which does not conform to its tenets does not really count as critical practice. In this sense, CDA seems to have staked a claim to the whole field of enquiry: it *is* critical discourse analysis, and there is no other, just as, in some people's minds, SLA *is* second language acquisition. In a way, there is no cause for complaint about that. A field will always tend be defined in the terms of its most vigorous development, which is all the more reason for questioning the equation, and this is what I propose to do in this chapter. I shall argue that CDA (in some of its manifestations at least), in seeking to extend its scope of analysis, actually ends up by being reductionist, and far from incorporating literary criticism into a more comprehensive concept of critical practice, it actually applies literary critical procedures in quite inappropriate and uncritical ways.

We may begin by noting that, historically, CDA originates in literary criticism, as Fowler (1996: 4) makes clear when speaking of its pioneering days: '. . . our education and working context made us familiar with the hermeneutic side of literary criticism, and we, like the literary critics, were working on the interpretation of discourse'.

It is therefore not surprising to find striking resemblances between the two enterprises. Both assume that there is significance in texts below the level of appearances, and seek to prise it out of the linguistic texture. Both draw on the concept of genre and have an eye for intertextual echoes and allusions. Both assume a privileged authority to provide an exegesis and reveal to unenlightened readers covert meanings which would otherwise escape their notice. The difference lies, Fowler tells us, in the toolkit they were using. The critical linguists had instruments to hand which enabled them to make more precise statements about the language; but they also, of course, were applying these for the interpretation of all discourse, whether recognised as literary or not, on the assumption that there was no real difference between them. The question is: How valid is such an assumption?

As we have seen, it is perfectly valid as far as Eagleton is concerned. So-called 'Literature' is simply a discursive practice like any other: just a label that people stick on certain kinds of writing for some obscure reason or other, signifying nothing. It is a name, not a concept, and what's in a name? There is, nevertheless, a curious contradiction here. The use of the *term* 'literature' is itself a discursive practice and it is precisely the purpose of critical analysis to infer what its use might signify. The point repeatedly made by sociolinguists, and not only those of critical linguistic persuasion, is that there is good deal in a name: that the way things are labelled marks sociopolitical values. They are not just randomly attached. So if people identify something as distinctive, then it *is* distinctive. If, for example, they say that what they speak is a distinct language, then that defines it as a language and there is no point in the linguist insisting that it is a dialect. By the same token, if people say that certain texts are literary, that defines them as such, no matter what literary theorists might say; and to identify texts as literary is to adopt a certain attitude to them and a certain way of reading them. So which way?

Let us enquire into the question by considering two texts. They are alike in that they are both in English and have a common topic (the death of a woman). They are comparable in length (both about 80 words) and in each case the text is vertically rather than horizontally aligned – that is to say, it does not extend over the whole page but is confined in a column of print.

Text A

> *Annabella, film actress,*
> *died on September 18*
> *aged 87, she was born on*
> *July 14, 1900*

Even from earliest childhood Annabella had a passion for cinema. As a child playing in the garden of her family home near Paris, the chicken shed

out in the yard became her
imaginary studio where, lost
in a world of imagination, she
would act out scenes from the
films she had watched, taking
upon herself the roles of director, cameraman and leading
lady all at once.

(From *The Times* 23.9.96)

Text B

She dwelt among the untrodden ways

1 She dwelt among the untrodden ways
2   Beside the springs of Dove,
3 A Maid whom there were none to praise
4   And very few to love.

5 A violet by a mossy stone
6   Half hidden from the eye!
7 – Fair as a star, when only one
8   Is shining in the sky.

9 She lived unknown, and few could know
10   When Lucy ceased to be;
11 But she is in her grave, and, oh,
12   The difference to me!

(From William Wordsworth,
Collected Poems)

We readily identify these texts as different in genre: the first as a newspaper obituary, the second as a poem. One immediate consequence of this is that we disregard the vertical arrangement in Text A as a feature of no significance. We know that columns of print are conventionally used in newspapers to save on space, or to provide convenient blocks of text for easy reading when folded. In Text B, on the other hand, we recognise that we do not just have an expedient disposition of print, but a pattern of metrically regular lines which are intrinsic to the text itself. Identifying the first text as a conventional obituary also leads us to overlook other textual features. We recognise that its purpose is to provide information about a particular person and that the language is effective to the extent that it succeeds in doing that. In other words we use the language indexically as a set of referential directions, and ignore any textual features which are not referentially functional. So it is that while we take note of structural features, we attach no particular importance to their sequential realisation. Consider the consequence of making *structural* changes to the heading of the text so that it read:

Annabella, film actress,
was born on September 18
aged 87, she died on
July 14, 1900

The text now fails in its indexical function: it directs the reader to a referentially impossible world, But a *sequential* alteration has no such referential effect. The sequence, we might say, has no consequence:

Film actress, Annabella
was born on July 14, 1900,
died on September 18 aged 87

Similarly, the structural change:

From   earliest   childhood
Annabella even had a passion
for cinema.

Completely alters the referential meaning and makes it presuppositionally dependent on some non existent context of shared knowledge. Not so with a sequentially different version:

Annabella had a passion for
the cinema even from earliest
childhood

So it would seem that Text A can be reformulated in different versions without changing its meaning in any substantial way. The differences do not matter and this suggests that there are features of conventional texts which readers edit out as of no pragmatic importance. What matters is that the texts should indexically refer, and this means that they should effectively refer readers to some context of situation that they can recognise in their world. Even structurally defective texts can be pragmatically effective. It is unlikely, for example, that newspaper readers would be disturbed by the dangling participle in Text A. *As a child . . . the chicken shed.* It is not the chicken shed that is playing in the garden. This is nonsense as grammatically signified; but it is nonsense that, pragmatically speaking, does not signify. None of the people to whom I have given the text to read (even abstracted from its normal appearance on the newspaper page) has noticed the structural non-sequitur.

It is a pragmatic truism that readers normally proceed on a least effort principle, and treat language in a fairly cavalier fashion: they pay attention to it only to the extent that it makes a satisfactory indexical connection for them. Writers also, of course, design their texts accordingly, assuming, for their part, that the Gricean co-operative principle is in place (Grice 1975) and that readers will not perversely dissect their texts and analyse the entrails. They assume that they are writing for readers not analysts. They do not realise that they might have critical linguists to reckon with. But I anticipate. We have yet to consider Text B.

As I have already mentioned, in identifying this as a poem, we recognise that its actual physical shape is intrinsically a part of the text. It is a series of metrically regular lines, which are ordered in a rhyme scheme. There is here a patterned texture, a secondary arrangement of language which is not informed by the requirements of the language code itself. There is significance here in the textual design which is not simply a matter of what the linguistic elements signify. With Text A you can meddle with sequence without altering the referential functioning of the text. Meddling with Text B, however, is a very different matter, for in so doing you inevitably alter the second order textual design (for further discussion, see Widdowson 1986):

1/2	She dwelt beside the Springs of Dove,
1	Among the untrodden ways,
3	A Maid whom there were none to praise,
4	And very few to love.

3/4	A Maid whom there were very few to love,
3	And none to praise,
1	Dwelt among the untrodden ways
2	Beside the Springs of Dove.

So why then should it matter if the textual design gets changed? If it does not affect referential functioning in Text A, why should it do so here? My answer would be that there *is* no referential functioning in Text B, and that the textual design in effect closes the text off from contextual connection. Thus although both texts are about women, their mode of existence is quite different. The description of Annabella in the obituary corresponds to a factual counterpart. She has independent existence quite apart from the text, and we could, if we chose, check up on the accuracy of the information we are given about her. The text is organised to achieve this referential purpose as effectively as possible. Thus Annabella is named at the start, and information about her is provided to establish her as the topic, and the pronoun *she* then functions anaphorically for subsequent reference in the normal co-operative way. But Lucy has no separate existence outside the poem: she is created in its very design. And so it is that her first appearance is not as a person at all but as a pronoun, a pro-person, and we are kept in the dark about who she is until the last verse, and even then we get only a name. Her identity is traced only in the patterns of negative phrases: *untrodden, none, very few, only one, few, unknown, ceased to be.* The language itself *represents* who she is.

I suggest, then, that the secondary patterns of language in the poem close it off from context and, in so doing, set up conditions for representation rather than reference. It would follow that if you wanted to be referential, you would avoid such patterns. And here one might cite the example of William Whewell, author of a learned work (published in 1819) entitled *Elementary Treatise on Mechanics* (quoted in Butler and Fowler 1971: Text 23). In it Whewell wrote the sentence: *There is no force, however great, can stretch a cord, however fine, into a horizontal line that is accurately straight.* It was pointed out to him that he had thereby produced inadvertent verse, the pattern of which could be made more evident by vertical alignment thus:

> There is no force, however great,
> Can stretch a cord, however fine,
> Into a horizontal line,
> That is accurately straight.

Whewell rightly assumed that the secondary patterning would be a distraction, and restored normal referential conditions by deleting the offending sentence in the next edition of his book. Where such patterning is apparent, the reader will, I argue, read the text as representation rather than reference. So, if we were to modify Text A in only quite minor ways to provide it with such patterning (changing the way the text is disposed on the page and giving metrical regularity to the lines of print), it would, even though its content remains essentially the same, no longer be read as an obituary, but as a poem, and Annabella would accordingly, like Lucy, be closed off within it, and take on a different existence.

> Even from her earliest childhood
> Annabella had a passion
> For the cinema and she
> As a child and playing in
>
> The garden of the family home
> The chicken shed out in the yard
> Became her studio and there,
> Lost in her imagined world,
>
> She acted out the scenes from films
> She had watched, while taking on
> In turn the different roles herself
> of film director, cameraman
> And leading lady all at once.

I would not claim much merit for this as a specimen of verbal art. It may not be adjudged to be a very good poem, but it is read as a poem nevertheless, and so understood quite differently from the way the original Text A is understood. You do not treat it indexically by using it as a set of directions for engaging some existing reality. In the reading of normal conventional texts your attention is directed *away* from the text and you take note of its linguistic features to the extent that they are referentially effective. But in reading a poem, your attention is directed *into* the text, and you seek significance in the very textual pattern. So, to take just one example, in the Annabella obituary, it does not matter in what sequence the noun phrases (*director, cameraman, leading lady*) occur. In the Annabella poem, it does: you read significance into the sequence. And it matters too that the last of them has a line all to itself.

The literary texts we have been concerned with so far take a poetic form, and here, of course, the secondary patterning and its enclosing effect are particularly apparent. But I believe that enclosure is a defining feature of all literature. So I would argue still (as I have argued with stubborn persistence ever since Widdowson 1975) that if you read something as literature, you recognise that it does not have any direct referential connection with your concerns. The text is essentially parenthetical and unpractical, and you are relieved of any obligation to take it seriously. It would not matter if you did not read it at all. Literature is an optional extra. It represents an alternative reality in parallel, which co-exists with that of the everyday world, *corresponds* with it in some degree, but does not *combine* with it. You do not have to act upon it, or incorporate it into the continuity of your social life, or make it coherent with conventional modes of thought. You do not have to worry about whether your interpretation corresponds with the author's communicative intention. You assume that the very existence of the text implies intentionality, some claim to significance, but you are free to assign whatever significance suits you. There is no possibility of checking out whether your understanding matches what the author meant, and no penalties for getting it wrong. In this respect, the literary text is in limbo: there is authorship but no ownership. As the French poet Paul Valery observed: 'There is no true meaning for a text. No author's authority. Whatever he may have wanted to say, he has written what he has written' (quoted in Butler and Fowler 1971: Text 542).

In literature, the text does not mediate between first and second person parties. It floats free in a state of vacant possession for readers to appropriate and inhabit. The reader engages *with* the text but cannot participate in interaction with the writer *through* the text. Literary interpretation, therefore, is not concerned with what the writer meant by the text, but what the text means, or might mean, to the reader. One might indeed hazard the proposition that what defines a literary text is that it is essentially vacuous, in the sense that it creates a vacuum for the reader to fill. Here, for example, is the beginning of Hemingway's story *The Short but Happy Life of Francis Macomber:*

> It was lunch time and they were all sitting under the double green fly of the dining tent pretending that nothing had happened.

Here a scene is textually set, with time and place location linguistically specified. The definite article signals shared contextual knowledge, but there *is* no shared contextual knowledge. The pronoun *they* presupposes that we know who the referents are, but we don't: the specification leads to no identification. They are pretending that nothing had happened, and this presupposes something *had* happened, a previous event to which this text refers, and that we are in the know. But we are not in the know, and there is no previous event. In short, the text creates the illusion of contextual space, a referential vacuum which the reader is drawn into to give imaginative substance to. It is this being drawn into a different contextual reality, being absorbed into a different order of things that is, I think, the essence of aesthetic experience. In this way, readers make the literary text their own.

Let me offer another example. This is R.K. Narayan's novel *The English Teacher*. Krishna, the hero, teaches at the Albert Mission College in the little town of Malgudi. He has a thick notebook in which he intends to write down the poetry he has ambitions to compose. Inspiration flags, however, and he has only ten pages or so to show for his pains. His wife, Susila, mocks him.

'The trouble is I have not enough subjects to write on,' I confessed. She drew herself up and asked: 'Let me see if you can write about me.'

'A beautiful idea,' I cried. 'Let me see you.' I sat up very attentively and looked at her keenly and fixedly like an artist or a photographer viewing his subject. I said: ' Just move a little to your left please. Turn your head right. Look at me straight here. That's right . . . Now I can write about you. Don't drop your lovely eyelashes so much. You make me forget my task. Ah, now, don't grin please. Very good, stay as you are and see how I write now, steady . . .'

Krishna then writes down in his notebook the following lines:

She was a phantom of delight
When first she gleamed upon my sight,
A lovely apparition sent
To be a moment's ornament . . .

and several more, thirty lines in all. His wife is most impressed.

'I never knew you could write so well.'

'It is is a pity that you should have underrated me so long; but now you know better. Keep it up,' I said. 'And if possible don't look at the pages, say roughly between 150 and 200 in the Golden Treasury. Because someone called Wordsworth has written similar poems.'

Of course his wife looks through these pages and discovers that the poem is word for word a copy of one by Wordsworth.

'Aren't you ashamed to copy?'

she asks, and Krishna replies:

'No. Mine is entirely different. He had written about someone entirely different from my subject.'

One reason why Krishna can make this claim is because the pronoun *she* that begins the poem is indeterminate. It refers to no person: it represents a persona, and so he can appropriate it to represent his wife. In conventional terms, third-person pronouns are used as tokens of more complete references. *She* encodes the semantic features of singular and female. That is a linguistic fact. In normal circumstances it can therefore be used to refer to some single female person who does not have to be explicitly identified because the addressee knows who it is. The pronoun is pro somebody. But who is *this* she? There is nobody around for the pronoun to be pro for. There is no indication of identity in the poem. *She* is used like a proper noun, as if referring to some specific and unique identity, a named person: Barbara was a phantom of delight . . . or Sally, or any other *she* who delights you. But the use of the pronoun as a proper noun is most improper, because it presupposes specific reference when there is none. So a referential vacuum is created and readers can fill it with whatever identity they choose, and notice, in passing, that it is not only a matter of investing this pronoun with unique significance as a term of reference. Krishna pretends to be composing the poem from life, as if it were a verbal painting. His wife is sitting for her portrait. 'Let me see if *you* can write about *me*', she says. 'Let *me* see *you*', Krishna says. The poem is thus made specific to this interaction and the pronoun in it therefore acts also as a term of address. Part of Susila's pleasure in the poem is that she takes it not just as *referring* to her but as *addressed* to her.

> *You* were a phantom of delight
> When first *you* gleamed upon my sight . . .

She is a third-person pronoun which encodes singular and female. This is a linguistic fact. In the absence of anybody that it can refer to, the reader can invest it with any singular and female identity. This is a literary effect. So in a way Krishna is right. He makes the poem his own. The text may be Wordsworth's, but it is a poem only because its meaning can be individually invested by other people. In performing the poem, they appropriate it.

The general point, then, is that a literary text is different because it does not mediate between first- and second-person parties as other texts do. This means therefore that Grice's co-operative principle, the normal contract between parties which enables them to converge on agreed meaning, is necessarily in abeyance. However, literature is not normal communication. We assume intentionality, but there is no way of assigning intentions. It makes no sense to ask whether the events are being presented as true, or according to normal expectations of economy or clarity of expression, or as relevant to what has been previously said or to the immediate context. We do not require of literature that it should be true, but only that it should carry conviction; we do not require of it that it should be relevant, but only that it should be consistent and coherent on its own terms and in its own terms. There is no point in trying to trace what is being referred to, because the point of literature is that it does not refer to actual worlds, but represents imaginary ones. Literary texts are not bound by the co-operative conditions of conventional communication because they are disconnected from the social contexts in which those conventions operate. They are of their nature untrue, uninformative, irrelevant and obscure. The maxims of quality, quantity, relation and manner are consistently denied, and consequently literary texts give rise to complex and unresolvable implicatures on a vast scale. It is this which constitutes their aesthetic effect.

Ordinarily, in the normal, non-literary business of communication, the text *does* of course mediate between parties in the general social process, and the co-operative principle *does* come into play. Authors assume first-person responsibility, mindful that they will be held accountable for the text, and that it can be referred back to them by the reader. Readers, for their part, co-operate by indexically interpreting the spirit rather than the letter of the text. To return for a moment to the Annabella obituary, as readers we would normally assume that the writer is not being deliberately untruthful and obscure, so we edit out of our reading any textual feature that might suggest otherwise. Thus the dangling participle referred to earlier is not fixed upon as evidence of obscurity, and we do not scrutinise the semantics of individual words for their truth value. Take the expression 'Even from earliest childhood'. *Earliest* childhood? From the moment of birth? When mewling and puking in her nurses arms? In her pram? The fact is that we relate what is said in the first sentence of the text to what is said in the second and realise that, whatever he may have actually *said*, what the writer *meant* was not the earliest period of childhood, but the one at which children are capable of playing on their own in a garden. We take this as read. We do not accuse the writer of falsehood.

But critical linguists do not take such things as read. They operate by denying the co-operative principle. They take a fix on specific textual features and assign them significance. Here are two typical examples.

Text C

Quarry load-shedding problem

> The grammatical form in which the headline is cast is that of nominalization: a process is expressed as a noun, as if it were an entity. One effect of this grammatical form is that crucial aspects of the process are left unspecified: in particular we don't know who or what is shedding loads or causing loads to be shed – causality is unspecified. (Fairclough 1989: 51)

What is left unspecified is crucial, according to Fairclough, because it 'avoids attributing any responsibility'. But significance is here assigned to the grammatical device of nominalisation per se in disregard of the fact that the use of this form is a matter of standard format, a convention for newspaper headlines, motivated by considerations of space and so on. It serves the same practical function, therefore, as the vertical alignment of text in columns, as in the Annabella obituary (and it is indeed this alignment which commonly requires headlines to be so compacted). If one is significant, then by the same token presumably the other ought to be so as well. No significance would normally be attached to either. Leaving all this aside, however, it should also be noted that although it is a semantic fact that nominalisation leaves aspects of the process unspecified, it does not follow at all that its pragmatic *effect* is necessarily to conceal such specification. Effect is a matter of reader response, and although we might not know who or what is doing the shedding, the readers of *The Lancaster Guardian* (from which the headline was taken) probably do, in which case there is no concealment. There is also some textual evidence that they do know, for in the body of the text reference is made to the fact that the load-shedding lorries are '*still* causing problems'. This text, therefore, has contextual and/or intertextual connections: it apparently refers to something already familiar to the community, and/or something already mentioned in the newspaper, and if this is so, then there would seem to be no reason to read an ulterior motive into its use here. Nominalisation is, after all, routinely used as a cohesive device, as is pronominalisation, in the interests of communicative economy: it serves not to establish reference but to maintain it, anaphorically, through second mention. Also, its use is essentially co-operative since, without it, texts would be clogged up with unnecessary information, and so its use for this purpose is considerate of the second-person reader. In short, referential *avoidance* is not the same as referential *evasion*.

Text D

> The black township of Soweto, which has been simmering with unrest since the riots on June 16 and the shooting of 174 Africans erupted again today.

> Note, too, that the emotions of individuals and the actions they give rise to are transferred onto the place where they live. It is the 'township' that has been simmering and that now erupts, rather than the Sowetans experiencing anger and deciding to march. (Lee 1992: 93)

The suggestion here is that to predicate the verb *simmer* of a township is to deflect attention from the fact that it is its inhabitants who are simmering. But this ignores the entirely normal and productive metonymic process whereby a place is routinely taken to refer to people in it: *France declared war . . . Britain claims fishing rights . . . Belgrade denies . . . The White House is worried* and so on. Nobody, presumably, would suggest that in these cases there is any devious attempt to conceal the human factor. It is also worth noting that on corpus evidence there is nothing particularly unusual about the collocation of the word *township* with *unrest* and *violence*. It would appear that, as with the other nominalisation we have considered, the expression *township unrest* would generally serve quite normally and co-operatively as a device for referential avoidance (not evasion) in the interests of economical topic continuity.

These are just two examples, but they are typical of much CDA work. The procedure is to fix on some particular linguistic feature, grammatical or lexical, and assign it ideological significance without regard to how it might be understood in the normal indexical process of reading. Indeed the analysis is designed to counteract this normality: critical analysts take up a deliberately non-co-operative position on the grounds that to co-operate is to collaborate in the hegemonic imposition of ideological values. Thus, the whole purpose of critical analysis of this kind[2] is to isolate the text from the contextual conditions that would normally be associated with it. In other words, it treats texts (or, more usually, text fragments – see Stubbs 1996: 129) as if they were literary.

The point about literary texts, as I have indicated earlier, is that they are *designed* to be contextually detached, so that, free of the constraints of co-operation, readers are licensed to focus selectively on whatever textual features they might fancy, and infer significance from them. Hence, of their very nature, literary texts will give rise to divergent interpretations, each a function of a particular textual fix. That is what is distinctive about literature: that is what it is *for*, but other uses of language are based on the assumption that co-operation is in place. The basic contradiction in CDA is that it detaches the text at the receiving end, by denying the normal process of co-operative reading, but keeps it firmly attached at the producing end by assuming it to be informed by ideological intent.

The fact is that textual data will always yield uncertain evidence. This is something that literary texts exploit, and conventional texts have to counter. Either way, the uncertainty can only be resolved by adopting a particular second-person position, and so it is that a quest for what the author intended by the text will always lead you back to your own interpretation. Your findings will effectively be inventions, and the further you need to quest, the more you will invent. This seems clear from the two examples I have considered here. The analysis is bent on uncovering what is going on behind the textual scenes and pays selective attention to particular details: a word here, a grammatical form there. There is no consideration of how these features act upon each other in the text, or upon contextual conditions outside it or, in general, how the text is actually discoursally processed. There appears to be no principled theoretical motivation for picking on particular features. So on what basis are they selected? The only basis, as far as I can see, is the analyst's own second-person position as interpreter. Critical analysts may claim that they are assigning significance on behalf of other readers, but they can only do so by imposing their own position in disregard of the response of readers for whom the text was designed. They exploit the text for their own ideological purposes. In a word, they colonise it.

So what, in effect, critical linguists do is to read themselves into texts, just as Krishna reads himself into Wordsworth's poem. The crucial difference, of course, is that Krishna does not claim special validity for his reading as revealing the real significance of the poem, which other readers have failed to notice. Of course, if he were a literary critic, and not just an English teacher, he might be tempted to do so, for literary critics, like critical linguists, have a way of claiming privileged status for their partial interpretations, similarly based on a selective attention to text, and, as Fowler points out, using a limited toolkit to boot. It was, in fact, the purpose of Widdowson (1975) to demonstrate how, in a stylistics approach to literature, such partial interpretations might be referred to more specific linguistic evidence. This, however, was not in order to close down on interpretation and confirm any particular reading as 'correct', as recovering the meaning that was 'really' there, embedded in the text; on the contrary, my purpose was to show how reference to textual patterns revealed how the diversity of literary effects was necessarily a function of the essential indeterminacy of language. This is what, to my mind, made it critical. It is an odd irony that critical discourse analysis is the name that is now given to the use of linguistic insights (the better toolkit) for the assertion of the same kind of privileged partiality of interpretation that is characteristic of the kind of literary criticism that I was seeking to counteract with my stylistics.

I believe that literary criticism and critical linguistics depend, for their validity as areas of inquiry, on recognising the nature of the texts they are dealing with and why they give rise to variable interpretation. Both are, to my mind, centrally concerned with how meanings are read into texts. What distinguishes the two activities is the *kind* of interpretative conditions that apply. As I suggested earlier, if people give the name 'literature' to a certain kind of writing, then they will read it in a particular way, and this, I have proposed, essentially involves recognising that the text is contextually disconnected and so the co-operative principle is in abeyance. So, whereas both activities must be centrally concerned with how meaning is variously derived from text by a process of pragmatic inference, critical linguistics has to show how this is done when the co-operative principle is in place, literary criticism when it is not.

Notes

1. It is not only appropriate for my argument to begin with reference to this book, it is also appropriate to the occasion: for in writing this chapter I replay the past and, in a way, return a favour. Twenty-five years ago, when Chris Candlin and I were both starting to make our way in the academic world, I submitted (with some trepidation) a manuscript to him for inclusion in the series he was editing. He accepted it, and thus this, my first book, was published.

2. Of this kind: an important proviso. I would not want to say that *all* critical analysis as currently practised is textually fixated in this way, nor that many of its practitioners are unaware of the limitations of an analysis that is. It might also be objected that in taking these particular comments out of context and subjecting them to critical appraisal, I am falling into the same trap of partial interpretation based on fragmentary evidence. There is the difference, however, that I am considering not the covert significance of textual features, but claims that are explicitly made; and the two examples I discuss here are not isolated instances but are representative of a very general tendency. For a discussion of other examples, see Widdowson (1996, 1998) and for other criticism along similar lines of this kind of analysis, see Hammersley (1996), Stubbs (1997) and O'Halloran (1999).

References

Brumfit, C.J. and R. Carter (eds) (1986) *Literature and Language Teaching*. Oxford: Oxford University Press.

Butler, Christopher and Alastair Fowler (eds) (1971) *Topics in Criticism*. London: Longman.

Caldas-Coulthard, Carmen and Malcolm Coulthard (eds) (1996) *Texts and Practices*. London: Routledge.

Carter, R. and P. Simpson (eds) (1989) *Language, Discourse and Literature*. London: Unwin Hyman.

Cox, C.B. and A.E. Dyson (eds) (1963) *Modern Poetry. Studies in Practical Criticism*. London: Edward Arnold.

Cox, C.B. and A.E. Dyson (eds) (1965) *The Practical Criticism of Poetry*. London: Edward Arnold.

Eagleton, Terry (1983) *Literary Theory: An Introduction*. Oxford: Basil Blackwell.

Fairclough, Norman (1989) *Language and Power*. London: Longman.

Fowler, R. (1986) *Linguistic Criticism*. Oxford: Oxford University Press.

Fowler, R. (1996) 'On critical linguistics'. In Caldas-Coulthard and Coulthard (eds), 3–14.

Grice, H.P. (1975) 'Logic and conversation'. In Cole, P. and J.L. Morgan (eds) *Syntax and Semantics 3: Speech Acts*. New York: Academic Press, 113–127.

Hammersley, M. (1996) 'On the Foundations of Critical Discourse Analysis'. *Language and Communication* 17(3), 237–248.

Lee, D. (1992) *Competing Discourses: Perspective and Ideology in Language*. London: Longman.

O'Halloran, K. (1999) Draft chapters, PhD thesis. University of London.

Stubbs, Michael (1996) *Text and Corpus Analysis*. Oxford: Basil Blackwell.

Stubbs, Michael (1997) 'Whorf's children: critical comments on critical discourse analysis.' In Ryan, Ann and Alison Wray (eds) *Evolving Models of Language. British Studies in Applied Linguistics*, 12. Clevedon: BAAL/Multilingual Matters.

Widdowson, H.G. (1975) *Stylistics and the Teaching of Literature*. London: Longman.

Widdowson, H.G. (1986) 'The untrodden ways'. In Brumfit and Carter (eds), 133–139.

Widdowson, H.G. (1996) 'Reply to Fairclough. Discourse and interpretation: conjectures and refutations'. *Language and Literature* 5(1), 57–69.

Widdowson, H.G. (1998) Review article: 'The theory and practice of critical discourse analysis'. *Applied Linguistics* 19(1), 136–151.

Chapter 10

Dialogue in the public sphere

Norman Fairclough

In a special issue of the journal *Marxism Today*, devoted to an assessment of the Labour Government (the journal closed down in 1991, but reappeared for this one-off issue in the autumn of 1998), one point of contention was whether New Labour has silenced or stimulated debate. Stuart Hall (Hall 1998: 13) argues that:

> Great Debates are announced which do not actually take place. Instead . . . we have a massive public relations and spinning exercise, and policy forums to speak over the heads of the much-abused 'experts and critics', directly to selectively chosen members of the Great British Public . . . . When in difficulties, the party faithful . . . are summoned to hear the message, not to state their views . . . . A terrifying and obsequious uniformity of view has settled over the political scene, compounded by a powerful centralisation of political authority.

An example of the 'public relations and spinning exercises' to which Hall is referring was an article by Tony Blair headlined 'It really is the end of the something for nothing days' which appeared in the *Daily Mail* on the day on which the Government's Welfare Reform Bill was published – which can be seen as part of an attempt to pre-empt and manage media coverage of the Bill.

But according to Geoff Mulgan (former Director of the Demos think-tank, now a member of the Prime Minister's Policy Unit):

> the debate about social policy has probably never been livelier . . . led by practical women and men and by intellectuals who are able to combine critique, vision and practical policy . . . Few have fallen for the idea that the only choices are co-option or opposition. Instead . . . the propagators of ideas have remained critical and independent, while also being engaged. Reading the marxists, by contrast, you sense the cloying atmosphere of the seminar room. (Mulgan 1998: 16)

Those who are disparagingly lumped together as the (lower-case) 'marxists' presumably include Hall himself and Eric Hobsbawm, also a contributor to the issue. Mulgan goes on to argue that one reason why *Marxism Today* closed was 'because critique was no longer enough . . . . It was no longer enough for arguments to be interesting or eloquent; they also had to be realistic and practical.'

So who is right, Mulgan or Hall? Of course Mulgan is right that there is debate within and around the 'new' Labour Government, but the things at issue are: How open is that debate?, Who can contribute and on what range of issues?, What can be questioned?, Who gets access to spaces where they are likely to be listened to? In more general terms, would one recognise it as democratic dialogue in a substantive sense? One might even read Mulgan's claims as helping to make Hall's point: if contributors are expected to be 'engaged' and 'practical' and arguments are to be 'realistic' and 'practical', those conditions imply some sort of policing of what counts as a contribution to the debate.

Despite its claim to constitute a 'Third Way', there are those (like the critics in *Marxism Today*) who see New Labour as, at bottom, a part of the constitution of new forms of governance and politics which accord with neo-liberalism, based upon the assumption that the neo-liberal form of the global economy is an immovable fact of life rather than (in a recent formulation – Bourdieu 1998a, 1998b) a rational utopia for finance capital which the latter is trying to impose upon reality and make real. Obstacles to its realisation – especially collective institutions with the capacity to resist, notably nation-states but also, for instance, trade unions – are according to Bourdieu relentlessly dismantled or disabled. In the process, the existing structures and forms of democracy are being destroyed and not being effectively replaced – for instance, national parliaments and parties are losing power and legitimacy without effective supranational replacements, e.g. within the EU. Habermas (1998) suggests a process in which politics is becoming increasingly subservient to economics.

For these writers and others (e.g. Benhabib 1996) there is a pressing need to reconstruct democracy, perhaps on an international (e.g. European Union) scale. They all link the debasement of democracy to the debasement of the public sphere (Arendt 1958; Habermas 1989, 1996), and see the reconstruction of democracy as hinging upon the reconstruction of the public sphere and civil society. I have argued elsewhere (Fairclough, 1999) that the problem and crisis of the public sphere is substantively a problem and crisis of discourse, a problem and crisis of dialogue: a matter of the absence of spaces for and forms of democratic dialogue in which people can address together matters of common social and political concern, outside the structures of the state (and of the market), and in ways which can shape the formulation and implementation of policy.

This raises the question of how those of us who are involved in critical discourse analysis should see the business of critique. Do we not need a critique which is, in Jameson's terms, not just ideological but also utopian (Jameson 1981) – in this case, both a negative critique of actual forms of dialogue, and a positive critique which seeks within them hitherto un- or under-realized potentials for democratic dialogue? *Pace* Mulgan, good critique in the Marxist and 'critical theory' traditions has never been just negative, it has also been oriented to seeing and fighting for achievable alternatives

171

– whereas the Thatcherite slogan 'there is no alternative' generally proves enticing for governments.

1 Governance as orders of discourse

To approach these issues, I want to suggest a discourse view of governance. The concept of 'governance' is increasingly used in political and sociological analysis (Giddens 1998) to refer in general terms to the governing of social organisations and institutions, not just the Government. This accords with a tendency of (national) government to be enacted through networks or 'partnerships' (in New Labour terminology) between the Government itself, business, voluntary organisations, and so forth (Jessop 1999).

A particular regime of governance is a particular configuration of social practices, one moment of which is an order of discourse – so a regime of governance is in part an order of discourse, that is, a particular configuration of genres, discourses and styles. On the dialectical view of social practices assumed here, and in particular the dialectic of discourse see Chouliaraki and Fairclough (1999) and Harvey (1996). Any such order of discourse can be characterised in terms of what is included, how it is articulated together, and what is excluded. This includes the crucial question of who can do what – or, more exactly, who can (or cannot) say (write, etc.) what to whom when, where, and how. One question, for instance, we can ask of a regime of governance is what it includes and what it excludes in the way of dialogue – i.e. how dialogically oriented and dialogically open it is.

Regimes of governance are more or less intrusive bids to regulate politics and political discourse, but that does not mean that governance and politics are one and the same thing (Dillon 1998; Ranciere, forthcoming). Indeed, an important issue is what space regimes of governance give for politics – one regulatory effect of regimes of governance is to depoliticise, to squeeze out the political (Beck 1994; Touraine 1997). I view politics as the domain of struggles amongst groups of people over substantive aspects of social life, including, centrally, struggles over the distribution of social 'goods' in the widest sense. A particular politics too can be envisaged as a configuration of social practices, one moment of which is an order of discourse. As an order of discourse, what characterises politics is disagreement, dissent and polemic (Dillon 1998; Ranciere, forthcoming), as well as transcendence of disagreement in alliances. The orders of discourse of governance and politics are in tension. While regimes of governance tend to exclude, marginalise or suppress disagreement, politics subjects the orders of discourse of regimes of governance to its own regime of disagreement – it opens them up to scrutiny, and exposes their exclusions and suppressions.

I referred to regimes of governance above as 'networks of practices'. A particular regime of governance is a particular networking of the practices of government in the narrow sense (legislative, executive, administrative) with, for instance, the media, business, voluntary work and politics. There are both 'external' and 'internal' aspects of networking: the 'external' relations between, for example, the field of governance and the field of politics shape the 'internal' constitution of the field of governance. Politics comes to be selectively and, as I am suggesting, reductively internalised within governance, as 'governmental politics', through a process of recontextualisation (Bernstein 1990, 1996). The political field as such may in this process be relatively enhanced or relatively marginalised, brought into a productive synthesis with governance or cut off from it. In the case of New Labour I am suggesting that governmental politics is impoverished and the political field is marginalised. At the same time, it is partly the political positions and policies taken up by New Labour that favour this regime of governance – for instance, their commitment to 'one nation' politics.

I envisage an order of discourse as a configuration of genres, discourses, and styles. Any social practice is a practice of production; it produces social life by applying certain means of production to certain material within certain social relations (Althusser and Balibar 1970; Mouzelis 1990). There is always a discourse moment within production, though its relative salience is variable. I see genres as discoursal means of production, which entails also that they are discoursal means of interaction. If a regime of governance is a configuration of social practices as I have suggested, that partly means that it is a configuration of genres, and discourse analytical research on genre is part of researching how it produces social life. Any social practice can further be characterised in terms of how it recontextualises (represents, incorporates and so transforms) other social practices (Bernstein 1990, 1996). I see different discourses (using 'discourse' now as a count noun) as different ways of recontextualising other social practices. To summarise the distinction between genres and discourses in rather different terms, genres are to do with the regulation of social interaction, discourses are to do with the classification and categorisation of the world (Bernstein 1990, 1996) – the discourse moment of any social practice always simultaneously figures in both. Social practices set up positions for social subjects (Bhaskar 1986), but these positions are variously occupied and produce various 'performances' depending on the social membership (social class, gender, etc.) and the social and individual life-histories of those who occupy them. In so far as these differences are discoursal, they are different 'styles'.

2 New Labour

The British Labour Party has responded to a string of defeats from the late 1970s to the early 1990s with a radical rethinking of its political positions and commitments, which has led it to a whole-hearted acceptance of the new global economy in its neo-liberal form, and a conception of the task of social democratic government not as to intervene to change or even modestly to inflect capitalism, but rather to equip the country and its people to compete successfully in the global economy (Ellison 1997; Hobsbawm 1998; Hall 1998). The stance of New Labour towards the traditional Labour concerns with inequality and poverty is to turn away from policies of redistribution and protective welfare towards policies oriented to liberty and equality of opportunity more than equality of outcomes, and based on a balance between rights and responsibilities – government should provide the educational and other forms of support to equip people to work and be independent of welfare; people have a responsibility in return to take the opportunities that arise and look out for themselves.

The new politics of the 'Third Way' claims to be an inclusive politics which transcends old divisions – it is characterized in terms of a mixture of New Right and Social Democratic discourse (see below). This is a 'one nation' politics, a politics for national success which incorporates all sections of the society. Unlike Thatcherism, there are no enemies. It has no time for fundamental differences of interest or inequalities, or for the redistribution of wealth needed to deal with them. It has no time for questions about power, domination or exploitation – there is no analysis (still less critique) of capitalism. There is a commitment to an inclusive society, to strong communities (ranging from national to local) based upon shared values, and a commitment to strengthening civil society and the family. The Government sees itself as a corporation providing services for customers ranging from the richest to the poorest (Barnett 1998) – even producing 'annual reports' (Blair 1998c). It sees governing as a 'partnership' between the Government and business on the one hand, and a revitalised civil society and voluntary organisations on the other. Hundreds of 'task forces' and reviews have been set up based on such 'partnerships', though certain sections of society are over-represented (especially business) while others (e.g. trade unions, women, black people) are under-represented (Platt 1998).

Political divisions are ascribed to the 'outmoded' ideological conflicts of the past, a stance which is facilitated by the size of the Government majority, the ineffectiveness of the Conservative opposition (which hitherto could largely be ignored), and the partial incorporation of the Liberal Democrats into the New Labour project (tied to an apparent aspiration towards unification within a restructured centre and centre-left on the part of some New Labour politicians, including Tony Blair). While there is of course debate, disagreement over basic aspects of New Labour policy and strategy is repressed in the sort of ways to which Hall refers. Government manages debate to an unprecedented extent, through public relations and media spin, as Hall says, but also through 'experiments in ("deliberative") democracy' which include use of focus groups and citizens' juries – what one might see as both a recognition of a crisis in the legitimacy of the political system and system of governance and the need for people to be involved, and a determination to manage and control the forms of their involvement through creating a simulated (and government-stimulated) public sphere.

New Labour has gone for a regime of governance which depoliticises, tends to squeeze out politics, and therefore tends to squeeze out democratic dialogue. This is not its particular achievement, it reflects rather a form of centre-left response to neo-liberalism which is evident elsewhere. Indeed, the main model for New Labour has been the Clinton Government in the USA. I want now to look at the order of discourse of the New Labour regime of governance in order to show in more detail how dialogue is squeezed out.

3   The discourse of New Labour

Analysis of the discourse of New Labour can proceed according to the distinctions drawn above. First, there is the question of the genres of this regime of governance; second, there is the question of the discourses through which other social practices are recontextualised in this regime of governance; third, there is the question of the styles in which governance is 'performed', including the question of the highly effective style of Tony Blair. All three are of relevance to the question of how dialogue is squeezed out in this regime of governance, but I shall limit myself to some necessarily partial comments on the first two. Just a note on the third: unlike Thatcher, Blair avoids polemic and the construction of enemies in his speeches, and is polite rather than gladiatorial in interviews – he has developed a style which accords with New Labour's consensus politics, but also excludes substantive dialogue.

4   Discourses

Fundamental political differences are represented as outdated in the discourse of New Labour, the 'old ideological struggles' which 'we cannot afford', 'tribal positions' which we have to give up (Blair 1998b). The 'Third Way' is represented in terms of a combination of Social Democratic and New Right discourses – for instance, one widely used formulation is 'enterprise with fairness', which combines the New Right commitment to 'enterprise' (the project of an 'enterprise culture' was a Thatcherite project, see Keat and Abercrombie 1991) with a covert rewriting of the social democratic discourse of the 'old left' – the aim of 'equality' is rewritten in this discourse as the more nebulous aim of 'fairness'. Fuller formulations of the 'Third Way' accentuate in various ways its reconciliation of what have been taken to be political opposites, for instance through the use of stressed *and* in the following example, which comes from a Fabian Society pamphlet by Blair on the 'Third Way' (Blair 1998a):

> In New Labour's first year of government we have started to put the Third Way into practice. Cutting corporation tax to help business *and* introducing a minimum wage to help the lowest paid. Financial independence for the Bank of England *and*

the biggest ever programme to tackle structural unemployment. New investment and reforms in our schools to give young people the skills they need *and* cracking down hard on juvenile crime to create secure communities. Reforming central government to give it greater strategic capacity *and* devolving power to bring it closer to the people. Significant extra resources into priority areas such as health and education *and* tough and prudent limits on overall government spending. Investment *and* reform in the public sector. A key player in the EU *and* hostile to unnecessary centralisation.

The Third Way as a discourse is inseparable from the rhetoric of the Third Way – a rhetoric of surprise, a presupposition of 'old' expectations plus a denial of those expectations. The pervasive meaning is 'not only but also', realised in a variety of linguistic expressions (e.g. stressed 'and', 'as well as', 'yet', and 'not only . . . but also' itself).

The message that fundamental political oppositions can be reconciled entails a marginalisation of the political domain and of substantive political dialogue. It also goes along with an inclusive construction of nation and national identity which seeks consensus and in so doing obfuscates the differences from which politics and dialogue arise. This is evident in the construction of an inclusive 'we'. One point is that equivalences are routinely set up between 'we', 'Britain', 'the people', and so forth, as, for example, in the following opening sentence from a speech by Tony Blair (1998b) to the Confederation of British Industry: 'I believe in this country, in its people and our capacity to renew Britain for the age in which we live.' 'This country', '(its) people', 'we' ('our') and 'Britain' are set up as equivalent in the sense that they substitute for each other rather like pronouns substitute for nouns. An indication of this is that we can rewrite the sentence substituting one of them for another without really changing the meaning – e.g. 'I believe in Britain, and in our people and their capacity to renew the country' . . . or 'I believe in us, in the people of Britain and Britain's capacity to renew this country' . . . .

There is often, however, a vagueness about who exactly 'inclusive we' includes. For instance, in the same speech, where 'we' is equated with 'Britain': 'If Britain is to succeed in the new world marketplace, it has no future as a low-skill, low-quality, low-value, low-wage economy. To be competitive, we have to aim high.' Who is the 'we' here? Perhaps those involved in the British economy? But then isn't it only those who control the economy, in conjunction with those who control the state, who set 'aims'? Yet such a narrow interpretation of the 'we' is at odds with: 'This is a challenge for all of us. Taking responsibility to improve our country's performance. Tackling the gap in our performance by doing something ourselves to close it.' But does the 'we' really include 'all of us' – what about the young, the sick, the retired, the unemployed? The apparent inclusiveness of the language is at the expense of a vagueness which obfuscates difference.

Inclusive 'we' as a device for avoiding division leads in some cases to incoherence. The following extract from the speech is a case in point:

Private sector income growth gives serious cause for concern. It would be the worst of short-termism now to pay ourselves more today at the cost of higher interest rates, fewer jobs . . . . It is really up to us: the greater the responsibility, the bigger the reward. We have learnt that lesson so often in the past. We cannot afford to learn it again.

Who is the 'we' here? It is an inclusive 'we', yet it is clearly not the British people as a whole who are 'paying themselves more'. The reference is specifically to the private sector. One division which 'we' covers over here is between private sector and public sector – the income gap between people who work in the private sector and people who work in the public sector is growing under New Labour. But there is also another division which 'we' covers over, though it is hinted at in the wording 'pay ourselves'. It is only really those in senior management who control pay who 'pay themselves'. The other division is between senior managers and the rest – that income gap is also growing under New Labour. But Blair is after all addressing the Confederation of British Industry, i.e. senior managers; they will no doubt pick up the hint without Blair needing to foreground the division for his wider audience. So, we might say that the inclusive language in this case causes obfuscation, it covers over social relations and divisions – except that the incoherence of 'pay ourselves more' leaves a trace of this obfuscation. It is not a trace which someone listening to the speech, or listening to or reading reports about it, will necessarily notice, but it is the sort of trace which some people will notice (maybe those whose pay is decreasing or not increasing, as well as Blair's audience in the CBI), and which may become more widely noticeable and noticed in a changing political climate. Of course, the contrast between the inclusive discourse and the exclusive club Blair is addressing on this occasion enhances its noticeability! What I am suggesting then is that an inclusive political discourse is difficult to sustain without incoherences, and that those incoherences may, in certain circumstances, expose it to risk.

There are also noticeable inconsistencies in inclusiveness. Contrast 'pay ourselves more' with 'We must end the deepening culture of a group of people, especially our youth, left out of the mainstream of society'. In the former, a particular section of the population is universalized into – made equivalent to – 'we'; in the latter by contrast a section of the population is particularized out of the 'we' to create a difference, an opposition between 'we' and 'our youth', all of us and part of us (again raising the question of who the 'we' really is). It is possible through a rewording to effect a slippage from particular to universal for excluded young people analogous to the slippage effected in the speech for (senior managers in) the private sector (e.g. 'We must end the deepening culture of a group of people, especially youth, finding ourselves left out of mainstream society'), but this does not sound like the discourse of New Labour.

There is also a constant ambivalence and slippage between exclusive and inclusive 'we' – the pronoun can be taken as refering to the Government or to Britain (or the British). For instance: 'Third, we intend to make Britain the best educated and skilled nation in the western world . . . This is an aim we can achieve, if we make it a central national purpose to do it.' The first 'we' is the Government – the reference is to what the Government intends, but the second and third uses of 'we' are ambivalent – they can be taken either exclusively or inclusively. This ambivalence is politically advantageous for a government which wants to represent itself as speaking for the whole nation (though not only for New Labour – playing on the ambivalence of 'we' is commonplace in politics).

New Labour discourse tends to be univocal, which is another way in which it is inimical to dialogue. I shall refer specifically to the process of reforming the welfare state which New Labour has embarked upon, and especially the Government's Green Paper on welfare reform, a consultation document published in March 1998 (I use the same example in discussing genre below). What I want to focus on is how the Green Paper represents what one might call the 'world of welfare' – the activities and processes which constitute the welfare system, including the process of welfare reform itself. The representation is univocal, and this univocality is textually manifest in the rarity of represented speech and thought in the document. There are various positions and perspectives within the world of welfare, and correspondingly various views on the process of welfare reform, but the representation of the world of welfare reduces its population virtually down to two major participants: the Government, and the claimants. Welfare staff feature very little, claimants' organisations and campaign groups hardly at all, and welfare professionals and experts never. One might say that an obvious opportunity for dialogue, which would seem to accord with the declared objectives of this consultation document, has been forgone – the opportunity to give voice to a range of perspectives on welfare and welfare reform.

It is instructive, however, to look at those rare points in the document where reported speech and thought do occur. The following is a paragraph from the third chapter, 'The importance of work':

> Lone parent organisations, employers and lone parents themselves have all welcomed this New Deal, and the staff responsible for delivering the service have been particularly enthusiastic. The staff have welcomed the opportunity to become involved in providing practical help and advice. The first phase of this New Deal has aroused considerable interest: lone parents in other parts of the country are asking if they can join in.

There is also a scatter of other examples of reported thought elsewhere in the chapter, where claimants are subjects of mental process verbs (e.g. 'the vast majority of single parents want to work', 'some people feel forced to give up their job'). A variable in reported speech is whether the practice that is recontextualised is explicitly identified. Here it is not. In fact the practice recontextualised is market research (opinion polls, surveys, perhaps focus groups) – the only practice reported in terms of what claimants (and staff) say (think). Notice, in particular, the way in which thought is reported, e.g. 'the vast majority of single parents want to work': not only is the practice where these 'wants' were expressed unspecified, so also is who expressed them (possible alternative: 'in a poll of single parent opinion, the vast majority of those asked said they wanted to work'). The Government speaks for these people. Part of the classification which divides the Government from claimants is that the latter do not act but do react (verbally, mentally), though both the ways in which they react and how reactions are represented are controlled by Government. One might say that this form of governance includes market research as a technology for legitimising the Government speaking for the public. Apart from these examples, the voices of others (including relevant others such as welfare professionals, claimant groups) are not reported.

5 Genre

A preliminary question with respect to genre is: what does governance as social practice (or rather configuration of social practices) produce? I want to suggest that governance produces social effects by way of producing political effects – it changes social practices, but in order to do so it gathers people around projects for changing social practices, it is oriented to producing a sufficient measure of consent (or acquiescence) to such projects. One way of producing a sufficient measure of consent is by shifting between governance and politics, seeking consent through dialogue in which disagreement can be more or less openly expressed. Although New Labour does represent its regime of governance (and welfare reform in particular) in these terms, this is not how it produces consent. Rather, it manages consent through promotion.

For example, the welfare reform Green Paper did not come out of the blue, it was framed by various other documents, speeches, interviews, press releases and so forth. One aspect of the discoursal moment of a practice of producing social life is its characteristic form of generic chaining – how it chains genres together in particular ways. In the case of the New Labour regime of governance (as in other regimes of governance), for instance, the generic chain is punctuated by press releases (and in some cases news conferences) – no major document or speech comes without an associated press release. What is striking about New Labour is the intensity of management of intertextual chains (Fairclough 1992). In the case of the Green Paper for instance, it was precededed in the early months of 1998 by a series of meetings around the country on the case for welfare reform organised by the Prime Minister, as well as a series of briefing documents, produced by the Department of Social Security, making the case for reforming various aspects of the welfare system, plus various other speeches, interviews, newspaper articles, etc., by key Government members. This intensity of management is itself promotional and inimical to politics and dialogue. It also highlights from a discourse analytical perspective the importance of summaries: a document like the Green Paper is extensively and repeatedly summarised both internally (it begins with a Preface by the Prime Minister which summarises it, then a Summary chapter) and externally (it is summarised in the press release, in media reports, in speeches, in interviews, and so on), and summarising is the process through which media spin is added, as well as the process through which differences within the Government are worked through and negotiated.

The process of welfare reform is, in Bernstein's terms, 'strongly framed' (Bernstein 1990), and the generic chaining is a part of that. So too is the genre of the Green Paper itself. Each of the central chapters (3–10) is structured as follows: a chapter title below which there is coloured box containing one of the eight 'principles' of the proposed welfare reform (e.g. 'Principle 1: *The new welfare state should help and encourage people of working age to work where they are capable of doing so*'). There is then an unheaded introductory section focusing on past and present welfare practices, and the case for reform; a section headed 'Policy Direction' taking up the bulk of the chapter and setting out proposed future welfare practices; and under the heading 'Measures for Success' a short list of criteria against which the success of the proposed reforms will be judged. Each of the chapters tells readers what the case is for welfare reform, but above all what the Government has done, is doing and intends or aims to do in the way of welfare reform. In these accounts, welfare reform is represented as a managerial process of problem-solving, finding solutions to obstacles in the way of the objectives formulated in the eight 'principles', with the problem-solver represented as virtually exclusively the Government itself.

Representing welfare reform as managerial problem-solving, and structuring these central chapters of the document in terms of problem-solving, is part of what makes the genre promotional: the Government's policies are sold as merely technical solutions to an agreed problem. The grammatical mood is declarative: although in the nature of things there are many unanswered questions at this consultative stage in the reform process, no questions are asked. (The potential for questions is indicated by their marginal presence at the end of the Summary chapter where the reform process is constructed as debate: 'it is also vital that reform is informed by full debate on the proposed framework. We are consulting widely on the content of this Green Paper and we want your views. For instance, how can we best deliver on our guiding principles? Are there ways in which the policy direction can be improved? Are our tracking measurements for success right?') Statements are categorical assertions – again, although in the nature of things there are uncertainties about what has happened or what is the case and hesitations about what should be done, there are no 'maybes' here. The Government is constructed as in full and solitary control. The simulation of certainty and being in control are part of the representation of welfare reform as problem-solving and part of the rhetoric of promotion.

Moreover, there is a slippage between the process of consultation over proposed welfare reform and the process of implementation, between consultation document, planning document, and publicity document. This is evident in the use of boxes in the chapters (there is an example below). These boxes contain bullet points or, in one case, numbered points, with or without headings. This device is widely used in planning documents. The clearest example of this sort of use is the 'Success Measures': in the chapter on 'The importance of work' (chapter 3) there is no discussion of 'success measures' as part of welfare reform, no statement of the Government's view that all policies should come with criteria for evaluating their sucess, just a raw list of four measures (the first is: 'A reduction in the proportion of working age people living in workless households'), as if this were itself a procedural document in the implementation of welfare reforms (which have not yet been agreed). Such boxes are also widely used in publicity. The document oscillates not only between consulting about the proposed welfare reform and implementing it, but also between these two and the subsequent stage of publicising particular schemes to potential claimants. There is a slippage in the scheduling of welfare reform, so to speak: treating the Government's desired outcomes as if they were already agreed policies is rather an effective way of promoting them.

These boxes figure as a structuring device: they mark and signal to readers careful authorial planning of and tight control over the text and the texturing of the text (I use 'texturing' to draw attention to the process of making texts and so making meanings as part of the process of production – see Fairclough, forthcoming). They are a resource for strong framing, strong unilateral control by the writer (the Government) over the texturing. For instance, the box in paragraph 5 of chapter 3 lists in their sequential order the main sections of the 'Policy Direction' part of the chapter, which takes up 35 of its 40 paragraphs:

5. The government aims to promote work by:
- helping people move from welfare to work through the New Deals and Employment Zones;
- developing flexible personalised services to help people into work;
- lowering the barriers to work for those who can and want to work;
- making work pay, by reforming the tax and benefit system, including a Working Families Tax Credit, reforming National Insurance and income tax, and introducing the national minimum wage; and
- ensuring that responsibilities and rights are fairly matched.

The boxes also figure as a pedagogical device, directing the reader to the main points and the main structures of the projected new world of welfare. These are 'reader-friendly' but also thereby reader-directive features, which construct the social relations of the document as asymmetrical relations not only between the one who tells and the one who is told but also more

181

specifically between teacher and learner, with strong classification (insulation) between the two subject positions (Bernstein 1990). The many section headings work in a similar way.

6 Implications for the analysis of dialogue

I have pointed to ways in which New Labour governance and discourse is inimical to dialogue and, by implication, to politics and democracy. At the beginning of the chapter I suggested that critical discourse analysis needs to be engaged in critique which is both ideological and utopian. With regard to the latter, what makes dialogue democratic? Let me provisionally suggest a set of necessary properties of democratic dialogue:

(a) it is accessible to anyone, and those who participate have equal rights to speak and obligations to listen;
(b) it is sensitive to difference, it gives rights for differences to be voiced and obligations for them to be listened to and recognised;
(c) it gives space for disgreement, dissent and polemic;
(d) it also gives space for new positions, identities, relationships, alliances, and knowledge to emerge;
(e) it is talk which can lead to action.

The emphasis on equality of access is familiar in the work of Habermas, but Habermas's influential early work on the public sphere is seen as insensitive to difference (Benhabib 1992, 1996; Calhoun 1992). The view of politics I introduced earlier following Ranciere entails seeing disagreement as inherent in democratic dialogue; but politics is not just about disagreeing, it is also about working through disagreements to alliances in which new collective identities are constituted. Finally, talk can be empty words unless it is tied to action (Arendt 1958; d'Entreves 1994).

This implies that the critical analysis of dialogue is not only interactional analysis, 'internal' analysis of dialogical interaction, but also analysis of practices and conjunctures of practices in their discursive aspect, i.e. analysis of orders of discourse. This is a way of picking up both Bourdieu's critique of 'discourse analysis', understood as interactional analysis and no more (Bourdieu 1992), and Ranciere's distinction between enunciation (interaction) and 'accounting' (which points to the concept of order of discourse). Putting it differently, critical discourse analysis is not a mere interactional analysis but an analysis of the dialectical relationship between the social structuring of semiotic variability (the order of discourse) and semiotic interaction, as a facet of the the broader dialectic between structure and action (Chouliaraki and Fairclough, 1999).

More specifically, we need a form of critique which is capable of mapping the relationship between actual interactions and orders of discourse in both ideological and utopian terms, i.e. in terms of both an understanding of how and why interactions fail as democratic dialogue and an understanding of what hitherto un- or under-realised potentials for democratic dialogue can be discerned (often just glimpsed) within them. Chouliaraki and Fairclough (1999) propose a form of discourse critique based upon the 'explanatory critique' developed by Bhaskar (1986), which consists of the following stages:

1. Identification of a language-related problem.
2. Specification of obstacles to its resolution in the conjuncture of practices it is located within (relation analysis).
3. Is the problem in fact functional for the conjuncture? (Does it 'need' it?)
4. Specification of possibilities for its resolution within the conjuncture (dialectical analysis).

Stages 2 and 3 correspond to ideological critique – they show how negative properties of interaction can be referred to the way social life and social relations are structured, how things hold together: they map the interactional instance onto an account of relations within the conjuncture (sense 'relational analysis'). Stage 4 by contrast is 'dialectical analysis' in that it is focused on the gaps, tensions and contradictions in the interaction and its framing conjuncture of practices, on the limits to how things hold together, and the possibilities for something different which are thus revealed (for instance, the difficulty in sustaining an inclusive 'we' which I discussed above). Such gaps, tensions and contradictions are there in the discourse of New Labour, and so therefore are possibilities for something different, but it is beyond the scope of this chapter to go into them (see, however, Fairclough, forthcoming).

References

Althusser, L. and Balibar, E. (1970) *Reading Capital*. London: Verso.

Arendt, H. (1958) *The Human Condition*. University of Chicago Press.

Barnett, A. (1998) All power to the citizens. *Marxism Today*. Special Issue on New Labour.

Beck, U. (1994) The reinvention of politics. In Beck, Giddens and Lash (eds) *Reflexive Modernization*. Oxford: Polity Press.

Benhabib, S. (1992) *Situating the Self*. Oxford: Polity Press.

Benhabib, S. (ed.) (1996) *Democracy and Difference*. Princeton University Press.

Bernstein, B. (1990) *The Structuring of Pedagogic Discourse*. London: Routledge.

Bernstein, B. (1996) *Pedagogy, Symbolic Control and Identity*. London: Taylor & Francis.

Bhaskar, R. (1986) *Scientific Realism and Human Emancipation*. London: Verso.

Blair, Tony (1998a) *The Third Way – New Politics for a New Century*. Fabian Society pamphlet.

Blair, Tony (1998b) Speech at the CBI Annual Dinner 27 May.

Blair, Tony (1998c) Speech at publication of the Government's Annual Report 30 July.

Bourdieu, P. (1992) *Language and Symbolic Power*, London: Polity Press.

Bourdieu, P. (1998a) A reasoned utopia and economic fatalism. *New Left Review* 227, 125–130.

Bourdieu, P. (1998b) L'essence du neo-liberalisme. *Le Monde Diplomatique*, March.

Calhoun, C. (1992) *Habermas and the Public Sphere*. MIT Press.

Chouliaraki, L. and Fairclough, N. (1999) *Discourse in Late Modernity: Renewing Critical Discourse Analysis*. Edinburgh: Edinburgh University Press.

d'Entreves, M. (1994) *The Political Philosophy of Hannah Arendt*. London: Routledge.

Dillon, M. (1998) *The objectification of politics*. Politics Department, Lancaster University.

Ellison, N. (1997) From welfare state to post-welfare society? In B. Brivato and T. Bale (eds) *New Labour in Power*. London: Routledge.

Fairclough, N. (1992) *Discourse and Social Change*. London: Routledge.

Fairclough, N. (1999) Democracy and the public sphere in critical reseach on discourse. In R. Wodak and C. Ludwig (eds) *Challenges in a Changing World*. Vienna: Passagen Verlag.

Fairclough, N. (forthcoming) *The Language of New Labour*. London: Routledge.

Giddens, A. (1998) *The Third Way*. London: Polity Press.

Habermas, J. (1989) (1962) *Structural Transformation of the Public Sphere*. Polity Press.

Habermas, J. (1996) *Between Facts and Norms*. London: Polity Press.

Habermas, J. (1998) There are alternatives. *New Left Review* 231.

Hall, S. (1998) The great moving nowhere show. *Marxism Today*. Special Issue on New Labour.

Harvey, D. (1996) *Justice, Nature and the Geography of Difference*. Oxford: Blackwell.

Hobsbawm, E. (1998) The death of neo-liberalism. *Marxism Today*. Special Issue on New Labour.

Jameson, F. (1981) *The Political Unconscious*. London: Methuen.

Jessop, B. (1999) *Reflections on globalisation and its (il)logic(s)*. Sociology Department, Lancaster University.

Keat, R. and Abercrombie, N. (1991) *Enterprise Culture*. London: Routledge.

Mouzelis, N. (1990) *Post-Marxist Alternatives*. London: Macmillan.

Mulgan, G. (1998) Whinge and a prayer. *Marxism Today*. Special Issue on New Labour.

Platt, B. (1998) Tough on soundbites, tough on the causes of soundbites: New Labour and news management. *Catalyst* pamphlet.

Ranciere, J. (forthcoming) *Disagreement*. London: Verso.

Secretary of State for Social Security and Minister for Welfare Reform (1998) *New Ambitions for Our Country: A New Contract for Welfare*.

Touraine, A. (1997) *What is Democracy?* Westview Press.

Chapter 11

Recontextualization and the transformation of meanings: a critical discourse analysis of decision making in EU meetings about employment policies

Ruth Wodak

1 Introduction: decision making in organizations

1.1 Organizational discourse

Previous analyses of talking have shown the importance of interaction in shaping and constituting organizations (Iedema and Wodak 1999; Boden 1994, 1995; Drew and Heritage, 1992; Drew and Sorjonen 1997; Wodak 1996; Firth 1995; Grant et al. 1998). It is through discursive interaction that meanings are produced and transmitted, that institutional roles are constructed and power relations developed and maintained. The ethnographic analysis of organizations has not been greatly developed in Discourse Analysis so far; most of the work has concentrated on either interviews between insiders and outsiders, or on small sequences of conversation (see Menz 1999b for an overview). In this chapter I present a critical approach to the study of organizations, from 'within', focusing on decision-making processes in terms of 'recontextualization' (Wodak 1999b; Bernstein 1990; Sarangi and Linell 1999) on employment policies in the European Union. We will follow the genesis of a policy paper in a European Union committee from its first stage to the final version.

Decision making constitutes the life of organizations; there is a continuity (intertextuality) from one event to the next, and transformations of written into oral and back again due to different lobbies, beliefs, interests and ideologies. In our analysis this context (and also the macro context of employment policies and globalization) has to be included in order to allow interpretations of the mechanisms of decision making in this particular case. In contrast to classical Conversational Analysis (see Schegloff 1997), we believe that understanding precedes the analysis, and that understanding touches the process and interaction as a whole and not only small sequential structures.

1.2 Decision making in organizations

The German sociologist Niklas Luhmann characterizes organizations primarily in terms of their decisions (Weiss and Wodak 1998; Menz 1999a). He claims that decision processes determine the day-to-day life in organizations, which, he says, are constantly reproduced through decisions: 'Organizations produce decision options which otherwise would not exist. Decisions serve as contexts for decisions' (Luhmann 1997: 830). The European Union is a very complex system with an extremely differentiated structure and 'with increasing complexity of decision making on decisions on decisions, the autopoesis creates conforming structures and develops a growing tendency towards a decision not to decide' (Luhmann 1997: 839). This may sound confusing at first, but what it means is that decisions are postponed, delegated, or shifted to other bodies – organizations may even choose not to take any decision at all, and this also is a decision. This is what happens at many meetings, as we all know only too well. The feeling that yet again 'nothing has been achieved' simply means that there has been a decision not to decide or at best to postpone the decision.

So far, two sociological theoretical approaches have been concerned with the decision-making processes in the European Union: (a) the 'institutional–functional approach' which emphasizes the legal aspect and the legislative procedure and explains decisions on the basis of these formal structures; (b) the 'behavioural–interactionist approach' which focuses on communication as it actually occurs in meetings. Van Schendelen (1996) argues that the functional paradigm concentrates merely on the 'skeleton' of institutions and neglects the actual 'flesh and blood'. In our view, only an approach which combines both aspects will yield satisfying results; a critical sociolinguistic approach has to consider both the structures and the functions of the organization and what is actually happening there in the discursive interactions at different levels of the hierarchy.

Decisions are taken at many times and places in an organization, at meetings, in the corridors, during telephone conversations or on social and informal occasions. It is very difficult to reconstruct individual incidents. However, organizations tend to stage their decision processes, much like a drama, orally at meetings as well as through their protocols, directives and other written bureaucratic genres (Iedema 1994/1996, 1998a). For the insider at least these scenes are comprehensible; but they are hierarchically structured and not everyone has unlimited access to everything – thus status and power are produced and reproduced. The linguist and sociologist Denis Mumby (1988: 68) characterizes the significance of meetings in organizations as follows:

> meetings are perceived as a necessary and pervasive characteristic of organizational life – they are events that people are required to engage in if decisions are to be made and goals to be accomplished. While this is the ostensible rationale for

meetings, they also function as the most important and visible sites of organizational power, and of the reification of organizational hierarchy.

Our current five-year interdisciplinary project explores discourses in supranational institutions of the EU.[1] In this chapter I will chart and reconstruct decision-making processes in the complex, multinational, multilingual organization by showing how a policy paper on employment policy and unemployment intended for the Council of Ministers in Luxembourg in November 1997 was produced in several drafts; i.e. the *genesis* of the paper. Compared to other organizations, the EU is characterized by even greater complexity, because a wide range of frequently conflicting political and ideological positions deriving from different lobbies and interest groups have to be added to the characteristics already mentioned (see below).

The prime objective of our research, however, is to develop discourse-theoretical approaches and assumptions. Although I cannot go into detail in this chapter due to space restrictions, I would like briefly to introduce our definition of discourse and provide a model – the discourse-historical approach – on which this research is based (Wodak and Reisigl 1999). I will then address the reconstruction of decisions by looking at the drafts of the policy paper and charting the 'life of arguments' in their recontextualization, so-called textual chains (Fairclough 1992), from the first proposal through the draft to the final version. This will be preceded by a short discussion of employment policies in the EU and by the role of globalization in the search for new 'European employment policies'.

2 Discourse-theoretical considerations

2.1 Critical Discourse Analysis: the discourse-historical approach[2]

The paradigm of Critical Discourse Analysis (CDA) is taken as the point of departure for our linguistic analysis. CDA is problem oriented and interdisciplinary (Wodak 1996, 1999a, 1999b; Fairclough and Wodak 1997). However, one has to bear in mind that 'interdisciplinary' does not mean a cumulation of eclectically selected approaches, but something entirely new in quality which emerges from integrating various positions, including epistemological ones, thus moving beyond superficial analysis and exploring new dimensions in an entirely innovative way. Looking at socially relevant areas of life, these studies focus on communication embedded in historical and social contexts rather than on the linguistic system as such.

In contrast to traditional quantitative sociolinguistics, which correlates linguistic phenomena with certain social variables (such as age, social class, sex [gender]), the aim of CDA is to show the complex dialectical interplay of language and social practice on many different levels. The complexities of modern societies can only be grasped by a model of multicausal, mutual influences between different groups of persons within a specific society. That is to say: If we take, for example, the politicians as specific and not at all homogeneous groups of elites, then they are best seen both as shapers of specific public opinions and interests and as seismographs that reflect and react to the atmospheric anticipation of changes in public opinion and on the articulation of changing interests of specific social groups and affected parties.

In recent years, the discourse-historical approach (Wodak et al. 1998, 1999; Wodak and Reisigl 1999; van Leeuwen and Wodak 1999) has increasingly been influenced by other schools and subdisciplines.[3] Apart from mainly linguistic subdisciplines, the discourse-historical approach adheres to the sociophilosophical orientation of Critical Theory (see Horkheimer and Adorno 1991[1944]; Benhabib 1992; Honneth 1994; Habermas 1996).

One way of minimizing the risk of critical biasedness, and of avoiding simply politicizing instead of accurately analyzing, is to follow the *principle of triangulation*: one of the most salient distinguishing features of the discourse-historical approach, as compared to most of the approaches already mentioned, is its endeavour to work interdisciplinarily, multi-methodically and on the basis of a variety of different empirical data and background information (see, for example, Wodak 1986, 1996; Mitten and Wodak 1993). Depending on the object of investigation, it attempts to transcend the purely linguistic dimension and to include more or less systematically the historical, political, sociological and/or psychological dimensions in the analysis and interpretation of a specific discursive occasion. A number of different genres, all related to the same problem domain, are investigated simultaneously. In the case of our project, interviews were tape-recorded, written texts analyzed, EMPs followed and observed in their daily organizational life, speeches of commissioners compared with their written statements, and debates in the European parliament investigated.

In examining historical and political topics and texts, the discourse-historical approach addresses the historical dimension of discursive actions in at least two ways. Firstly, it attempts to integrate much available knowledge about the historical sources and the background of the social and political fields in which discursive 'events' are embedded. In our case, the whole development of 'unemployment policies' in the EU was reconstructed. Secondly, it explores the ways in which particular genres of discourse are subject to diachronic change – a topic which has been studied in a number of previous investigations (Wodak et al. 1990, 1994; Matouschek et al. 1995). This is one point where intertextuality and recontextualization have their specific relevance as methodological and theoretical concepts.

In accordance with other approaches devoted to Critical Discourse Analysis, the discourse-historical approach perceives both written and spoken language as a form of social practice (Fairclough and Wodak, 1997; Wodak, 1996; van Dijk 1998). To put it more precisely: 'Discourse' is understood as a complex bundle of simultaneous and sequential interrelated linguistic acts which manifest themselves within and across the social fields of action as thematically interrelated semiotic (oral or written) tokens (i.e. texts), that belong to specific semiotic types (genres). 'Fields of action' (Girnth 1996) may be understood as segments of the respective societal 'reality' which contribute to constituting and shaping the 'frame' of discourse. The spacio-metaphorical distinction among different fields of action can be understood as a distinction among different functions or socially institutionalized aims of discursive practices.

Thus, in the area of political action – the case study with which I am dealing here is, in a wider sense, 'localized' within this area – we distinguish among the functions of legislation, self-presentation, the manufacturing of public-opinion, developing party-internal consent, advertising and vote-getting, governing as well as executing, and controlling as well as expressing (oppositional) dissent (see Figure 11.1).

A 'discourse' about a specific topic can find its starting point within one field of action and proceed through another. Discourses and discourse topics 'spread' to different fields and discourses. They cross between fields, overlap, refer to each other or are in some other way socio-functionally linked with each other. We can illustrate the relationship between fields of action, genres and discourse topics with the example of the area of political action in Figure 11.2.

In this figure, interdiscursivity (e.g. the intersection of discourses A and B) is indicated by the two big overlapping ellipses. Intertextual relationships in general – whether of an explicitly referential kind, a formally or structurally iconic (diagrammatical) kind, or in the form of topical correlations, evocations, allusions or (direct and indirect) quotations, etc. – are represented by dotted double arrows. The assignment of texts to genres is signalled by simple arrows. The topics to which text A refers are indicated by small ellipses. Simple dotted arrows point to the topical intersection of different texts. Finally, the specific intertextual relationship of thematic reference of one text to another is indicated by simple broken arrows.

Through discursive practices, social actors constitute knowledge, situations, social roles as well as identities and interpersonal relations among various interacting social groups. In addition, discursive practices are socially constitutive in a number of ways. First, they play a decisive role in the genesis and production of certain social conditions. This means that discourses may serve to construct collective entities like organizations, nations, ethnicities, etc. Second, they might perpetuate, reproduce or justify a certain social status quo (and organizational identities related to it). Third, they are instrumental in transforming the status quo (in the whole process of decision making). Fourth, discursive practices may have an effect on the dismantling or even destruction of the status quo (in conflicts, see Wodak 1999e). According to these general aims one can distinguish between constructive, perpetuating, transformational and destructive social macro-functions of discourses.

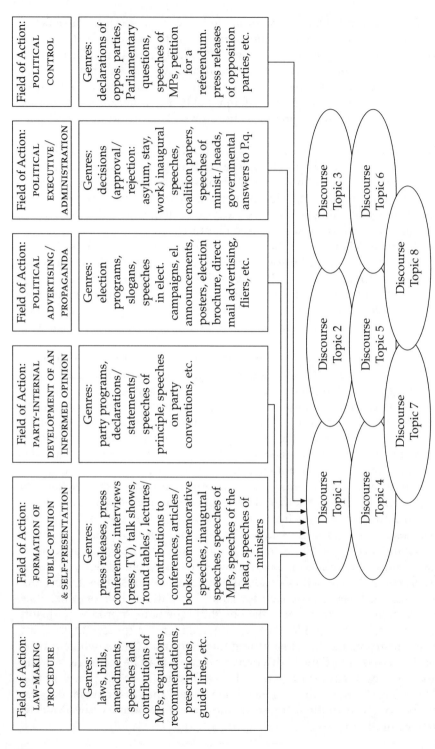

Figure 11.1 Selected Dimensions of Discourse as Social Practice

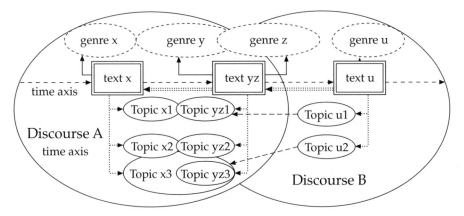

Figure 11.2 Interdiscursive and intertextual relationships between discourses, discourse topics, genres and texts

In order to analyze the genesis of the policy paper, I will make use of the principle of triangulation in the following way: I will analyze different sequences of the drafts within the framework of Functional Grammar (Halliday 1994; Thompson 1996) and talk about the meetings where these drafts were discussed, illustrating with several sequences from the discussions. Some quotes from an interview with the chairperson of the committee will allow for the self-assessment of the committee members themselves.

In the linguistic analysis, two concepts are of particular importance: the distinction between 'theme' and 'rheme' and the information conveyed by 'transitivity' choices. For Halliday, the theme is the given, the starting point for the message or 'the ground from which the clause is taking off' (Halliday 1994: 38), whereas the rheme is the new information introduced in the clause. The theme constitutes the beginning of the clause and is very often coterminous with the subject (see Thompson 1996: 119f). Changes in the structure of theme and rheme can be interpreted by focusing on given and new information – theme is what is understood as presupposed and not questionable, while rheme contains the new information which should be focused upon.

If we also take transitivity into consideration, we turn from the textual to the ideational function because the latter shows how the 'world' is represented in language in a text, and ultimately in the clause: 'from the experiential perspective, language comprises a set of resources for referring to entities in the world and the ways in which those entities act on or relate to each other' (Thompson 1996: 76). These process types illustrate how certain agents act and what kind of semantic constructions are created to relate actions to agents. In our case, this is of great importance: Who are the actors and what do they do? What kind of actions are ascribed to which agents? As will be shown, experts act rationally, whereas the 'European citizens', the non-experts, act irrationally, which is manifested in different verb processes.

2.2 Recontextualization

Intertextuality, a concept which goes back to Bakhtin, connects texts both synchronically and diachronically. Each text, according to David Harvey (1996), is anchored in time and space and relates to texts produced previously, synchronically or subsequently. Here the concept of recontextualization, which was developed by Basil Bernstein (1990: see Mehan 1993; Iedema 1997; Sarangi 1998; Fairclough 1999; van Leeuwen and Wodak 1999) in his most recent work on pedagogy, is particularly useful as it can be applied to chart shifts of meanings either within one genre – as in different versions of a specific written text – or across semiotic dimensions: in an organizational context, for example, from discussion to monologic text to implementation of content to acts which may even belong to a different semiotic mode. The shift from design to building, for example, has been investigated by the systemic linguist Iedema (1998b: 6):

> In the context of organizational planning, this is also the case: talk becomes writing becomes design becomes physical construction. The logic here resides in the fact that each recontextualization moves the relevant meanings (contents) into an increasingly solid materiality, an increasingly non-negotiable materiality. If we think about how congruent language may become metaphorized, then I think these organizational recontextualizations are metaphors.

Iedema (1998b: 7) further points out

> that organizations reproduce themselves by means of not only processes of repetition, but also and primarily processes of production. This productive imperative governs which modes/semioses can recontextualize which others. Generally, organizational recontextualizations move towards increasingly non-negotiable and unchangeable modes/semiotics.

Thus interaction during a meeting, for example, may not only be recontextualized in a written text, but meaning shifts are also observable from dialogue to monologue (monologizing), from dynamic to static, from process to entity, from negotiable to fixed. Many 'voices' (in the Bakhtinian sense) coalesce to form one continuous strand, where violations of text coherence in the document in question indicate the different stances, views and interests voiced by those who took part in the meetings.

In summary we can say that we are concerned with semiosis if we look at the construction of meanings, the reconstruction and making of decisions in organizations (Wodak 1999a, 1999b). Although organizations involve, to a great extent, movements of information from talk to print, written documents are not necessarily the end-product of such recontextualizations. Actions, buildings, speeches, etc., may also represent the final stage. By contrast with what Iedema (1999) found, the genre of policy papers takes stages in abstraction and in the transformation of meanings, different from those found in bureaucratic language. Iedema was able to show how 'mustness' and directives get nominalized and abstracted in grammatical metaphors. If one accounts for the genre of an argumentative text and the field of politics, the processes work differently, due to the different beliefs, negotiations and ideologies involved. We get – as will be shown – very different tendencies of recontextualization. In our specific case (see below), employers, politicians and delegates of the trade unions have to find a consensus and take a decision on a policy paper. It is exactly these conflicts of interest which manifest themselves in the recontextualization processes. Only a critical analysis which takes this whole context into account can make the transformations of meanings transparent and understandable.

3   The Competitiveness Advisory Group (CAG) and employment policies

3.1   The CAG

The CAG, i.e. the body under investigation, was set up by President Santer in order to prepare specific drafts and proposals directly for the Council of Ministers. The group consists of 12 members, two women and ten men, who represent industry, politics and the trade unions; while the Commission itself is also represented by one member. These representatives discuss highly sensitive issues and draw up a report every six months. The CAG is chaired by Jean Claude Paye, former Secretary-General of the OECD, whom I interviewed in Paris in September 1998. Meetings are audio-taped, there are handwritten protocols as well as resolution papers. In summer 1997, the CAG was asked to draw up an employment policy paper for the Council of Ministers in November 1997.

Figure 11.3 shows the data that were available to me and allows a reconstruction of the text genesis, from the first draft, which simply lists the relevant issues, to the final version of the document.

The meetings were held in three languages, Italian, English and French; the chairman edited each version of the document in English, although his native language is French. I interviewed Jean Claude Paye, about the structure of the group and the conflicts which occurred, as well as about the drafting process:

I: and do you have the impression that from a point-
I: of view of the social partnership that (xxx xxx) BALanced the group?
P: yes I think the group 'h I find the group very well
I: ja.
P: BALanced. of COURSE 'h in so small a group, 'h the personalities and I 'h do THINK this is 'h of the of, of the people are very very imPORTant. and 'h. some of THEM are
I: ja.
P: quite 'h: STRONG well ALL of them are quite strong
I: ja,
P: persoNALities. and sometimes there are some 'h: let's say differences of views
     [*both laugh*]

Competitive Advisory Group 1997

The Dynamics of Text Genesis

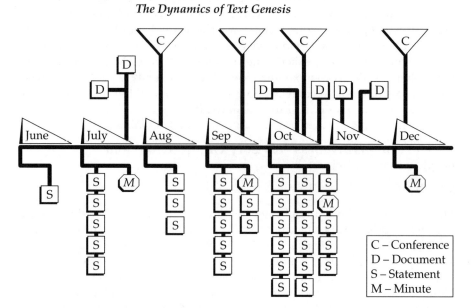

Figure 11.3 Reconstruction of the text genesis

Here, Paye already hints at the conflicts between 'strong personalities', specifically between the representatives of the trade unions and employers. We will illustrate these conflicts in the meetings below. It is naturally also difficult to get such important people together; this is why a lot of written correspondence is circulated and many statements sent in, because the members sometimes cannot attend the meetings. The chairperson emphasizes that he always took account of the written statements during the drafting process.:

P: are not (implied) 'h: either they ha/ well often they have
I: no TIME ja.
P: no TIME but but more frequently they say that they will COME but they have an: urgent matter to deal with, 'h and 'h they drop out 'h just 'h 'h the day beFORE,
I: Yeah.
P: so we have to to make recourse to: [*laughs*] written proCEDURE as 'h as I said,

3.2   Employment policies in the EU and the impact of globalization

The economic and currency union lies at the core of European Union integration and has been central in shaping the policy making of the various member states since the Treaty of the European Union (TEU, 1992). The builders of the economic foundation for European integration cannot, however, ignore what is widely reported in the media to be the EU's most critical social issue, the unemployment of 18 million or more of its citizens. Unlike fiscal and currency matters, employment in the EU was not an operationalized policy goal; employment figures (or unemployment rates) did not constitute a convergence criterion, and EU-wide coordination of employment matters was largely lacking.

However, beginning with the publication of Jacques Delors' White Paper (1993), and the Essen Summit of the European Council (1994), through to the recent Treaty of Amsterdam (June 1997) and its inclusion of a chapter on employment, the EU's role in employment policy making at the supranational level appears to be expanding, indeed becoming institutionalized. As a follow-up to Amsterdam, in November 1997, the European Council met in Luxembourg for an extraordinary meeting – the so-called Jobs Summit – devoted exclusively to the issue of (un)employment. These changes in the EU's orientation to employment policy coincide with the rising unemployment figures, pressure from labour unions, advocacy groups and others, as well as political agitation among the unemployed themselves (e.g. in France in 1997 and in 1998). Thus, where employment policy making at the supranational level of the EU had previously been almost non-existent, it is now being given increasingly more attention. The basic problem lies in the creation of a new 'European' policy which is different from the neo-liberal policies of Japan and the USA, even though it might contain elements of such economic concepts. The trade unions are anxious not to give up the European traditions of the welfare state and Keynesianism. Thus, the CAG is characterized by a conflict between the employers and politicians on the one hand, and the trade unions on the other. All parties agree that unemployment has to be attacked, but the preferred methods and tools are different. Discussion in the CAG is marked, therefore, by a tension between maintaining 'social cohesion' and giving up social welfare policies in order to be able to compete worldwide, as now required by globalization. Therefore, globalization becomes a central argument and topos throughout the discussion and is also used as an introduction to the policy paper (see analysis of example below). In this context, we will call the problem of globalization 'globalization rhetoric' in political and economic discourses (see Weiss 1999b). This rhetoric has clearly become an argumentative vehicle for controlling the aims of workers and trade unions. Usually, the argumentation goes as follows: There are international/global constraints, and because of these constraints, higher wages are not possible, the number of jobs has to be reduced, as well as social benefits. The social partners should thus be 'realistic' in the face of a 'changing world', they should also be 'co-operative'; international competitiveness is the precondition for growing employment; and in order to become competitive 'we' have to keep our currency strong by all possible means, and be flexible. We all 'must swim in the same Darwinian ocean' (Thurow 1996: 166). This rhetoric dominates today's political arena, and, as will be shown, also the CAG. Due to space restrictions, I will focus on the written texts only, and even there only on one paragraph concerning globalization and competition as well as social cohesion, and will illustrate the oral debates in the meetings with only two sequences which are then recontextualized into the written text.

3.3 The policy paper

This document, which generically can be classified as a policy paper, consists of four parts. First, an introduction, which discusses the implications and consequences of globalization. It is argued that globalization should be regarded as a positive phenomenon, and that Europe should be aware of and respond effectively to this challenge. The USA and Japan are mentioned as Europe's competitors. In part 2, the emphasis is on Europe's previous mistakes, starting with common-sense views rendered in highly generalizing and hyperbolic rhetoric, which are, however, later refuted. Thus, unemployment is not regarded as a consequence of globalization, but rather as a result of too strict and rigid employment laws and of too high taxation. Part 3 focuses on the construction of a European identity: the attractions of the 'European marketplace' are praised in phrases resembling those of advertising brochures: notwithstanding high taxation, there are numerous arguments in favour of investment in Europe, primarily in the level of education, the know-how, the culture, the fairness, the traditions of equal treatment, equality and democracy. In part 4, proposals for reducing unemployment are put forward. At the CAG meetings, different versions of the document were discussed and various modifications were suggested. The entire process of text construction was marked by a conflict between the trade union representatives, who wanted to retain the 'status quo' and demanded 'social cohesion', and those group members who represented the employer's side and advocated a liberalization of the labour market.[4]

In what follows I would like to discuss the 'life of arguments', drawing on the systemic-functional theory of M.A.K. Halliday (see Thompson 1996), among others, in order to describe and explain the semantic recontextualizations.

4 The 'life' of arguments

Before analyzing some changes and recontextualizations from two drafts, I will focus on the discussion of the title of the document. I will then concentrate on the first and second paragraphs, which clearly manifest the different voices participating in the discursive interaction. The first suggestion for a title was 'Ambition for employment'. This became 'Ambition for employment. Competitiveness as a source of jobs', and was finally changed to 'Competitiveness for employment'. According to van Dijk (1998), titles function as macro-propositions, i.e. they summarize the content, provide signals for the reader and anticipate what will be said; their additional function is to arouse the addressee's interest. Consequently, titles are predominantly located in the interpersonal metafunction, to use Halliday's terminology. The interpersonal metafunction defines the relational level, in our case between the reader and the text.

I will come to the textual metafunction. Theme and rheme organize a text according to the assumed knowledge and the new information. Thus the theme–rheme pattern in a sentence is of profound importance. Whatever is perceived as theme is taken for granted. This is significant in our case. 'Employment' constituted the rheme, the new information, which was to be discussed, without, however, narrowing down the number of possible options at this point. At this meeting, the participants decided – as befits the name of their own group – to include 'competitiveness' as a subtitle in the title and thus limited possible decisions and options. In the final version, only 'competitiveness' and 'employment' are highlighted. A connection is made between them, although it remains open whether this relation is causal or functional. Throughout the entire policy paper, competition and competitiveness are assumed to be the bases of the new employment policy; therefore the paper includes a discussion of how competitiveness might be increased and this resulted in the final title 'Competitiveness for employment'.

The next example illustrates the impact of globalization rhetorics:

Topic list: The globalization process
a) is natural: it is the continuation and spread of the process of economic development and social progress on which the prosperity of our countries is based;
b) is a good thing since it
c) helps to satisfy consumer needs,
d) enables an increasing number of countries throughout the world to take part in the economic development process, thereby raising their living standards and thus giving us increasingly attractive trading partners;
e) is therefore inevitable and irreversible.

This is recontextualized following the meeting in September where conflicts between trade unions and employers occurred in a much more abstract and euphemistic form. As a result, the monocausality of the link between globalization and necessary change of employment policies and the metaphor of 'globalization as natural' were deleted and the argument was recontextualized into economic terms; moreover, globalization is now marked as 'so-called', which emphasizes that the members of the CAG do not agree on the meaning of the term:

Outline:
The so-called globalization is the result of interaction between two main factors: liberalization of trade and technological progress in all its forms (innovation in products services management). This makes competition even fiercer.

Now let us take a quick look at the third paragraph. In the following, two versions – 14 October 1997 and 28 October 1997 – are presented. A third meeting took place in between, which was marked by the above-mentioned conflicts between the trade unions and the employers' side:

1 But it [globalization] is also a demanding one, and often a painful one.
2 Economic progress has always been accompanied by destruction of obsolete activities and creation of new ones.
3 The pace has become swifter and the game has taken on planetary dimensions.
4 It imposes on all countries – including European countries, where industrial civilization was born – deep and rapid adjustments.
5 The breadth and urgency of the needed adaptations are indistinctly perceived by public opinion, which explains a widespread sense of unease.
6 The duty which falls on governments, trade unions and employers is to work together
   – to describe the stakes and refute a number of mistaken ideas;
   – to stress that our countries have the means to sustain high ambitions; and
   – to implement, without delay and with consistency, the necessary reforms.

This paragraph is transformed and recontextualized as follows:

1 But it is also a demanding *process*, and often a painful one.
2 Economic progress has always been accompanied by destruction of obsolete activities and creation of new ones.
3 The pace has become swifter and the game has taken on planetary dimensions.
4 *It imposes deep and rapid adjustments on all countries – including European countries, where industrial civilization was born.*
5 *Social cohesion is threatened.*
6 *There is a risk of a disjunct between the hopes and aspirations of people and the demands of a global economy.*
7 *And yet social cohesion is not only a worthwhile political and social goal; it is also a source of efficiency and adaptability in a knowledge-based economy that increasingly depends on human quality and the ability to work as a team.*
8 *It has been difficult for people to grasp the breadth and urgency of necessary adaptations.*
9 *This explains a widespread sense of unease, inequality and polarization.*
10 *It is more than ever the duty of* governments, trade-unions and employers to work together
   – to describe the stakes and refute a number of mistakes;
   – to stress that our countries should have high ambitions and they can be realized; and
   – to implement the necessary reforms consistently and without delay.
11 *Failure to move quickly and decisively will result in loss of resources, both human and capital, which will leave for more promising parts of the world if Europe provides less attractive opportunities.*

What, then, are the transformations? Basically, we distinguish between four types of transformation which result from recontextualization: addition of elements, deletion of elements, rearrangement of elements and substitution of elements (van Leeuwen and Wodak 1999). Thus, in sentence 4 of the final version we observe a change in word order, which refers to the rheme: Now the emphasis is on 'European countries' and no longer on 'adjustments'. This allows for at least two readings, and we can only select an interpretation if we are familiar with the entire context: first, it may be interpreted as a purely stylistic change, as a tendency towards making plain English more comprehensible and efficient. Efficiency characterizes the entire document, the content as well as the form. This is business speak. Or, it can be interpreted as highlighting Europe and its tradition in an attempt to construct a new identity.

Sentence 5 is missing in the initial document. In this sentence, the trade union voice – in the Bakhtinian sense – makes itself heard; therefore this constitutes a concession to the unions, as becomes clear if we look at the union representative's turn during the meeting. The inclusion of social cohesion as an important objective is demanded and it is claimed that the welfare state is under threat. This topos of danger is further developed and justified in the following two sentences. The trade union argues that social welfare must not be perceived as a burden, but as something intrinsically efficient. Consequently, investment in human capital will improve competitiveness. Unfortunately, I do not have the space to discuss the syntactic and semantic structure of this argument in detail. However, I would like to point out two elements which pervade the entire text like a motto: first, the tension between people's hopes and the implications of globalization (please note the multiple embedding of nouns, the presentation of people as an anonymous group and their characterization in terms of irrationality); second, the 'knowledge-based economy', which is presented as a European trademark.

The following sentence (Figure 11.4) in the initial version of the document is complex and appears as two sentences in the new version, i.e. in a transformed and rearranged form.

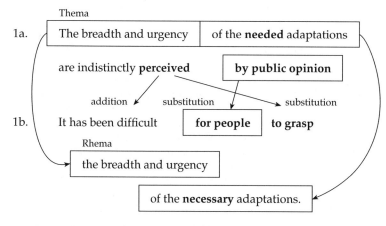

2a.   **Which** explains a widespread sense of unease.
2b.   **This**   explains a widespread sense of unease, **inequality and polarization**.

Figure 11.4   Changes from the draft dated 14.10.1997 to the draft dated 28.10.1997.

At the same time, a shift occurs from theme to rheme. Again, this is a case of business speak, a simplification, but on the other hand the information is transformed. There are further additions, for example in the description of the atmosphere and of the feelings of the people. The transformation of the nominal group 'public opinion' to 'people', i.e. to actors, is also important. Throughout the document, 'people' are consistently described by means of 'sensing processes', or characterized by their hopes and beliefs, whereas knowledge and mental processes form the basis of the rational arguments of the experts. Although the distance *vis-à-vis* 'ordinary people' is reduced, the group referred to as 'people' still remains anonymous and we do not know who is included in this group. Also note that 'perceive' is replaced by 'grasp', i.e. a mental process is replaced by a material one.

The last sentence has been added in the final version: the topos of danger, which is conjured up here, is a rhetorical device used to persuade politicians to act quickly. The topos of speed and urgency also pervades the document, as does the semantic field 'urgent, rapid, quick', etc.; efficient, urgent action is needed. The basic message of this document, then, is that action is required, mere thinking is not enough, otherwise Europe will no longer be able to keep up with competition and primarily, as is often mentioned in the document and the meetings, with Japan and the USA.

In the following two turns of the meeting on 17 October, the notion and concept of globalization is put forward and discussed. We will analyze these clauses carefully and neglect other interesting aspects of the dynamics and discussion.

Paye:
J'aimerais avoir votre sentiment parce que eh, je, je suis moi-même peut-être un peu, un peu biasé, eh, a cet égard eh, je me suis battu eh, a l'OECDE pendant des années pour essayer de faire reconnaître que, eh, il y avait quelque chose qui était en train de changer dans la manière dont fonctionnait l'économie. Alors qu'on l'appelle globalisation, c'est un, un catchword qui est, qui est commode, mais eh, je crois que eh, il y a vraiment dans la manière que fonctionne l'économie quelque chose qui a changé c'est à dire une concurrence qui est eh, eh, de plus en plus présente, de plus en plus forte, eh, une concurrence non seulement présente mais potentielle quand on discute avec les chefs d'entreprise, on s'apperçoit que non seulement ils se préoccupent de résister à la concurrence, de concurrence qui existe déjà, mais ils se préoccupent des concurrents qui peuvent naître et surgir, eh, brusquement donc c'est la 'contestability of markets' qui, qui est une, une notion nouvelle. Et tout cela je crois a, a changé fondamentalement le paysage parce que ça veut dire que la pression pour eh, le, l'innovation, pour l'adaptation, pour le changement, pour le streamlining etcetera, n'a jamais été aussi forte. Et donc, eh, eh, les effects, eh, perturbateurs eh, de, de l'ajustement structurelle que, on les a toujours connus depuis les, les, les débuts de l'activité économique, il y a des métiers qui ont disparu et d'autres qui sont apparus, mais cette déstruction créatrice eh, eh, est est, beaucoup plus brutale et beaucoup plus rapide maintenant qu'elle ne l'a été.

Paye starts out with a very personal statement and relativizes his point of view by admitting that he had worked in the OECD and that his view might be biased for that reason. He had fought for the realization that things were starting to change in the economy. An important rhetorical device is used: by marking this statement as a very personal opinion, Paye makes it discussable and also refutable. On the other hand, by using and referring to the outside, to another very important organization, he claims the topos of authority for himself and implicitly indicates that he has a lot of experience and know-how. Paye is a diplomat and diplomats typically refer to other organizations, committees and negotiations in which they have been involved (Wodak and Vetter 1999). This is the social capital of diplomats, the knowledge of international organizations and their experience with negotiations. Paye continues and switches to impersonal mode, distancing himself from the concept of globalization, which is a 'catchword'. The labelling of globalization as catchword is derogatory, it is even a comfortable catchword, something one can use in many situations. However, Paye remarks, it is true that – without defining globalization more precisely – there have been changes in the economy, and competition has become stronger.

This recontextualizes the draft analyzed above; globalization as theme is linked to competition as rheme in the text. The competition has to be met and to be adapted to the 'contestability of markets'. Again Paye introduces a precise English economic term into the discussion. Then follow characteristics of globalization and competition, now presented as analogous: innovation, adaptation, change, streamlining, which are all much swifter and more brutal then they used to be. These notions continue throughout the whole meeting. Paye ends his turn with an optimistic twist: it is possible to discuss much more now than four years ago, thus emphasizing the here and now, the 'window of opportunity' which has opened for change and adaptation. This suggests that it is high time to act, NOW! Furthermore, he states that dialogue should be possible between the social partners, 'un effort solidaire'. The notion of *solidarity* is a most important topos throughout the whole drafting process, which seems to contradict the responsibility of the individual which had been proposed beforehand. But they go together: responsible individuals decide to act together, in contrast to the American and Japanese way of economies. This implies the specific European road which should be taken and decided upon.

The next speaker, whose paper had not been distributed, is M9, a British employer. M9 characterizes himself as coming from a very narrow sector, telecommunications. He then continues to define two approaches to globalization:

> Ehm and there is one very important point I think we need make about globalization, and that is that you can take two basic approaches to it. One of which is to be defensive and to see it as a threat and there is a tendency I detect within Europe to look at it in that way. And the other is to be offensive, and to see

it as an opportunity. Eh, frankly, I think there is only one sensible way of viewing it and that is the latter. Ehm, I detect worries that United States are getting further ahead of Europe, that Japan may be getting further ahead, that other Asian-Pacific countries may be getting further ahead. You will not succeed in a global market unless you aim to do better than the Americans, better than the Japanese, better than the, the Asian Tigers. And I think a key message we need to get over to heads of state is that we can.

M9 stays in the explicit declarative mode which is implicitly directive and makes a very general statement, not mitigated by any particles or by using the first person very rarely. The theme is the basic approaches to globalization, in a relational clause he explains the first approach, using 'defensive' and 'threat' as rheme. He then continues to state that there is a tendency in Europe to view globalization in this way. This is an insinuation to the public opinion from the outline which is recontextualized as an agent's process. The next clause, again relational, has 'offensive' as rheme and 'opportunity', two positively connotated attributes among the business speak. Then he switches to personal mode and suggests the latter view to be the only one which is sensible, a very evaluative judgement, clearly marking the other approach as the contrary, as insensible and irrational. This is a juxtaposition which we encounter in the next draft, the contrast between insensible and irrational tendencies, i.e. beliefs of many people, and the rational and sensible opinions of the experts. M9 takes this argument further: he 'detects worries' which are agentless and anonymous, irrational and without evidence that the Americans and Japanese might get ahead. And then he makes a very general statement that one has to compete and win the competition with the two most important competitors. He phrases this as a rhetorical address, using 'you' where it is not clear who is actually addressed – the CAG, Europe, the people, or the politicians. The next clause makes the addressee clear and reduces the options, the 'heads of state' are the rheme, the document should be directed at them. M9 ends his statement with a very direct, imperative and emphasized appeal: 'it [Europe] has to win, it actually has to be best'. And the topos of threat continues: 'unless you set your sights at that, you will lose'. The message which he conveys is taken up by the next speaker, M3; thus M9 has positioned himself and the employers' side very well in this meeting.

5 Conclusions

In this brief illustrative analysis of the recontextualization of arguments in two versions of one paragraph where a meeting occured in between, I have only been able to sketch out a small number of linguistic characteristics. A more detailed discourse analysis of the whole document, however, reveals four contradictory recontextualization tendencies, which can be interpreted on the basis of the interaction, the negotiations and compromises occurring at the meetings:

- static versus dynamic quality
- simplicity versus complexity
- precision versus vagueness
- argumentation versus statement and generalizing claims.

In other words, recontextualization depends to a large extent on the semiosis at the meetings. The transformations from oral to written constitute a mono-logizing process which leads to materialization. In contrast to Iedema (1999), I would like to emphasize that the tendencies are contradictory and not unidirectional. They display the same contradictions and incoherences which are manifested in linguistic interaction. Thus, recontextualization processes have to be viewed as context-dependent.

Each document, then, ultimately mirrors a structure of interaction which can only be made transparent through detailed linguistic analysis. As I have indicated, such analyzes highlight the decision-making processes which we as 'ordinary European citizens' are never informed about, since we are always confronted with decisions 'from above'.

Our ethnographic study has provided us with data from the 'inside', we get a glimpse of what happens behind 'closed doors'. The issue of transparency is an important theme within the European Union, on which great emphasis was also placed during the Austrian presidency (1998). However, 'citizens' Europe' has remained only a political slogan to date. I would like to end by quoting Juergen Habermas on the conflict between trade unions and employers, between neo-liberalism and Keynesianism:

> 'Terminating the social pact inevitably means that those looming crises which so far have been buffered by the welfare state will flare up again. This will lead to social costs threatening to overstretch the integration capacity of a liberal society' (Habermas 1998: 68). And he argues, 'In the context of a globalizing world economy, nation-states can only improve their international competitiveness by reducing the state's operational power, i.e. by implementing "dismantlement policies", which damage social cohesion and jeopardize a society's democratic stability'. (ibid.: 69)

It is this conflict – reflected in our document – that politicians in the European Union member countries are confronted with. Incorporating a variety of different 'voices', including those of the European citizens and their hopes and beliefs, therefore would indeed serve essential democratic principles.

Finally, I would like to stress that carrying out critical discourse-theoretical sociolinguistic analyses will not help us to solve these problems; however, by using an interdisciplinary, applied linguistic approach we will be able to make these processes more transparent – and this is a very important contribution, in accordance with our notions of critical research.

Notes

1. This project is part of the Wittgenstein Research Center 'Discourse, Politics, and Identity', directed by the author and funded by the Wittgenstein Prize which she

received in 1996. The whole project runs for five years (started in 1997) and a first book is in preparation about the Meeting of the European Council of Ministers on Unemployment, November 1997, in Luxembourg (Muntigl, Weiss and Wodak, 1999).

2. I am very grateful to Martin Reisigl for comments and important contribution to this section. (See Wodak and Reisigl forthcoming for an extended discussion of this model.)

3. The British tradition was important (Hallidayan Functional Systemic Linguistics), Argumentation Theory and 'Politolinguistics' of a German nature.

4. A content analysis and a quantitative analysis of the most 'prominent turns' in the two tape-recorded meetings brought some significant results about the alignments in the CAG: thus employers and politicians formed a group against the members from the trade unions. In the third meeting a conflict occurred between these two interest groups which had a big impact on the drafting process. The biggest changes occur from Document 2 to Document 3, some of which we will illustrate below.

References

Benhabib, S. (1992) Kritik, Norm und Utopie. *Die normativen Grundlagen der Kritischen Theorie*. Frankfurt am Main: Fischer.

Bernstein, B. (1990) The structure of pedagogic discourse. *Class, Codes and Control*, Vol. VI. London: Routledge.

Boden, D. (1994) *The Business of Talk*. Cambridge: Polity.

Boden, D. (1995) Agendas and arrangements: Everyday negotiations in meetings. In A. Firth (ed.) *The Discourse of Negotiation: Studies of Language in the Workplace*. Oxford: Pergamon, 83–99.

Drew, P. and Heritage, J. (eds) (1992) *Talk at Work: Interaction in Institutional Settings*. Cambridge: Cambridge University Press.

Drew, P. and Sorjonen, M.-L. (1997) Institutional dialogue. In *Discourse as Social Interaction: Discourse Studies*, Vol. 2. London: Sage, 92–118.

Fairclough, N. (1992) *Discourse and Social Change*. Oxford, UK/Cambridge, MA: Polity Press/Blackwell.

Fairclough, N. (1999) Democracy and the Public Sphere in Critical Research on Discourse. In Wodak, R. and Ludwig, Ch. (eds) *Challenges in a Changing World*. Vienna: Passagen Verlag, 63–85.

Fairclough, N. and Wodak, R. (1997) Critical Discourse Analysis. In T. van Dijk (ed.) *Discourse as Social Interaction. Discourse Studies: A Multidisciplinary Introduction*, Vol. 2. London/Thousand Oaks/New Delhi: Sage, 258–284.

Firth, A. (1995) *The Discourse of Negotiation*. London: Pergamon.

Girnth, H. (1996) Texte im politischen Diskurs. Ein Vorschlag zur diskursorientierten Beschreibung von Textsorten. *Muttersprache* 106(1), 66–80.

Grant, D., Keenoy, T. and Oswick, C. (eds) (1998) *Discourse and Organization*. London: Sage.

Habermas, J. (1998) Die Einbeziehung des Anderen. *Studien zur politischen Theorie*. Frankfurt am Main: Suhrkamp.

Halliday, M.A.K. (1994) *An Introduction to Functional Grammar* (2nd edn). London: Edward Arnold.

Harvey, D. (1996) *Justice, Nature and the Geography of Difference.* London: Blackwell.

Horkheimer, M. and Adorno, T.W. (1991[1944]) Dialektik der Aufklärung. *Philosophische Fragmente.* Frankfurt am Main: Fischer.

Iedema, R. (1994/1996) The Language of Administration: Write it Right. *Industry Research Report,* Vol. III. [Disadvantaged Schools Program (Met.East)]. Sydney: Erskinville.

Iedema, R. (1997) *Interactional Dynamics and Social Change; Planning as Morphogenesis.* Unpublished PhD Thesis, University of Sydney.

Iedema, R. (1998a) Bureaucratic Planning and Resemiotisation. In E. Ventola (ed.) *Proceedings of the Halle Systemic Functional Workshop* 1997 [Pragmatics and Beyond Series]. Amsterdam: Benjamins.

Iedema, R. (1998b) 'Multimodal Semiotics and Social Processes: Analysing a Graphics Interface Web Site in Relation to the Process of User Navigation', keynote address to the Australian Systemic Functional Congress, Adelaide, 26–28 September 1998.

Iedema, R. (1999) Formalizing organizational meaning. *Discourse and Society* 10, 49–65.

Iedema, R. and Wodak, R. (1999) Introduction. In R. Wodak and R. Iedema (eds) *Organizational Discourse.* Special Issue of *Discourse and Society* 10, 5–19.

Linell, P. and Sarangi, S. (eds) (1998) Discourse Across Professional Boundaries. Special issue of *Text* 18, 2: 143–318.

Luhmann, N. (1997) *Die Gesellschaft der Gesellschaft.* Frankfurt am Main

Matouschek, B., Wodak, R. and Januschek, F. (1995) Notwendige Maßnahmen gegen Fremde? *Genese und Formen von rassistischen Diskursen der Differenz.* Wien: Passagen.

Mehan, H. (1993) Beneath the skin and between the ears: A case study in the politics of representation. In S. Chaikin and J. Lave (eds) *Understanding Practice: Perspectives on Activity and Context,* 241–68. Cambridge: Cambridge University Press.

Menz, F. (1999a) *'Was soll denn das Chaos?' Selbst- und Fremdorganisation durch Kommunikation in Wirtschaftsunternehmen.* Habilitationsschrift (unveröffentlicht).

Menz, F. (1999b) 'Who am I gonna do this with?' Self-organisation, ambiguity and decision-making in a business enterprise. In R. Wodak and R./Iedema (eds) *Organizational Discourse.* Special Issue of *Discourse and Society,* 101–128.

Mitten, R. and Wodak, R. (1993) On the discourse of racism and prejudice. Discourse analysis and racist talk. In: *Societas Linguistica Europaea,* Berlin: de Gruyter, 191–251.

Mumby, D.K. (1988) *Communication and Power in Organizations: Discourse, Ideology and Domination.* Norwood, NJ: Ablex.

Muntigl, P., Weiss, G. and Wodak, R. (1999) *Snapshot of an Emerging Organization.* Amsterdam: Benjamins (in press).

Reisigl, M. (forthcoming) 'Austria First' – A discourse-historical analysis of the Austrian 'Anti-foreigner-petition' in 1993. In M. Reisigl and R. Wodak (eds) *The Semiotics of Racism.* Wien.

Reisigl, M. and Wodak, R. (eds) (forthcoming) *The Semiotics of Racism.* Wien.

Sarangi, S. (1998) Rethinking Recontextualization in Professional Discourse Studies: An Epilogue. Special Issue of *Text* 18(2), 301–318.

Schegloff, E.A. (1997) Whose text? Whose context? In *Discourse and Society,* 8, 165–187.

Straehle, C., Weiss, G., Wodak, R., Muntigl, P. and Sedlak, M. (1999) Struggle as Metaphor in EU Discourses on Unemployment. In R. Wodak and R. Iedema (eds) *Organizational Discourse.* Special Issue of *Discourse and Society* 10, 67–99.

Thompson, G. (1996) *Introducing Functional Grammar.* London, Arnold.

Thurow, L. (1996) *The Future of Capitalism. How Today's Economic Forces Shape Tomorrow's World*. London: Penguin.

Titscher, S., Wodak, R., Meyer, M. and Vetter, E. (1998) *Methoden der Textanalyse*. Opladen: Westdeutscher Verlag.

van Dijk, T.A. (1998) *Ideology*. London: Sage.

van Leeuwen, T. and Wodak, R. (1999) Legitimizing immigration control: A discourse-historical analysis. *Discourse Studies*. 1(1), 83–118.

van Schendelen, M.P.C.M. (1996) EC Committees: Influence counts more than legal powers. In R. Pedeler and G.F. Schaefer (eds) *Shaping European Law and Policy. The Role of Committees and Commitology Processes in the Political Process*. Maastricht, 25–38.

Weiss, G. (1999a) Some remarks on decision making in committees of the European Union. In R. Wodak and C. Ludwig (eds) *Challenges in a Changing World*. Vienna: Passagen Verlag.

Weiss, G. (1999b) *Unemployment, Globalisation and European Union Decision-Making* (forthcoming).

Weiss, G. and Wodak, R. (1998) Organization and communication. On the relevance of Niklas Luhman's systems theory for a discourse-hermeneutic approach to organizations (forthcoming).

Wodak, R. (1986) *Language Behaviour in Therapy Groups*. Los Angeles: University of California Press.

Wodak, R. (1996) *Disorders of Discourse*. London/New York: Longman.

Wodak, R. (1999a) Rekontextualisierung und Bedeutungswandel. *Diskursive Entscheidungsprozesse in der EU* (forthcoming).

Wodak, R. (1999b) *Theories in Applied Linguistics* (forthcoming).

Wodak, R. (1999c) From conflict to consensus? The co-construction of a policy paper. In: Muntigl, P., Weiss, G. and Wodak, R. (1999) *Snapshot of an Emerging Organisation*. Amsterdam: Benjamins (in press).

Wodak, R. and Reisigl, M. (forthcoming) *Discourse and Discrimination*. London: Longman.

Wodak, R. and Vetter, E. (1999) The small distinctions between diplomats, politicians and journalists: the discursive construction of professional identity. In R. Wodak and C. Ludwig (eds) *Challenges in a Changing World*. Wien: Passagen, 209–237.

Wodak, R., Menz, F., Mitten, R. and Stern, F. (1994) *Sprachen der Vergangenheiten*. Frankfurt am Main: Suhrkamp.

Wodak, R., De Cillia, R., Reisigl, M. and Liebhart, K. (1999) *The Discursive Construction of National Identities*. Edinburgh: Edinburgh University Press.

Wodak, R., De Cillia, R., Reisigl, M., Liebhart, K., Hofstätter, K. and Kargl, M. (1998) *Zur diskursiven Konstruktion nationaler Identität*. Frankfurt am Main: Suhrkamp.

Wodak, R., Nowak, P., Pelikan, J., Gruber, H., De Cillia, R. and Mitten, R. (1990) 'Wir sind alle unschuldige Täter.' *Diskurshistorische Studien zum Nachkriegsantisemitismus*. Frankfurt am Main: Suhrkamp.

Chapter 12

Relational frames and pronominal address/reference: the discourse of geriatric medical triads

Nikolas Coupland and Justine Coupland

In one of Christopher Candlin's formulations of 'discourse', he captures the tension between creativity and constraint in how social actors and social practices function:

> 'Discourse' . . . refers to language in use, as a process which is socially situated. However . . . we may go on to discuss the constructive and dynamic role of either spoken or written discourse in structuring areas of knowledge and the social and institutional practices which are associated with them. In this sense, discourse is a means of talking and writing about and acting upon worlds, a means which both constructs and is constructed by a set of social practices within these worlds, and in so doing both reproduces and constructs afresh particular social-discursive practices, constrained or encouraged by more macro movements in the overarching social formation. (Candlin 1997: viii)

In the social context of medical geriatrics, with which we are concerned in this chapter,[1] Candlin's perspective takes us to the heart of what we would want to achieve through discourse analysis. The 'institutional practices' here are most obviously those that define geriatrics as a distinct domain of medicine and social care (Hall et al. 1993) – their presuppositions, their priorities, and their routines. Many aspects of these practices are made visible in the talk that constitutes geriatric medical consultations, and it is a sample of these that we take as data here.

But Candlin's phrase, 'the overarching social formation', locates the data we are dealing with in a more general and more fundamental sense than linking it to the institution of medical geriatrics. The overarching social formation that constrains our data is social ageing. Participation in geriatric medical consultations is structured to deal with age and its associated circumstances, cultural values and attributions. We have come to see these consultations as focused age-negotiations – as a forum for representing and recontextualising what ageing entails for older people and their social networks (Coupland and Coupland 1999). Old age is often an experience loaded with physical, material and practical relevancies. It is nonetheless a socially structured and socially structuring process. We are interested in the discourses of geriatrics as much for what they reveal about the ideological conditions of ageing as for what they can explain about doctor–patient interaction itself. Candlin's broad theorising of institutional discourse has been important in helping us to construe our work in this way.

One acknowledged material characteristic of geriatric medical consultations is that 'third-parties' are often present.[2] In more than 40 per cent of our sample of 107 instances, elderly patients are accompanied to the consultation by a close relative, a friend or a carer. Several US studies confirm this general distribution (Beisecker 1989; Coe and Prendergast 1985; Greene et al. 1994; Hasselkus 1992). The dominant demographic pattern in our data is an elderly female patient mother conversing with a doctor in the presence of her daughter (full details are available in other papers – Coupland and Coupland 1997, 1999, forthcoming). This frequent triadic participation structure is superficially similar to, for example, the one Silverman (1987: 161ff) describes in a cleft-palate clinic involving doctors, adolescents and their parents. These parents, like the daughters in our data, might be said to be present in a 'chauffeuring' capacity, and this is a concept we return to at the end of the chapter. But a unitary, role-based concept like 'chauffeuring' under-represents the diversity and subtlety of structuring effects produced in the consultation discourse. It also implies that the significance of the triadic constitution is relatively local, linked to the practicalities of transport and mobility. Alternatively, and in the spirit of the Candlin quotation, we shall try to show how geriatric medical discourse constructs diverse social positions for participants, and how these are far more than rhetorical positions (who speaks to whom about what). We are interested in the social alignments and confederations that are discursively constructed, and the moral rights and obligations that are thereby implied to exist for participants.

1   Relational framing

Goffman's idea of activity frames as 'organizational premises', as participants' 'understanding of what is it that is going on' in an interaction (Goffman 1997: 158; also Goffman 1981; Tannen and Wallat 1993), as the constellations of participants' assumptions and understandings in the light of which talk proceeds, is central to our analysis. In an earlier report based on data from this same source we have shown, for example, how doctors and patients move in and out of social frames, especially at the periphery of these encounters. We showed how social (versus medical) frames are signalled by participants, and how agreement about which frame obtains conditions the nature of talk and the inferences participants draw from it. Frame management can be analysed in the textual dimension because frames are often marked, through formal and functional elements of language. Through verbal and non-verbal markers, and conversational inferencing work linked to them, participants in triadic consultations can index and potentially impose a particular frame – a particular set of understandings about how talk is being entertained. This includes framing social relationships among speakers. Relational frames will be partly given by consensual definitions of an encounter (e.g. what it means for an encounter to be taken as 'a geriatric medical event'), but partly negotiated by participants to particular ends.

Goffman's account of the multiplicity of speaking and listening roles which may be operative at any given point in a social encounter is well known. For example, he distinguishes categories of 'listener' such as ratified versus non-ratified listeners, or addressed versus unaddressed listeners. He writes that 'an utterance does not carve up the world beyond the speaker into precisely two parts, recipients and non-recipients, but rather opens up an array of structurally differentiated possibilities, establishing the participation framework in which the speaker will be guiding his delivery' (1981: 137). These conceptions have an obvious importance for analysing triadic interactions. In three-party talk, participants will inevitably frame themselves and others into different communicative relations, at different points. However, in the context of geriatric medicine, any one relational frame potentially establishes more than particular speakership and listenership roles. It establishes a social position and identity for each participant, affecting how each is heard or silenced, validated or side-lined. Relational frames establish entitlements and responsibilities. Frame analysis can therefore access some of the discourse strategies by which patients, third-parties and doctors claim positions for themselves, or deny them, foist them onto others, or deny them to others. Frame constitution and frame shifting are central to the practice of geriatrics as an age-negotiative institution. For example, they allow subtle and sometimes fleeting confederations to be constructed to signal social support or promote coping. At the other extreme, they can implement social division and disempowerment. Frame management therefore has a moral dimension, constructing age-values, both positive and negative.

Of the linguistic features and strategies with potential to mark relational frames, pronominal address and reference are probably the most obvious and the most powerful (cf. Harre 1992). A classic 'address complexity' in all triadic interaction, even where (as in our data) all three participants are ratified within the encounter, is ambiguity of inclusiveness. A doctor's utterance beginning with *you* may, depending on content and context, identify one or both of the other participants (or neither, if it is a generic *you*). In Goffman's terms, the two hearers will each need to decide whether, at that moment, they are being framed as addressees or alternatively as overhearers, with all that that distinction might entail. The direction of a speaker's gaze can sometimes disambiguate, but there is no necessary correlation between gaze and addresseeship (Goodwin 1981). Where a doctor's *you* address is interpretable as inclusive (addressed to both the other main participants), the relational effect may be to corral a third-party into shared responsibility for a treatment regime. Where it is interpretable as exclusively addressed to a third-party, the effect may be to frame the patient him/herself as excluded from such responsibility (cf. Lerner 1996; Levinson 1988). 'Complexities' over third-person reference in triadic encounters also arise. A third party referring to a patient as *she* or *my mother*, or to a medical or emotional problem as *her difficulty in walking* or *her depression*, in that person's presence, will frame relationships differently from a second-person pronoun address (*you*) to the mother in specific circumstances. Agency, responsibility, credit or blame can be apportioned (or be assumed to be apportioned) or denied, empathy and exclusion can be signalled by these means.

In the presence of a 'chauffeuring' daughter, a basic question is whether the doctor's address is (regularly or variably, when and why) to the patient or to the daughter. We can immediately sense the socio-political issues attendant on this strategic decision, linked to beliefs and expectations about an older person's rights to autonomous decision-making and judgement. There is a potential imputation of ageist practice here (implied in analyses of 'patronising talk' to older people – cf. Hummert 1994; Ryan et al. 1991). That practice is opposed in the institutional ideology of geriatrics, which is reflexively anti-ageist, and clearly so in the clinic we are studying. But what of the holistic remit of the geriatric enterprise? Is the boundary between daughter-carers or spouse-carers and caring medics potentially blurred, and might third parties have a legitimacy in the consultation discourse, even in 'speaking for' elderly patients in some circumstances? How do they make their voices heard in the consultations, and how do they manage their address? Listening to the data, we sometimes ask: 'Whose illness is it?' As Sidell (1995: 65) says, 'the disruption chronic illness brings to the reciprocity in social relationships requires the renegotiation of pre-illness roles'. Chronic illness can be a 'dis-ease' of the social network and forces redefinitions of social patterns and possibilities. Are there discursive means by which participants can refashion the normatively presumed medical dyad ('the doctor–patient relationship') as a more open network, with more delicately apportioned responsibilities? We shall consider some data extracts which show different social and ideological formations which are linked to different strategic uses of pronominal address and reference.

2 A caring son: speaking for

In Extract 1[3] there is a dominant pattern of the doctor and patient doing mutual address.

2.1 *Extract 1*

Doctor H: (registrar) male, in his thirties
Patient 41: female, aged 87
Triad: with the patient's son, in his sixties

(*A nurse brings the patient into the consulting room. The patient has a heart problem and diabetes. She is slightly deaf and appears very frail.*)

1   Doctor: (*loudly and brightly*) he<u>llo</u> there! (3.0) (*door closes*) (*much more quietly*) hello

2   Son: hello

3   Patient: hello doctor

4   Doctor: hello Mrs W—— (.) take a seat
                             [
5   Son: I'm her I'm her <u>son</u>

6   Doctor: (*slowly, clearly*) Dr H—— pleased to meet you and (.) (*quieter*) pleased to meet you
                [
7   Patient: (*breathlessly*) pleased to meet you (.) doctor

8   Doctor: just having a quick look at things here (*referring to notes* 3.0)

9   Patient: (*gasping as if in pain*) oh (.) oh (.) oh

10 Doctor: well you certainly had a (.) (*louder*) <u>compl</u>icated course in hospital (.) but you look quite <u>well</u> now (.) how <u>are</u> you feeling?

11 Patient: oh I don't feel too <u>bad</u> doctor (.) but I could be <u>bett</u>er you know what I mean

12 Doctor: what are the <u>main</u> <u>prob</u>lems?

13 Patient: (turns to Son) (quietly) oh I don't know
                               [
14 Son: well er it's her <u>ank</u>les doctor
                                            [
15 Patient: er my ankles
              have sw=

16 Doctor: =swelled yes=

17 Patient: =my ankles have swelled (.) see

18 Son: er (.) I had the local doctor er doctor (.) and er he come he come and he give her some <u>wat</u>er tablets to take

19 Doctor: <u>right</u>=

20 Son: =the tablets like and they dissolve in water

21 Doctor: yes
                [
22 Son: and she's got um (.) she's got to take it <u>twice</u> daily=

23 Doctor: =yes

24 Son: and he give her some tablets for the (.) <u>heart</u> like (2.0) but er sh

25 Doctor: have they <u>helped</u>?

26 Son: well it <u>have</u> helped (.) I don't know if they've gone down a bit (.) but
              they've gone
                                                                                    [
27 Patient: no
              they've <u>not</u> gone down now ((yet))

28 Doctor: have you been short of breath?
              (1.0)
29 Son: <u>yes</u> when she <u>do</u> walk a bit like doctor yes
                                 [
30 Patient: yes <u>some</u>times I do doctor

31 Doctor: are you more short of breath than you were before hospital?
              (4.0)
32 Patient: (*turns to Son*) oh I don't remember

33 Son: uh?

34 Patient: much I don't think I am
                          [
35 Doctor: OK that's alright

36 Son: nah

37 Patient: I don't remember much though

38 Son: no
              (3.0)
39 Doctor: now <u>when</u> we had you in hospital we <u>didn't</u> have you on any fluid
              tablets (.) just the diabetic tablets and the (*name of drug*) are you <u>still</u>
              taking both of those?

40 Son: er <u>yes</u>

41 Doctor: right (.) and do you test your urine for sugar?
              (1.0)
42 Son: <u>no</u> I don't s (.) I didn't I didn't <u>know</u> that doctor
                                                [
43 Patient: no don't take ((much))
                                                            [
44 Doctor: don't (.) nobody tests it (.)
              right

45 Son: I didn't er (.) didn't know that
              (36.0) (*Doctor reads through case notes*)
46 Doctor: (*loudly and clearly*) so (.) did <u>any</u>body get a chance to talk to you about
              the diabetes in hospital?
              (3.0)
47 Doctor: no
              [
48 Son: did anybody come to you mum? (.) did anybody come to you to talk
              to you about your illness?

49 Patient: I don't think so . . .

(*After five minutes, near the end of the consultation*)
50 Doctor: we'll <u>see</u> you again Mrs W—— in <u>two</u> months

51 Patient: two months yes

52 Doctor: and if everything's going well then we can discharge you back to
              your doctor

53 Patient: oh <u>right</u> you are
                   [
54 Son: <u>oh</u> well

55 Doctor: er is there <u>any</u>thing else you're worried about?=

56 Son: =er she <u>want</u>ed to know (.) could she er is there any ch chance of
              going out doctor? (1.0) or is it ((unwise))?
                                     [
57 Doctor: <u>yes</u> she can do whatever she feels like doing

58 Son: she can go out can she?

59 Doctor: abso<u>lutely</u>

60 Son: oh that's alright then

213

In the initial social or phatic sequences (up to turn 8), the doctor's two uses of *you* (in turn 6) are audibly individualised to the patient and the patient's son. The patient is hard of hearing and the quieter, second *pleased to meet you* is addressed to the son. However, once diagnostic and evaluative talk begins, the doctor's address, marked in his pronoun usage, is uniformly to the patient throughout the extract. His *you*s in turns 10, 28, 31, 39, 41, 46, 50, and 52 are all unambiguously addressed to the patient, on the evidence of content and context information (e.g. referring to her time in hospital, her state of health and at one point mentioning her name within these turns). And if turn 55 is ambiguous in terms of address, the son's turn 56 *er she wanted to know* at least orients to it as having been exclusively addressed to his mother. While at one level this pattern of address is unexceptional, at another level it has an ideological loading, as we suggested above. It is part of what we might call *routine anti-ageist discourse practice* in geriatrics (cf. Coupland and Coupland 1999).

Silverman's (1987) cleft-palate clinic data raise similar issues, although the discursive politics of address to young people and old people as patients are different. Young people with facial disfigurement in the cleft-palate clinic are treated as arbiters of their 'feelings' about their 'looks'. Silverman suggests they have specific, limited rights over this non-clinical aspect of what is negotiated. In our data, the base-line institutional assumption is that elderly patients have autonomy – as far as this is ever possible – in reporting and appraising their own health. All the same, in our data as in Silverman's, family members as third parties do also become significantly involved in the consultations.

In Extract 1 the son's talk, when he is involved, is very largely addressed to the doctor rather than to the patient, and this is another general feature of our sample of 44 triadic interactions. We can list the discourse functions performed by the son's turns at talk. He focuses attention on the patient's problems (turn 14), reports aspects of the patient's previous involvement with other doctors, medicines and treatments (18, 20, 22, 24, 40, 42, 45), evaluates the success of treatment regimes (26), evaluates the patient's breathing (29), and confirms the patient's evaluative responses (36, 38). At one point, near the end of the encounter (turn 56), the son establishes the topic of whether the patient can go out, asking a question about this on his mother's behalf. As this sequence develops he then clarifies his question (turn 58) and marks receipt and understanding of the information he has requested (60). All these discourse functions are basically information-reporting or information-requesting moves, with the doctor as their target.

The son's limited address to his mother throughout the extract is restricted to prompting her to answer a doctor's question (33, 48). Other than this, the son fills spaces in the discourse which could in principle be filled by his mother. At many points, and particularly when he is voicing *her* experiences, he is 'speaking for' his mother. This is to say that something like a traditional doctor/patient frame for talk is maintained within the encounter, but that the son, at various points, positions himself within that frame in place of the patient. There is therefore a general framing conflict within the encounter. What does this tell us about the relationships constituted in this consultation, and how we should evaluate them? Important evidence is available in local contexts of the son's reportings.

The doctor's open-ended elicitation at the end of turn 10 (*how are you feeling?*) triggers a hedged-negative response from the patient. 'Not too bad' and 'could be better' are two of a small set of conventional responses to 'how are you?' openings in medical encounters which we have considered in detail elsewhere (Coupland et al. 1992, 1994). At turn 12 the doctor specifies his earlier question by requesting information about the *main problems*. The patient physically orients to her son and, partly through lowered voice and partly through a further non-committal answer (*oh I don't know*), offers the doctor's elicitation and the floor for a response to her son. After this, she seems content to echo and then elaborate (turns 15 and 17) on her son's response. The son then holds the floor for several turns, reporting his mother's experiences through third-person reference (*she, her*). The doctor complies with this participation frame, marking recipiency and acknowledgement of the son's information (turns 19, 21 and 23). We cannot tell whether the doctor's question at turn 25 is designed for the patient or for the son, but the son clearly assumes response rights and fills out turn 26.

The patient does not retire from the conversation at this point, and in fact she interrupts her son during his turn 26 to clarify his rather hedged, uncertain response. Yet she leaves a one-second pause after the doctor's next question (turn 28) which again provides a floor opportunity for the son. His response, in her conversational space, produces the pronominal dissonance of the doctor's patient-designed *you* (turn 28) being followed by the son's *she* (turn 29). The next few turns repeat the progression we have described, with the patient again forgoing a response (the longer pause after the doctor's turn 31) and again offering her response role to the son (turn 32). There is another instance at turn 46, where the mother's reticence to respond to the doctor's question sees the son attempting an elicitation of his own. Here he has been unable to provide the answer to the question. But more generally, the son's readiness to fill such spaces and provide quite detailed accounts of his mother's problems and activities is therefore compatible with, and at least partly occasioned by, her own reticence. This reticence is displayed not only by silence at points where the doctor has designed her to be next-speaker, but also by non-committal responses which mark low authority to comment (e.g. *oh I don't remember, I don't remember much though, I don't think so*).

It would be difficult to conclude that the elderly patient's conversational and functional autonomy is being compromised in this extract by an 'over-talking' son, and to invoke ageist practice. He is certainly operating in her space, both rhetorically and experientially. We get an impression of *surrogacy* here, particularly when the son assesses his mother's swollen ankles and shortness of breath. These assessments would normally be considered appropriate only for first-person accounts. But the son is invited into the surrogate role at crucial points. In the closing section (from turn 50), it is the son who asks whether his mother can *go out* (turn 56), following the doctor's pre-closing *is there anything else you're worried about?* On this occasion there is no pause in the mother's response space and the son's response is latched to the end of the doctor's turn. However, he prefaces his response with *=er she wanted to know*, which proposes that he is in any case voicing her concern, not his. He is again speaking for his mother, but the suggestion is that this is warranted by the concern being his mother's. In Goffman's terms for participation frames, he claims to be animating concerns which she has principalled (Goffman 1981: 144). It is interesting that the doctor is briefly drawn into third-person reference to the patient at this point (in his turn 57). But this is within a response to a question (the first in the consultation) asked by the son (turn 56), and where a response using second-person reference would have seemed inappropriate. The doctor in any case then reverts to the dominant participant design using *you*.

These moments of surrogate communication are interspersed with a patient–son alignment that is better described as *role-shared* or *co-articulated*. These include the echoic utterances we noted at turns 14 and 15, and the editing the patient does of her son's response at turns 26 and 27. Similarly, the answer to the doctor's question about being short of breath is jointly produced by son and patient (turns 29 and 30), with similar alignment in responses to the doctor's question about urine testing (turns 42 and 43). In the closing sequence, the discourse is more evenly voiced. But the 'closing sequence turns' are arguably highly reactive in any case, as all are produced in response to information giving and confirming by the doctor, and occur as *oh*-prefaced change-of-state markers (Heritage 1984). In general, it is quite possibly true that the son's conversational activity further represses the mother's involvement, which the doctor, as we saw, is keen to promote. But there is also textual evidence that the son is compensating for his mother's low involvement, and certainly that, in this interaction, she initially creates the opportunity and the need for him to be conversationally active – either with her or on her behalf.

3 A caring daughter: speaking with

Doctors in the data seem generally more ready to design daughter third parties into consultation discourse than we saw with the son in Extract 1, but generally not to the extent of forgoing the principle of second-person address to patients. All third parties and patients in the remaining extracts we consider are female.

3.1 Extract 2

Doctor H: (registrar) male, in his thirties
Patient 37: female, aged 85
Triad: with daughter, in her fifties

(The patient and her daughter have just entered the consulting room. They have exchanged greetings with the doctor and the doctor has gained permission to record the consultations. The patient is a little deaf.)

1 Doctor: good (2.0) erm (looking at patient's notes) (2.0) right I notice that
               we had a bit of a slow (1.0) noted a bit of a slow pulse when you
               were in hospital (.) have you had any problems since you've gone
               home?

2 Patient: no

3 Doctor: right (.) and (.) *(to daughter)* how's she been?

4 Daughter: yeah you had a bit of er

5 Patient: <u>oh</u>! er er=

6 Daughter: =yeah giddy=

7 Patient: =j j just a little (.) not not er a <u>pain</u> but (.) just a pressure (.) you know
                                                                              [   ]
8 Daughter: ((1 syll))

9 Daughter: a pressure (.) you know in her head she (.) for a couple of days it's
               passed now
                                                                        [
10 Doctor:
                                                                  did you
               actually (.) did you actually (.) be have the (.) the dizziness? (.) the=
                                                                  [
11 Patient: no giddiness
                                                                        [   ]
12 Daughter: no

13 Doctor   =the sickness that you had before?
                        [   ]
14 Daughter: no

15 Patient: no

Extract 2 shows how the same doctor as in Extract 1 elicits an evaluative response from the patient's daughter early on in the consultation with patient

37. The patient has produced a brief *no* in response to the doctor's question in turn 1, and it is at that point that the doctor offers a more open reformulation to the daughter, *how's she been?* Differently from the son's talk-design in Extract 1, the daughter then makes a response which initially offers the floor back to her mother, using *you* address to her. The account of giddiness that ensues is co-constructed by the two women over turns 4 to 9. In fact, this pattern of role-shared response is repeated in dealing with the doctor's next two questions (turns 11 and 12, and 14 and 15), and it persists across later turns (not extracted). The patient is, this time, the primary account-giver, for example in offering the first detailed response after the daughter's brokerage of the doctor's question (turn 7). The daughter's main roles in the extracted talk, after facilitating her mother's response, are to add detail to her mother's account (turn 9) and to provide small utterances of general endorsement (turns 12 and 14). A subtly different frame is constructed from the 'doctor–patient frame with patient surrogacy' of Extract 1. The daughter-carer in Extract 2 has her own position within a more resolutely triadic structure, albeit a subordinate position, facilitating and endorsing. 'Speaking with' is a more appropriate general concept to summarise her contributions to Extract 2 than 'speaking for'. Her talk frames her as co-narrator of her mother's problems, symptoms and histories, and less as a discursive surrogate. She facilitates her mother's own account as much as she contributes to it.

4   Framing agency

Both the third parties we have encountered so far undoubtedly feel they have legitimate voices in the consultations. They are family members who have witnessed, and in that sense co-experienced, at least some aspects of the health problems patients are presenting at the clinic. Many of the accounts they give, or share in giving, relate to physical and externally visible problems, and this suggests they may feel they have not only rights but a duty to report problems and symptoms to doctors as they have seen them. In the different ways we have examined, they stand in the place of or alongside elderly patients, offering extended informational and interpretive accounts for the doctor to assimilate and work into diagnoses and recommendations for later care.

Not surprisingly, there are instances in the data when the 'third-party-as-carer' role is expressed very directly in the discourse, to the extent of marking family members' agency and felt responsibility in care taking. This responsibility is sometimes framed by third parties adopting a mediating role between doctor and patient. They orient to treatments and regimens that the doctor authorises as practices they have to inculcate or police.

4.1 Extract 3

Doctor E: (professor) male, in his sixties
Patient 117: female, aged 76
Triad: with daughter, in her fifties

(*The doctor is discussing the patient's need to lose weight.*)

1 Doctor: <u>great</u> (.) because I think we had a long chat about that some time ago how important this <u>was</u> because this is quite crucial to those nasty pains in your knees=

2 Patient: =yeah=

3 Doctor: =to get the <u>load</u> off your joints=

4 Patient: =yes=

5 Doctor: =um (.) are you still sticking fairly strictly to your diet?

6 Patient: yes haven't I? but I ((2 sylls))
   [

7 Doctor: good good
        [

8 Daughter: (*loudly*) <u>yes</u> and we've <u>really</u> tried <u>this</u> time=

9 Doctor: =I'm sure well er it's clearly being successful
       [   ]   [   ]

10 Patient: yes   but
       [

11 Daughter: we really have tried but yeah

12 Doctor: I can see that by the different weight
      [

13 Daughter: <u>yes</u> I wish I could get her to do a bit more exercise doctor but I can't doctor she'll
       [

14 Doctor: <u>yes</u>

15 Daughter: come down to the shops with me one time

16 Doctor: yes

17 Daughter: fine she'll go all the way back and when she comes back it might be a month again before she'll=

18 Doctor: =yes

19 Daughter: make the effort to go back down again

20 Doctor: yes

21 Patient: I get so out of breath like you know walking
                          [
22 Doctor: do you?

23 Doctor: yes
              [
24 Daughter: she perspires a lot she do
                          [
25 Doctor: yes
                          [
26 Patient: and er the perspiration pours off me then
                          [
27 Doctor: yes yes (.) you see really what it's best to
            do is er kind of little and often (.) erm it's obvious that while your
            weight is what it is you can't do large amounts of exercise

28 Patient: no

Extract 3 is initially framed as the normative doctor–patient dyad, with the doctor asking the patient (turn 5) if she has been keeping to her diet, the patient replying that she has done this (turn 6). At this point the patient looks to the daughter for confirmation *haven't I?*, which overtly endorses the daughter's potential role as witness. The doctor's supportive endorsement in the follow-up slot (turn 7) is overlapped by an explicit marker of involvement by the daughter in the practice of maintaining the diet. She says *we've really tried this time*, pronominally reinterpreting the agency implied in the doctor's singular *you* in turn 5 as a matter of shared involvement. She repeats this in turn 11. As she elaborates on how much exercise her mother takes (another part of the regimen previously discussed), she casts herself in the causative role, relative to the walking which her mother does (or doesn't do). Her grammatical representation of their roles is very direct: *I wish I could get her to do a bit of exercise* (turn 13), and she repeats it later in the extract (beyond the extracted text): *I can't get her active; try to get her going*.

The daughter's third-person reporting on patient circumstances takes on a different quality from the previous instances. She has established that she views her own role as causative, wielding the doctor's authority by proxy. As a result, her later reporting references to her mother (e.g. *she'll go all the way back*, turn 17; *she perspires a lot*, turn 24) go well beyond surrogacy and co-articulation. She is not speaking for or with the patient, but from an independent position which she assumes allows/requires her to evaluate the patient's practices as well as report on them. She is effectively exposing the patient to the doctor for her non-compliance. Note how the doctor for the most part maintains his second-person address to the patient and says very little that could be construed as supporting the daughter's framing of her own role in the triad. His main turns, after the daughter has asserted her causative role, are resolutely patient-addressed (turn 27 and later, beyond the extracted text).

5 Third-party/doctor confederations

Radically different alignments emerge within the data. Particularly distinctive are those events where third parties align with doctors, and we can consider two instances.

5.1 Extract 4

Doctor A: (registrar) male, in his thirties
Patient 059: female; aged 81
Triad: with daughter

(The patient has had a stroke which has affected her eyesight. She is depressed and reports that the anti-depressants prescribed are not helping.)

1 Patient: <u>no</u> (.) um what you (.) I can't see how those things are gonna make
            what you <u>think</u> (.) it's er the <u>trouble</u> I've had (.) <u>that's</u> the trouble
            <u>that's</u> the cause of my depression (.) nothing else . . .
            (The doctor acknowledges her feelings, pauses and continues)

2 Doctor: *(referring to tablets)* now we find sometimes that those <u>help</u>

3 Patient: well perhaps they <u>are</u> helping me I don't know

4 Daughter: well <u>I</u> think I think she's better
                            [
5 Doctor: I think she's er
                                  [
6 Daughter: Christmas time she just sat used
            to sit and sort of erm=

7 Doctor: =I think she a little bit improved since
                      [
8 Daughter: she didn't want to do things (.) yes

9 Doctor: since I saw you last time

10 Daughter: <u>yes</u>
            (2.0)
11 Doctor: how do <u>you</u> think things are going?

12 Patient: *(sighs)* (2.0) well sometimes I feel alright and sometimes (.) I feel (.)
            er oh it's not what the hell's er living in when you put the <u>news</u> on
            what do you get? (.) it's <u>all</u> trouble here and (.) everywhere in the
            world is is <u>misery</u> and trouble (.) you think what the <u>hell's</u> the good
            of living (.) in a world like this?

221

In the first transcribed turn of Extract 4, the patient is expressing her frustrations about taking the anti-depressant medication she has been prescribed. She is putting the case to the doctor that her depression relates to her past personal troubles, and will not respond to drugs. If, once again, we begin by examining pronoun-indexed address and reference, we see a relational pattern develop early in the extract that is very untypical of the data as a whole. The daughter embarks on third-person reference, *she*, in turn 4. The doctor and the daughter then maintain mutual *she* through turns 5, 6, 7 and 8, and it returns in the closing sequence of the consultation (not extracted).

The mutuality of third-person reference is important in itself. It allows the doctor and the daughter (who instigates it) to articulate a shared stance – a *confederation*. The stance is to argue that the patient's morale has in fact improved over time, to counter the patient's own account that her depression is not responding to drug treatment. Doctor and third party are attempting to 'talk the patient up'. They cast her in the discourse role of overhearer, albeit intended overhearer. This is an instance of Goffman's 'byplay' – 'subordinated communication of a subset of ratified participants' (Goffman 1981: 134). What's more, it is a particular form of 'collusive byplay' (ibid.), because the doctor and daughter make quasi-dyadic, quasi-objective evaluations of the patient's progress, but within her hearing. The strategy frames the patient as a non-addressed observer of an apparently 'neutral' assessment of her improving circumstances. However transparent the participation framework device is, it may be responsible for the patient's more positive self-assessment, at least at the onset of turn 12.

The discourse of this sequence has a strongly non-institutional quality. In fact, because boosting morale defines their main local objectives, the daughter and the doctor have an investment in breaking clinic norms, which are themselves mainly driven by the doctor's institutional authority and interactional control – for the purposes of orderly symptom-getting, evaluation, decision making, and so on (Silverman 1987). But this normative institutional order is redundant, and unhelpful, at this moment. Doctor and third party need to present themselves in non-institutional roles, presenting 'what anyone would observe' about the patient's improving situation. A further indication of how the institutional frame has lapsed is the patient's repeated self-talk within the extract. In turns 1 and 12 (and at several later points, not extracted) her talk is not obviously designed as addressed to either of the other participants. Her use of *you* in turn 12 is, in context, clearly non-second person.

This extract's relational confederation is no doubt positively motivated. The doctor collusively enters the confederation because it is potentially in the patient's interest to do so. In contrast, a final instance from a different interaction shows a daughter seeking collusion with a senior doctor much more destructively.

5.2 *Extract 5*

Doctor E: (professor), male, in his sixties
Patient 115: female, aged 75
Triad: with daughter

(The patient has been describing pins and needles in her leg when she tries to walk. The transcript begins about five minutes into the consultation, during which the daughter has said very little, while the doctor and patient discuss symptoms and medication another doctor has so far prescribed.)

1 Patient: now when I first went there (.) he told me to take <u>them</u> (*puts the second bottle of pills down on the table*)
                                              [
2 Daughter: (*irritatedly*) put them all on the <u>table</u>

3 Patient: for the high blood pressure right?

4 Doctor: yes

5 Patient: then they (.) it couldn't bring the blood down so he told me to take <u>those</u> with it (puts a bottle of pills on the table) (.) right?

6 Doctor: yes

7 Patient: they're a different colour doctor=

8 Doctor: =yes=

9 Patient: but um they're the same thing . . .

(Several minutes later the doctor has finished taking the history.)
10 Doctor: no (.) right okay fine (.) right would you like to pop onto the couch (.) we'll pull the curtain around you and we'll come and have a little look at you

11 Daughter: it'll be alright don't worry (.) (*to doctor*) if I wasn't here she wouldn't speak at all (*laughs slightly*)

12 Doctor: (*laughs slightly*) yes (.) they do get a bit nervous don't they? (.) strange places
                                                                    [
13 Daughter: yeah
                they do ((get a bit))

                (20.0) (*The doctor goes through notes and nurse can be heard helping the patient to get undressed*)

14 Daughter: she's a <u>worri</u>er

15 Doctor: pardon?

16 Daughter: she is a worrier

17 Doctor: yes (.) gets a bit <u>an</u>xious does she?
              (15.0)

18 Daughter: she's not quite sure whether she's got angina or no this is what
              ((could be))

                                                              [
19 Doctor: yes
              well we'll sort all that out (.) yes now (3.0) yes it's difficult when
              you know (.) when one's not quite certain what <u>is</u> wrong (.) then
              people get much more <u>an</u>xious about (.) er

20 Daughter: I think when you get to her age you get a bit confused actually
                                      [   ]
21 Doctor: yes yes

22 Doctor: well it's difficult if we're (.) you know sometimes somebody's con-
              ditions need a little bit of treatment (.) her blood pressure does (.)
              her doctor really was quite right (.) I mean to chop and <u>change</u>
              things because
                                              [
23 Daughter: ((he tried to
              regulate it))

At turn 10 of Extract 5 the doctor and the patient's daughter remain at the
doctor's desk while the patient, out of earshot, moves to a cubicle with a
nurse who will help her to get undressed. The daughter then instigates a
discussion with the doctor about her mother's emotional, bio-medical and
cognitive condition, some of it clearly stereotype-driven and age-prejudicial.
Within turn 11, the daughter frame-switches from addressing her mother to
commenting about her mother to the doctor. The switch is marked stylistically (cf. Tannen and Wallat's 1993: 65 discussion of 'register shifting'). The
mother is reframed by this switch, from ratified second-person addressee to
non-ratified third-party referent. But the relational definitions attached to
this switch are radical. The mother's constructed addressee role as 'a recipient
of endearment' (*it'll be alright don't worry*) is reconfigured, within the turn,
as 'nervous or incompetent old person' (*if I wasn't here she wouldn't speak at
all (laughs slightly)*). The daughter's slight laugh at the end of that same turn,
in the context of the imputation she makes that her mother is nervous or
incompetent, is important to reading its relational effect. The laughter gives
her utterance a collusive quality, and it is interesting that the doctor echoes
the laugh at the beginning of his turn, seeming to agree to collude. His utterances in turn 12 do agreement (*yes*), and accounting (*they do get a bit nervous*

don't they? (.) strange places). He implies that the patient's nervousness is attributable to the circumstances of the clinic (*strange places*) but also, surprisingly, to her group membership (*they*), which must refer to elderly people or elderly patients. Even if we interpret the doctor's strategy as being to minimise the daughter's imputation of nervousness/incompetence by accounting for it, he nevertheless uses a way of referring to her which is age-group based and de-individualising. Since the daughter agrees in similar terms (turn 13), doctor and daughter have now entered a relational frame where they, as 'younger people', are jointly evaluating the patient in intergroup terms. This pattern again runs directly counter to the anti-ageist ideology of the clinic, where age-group directed reference is generally considered age-prejudicial. The clinic, meta-ideologically, commits itself to 'treating patients as individuals'.

While the patient remains out of earshot (from mid-turn 11 to the end of the extract), the daughter tries to construct further forms of collusion with the doctor, inviting him to endorse several of her own typological perceptions and even diagnoses of her mother. She suggests to the doctor that her mother is *a worrier* (turns 14, 16), that her 'confusion' is typical of old people (20). At one point she suggests (not transcribed) that older people lack understanding (*when they get to their age they think well why are they doing it . . . they don't know*). The doctor does discursive work throughout this later sequence to withdraw from the constructed collusion. Most of his turns propose reformulations of the daughter's typologies. For example, he proposes an individuated characterisation (*gets a bit anxious*, turn 17) in place of the daughter's group label (*a worrier*, turn 14); and similarly in reformulating the daughter's *when you get to her age* (turn 20) with *somebody's conditions* (turn 22). He works to retrieve a medical context for evaluating the patient's circumstances, in place of the daughter's age-referenced generalisations.

6   The 'chauffeuring' model of medical triads

The framing of participation in triadic consultation discourse is highly variable, across and within the extracts we have examined. Their roles and alignments are not definitively given by the institutional or intergenerational structure of the encounters themselves, although normative configurations are apparent. Non-normative frames can be actively proposed, and in some cases resisted.

We can ask whether third-party participation, as lived out in the data, is consistent with what has been called *a chauffeur role* (e.g. Silverman 1987). Silverman develops a rather literalist interpretation of the chauffeur role in medical/clinical interactions, in his analysis of paediatric outpatients' interactions (involving babies or very young children). He considers a direct analogy between accompanying a young child to a paediatric clinic and 'what happens when a motorist takes a car to a garage workshop' (1987: 35), where the third party equates to the motorist, the doctor to the mechanic, and the patient to the car. With important caveats about the 'deeper moral and emotional basis' (ibid.) in the medical case, Silverman sees some power in the analogy. It allows him, he says, to appreciate a distinction between 'fault-repairing' and 'servicing' events, parallelled by clinical visits which are symptom-specific and those that are asymptomatic (check-up visits). In the first set, parents as chauffeurs may expect doctors to assume responsibility for 'fixing' problems, and they themselves will be relatively inactive in the discourse. In the second set, medical and other processes will be more negotiable, and Silverman expects third-parties to be more conversationally active as a result.

The direct analogy clearly does not capture the complexity of our data. There is no clear division between symptomatic and asymptomatic instances in our context. Very few of the elderly patients at the clinic we observed have no medical or social problems of any degree of severity to report. Elderly patients are not 'chauffeured' in anything resembling the same sense as babies or young children might be, and we have commented on the dominant ideology at the clinic that patients should be the arbiters of their own health decisions and outcomes. But could an alternative analogy based on the concept of chauffeuring be useful, at least in mapping out some of the relationships between patients and third parties framed in our data?

If we see a chauffeur as a 'mobiliser' (providing the service of moving another person from one position to another, discursively as well as physically), then some third parties' communication, and the relational positions constructed through it, do seem to fall within the scope of the concept. Chauffeurs, after all, have to be 'front seat drivers', but they are also in the service of the people they mobilise, and they may adopt relatively powerless or powerful roles. Some third parties, notably the daughter in Extract 4, represent their caring role as a causative one, mobilising patients to comply with courses of treatment or lifestyle changes doctors have recommended ('getting the patient to do something'). This daughter positioned herself as having a powerful role to play, in many respects relegating her mother to a powerless 'back seat', despite exposing her mother to the doctor for her passivity in sitting there. The Extract 5 daughter, seen as a chauffeur, framed her mother as one of a set of elderly 'non-drivers', firmly *denying* her access to the 'front seat'. Other third parties are less assertive in their chauffeuring roles. They exchange decisions about route and speed with their parents, variously deciding for them (as surrogate patients) and sitting alongside them, negotiating with them, making some of the relevant decisions about speed and route, as what we called 'co-articulators'.

The chauffeuring analogy is still inadequate, however, because it fails to indicate how important the multi-party context is for understanding *all* the relationships constructed in the data – even those constructed in what appear to be simple dyadic exchanges (e.g. when daughters and doctors talk, out of earshot of elderly patients). The Extract 5 daughter, for example, would be better described as seeking to assert her front-seat chauffeuring position in the eyes of 'a driving instructor' (if this is at all a plausible analogy for the doctor). Her ageist construction of 'the back-seat elderly client' is far more adverse when the client cannot hear her talk. The patient in Extract 1 is, over many sequences of talk, not involved in 'steering' or 'navigation', when her son shows himself quite enthusiastic to talk on her behalf. The Extract 4 daughter and doctor (viewed as chauffeur and instructor) actively remove themselves from the front seat to the back seat, to chat about the mother's improving driving competence. They try to boost her driving confidence and encourage her to resume a driving position (achieve greater control over her emotional life).

The data we have considered show that social roles in the care of elderly people are interdependent and, at least to some extent, negotiable. For example, we can see how the 'back seat' role becomes natural or even inevitable when another person moves, communicatively, to take the driver's seat. But even then, participants are able to negotiate a set of particular stances which vary, in terms of the chauffeuring metaphor, between 'front seat co-driver' (navigating, deciding on route and speed) and 'back-seat passenger' (a passive role whose occupant takes little or no role in decision making or responsibility). It certainly appears that these roles are products of communication practices. 'Chauffeurs', 'passengers' and 'instructors' can and do reconstruct their roles within relational frames during their (consultative) journeys.

The analysis perhaps suggests a wider conclusion, one relevant to the notion of dependency in old age. In one of its senses, dependency is an economically based concept. In the context of ageing it often points to the absence of a 'full' or legitimising contribution to the social system. It is, alternatively, definable in physical terms. Many of the people we listen to in the data seem to match these criteria, and this tends to essentialise them as 'elderly patients'. But the way we have approached our data, through frame analysis, emphasises the social and communicative senses of dependency. Seen in this light, dependency has a more malleable form (though by no means less impact on self-definition and morale). It is more obviously a product of social practice – a structural position that we can, within limits, discursively manufacture and mould. In the context of social ageing, the truism of human communication – that we are all (inter)dependent social actors – has a particular resonance (cf. Bytheway and Johnstone 1990).

Notes

1. We have tried to avoid the term 'geriatrics' because of its generally pejorative uses. On the other hand, it is the term that has become established in medical domains specialising in health care for the elderly. It is part of the official designation of the outpatients clinic where we did our ethnographic research and collected the present body of audio-recorded data.

2. Reference to 'third parties' is misleading because their contribution to the discourse of these events is, as we shall see, often far from peripheral. But we will persist with the term, in the absence of a better one.
3. Transcription conventions used in the extracts are:

(.)	un-timed short pause
(1.0)	pause timed in seconds
(*quietly*)	informal commentary on style or context of following utterance(s)
?	indicates question function (not grammatical interrogative)
[	overlapping speech
[ ]	entirely overlapped speech
((. . .))	unclear speech
Underlining	shows unusually heavy emphasis
=	shows 'latching' (utterances following each other without perceptible pause)
Line numbers	indicate speaking turns in a particular extract

References

Beisecker, A.L. (1989) The influence of a companion on the doctor–elderly patient interaction. *Health Communication* 1, 55–70.

Bytheway, B. and Johnstone, J. (1990) On defining ageism. *Critical Social Policy* 29, 27–39.

Candlin, C.N. (1997) General editor's preface. In Gunnarsson, B.-L., Linell, P. and Nordberg, B. (eds) *The Construction of Professional Discourse*. London: Longman, vii–xiv.

Coe, R.M. and Prendergast, C.G. (1985) The formation of coalitions: Interaction strategies in triads. *Sociology of Health and Illness* 7, 237–347.

Coupland, J. and Coupland, N. (forthcoming) Roles, responsibilities and alignments: Multi-party talk in geriatric care. In Hummert, M.L. and Nussbaum, J. (eds) *Aging, Communication and Health*. Mahwah, NJ: Lawrence Erlbaum Associates.

Coupland, J., Coupland, N. and Robinson, J. (1992) 'How are you?': Negotiating phatic communion. *Language in Society* 21, 201–230.

Coupland, J., Robinson, J. and Coupland, N. (1994) Frame negotiation in doctor–elderly patient consultations. *Discourse and Society* 5(1), 89–124.

Coupland, N. and Coupland, J. (1997) Discourses of the unsayable: Death-implicative talk in geriatric medical consultations. In Jaworski, A. (ed.) *Silence: Interdisciplinary Perspectives*. Berlin: Mouton de Gruyter, 117–152.

Coupland, N. and Coupland, J. (1998) Reshaping lives: Constitutive identity work in geriatric medical consultations. *Text* 18(2), 159–189.

Coupland, N. and Coupland, J. (1999) Ageing, ageism and anti-ageism: Moral stance in discourse. In Hamilton, H. (ed.) *Language and Old Age*. New York: Garland Publishing Inc., 177–208.

Goffman, E. (1981) *Forms of Talk*. Oxford: Blackwell.

Goffman, E. (1997) Frame analysis. In Lemert, C. and Branaman, A. (eds) *The Goffman Reader*. Oxford: Blackwell, 149–166.

Goodwin, C. (1981) *Conversational Organization: Interaction between Speakers and Hearers*. New York: Academic Press.

Greene, M.G., Majerovitz, S.D., Adelman, R.D. and Rizzo, C. (1994) The effects of the presence of a third person on the physician–older patient medical interview. *Journal of the American Geriatrics Society* 42, 413–419.

Hall, M.R.P., Maclennan, W.J. and Dye, M.D.W. (1993) *Medical Care of the Elderly* (3rd edition). Chichester: Wiley.

Harre, R. (1992) What is real in psychology: A plea for persons. *Theory and Psychology* 2, 153–158.

Hasselkus, B.R. (1992) Physician and family caregiver in the medical setting? Negotiation of care? *Journal of Aging Studies* 6, 67–80.

Heritage, J.M. (1984) A change-of-state token and aspects of its sequential placement. In Atkinson, J.M. and Heritage, J. (eds) *Structures of Social Action: Studies in Conversational Analysis*. Cambridge: Cambridge University Press, 299–345.

Hummert, M.L. (1994) Stereotypes of the elderly and patronising speech. In Hummert, M.L., Wiemann, J.M. and Nussbaum, J. (eds) *Interpersonal Communication in Older Adulthood: Interdisciplinary Research*. Newbury Park: Sage, 162–184.

Lerner, G.H. (1996) On the place of linguistic resources in the organisation of talk-in-interaction: Second-person reference in multi-party conversation. *Pragmatics* 6(3), 281–294.

Levinson, S.C. (1988) Putting linguistics on a proper footing: Explorations in Goffman's concepts of participation. In Drew, P. and Wootton, A. (eds) *Erving Goffman*. Oxford: Polity Press, 161–227.

Ryan, E.B., Bourhis, R.Y. and Knops, U. (1991) Evaluative perceptions of patronising speech addressed to elders. *Psychology and Aging* 6, 442–450.

Sidell, M. (1995) *Health in Old Age: Myth, Mystery and Management*. Buckingham: Open University Press.

Silverman, D. (1987) *Communication and Medical Practice: Social Relations in the Clinic*. London: Sage.

Tannen, D. and Wallat, C. (1993) Interactive frames and knowledge schemas in interaction: Examples from a medical examination/interview. In Tannen, D. (ed.) *Framing in Discourse*. Oxford: Oxford University Press.

Chapter 13

New dynamics in the nurse–patient relationship?

Sally Candlin

1   Introduction: nurses and patients

This chapter concerns a professional group whose history has been one of powerlessness and professional domination. Nurses are in a paradoxical situation since, as the largest professional group within the health care system, their voice for many years frequently was not heard. A number of reasons have been cited to account for this, only one of which concerns the gender imbalance occasioned by the predominance of women in the ranks of its members. As a group nurses have traditionally been 'managed', not only by another professional group (medicine) but as a consequence of nursing's hierarchical organisational structure. Nurses, however, face another paradox. As professionals with their own body of knowledge, they have been considered powerful members in the asymmetric relationship between themselves and patients. As a counterweight to this, and in support of a new kind of workplace relationship, we see a current patient-centred approach (cf. Ragan, forthcoming) where nurses facilitate trusting relationships by patient-empowering strategies. Rather than empowering patients, however, I argue that the strategies employed by nurses in this changed practice serve to maintain the status quo and result merely in a new manifestation of the traditionally asymmetric nurse–patient relationship.

2   Nursing and discourse practice

Until relatively recently, scant attention has been paid to the crucial nature of the contribution of discourse practices to nursing practice, with much of the work in conversational and discourse analysis being focused on doctor–patient interactions. This demands explanation, if only because it is the nurse who spends many hours relating to the patient and performing the most intimate aspects of care. Henzl (1989), for example, found that following a medical consultation, which may last for only 5 minutes and rarely for longer than 35, it was the nurse to whom the patient was directed for continuing care and often for the interpretation of instructions. It is upon the nurse's interactive skills that the success of treatment frequently depends and it is the nurse who often facilitates an improvement in the patient's quality of life. One explanation for the biased focus may be that discourse analysts find it easier to target their research at doctors and their practices, in part perhaps because doctor–patient interactions are of short duration and usually in private offices, where nursing involvement, at least in the hospital environment, is on-going and 'around the clock', usually in a public ward. Possibly, also, the doctor–patient interaction is an attractive option in that both doctors and discourse analysts have a joint base in the academy while, in most countries, nurse education has only recently been transferred into the tertiary education sector. There is also an assumption that doctors are the main contact point with patients. This imbalance in research studies' focus is now being somewhat redressed by, for example, Bredmar and Linell (1999) and Heritage and Sefi (1992), who have, respectively, analysed the conversations of midwives and health visitors with their clients. Similarly Grainger (1992) has examined the conversation of nurses when caring for elderly patients. This change in focus is of interest since studies of nurse–patient interactions appear to parallel fundamental changes taking place in professional practice (cf. Benner 1984; Paterson and Zderad 1976). Such changes in practice inevitably impact upon professional discourse since they relate to the move from a task-based approach to care (where emphasis is placed on physical care) to a process or holistic approach where emphasis is placed as much on the patient's psycho-social needs as on physical needs. These changes were exemplified by Alfano (1971) and adapted by Pearson (1991), who proposed no fewer than 37 distinctions between task-oriented nursing (where emphasis is placed on the task to be performed), and therapeutic nursing where the total needs of the patient are considered.[1]

These changes imply an ideological shift in nursing practice, and, ultimately, in the nurse–patient relationship. Where nurses have traditionally been regarded as the decision makers and gatekeepers to resources, now the patient is encouraged to be a co-partner in care. This shift suggests a potential for tension since patients (and some nurses too) frequently believe that in sickness people want to be 'cared for' and have the weight of decision-making taken from them. Linked to this is the belief that the nurse is the expert and 'knows best'. Whether such responses are the result of being sick, or stem from a genuine belief that the patient's knowledge base is inadequate, is a moot point. Linked to the changed focus of patient care is an acknowledgement that the identity of the nurse must change from one who is managed to a manager, from a keeper of information to one who is also an educator, a facilitator and counsellor. This suggests that the nurse adopts a multiplicity of functions to facilitate the caring role, as can be seen in Figure 13.1.

While the central role of the nurse is that of a clinician, it is enacted by the engagement in one or more functions. Those illustrated here – caring,

Figure 13.1 The role and functions of the nurse (*adapted from Candlin, S., 1992*)

advocating, counselling, educating, etc. – are by no means all-inclusive, yet none of these functions is necessarily discrete since a number of functions may be performed simultaneously. Such a hybrid functionality gives rise to polyphonic discourse (cf. Bakhtin 1981) as the voice of the healer/carer may also be, for example, the voice of the counsellor, educator and/or technologist, depending on the caring environment. Similarly, dependent upon the situation, the nurse does not necessarily engage in all of these functions. A situation may require engaging in the counselling function, but not the technical, policy-making, or research functions. Counselling, however, requires critical thinking skills, often the skills of the educator, and *always* involves communication skills. Discourse, therefore, is not only central to nursing care, it often *constitutes* the care. Responding to the needs of each clinical situation, nurses bring not only their education, training and practice experiences, but also their varying and individual life experiences. There is therefore potential for, and actual differences in, both practice styles and discourse strategies.

But as the nursing role is becoming more complex, so too is the patient's role changing. From being a passive recipient, the patient is expected to participate actively in care. Such changes are not merely ideologically invested professionally, but represent a shift in power relations since any decision making involves a degree of control and power. We see therefore the potential for confusion in the expectations of each partner, resulting in possible tension in the changing power structure of the relationship. Changes in expectations and ideological shifts in power exert pressure on the communicative skills of the participants. Two extracts of discourse (examples 1 and 2) between a registered nurse (N) and patient (P) demonstrate this apparent shift, with the patient dominating the conversation.

2.1 Examples

Transcription Notes.
The following symbols have been used in the transcription of data:
(.) seconds of silence;
(*) seconds of indecipherable talk;
(**bold font**) indicates Thematic structure.

Example 1
N (registered nurse) is assessing P (patient) at home

N:	1	How did **you** feel in **yourself** when
	2	all this was happening
	3	you know you
P:	4	Of course **I** couldn't believe
	5	this was really happening to **me** you know
	6	and then in the hospital em it was the first time (***)
	7	doctor was talking to **me** and
	8	one of them asked **me**
	9	what was **my attitude** towards (*) and all this (***) and
	10	**I** thought oh if **I die I die**
	11	**I** suppose there's nothing **I** could do about it but
	12	**I** still couldn't see it happening to me
	13	well nobody can can they
	14	it's always someone else

Example 2

N:	1	Yes it's not easy today with things (. . . . .)
P:	2	But it was after **I** was retrenched actually
	3	it was five months after mum because because
	4	mum because me mum passed away a week or so after
	5	and then **I** was crook
N:	6	yeah it must have been very hard for you
	7	that happening and
	8	then getting sick yourself
P:	9	**I** suppose
	10	that's the lot that's dealt out to **you**
	11	**you**'ve got to take it haven't **you**

2.2 Background to the situation

The patient is being visited in his home by a registered nurse who is performing a nursing procedure (dressing a surgical wound) and assessing his health status following discharge from hospital.

The development of a therapeutic relationship demands that the attitudes of the patient are recognised by the nurse. The identification of care-needs and the achievement of both nursing and discoursal goals hinge on this recognition. Attitudes are reflected in discoursal choices, and responses are made on the basis of the nurse's interpretive understanding. This is a crucial point to understand because although it is conceivable that this conversation might take place between friends (or some professional person other than a nurse), the information disclosed by the patient takes on a different meaning according to the orientation of the interlocutor. Knowing that the interlocutor is a nurse immediately takes the conversation out of the realms of a friendly interaction. What the nurse does with the information is professionally prescribed and enables her to 'do nursing'. At the same time, the patient enacts the patient-role. The conversation prior to these two extracts had consisted of 160 exchanges during which the nurse and patient had discussed his social situation. The interaction was friendly and conducted in a semi-structured manner, topics being raised by the nurse and developed by both parties. As the interaction proceeded, the patient's turns became longer as he volunteered considerable health-related information. On closer examination, although it appears that the patient and the nurse are co-constructing the discourse, the patient ostensibly being empowered, it is the nurse who controls and maintains the topic content, thus retaining a powerful position. The subtle nature of this seemingly changed relationship is one which is not immediately obvious, but becomes clear to an astute member of the professional group (i.e. any nurse who shares values, beliefs and knowledge base with this practitioner). For example, it becomes apparent that both participants align to the goals of the interaction. It is however, the nurse, in example 1, lines 1–2, who sets the parameters in this extract.

A more detailed analysis of the text demonstrates that not only is the nurse in a controlling situation but the patient indeed is very powerless. A functional approach to the analysis of the grammatical structures supports the intuitive and initial observations, enabling further explanation of the underlying dynamics of the interaction. Using a Hallidayan model of functional grammar to analyse the discourse I demonstrate that the apparent dominance of the patient in the discourse does not in fact represent a shift in power from nurse to patient. On the contrary, what we are seeing played out in this context is an example of what Fairclough (1992) calls the 'democratisation' of discourse, where, in his view there is an apparent

> removal of inequalities and asymmetries in the discursive and linguistic rights, obligations and prestige of groups of people. Democratization in discourse, like democratization more generally, has been a major parameter of change . . . but in both cases . . . there are questions about how real or how cosmetic the changes have been. (Fairclough, 1992: 201)

3   A functional approach to the analysis of the text

The grammatical model proposed and developed by Halliday (1985, 1994) requires examination of the lexico-grammatical choices, the meaning of the clauses and the metafunctions[2] of language, adding meaning and depth to initial observations of the surface structures. Halliday (1985: xvii) asserts that: 'a discourse grammar needs to be functional and semantic in its orientation with the grammatical patterns explained as the realization of the semantic patterns'.

The need to generate understanding of the complexity of the interaction motivates recourse to a functional grammatical analysis so as to illuminate the strategies employed by the patient to convey his or her needs to the nurse, and, in addition, to offer insights into the individual's relationship with his or her environment. This involves accounting for the functions of language and not merely its word classes (noun, verb, etc.). In Hasan's (1971) words, such a grammatical approach emphasises the social nature of language and the discoursal choices which are available to the speaker to create new meanings in the representation of his or her world. An analysis of the metafunctions of discourse – the textual, the ideational and the inter-personal – will help us to understand the meaning of life events and to place them within the social context of the wider society.

3.1   The Textual metafunction of language and the Thematic structure[3]

Analysis of the text displays how both participants align to the goals of the interaction. It is, however, the nurse, in lines 1–2 (example 1), who sets the parameters for the interaction. This talk is about the patient, his feelings and his health. Neither party deviates from those parameters. The patient discusses both health status and feelings, with the nurse in example 2, lines 1, 6, 7 and 8, commenting upon his responses. The Thematic structure of this text indicates that it is the patient who is generally Thematised (in boldface) and is foregrounded throughout. In other words, the clause is about the patient. He is the psychological subject, as distinct from the gram-matical subject. The clauses are unmarked, with the Theme of ten of them being the personal pronoun 'I' and in the last three, the existential 'you'. In the remaining clauses, 'one of them', 'it', 'nobody', 'my mum', 'that', 'you', are foregrounded and placed in Thematic position.

Each of these Themes in the corresponding Rheme is seen to relate to the patient, 'one of them asked me' (example 1, line 8), where the doctor ('one of them') was not spoken about as somebody who changed the patient's situ-ation. The patient is the recipient in both that clause and the next one: 'it was happening to me' (example 1, line 12).

'Me mum' (example 2, line 4) is a reference to the relationship of the mother's death to the patient's situation. When we examine the projected clauses, we see that the patient is in the projection,[4] for example, *'I suppose there's nothing I could do about it'* (example 1, line 11) where the patient *'I'* is the actor in an impossible situation and *'I suppose that's the lot that's dealt out to you'* (example 2, lines 9–10). The grammatical metaphor *'I suppose'* is followed by the general *'you'* as a recipient of *'that'*, implying that the patient is included in *'you'*. Similarly, we see that *'nobody'* is used as a general pronoun, which aligns the patient with all people in similar circumstances to his, *'well nobody can can they'* (example 1, line 13). The patient, by drawing upon the general pronoun *'nobody'* and the personal pronoun *'you'*, appears to be attempting to justify his attitude. As such, the use of these pronouns might be seen as an attempt to mitigate his attitude reflected in the response to the situation.

There appears to be an expectation by the patient that the nurse has certain rights and obligations. In particular she has a right, and indeed is obliged, to listen to his painful self-disclosures (PSDs) (cf. Coupland et al. 1991). PSDs are face threatening, placing the patient immediately in a weak position. But this patient's situation results not only in an admission of weakness; the resulting powerless position is magnified in that his disclosures are made to (i) a woman and (ii) a person younger than himself. I suggest, however, that the patient can make these disclosures precisely because he acknowledges the institutional power vested in the nurse by reason of her professional education and training. Moreover, he has a right to make PSDs because the roles of both participants are legitimised by the institutional power and the resulting rights and obligations of both parties. In such a situation there is no necessary perceived loss of face. From observations of the Textual meta-function of the discourse, we can evidence how the nurse and the patient align with the expectations set down by the institution. These expectations are related to the nursing functions outlined in Figure 13.1 since listening to such disclosures is firmly linked with the counselling function (where coun-selling involves active listening, values clarification and facilitation of the grieving process [S. Candlin 1995]). What we are observing, therefore, is a re-enacting of the cultural norms and expectations of the nursing situation.

3.2 Attitude to life events realized in the Ideational metafunction[5]

Analysis of the data enables us to observe the realisation of the patient's attitudes to his experiences as they are expressed in his use of psychological processes. In particular, the patient uses Mental processes more than any other, and in each of these processes he is the senser: feeling, thinking, seeing. When using the Material process (of which there are five), the patient is the actor on only two occasions: *'I was retrenched'* (example 2, line 2), and *'I was crook'* (example 2, line 5). (*'crook'* is a local word for *'sick'*). Each time, however, the clauses are framed in passive voice, again suggesting his lack of control over the situation. The actor in other clauses is either 'general' *'you'* or *'this'*, e.g. *'you've got to take it'* (example 2, line 11) and *'this was really happening'* (example 1, line 5). We can thus see that the patient's world is mentalised and has yet to be determined (*'I suppose'*, *'I think'*, *'I don't be-lieve'*). In these two brief extracts, there are six Mental and only five Material processes. In short, the patient is 'reflecting' rather than 'doing'.

3.3 The Interpersonal metafunction[6]: Attitude to life events realised in the modality of the clause

We see in the examples that the patient uses subjective modality: *'I couldn't believe'*, *'I thought'*, *'I suppose'*. Here there is a demonstration of a low affinity to the proposition, and evidence of doubt. It does not represent the same degree of power, for example, as another patient who, when demonstrating her rehabilitation progress, said: *'I can do ...'*, *'I can walk ...'*, *'I am now able to cook ...'*. High modality auxiliary verbs demonstrate an intrinsic ability and thus demonstrate the potential control which a person might have over a situation. However this patient does not use high modality auxiliary verbs, leading one to conclude that he does not believe that he is in control of his situation. The lexico-grammar of his discourse reflects this: *'nothing I can do'* (example 1, line 11), *'I still couldn't see it happening to me'* (example 1, line 12). By using negative polarity, he has removed the possibility of taking any action which might facilitate a change in his circumstances leading to a possible strengthening of his powerless position. His discourse is framed in the passive voice and although he is Thematised, agency lies not with him but with others, evidencing his lack of control, as does his use of the modal theme *'I suppose'* (example 1, line 11). His powerlessness is emphasised in the following clause, *'that's the lot'*. In the context of this discussion, his utterance in example 2, line 11: *'you've got to take it haven't you'*, is especially interesting. This is a clause which expresses high modality and obligation, but by using the second-person, namely, general *'you'*, rather than the first person *'I'*, he emphasises his position. Perhaps in this situation of aloneness and hopelessness he is looking for support from his interlocutor. He affili-ates with others ('general' *'you'*), leading one to conclude that the second-person plural is used in mitigation. The situation where the probability of being a victim is high, contributes to his placement in a passive position. He looks for support by using the tag *'haven't you?'*. Is he presupposing that the nurse will agree and thus demonstrate an affiliation with him? There may be other considerations, however. I propose that his high use of modality can also act as a face-saving exercise. *'You've got to take it'* exemplifies his situation of powerlessness, but it also places causality elsewhere. The choice of tense further reinforces his attitude. Modality is expressed in the choice of past tense in the narrative form, use of past tense suggesting that the situation is one which is over and cannot be controlled. He uses the present tense only once (example 2, line 11) *'you've got to take it haven't you'*. This in itself connotes helplessness. The present tense is not used to demonstrate that he can start making changes. He still has no control over the situation.

The analysis thus far has confirmed initial impressions of passivity and lack of control of events. With the patient admitting his powerlessness to one with institutional power, the nurse has two options: the first is that she maintains the status quo, the implied expected action of the 'old order' (cf. Alfano 1971) or, by adopting a different approach and engaging in therapeutic nursing strategies, she can place 'emphasis upon his feelings . . . giving him the opportunity to find out and understand himself' (cf. Alfano 1971, cited in McMahon and Pearson 1991: 195–8). It appears that she has taken the latter option, but the power was hers to decide, not the patient's. Such a decision is the first step in the empowering process. Power, therefore, might be conceptualised dynamically as a chain (Foucault 1980: 98), passed from one to another, or in terms of capillary structures which can infiltrate other structures or people. The implication is that the individual (in this context, the nurse) by drawing upon her resources, is in a position to empower another (the patient).

Power can be seen, then, as a reflection of a relationship between individuals, or between an individual and the environment, and realised through the Interpersonal metafunction of the text. The relationship of the patient with his circumstances can be more clearly demonstrated if we turn to another analytical scheme drawn from functional grammar, namely Hasan's (1985) Cline of Dynamism.

4   A suggested explanatory framework: the Cline of Dynamism

Attitudinal differences realised through the Ideational and Interpersonal metafunctions can be analysed and formalised by referring to the concept of the *Cline of Dynamism* offered by Hasan (1985). Seeking to compare the effectuality of individuals as it is reflected in the syntactic structure of the clause, she defines 'effectuality – or dynamism – as the quality of being able to affect the world around us, and of bringing change into the surrounding environment' (Hasan 1985: 45). Hasan proposes that the clause can be represented on a continuum where DYNAMIC is one end point and PASSIVE the other (she is not, of course, equating this with passive voice). In comparing two literary texts she argues that the construction Actor+Inanimate Goal is at the most DYNAMIC end of the continuum, and Circumstance (surrounding an event) is at the least DYNAMIC end. She identifies 13 points on the continuum, stressing that adjacent points on it are not always easily distinguished, but nonetheless illustrate a general tendency. She demonstrates the 'effectuality' of subjects, in the specific literary texts in her study, by reference to their discourse. Note that 'effectuality' as described by Hasan does not include a comprehensive range of grammatical structures. For example, her data does not account for the effects of negative polarity or modality in the individual's display of effectuality, since no modal or negative clauses are identified in her texts. I earlier stated, however, that it was the strength of the modality in the discourse of the patient that indicated the individual's perception of self-control. Use of either negative polarity or modality, therefore, can increase or decrease the DYNAMIC or PASSIVE nature of the clause. By comparing the grammatical structures of the patient in relation to Hasan's model, I demonstrate below how the individual's perception of power potential is measurable and can be a useful tool when assessing a person's psycho-social state. It thus has utility in the nurse-patient situation, or indeed in any situation where the delivery of service, be it counselling, social work, or medicine, for example, is dependent upon an accurate psycho-social assessment. The grammatical analysis of the extracts of data allows the construction of a Cline of Dynamism based on Hasan's model and demonstrates the patient's degree of effectuality. This is illustrated in Table 13.1 and is seen to support the observations that the patient is powerless.

Table 13.1   The Cline of Dynamism (*adapted from Hasan 1985: 46*)

	Examples from the data		
Dynamic			
1 Actor + Animate Goal	(none evidenced)		
2 Actor + Inanimate Goal/Effected	(none evidenced)		
3 Sayer + Recipient	(none evidenced)		
4 Sayer + Target	(none evidenced)		
5 Sayer	(none evidenced)		
6 Actor + Circumstance	(none evidenced)		
7 Actor + Phenomenon	(none evidenced)		
8 Phenomenon + Senser	(none evidenced)		
9 Senser	(evidenced 5 times)	I thought	(ex. 1 line 10)
10 Actor – Goal	(evidenced once)	I was crook	(ex. 2 line 5)
11 Possessor + Animate Possession	(none evidenced)		
12 Possessor + Inanimate Possession	(none evidenced)		
13 Behaver	(evidenced twice)	I die	(ex. 1 line 10)
14 Carrier (Relational)	(none evidenced)		
15 Goal/Target	(evidenced once)	I was retrenched	(ex. 2 line 2)
16 Range	(none evidenced)		
17 Circumstance	(none evidenced)		
18 Recipient/Beneficiary	(evidenced 4 times)	The doctor was talking to me (ex. 1 line 7)	
19 (Part of) Phenomenon	(evidenced once)	I couldn't see it happening to me (ex. 1 line 12)	
20 Actor + Circumstance (negative polarity)	(none evidenced)		
21 (part of) Existential	(evidenced twice)	There's nothing I could do (ex. 1 line 12)	
Passive			

In contrast to Hasan's thirteen points on the continuum, an additional eight points are identified from the extracts presented here. Actor+Animate Goal is at the most DYNAMIC end, and (part of) the Existential is at the least DYNAMIC end, i.e. at the extreme PASSIVE end of the continuum. Some of the clauses identified by Hasan in her data (for example, Sayer+Recipient) are not evidenced in this data. There are some forms which Hasan did not identify in her analysis but which are apparent in these extracts, for example the Existential: *'there's nothing I could do about it'*, representing the extreme PASSIVE end of this continuum.

Table 13.1 demonstrates that the most DYNAMIC clauses are realised by the Actor+Animate Goal structure, and the least by an Existential clause (where the situation is PASSIVE). The application of this concept of a Cline of Dynamism does indeed appear to confirm that the patient's behaviour is PASSIVE. Only two clauses relating to him fall in the DYNAMIC range of the continuum, i.e. within the first ten points (*I thought* and *I was crook*), and these are towards the PASSIVE end of the *dynamic* range (points 9 and 10). The patient's reactions are noteworthy since he does not seem to be a person in control of his life at all, his utterances falling mainly towards the PASSIVE end (within the range 9 and 21). Indeed a clear pattern emerges displaying his PASSIVITY. He uses more Mental processes with negative polarity, placing one of his utterances near to the lowest point of PASSIVITY. His least PASSIVE clauses fall midway between the two points on the continuum. The overall impression one receives of his situation from this extract of his discourse is one of hopelessness and aloneness in his situation. Other people are nominated only three times in his narration of events: his mother and the doctor.

While these extracts represent only a small proportion of the interaction, the patient's PASSIVITY continues throughout. His achievements have been in the past and he now appears to be content to allow the nurse to be in control. In response to her asking him, at the close of the interaction, if he had any more questions, he answers in the negative and confirms the nurse's power by congratulating her on the work that she is doing. He further re-enforces his powerlessness by suggesting that he would dress his wound himself if he could, if only to relieve the nurse of some work. His final statement is to confirm his PASSIVITY (and powerlessness) and to re-inforce the nurse's role as one of power.

5   Towards an explanation of discoursal practices in nursing

The collaborative nature of the interaction is displayed in the elicitation of information and the questions and responses of the nurse. Confirmation by the nurse of the patient's apparent lack of control and personal power is shown in the use of nominalisations, modality and tense. I suggested earlier that a resulting loss of face was avoided because of the recognition of the rights and responsibilities of both partners and the recognition of social and cultural norms within the specific situation. But the saving of face also in no small part relates to the discourse genre adopted by the nurse. This is the genre of caring – where the total situation and needs of the patient are considered. In fact this is an example of what one might term ecologically sensitive communication and is related to the goals of holistic care and meeting total needs. This can only be achieved by acknowledging the centrality of the relational function of talk. Scollon (1998: 33) asserts that

> any social encounter . . . has as its logically first and interactionally ongoing highest priority to position the participants in the social encounter in relationship to each other. Whatever else we do in speaking to each other, we make claims about ourselves as a person, we make claims about the person of our listeners, we claim how those persons are related to each other at the outset of the encounter.

Such claims are underwritten by strategies which the nurse utilises to achieve goals and the recognition of her professional role and that of the patient as recipient of care. Being aware of the patient's history, it is not unreasonable to suggest that she was aware of his potential need for counselling. At the beginning of the interaction she had taken a brief social history and homed in on his illness by saying: '. . . *when you first became ill tell me a little bit about that'*. By establishing the frame she was able to ask: *'how did you feel . . .'*. It is the nurse, who initiated the counselling genre, encouraging the patient's use of Mental processes in response, thereby aligning with institutional goals.

His responses are related to the beliefs of many about appropriate and acceptable role behaviours. These prescribed behaviours relate not only to the patient but to the institution of nursing. The nurse brings to the situation her institutionally constructed identity which is mediated through the superimposition of the patient's needs in which the institution is embedded (cf. Sarangi and Slembrouck 1996). Thus in response to the patient's powerlessness, the nurse enacts the counselling function, fulfilment of which, however, represents a change in the order of nursing discourse, in particular how the counselling is articulated in the conversational genre, increasingly common in nursing practice. Casual conversations therefore are used for professional purposes, the implications of which are addressed as we attempt to explain the observations highlighted here.

Overt markers of power do not appear to be in evidence in the discourse of the nurse, but there are covert markers of asymmetrical relationships. There is an unspoken recognition by both parties that the nurse with institutional power has a right to information, and the patient, in his sick position, will benefit from making disclosures. In this situation, both nurse and patient resolve any tension which the 'new order' is imposing on them (that of patient autonomy and self-determination), by accepting the situation and working within the constraints which the order presents.

Although conducted as an informal conversation, on closer examination the technological 'shape' of nursing discourse can be identified. The apparent informality belies the technological structure of a nursing activity. While the discourse is friendly and the patient is allowed the floor, the information is one way. The rules governing its structure are strictly adhered to and reflect not just the rules of politeness, but demonstrate that information and particularly painful self-disclosures are given by the patient about the patient, not by the nurse about the nurse. Participants are acting out a script where roles are pre-determined, suggesting that little has changed within the nurse–patient relationship. What has changed, however, is the structure of the discourse and the discourse technology.

The discourse takes on a hybrid nature, at one and the same time the rules which determine who is allowed to ask questions and who is obliged to answer, are set by the institution, but the discourse is structured as an informal and private conversation. It is not therefore the overtly informal conversation it purports to be, it takes on a covert controlling nature. There is, therefore, less democratisation of the discourse than is at first suggested.

6 Conclusion

The discourse model which is emerging as illuminative for the understanding of successful nursing practice is one which draws on Fairclough's notion of hegemonic struggle (Fairclough 1992). Specifically, what is being called for is the disarticulation of existing configurations of the discourse type and elements in the practice of nursing, and the rearticulation of a new configuration, where the discourse types are appropriate to facilitate changes in nursing practices. It is important to emphasise that while some nursing practices are enhanced by quality discourse, in other instances, discourse **is** the nursing practice. The two data extracts analysed above display this. Such changes in nursing discourse are not easily achieved. They can only be effected by appropriate changes in the educational process and practice experiences of the developing practitioner. This change in practice is not something which 'just happens', it is a change which demands adequate preparation and practice.

Grounding the argument presented here in the crucial site of nursing practice and engaging theoretical aspects of discourse analysis with nursing practice in order to inform practice results in a commitment to *praxis*. Praxis demands a response if practice is to change. An appropriate response is to evaluate critically the educational preparation programmes of undergraduate nursing students in the tertiary sector of education. A communication component of a curriculum should be based on authentic data (being mindful of legal and ethical constraints) and should critically examine the language for meanings, hidden and overt, and for controlling and enabling devices by which patients are empowered, and nurses in their practice can be emancipated and freed from any unnecessary constraints imposed by the powerful institution. Emancipatory practice will only happen when nurses develop a critical and explanatory awareness of the power potential of discourse.

Notes

1. Many of the differences identified by Alfano have also been documented elsewhere (see Candlin, 1995), but of particular interest to this chapter are the following:
   Task oriented nursing . . . supports patient's expression of helplessness . . . sets limits and restrictions upon the patient . . .
   Therapeutic nursing where there is . . . major emphasis of care upon patient's feelings, concerns, goals and assisting him and his family through medical therapy . . . concern with giving patient opportunity to find out about and understand him or herself . . . . (adapted from Alfano, 1971 and cited in Pearson 1991: 195–8)
2. For a detailed discussion of the concept of metafunctions see Halliday (1994) but in brief we might say that the English clause is a combination of three different structures deriving from distinct functional components (called 'metafunctions' in systemic theory). The three metafunctions: 'the ideational (clause as representation), the interpersonal (clause as exchange) and the textual (clause as message) serve to express three largely independent sets of semantic choice: 1) Transitivity structures express representational meaning (what the clause is about), which is typically some process, with associated participants and circumstances; 2) Mood structures express interactional meaning: what the clause is doing, as a verbal exchange between speaker, writer and audience; 3) Theme structures express the organization of the message: how the clause relates to the surrounding discourse, and to the content of the situation in which it is being produced.' (Halliday 1994: 179)
3. Theme and Rheme, are elements of the *Textual metafunction* used in a systemic grammar. Halliday states that: 'The Theme is the element which serves as a point of departure of the message; it is that with which the clause is concerned. The remainder of the message, the part in which the Theme is developed, is called . . . the Rheme.' (Halliday 1994: 37)
4. . . . any one pair of clauses related by interdependency, or 'taxis', is referred to as a CLAUSE NEXUS. The clauses making up such a nexus are PRIMARY and SECONDARY. The primary is the initiating clause in a paratactic nexus, and the dominant clause in a hypotactic; the secondary is the continuing clause in a paratactic nexus and the dependent clause in a hypotactic. (Halliday 1994: 218)
5. The *Ideational metafunction* of language is that component of meaning which is also realised throughout the grammar. It is concerned with what the clause is about, 'which is typically some process, with associated participants and circumstances' (Halliday 1994: 179). Psychological processes, therefore, may be said to be contained in the Ideational metafunction of language. Language enables us to express and reflect on experiences: what is happening, what we are doing, sensing, meaning, being and becoming. Halliday refers to them as: Material processes, i.e. processes of doing (happening, creating, changing, doing [to], acting); Mental processes, i.e. processes of sensing (feeling, thinking, seeing); Relational

processes: processes of being (having identity, having attributes, symbolising); Behavioural processes, i.e. behaving; Existential processes, i.e. existing; Verbal processes, i.e. saying. (For further discussion see Halliday 1994, chapter 5.)

6. Attitudes towards any event embedded in a proposition are expressed via the modality of the clause. Halliday (1994) subsumes this within the *Interpersonal metafunction* of language. Modality determines the probability or usuality of the truth of the proposition, and as such bears a *relationship* to reality rather than being a categorical statement of reality. It is also a means of negotiating one's position, aligning with a position or a person and realigning as the interaction proceeds.

References

Alfano, G.J. (1971) 'Healing or caretaking – which will it be?' *Nursing Clinics of North America* 6, 273.

Bakhtin, M. (1981) *The Dialogical Imagination* (ed. M. Holquist, trans. C. Emerson and M. Holquist). Austin: Austin University Press.

Benner, P. (1984) *From Novice to Expert. Excellence and Power in Clinical Nursing Practice.* Menlo Park: Addison Wesley.

Bredmar, M. and Linell, P. (1999) Reconfirming normality: The constitution of reassurance in talks between midwives and expectant mothers. In S. Sarangi and C. Roberts (eds) *Talk, Work and Institutional Order: Discourse in Medical, Mediation and Management Settings.* Berlin: de Gruyter Mouton, 237–270.

Candlin, S. (1992) Communication for nurses: Implications for nurse education. *Nurse Education Today* 12, 445–451.

Candlin, S. (1995) *Towards excellence in nursing: An analysis of the discourse of nurses and patients in the context of health assessments.* Unpublished PhD thesis, University of Lancaster.

Coupland, N., Coupland, J. and Giles, H. (1991) *Language, Society and the Elderly: Discourse, Identity and Ageing.* Oxford: Blackwell.

Fairclough, N. (1992) *Discourse and Social Change.* Cambridge: Polity Press.

Foucault, M. (1980) *Power/knowledge: Selected Interviews and Other Writings. 1972–1977.* New York: Pantheon.

Grainger, K. (1992) Reality construction in the discourse of elderly carers. Paper presented at the International Conference, *Discourse and the Professions*, Uppsala University, Sweden.

Halliday, M.A.K. (1985) *Introduction to Functional Grammar* (1st edn.). London: Edward Arnold.

Halliday, M.A.K. (1994) *Introduction to Functional Grammar* (2nd edn.). London: Edward Arnold.

Hasan, R. (1971) Syntax and semantics. In J. Morton (ed.) *Biological and Social Factors in Psycholinguistics.* London: Logos Press, 131–157.

Hasan, R. (1985) *Linguistics, Language and Verbal Art.* Victoria: Deakin University Press.

Henzl, V.M. (1989) Linguistic means of social distancing in physician–patient communication. In W. von Reffler-Engel (ed.) *Doctor–patient Interaction.* Amsterdam/ Philadelphia: John Benjamins Publishing Co, 77–92.

Heritage, J. and Sefi, S. (1992) Dilemmas of advice: Aspects of the delivery and reception of advice in interactions between health visitors and first time mothers.

In P. Drew and J. Heritage (eds) *Talk at Work: Interaction in Institutional Settings*. Cambridge: Cambridge University Press, 359–417.

McMahon, R. and Pearson, A. (eds) *Nursing as Therapy*. London/New York: Chapman & Hall, 170–191.

Paterson, J.G. and Zderad, L.T. (1976) *Humanistic Nursing*. New York: John Wiley & Sons Inc.

Pearson, A. (1991) Taking up the challenge. In R. McMahon and A. Pearson (eds) *Nursing as Therapy*. London/New York: Chapman & Hall, 192–210.

Ragan, S.L. (forthcoming) *Sociable Talk in Women's Health Care Context: Two Forms of Non-medical Talk*.

Sarangi, S. and Slembrouck, S. (1996) *Language, Bureaucracy and Social Control*. London, New York: Longman.

Scollon, R. (1998) *Mediated Discourse as Social Interaction: A Study of News Discourse*. London, New York: Longman.

Chapter 14

The case of the long-nosed potoroo: the framing and construction of expert witness testimony

Yon Maley

1 Introduction

Much of the literature on courtroom discourse has concentrated on question form, as the structural unit through which evidence is elicited in court, and on patterns of question-and-answer sequences. Much of that literature has been preoccupied with the coerciveness of different question forms and the asymmetries of power that such questions reflect; other studies have focused on the strategic nature of lawyers' questioning techniques (Danet et al. 1976; Dunstan 1980; Phillips 1984; Maley and Fahey 1991; Drew 1992). Another focus of study has been the discourse of the judge or magistrate as he or she intervenes in examination proceedings or sums up to the jury at the conclusion of the trial (Wodak 1985; Phillips 1990; Harris 1994). These studies also have been concerned with asymmetries of power.[1]

This chapter takes a wider perspective on what goes on in court. While analysis of selected question–answer sequences shows us how court talk is managed and provides necessary insights into the strategies of eliciting witness testimony, it provides only the researcher's interpretation of the effect of that testimony on the court itself. That is to say, it does not show us why those questions were asked and how they influenced the perceived truth or credibility of the witness testimony, and therefore the final decision of the court. A court case is a complex, purposeful event, constructed in clearly delineated stages, each with differentiated functions and participant roles. The elicitation and management of witness testimony should be seen in relation to general institutional rules and structural constraints as well as case-specific ends and strategies – since even a moderately experienced barrister will be working with a game plan (Napley 1975; Evans 1983). Similarly, the interpretation and evaluation of witness testimony should be seen in relation to recognised cultural values and case-specific patterns of expectations established and maintained in the different stages of the trial.

I shall look at courtroom discourse from the perspective of genre theory and text linguistics (Halliday and Hasan 1985; Halliday 1994; Fairclough 1995), that is, as the realisation of a generic situation-type, a purposeful discoursal event with structurally and discoursally differentiated but related elements or stages. In order to show how and why the links between stages are triggered for the benefit of the court, I shall call upon the insights of frame theory (Goffman 1974, 1981; Tannen 1993). And, in order to show this integrated process in an intense form, I shall focus on the elicitation and interpretation of the evidence of a particular category of witness – the expert witness.

In what follows, Section 2 discusses the setting of the courtroom in terms of its basic principles, structure, and processes; Section 3 takes up the participant structure and in particular the role and status of the expert witness; Section 4 sets out the structural stages of a hearing; and Section 5 applies this framework to the analysis of data from a single case in the Land and Environment Court, New South Wales, Australia. The terminology of the court refers to the 'hearing' of a case ('trial' is reserved for criminal cases), so 'hearing' will be used here.

2   The setting: the courtroom as institutional discourse

Courtrooms based upon the English common law system are characterised by a culture of argument and persuasion (Napley 1975; White 1990). This strongly developed institutional culture follows from the court's basic organising principle of the adversary system which sets up two (at least) opposing parties, an impartial third party to decide on the relevant law and often a jury to decide on the facts of the case in issue. The rules of court and the laws of evidence are a direct result of this adversarial principle. They are *intended* to meet the requirements of formal justice; they are *intended* to ensure fairness and impartiality for both parties.[2] There is no room in the courtroom for the give and take and spontaneity of everyday conversation. Instead there is an institutional setting, formally structured with deeply entrenched and strictly enforced rules and conventions. These rules and conventions and the constraints which they impose are discourse rules, conventions and constraints. Despite popular belief about the esoteric nature of legal language, courtroom discourse may not be – except in specialised areas like tax or property law – technical at all. But the unique and to most newcomers most inaccessible aspect of what goes on in court lies in its discourse rules. The central business of the court, the examination of witnesses, is conducted by sequences of question and answer. Neither witnesses nor counsel can say what they like. They are highly constrained by well-established evidential rules. Not only are there constraints on what topics can be broached and by whom, but also there are constraints on the way in which the permissible topics can be introduced and talked about. And of course the jury for whom all the information and argument is intended (but not directed, for the judge is the ratified addressee (cf. Goffman 1981: 137)) has the least speaking role of all, in the courtroom at any rate.

All these interactional discourse rules, as well as the differing degrees of interventionist and directorial power that they realise, are well known and indeed fiercely enforced. They are in the strictest sense institutional rules, in that they serve well-known, entrenched and established legal/institutional functions and ideology (Giddens 1994: 80). We see here the complex inter-action and interrelationship between the institution of law in its procedural and substantive sense, and the institutional discourse or discourses. These prescriptive and exclusionary rules constitute the laws of evidence – that is to say, the rules of substance and procedure which must be followed. Dis-course rules are legal rules. One constitutes and defines the other.

Constraints upon practice always produce strategies and tactics which are designed to exploit or to overcome the restrictions that such constraints create. Over the centuries, within English-derived common law courts, a resource of forensic rhetorical strategies has been built up, which counsel characteristically draw upon, according to their *adversarial role and the context or stage of the hearing in which they are appearing*. Counsel build up their own repertoire of strategies which their own skill and experience, as well as the received wisdom of the profession, have shown to be effective.

3   The participants: counsel and expert witnesses

The courtroom operates with a recognised participant format of distinct institutional participant roles, i.e. Judge, Jury, Counsel, Witness (Goffman 1981: 136; Levinson 1988: 197). Each role realises its own quite distinct rules of lexico-grammar and discourse, so, as noted above, each is constrained by rules and conventions about what can be said, when and in response to whom. Witnesses, for example, can only respond in pre-allocated turns, must answer factually and relevantly, and are rarely allowed to elaborate or explain (Maley and Fahey 1991). It is somewhat of a paradox that the expert witness, whose contribution to the case is the concern of this chapter, is in some respects the least constrained and in others the 'most easily assailable' of all witnesses (Napley 1975: 31).

Historically, in the common law, the practice of using experts to interpret and evaluate matters of fact requiring specialised knowledge or experience has been observed for a very long time. In the sixteenth century, in *Buckley v. Rice Thomas*, Saunders J. stated that

> If matters arise in our law which concern other sciences or faculties, we com-monly apply for the aid of that science or faculty which it concerns, which is an honourable and commendable thing in our law.
>
> ((1554) Plowd. 118, quoted in Hodgkinson 1990: 7)[3]

These days the range of expertise which may be called upon is very wide. It is quite possible for some professionals to earn their living as expert witnesses. The ideal expert witness has been characterised by a famous English advocate in these terms:

> Quite the best kind of expert, and they are unfortunately anything but thick upon the ground, and as a result anything but thick in the witness box, are those who have devoted time and study to their subject, have a wide experience in it, understand the purpose of a trial at law, have experience at giving evidence and, above all, are clearly apprised of their own limitations. (Napley 1975: 35)

The evidence given by experts may be medical, psychiatric, scientific or linguistic (Hodgkinson 1990; Levi 1994a). Because their role is to provide the benefit of their specialised knowledge, experience or research, expert witnesses enjoy, if that is the word, a rather different status and role in court proceedings from that of lay witnesses. The evidence of experts has high 'probative' value. That is:

> Expert evidence on a particular matter is admissible if it has both relevance and probative value in relation to it. The question of relevance is decided according to precisely the same criteria as for evidence generally, though the expert evidence may be different in form, in particular where it consists of opinion rather than fact. (Hodgkinson 1990: 4)

High probative value here may simply mean that expert testimony is more likely to be listened to just because it emanates from an expert, but even so 'it is particularly persuasive in its tendency to prove or disprove matters in issue' (Hodgkinson 1990: 4). However, the most significant difference between expert and lay witnesses is that, unlike lay witnesses, expert witnesses are invited as a matter of course to give opinions and evaluations of situations, research and even other experts' work and reputation (Jackson 1995: 419). The modern law of expert evidence rests upon an assumption that, insofar as experts may express opinions and draw inferences, they do so by way of an exception to the rule that witnesses may only give evidence of what they have themselves perceived (Hodgkinson 1990: 8).

Because of this special value and weight which attaches to their evidence, expert witnesses find themselves in the firing line in controversial and strongly contested cases. Their interpretations and opinions, and frequently their experience and qualifications, can be fiercely challenged. That is why they are, as Napley commented, above, 'especially assailable'. In these contested cases, expert witnesses are called by the opposing parties and then the court must assess which of the conflicting versions of reality – which interpretation, argument or story – is more likely to be 'credible' or 'true'.

Credibility has both a non-linguistic and a linguistic, or discoursal, basis. The non-linguistic basis of the assessment of credibility depends on the highly subjective and controversial factor of witness demeanour. The extent to which judges and juries are influenced by witness demeanour is very difficult to gauge and will vary from case to case and between national legal systems. One difficulty is to identify just what the notion of demeanour should include. At its widest, demeanour includes style, paralinguistic clues and non-verbal behaviour. Accent and speech style, more properly linguistic, may also be considered part of demeanour by some listeners. The studies of O'Barr and Conley in the United States (O'Barr 1982; Conley and O'Barr 1998) have shown that juries can be significantly influenced by such factors. However, they are outside the scope of this chapter and in any case there is reason to believe that they play a lesser role in the assessment of the credibility of expert witnesses.[4]

Discoursally, credibility is complex. It is not what the witness *wishes* to say that is assessed for credibility, but rather what the witness has been *able* to say in the circumstances of examination and cross-examination (Jackson 1995: 419). Credibility is built up or destroyed by the strongly constrained and constraining processes of courtroom examination and the forensic strategies which seek to shape and control the production and interpretation of evidence. The evidence of both lay and expert witnesses is affected by these factors but expert witnessing is, as we have seen, especially significant and therefore especially vulnerable.

Expert witnesses themselves, particularly if they are new and inexperienced, tend to be quite unaware of the extent to which this process of shaping and construction of evidence goes on. They assume that their privileged status allows them special leeway in the evidential process, which to some extent it does, but all too often they emerge frustrated from the courtroom believing that they have not been able to give evidence in the way they would like and that their evidence has been twisted or disbelieved. And often it has been. A lawyer comments:

> It is a commonplace among forensic experts that they do not receive the reception that they think is appropriate in the courtroom. (Freckleton 1987: 123)

Because my aim in this chapter is to describe and explicate the linguistic and discoursal processes which give rise to this problem, my focus here will be not so much on the expert testimony itself but on the 'norms of advocacy and the permissions of the formal law' (Jones, C.A.G. 1994: 224) by which expert testimony is constructed – or demolished.

4 Generic structure: the stages of the hearing

There are four central stages in a hearing. They are:

1. Opening address by counsel on both sides.
2. Examination of witnesses
   (i)   Examination-in-chief
   (ii) Cross-examination
   (iii) Re-examination.
3. Closing addresses by counsel.
4. Judge's decision.

These stages are obligatory and serve to define the hearing as a genre (Halliday and Hasan 1985). Each stage is constructed by discourse; only stage 2 is constructed interactively between counsel and witness, although there may be interventions by the judge in stage 1 or 2 or objections from opposing counsel in stage 2. The motivation for the structure derives directly from the adversary system and is intended to provide equal opportunity – a level playing or jousting field, as it were – for opposing sides to present argument and evidence.

5   Data: the discoursal construction of the long-nosed potoroo

In order to show how the production and interpretation of expert evidence is shaped by both evidential constraints and forensic strategies, I shall examine extracts from a single case where a number of expert witnesses were called. This was a case considered in a hearing before the Land and Environment Court of New South Wales, Sydney, concerning a development application.[5] The local government Council had granted permission for the development of a quarry on a large tract of untouched bushland. The development application was opposed by a group calling themselves a Protection Committee, who for various reasons did not wish the quarry to proceed. In such cases, almost all the evidence is given by expert witnesses in the various fields likely to be relevant to the affected areas, such as noise, water pollution, flora and fauna. I shall concentrate on one small, but very important element of that evidence. A Fauna Impact Study had been done, but was in some respects incomplete. The question was: had the Impact Study adequately established whether part or all of the quarry site was the habitat of a rare small marsupial, the elusive long-nosed potoroo?

There was no question that, if it could be established that part of the quarry site was the habitat of the long-nosed potoroo, then the development would be at worst quashed, or at the very least in need of considerable alteration in order to mitigate any significant impact on the survival of the long-nosed potoroo.

Three counsel appear in the hearing. They are:

What potoroo?
- **Counsel C:** for the Council and supporting the quarry.
- **Counsel H:** for a property owner also supporting the quarry.

Save the potoroo!
- **Counsel W:** for the Protection Committee, who wish to prevent the building of the quarry and protect the environment, including the habitat of the potoroo.

Readers unfamiliar with Australian fauna may find Figure 14.1 useful as it illustrates and describes the long-nosed potoroo.

Figure 14.1   Potorous tridactylus LONG-NOSED POTOROO

Potorous tridactylus
This squat rabbit-size kangaroo-like marsupial has a prehensile tail used to gather
nesting material, well-developed upper canine teeth and upper and lower incisor
teeth that bite against each other. The fur is grey to brown above (dark rufous
brown in Tasmania) and paler below. They have a long tapering nose with a
naked tip, rounded ears and a scaly tail furry at the base.
Behaviour: Nocturnal, they sleep in simple nests of grass and other vegetation
carried in the curled tail and placed in scrapes below dense scrub, grass tussocks
or grass trees. Solitary and sedentary, they have overlapping home ranges of 5–10
ha, rarely venture far from cover and sometimes gather in small groups. They
move quickly with a bipedal hopping gait assisted occasionally by the forelimbs.
Habitat: Rainforest, open forest, woodlands with dense understorey to 1600 metres.
Status: Common, patchy distribution.
(Leonard Cronin. *The Australian Museum Complete Book of Mammals.*
Illustrator: Marion Westmacott.)

5.1   Opening address by counsel on both sides

Let me then begin with an extract from stage 1, from the opening address of
the counsel who argues for the building of the quarry. Because he needs to minimise its impact on the flora and fauna of the property concerned, his attitude
is 'What Potoroo?'. The potoroo makes its first appearance in his address.

Transcription conventions in this chapter are adapted from Tannen (1993):

.	indicates sentence final intonation.
. . .	indicate brief pause, less than a second.
. . . .	indicate pause of more than a second.
,	indicates a clause final intonation.
/ /	indicate overlapping speech.

Transcript 1
Opening Address: Counsel C. (*For the Council and supporting the quarry. 'What potoroo?'*)

1 **Counsel C:** [the council] believes that the application can be carried out in a
2 way such that the impact upon fauna, particularly some suggestion of endan-
3 gered fauna, is such that no real problem should emerge. There are some areas
4 that have been identified in most recent studies, I think, of a potential bat
5 colony, and in respect of that ubiquitous animal that seems to arise in almost
6 every one of these cases that I've ever encountered, namely a potoroo

7 **Her Honour:** yes I knew/

8 **Counsel C:**   /they're endangered but they seem to be everywhere
9 in New South Wales that ever anybody has brought about some extractive
10 operation. But I think someone's being diligent . . . . yes but the same potoroo is
11 probably transported around the state in order that his hair or its hairs can be
12 entrapped by someone undertaking a survey in order to ensure that there is at
13 least a faint suggestion that the potoroo exists in the area. Now Your Honour I
14 dont say it flippantly, but . . .

15 **Her Honour:** I . . . (not transcribable) your note of flippancy Mr A [i.e. Counsel C]

16 **Counsel C:** we doubt very much if this ubiquitous potoroo will in fact cease to
17 exist by reason of this application.

In this stage of the hearing, each counsel addresses the judge, setting out the argument for his client. This is a discourse of argument and persuasion. Occasionally, as here, the judge may comment or intervene, but in general the floor belongs to the counsel. Counsel C's argument is based upon a disclaimer about the threat to fauna; *no real problem* should emerge (l. 3). The mitigation in *some suggestion* of endangered fauna (l. 2) minimises any threat to fauna, as does *potential* bat colony (l. 4), and *a faint suggestion* (l. 13). Apparently, nothing can be established as a firm threat. When he comes to the potoroo, counsel resorts to heavy irony, or as he and the judge call it, flippancy. He produces a fantasy scenario of a potoroo being transported around the state and its hairs left around in order to suggest its habitat. We note the modulation (Halliday 1985), suggesting doubt and probability, of *we doubt* (l. 16), *ubiquitous animal that seems to arise* (l. 5), *probably transported around the state* (l. 11), *they seem to be everywhere* (l. 8). Finally, in ironically labelling the potoroo *ubiquitous*, and repeating the label for added effect, he has struck a note of scepticism that will characterise his approach to the question of the potoroo's existence throughout the hearing. The judge now knows how his argument will tend in the following sequences of examination-in-chief and cross-examination, because Counsel C's opening address has provided a FRAME, which is intended to influence the inter-pretation of what follows. Addressed directly to the judge, the lexicogrammar of the address realises meanings of irony, scepticism and probabilities which will be sustained throughout the hearing.

The notion of a frame, or frame theory, owes its origin to Bateson (1954) and Goffman (1974, 1981). More recently Tannen has defined it as 'a structure of expectations' (1993: 16). As such, it has the status of product, but Tannen herself emphasises the non-static, dynamic aspect of frames and the ways in which they are interactively produced. In this chapter I distinguish two aspects of frames. There is first a frame as *a resource for interpretation*, which may be social, cultural or institutional. Clearly legal frames, or frames for courtroom behaviour, demeanour and discourse, are highly specialised institutional frames which legal professionals have acquired by education and experience (although most movie-goers or television viewers have acquired a reasonably sophisticated idea of what goes on in court). The concept of a frame as a practitioner's resource provides a way of describing the closed guild-like and craft-bound character of much of legal discourse that lawyers and others frequently comment upon (Maley 1987; Goodwin 1997). In addition, the issues that the court deals with are real-world issues, so there will always be an interaction between the specialised, technical knowledge of court participants and the moral and practical frames that each case throws up. Frames, consisting as they do of information, behavioural real-world expectations, and moral and ideological values, are not themselves linguistic but are implied by or brought into play by the meanings of the discourse.

Secondly, there is the dynamic interactive aspect of *framing*, which is a process and an activity. Framing as an activity is both information-giving and persuasive, particularly in courtrooms, as counsel strive, as in Transcript 1, to construct for the court a view of the issues that are favourable to their case. This notion of framing is familiar to legal practitioners who are taught in law school that a good opening statement is designed to inform the court of the case and to explain what the court can expect to hear during the trial or hearing (Napley 1975; Evans 1983).[6] In the rapidly growing field of alternative dispute resolution, i.e. community and court-annexed mediation, framing (and reframing) is considered to be the most important tactic in the lawyer/mediator's repertoire, where it is used to present the participants with the best possible version of events or behaviour (Candlin and Maley 1994; Greatbatch and Dingwall 1994; Jones, T.S. 1994; Rifkin 1994; Maley 1995). Also, frames usually carry an evaluative as well as an informative content. The stance or tenor (Halliday and Hasan 1985) which the speaker adopts towards the addressee and the subject matter is an integral part of the frame projected, here, to the court (Tannen and Wallat 1993; Jackson 1995: 419). This is apparent in Transcript 1 as Counsel C adopts a flippant, derisory tenor in his opening address. The judge and other ratified participants are invited to see and interpret the following evidence in the same, sceptical, non-serious way.

Because of the argumentative and persuasive culture of the courtroom, framing is always an ongoing and dynamic process and, as we will see, the counsel for each side will attempt to establish their own frame (as an alternative to their opposition's frame) to influence the perceptions and expectations of the judge. Counsel W, who represents the Protection Committee and opposes the quarry because he wishes to save (among other things) the potoroo, presents his argument in quite different terms and with a quite different tenor.

Transcript 2
Opening Address: Counsel W. (*For the Protection Committee and opposing the quarry 'Save the potoroo!'*)

1 **Counsel W:** as the evidence will emerge, there is an extraordinary number
2 of endangered species. This includes migratory endangered species as well as
3 resident species which will be directly affected and with the greatest respect to
4 my friend's comment about the potoroo, the evidence will indicate that there
5 is direct and clear evidence of the potoroo on this land and no adjoining
6 land . . . proceedings are not assisted by attempts to trivialise impacts upon
7 endangered species.

Counsel W uses direct unmodulated assertions, in strong contrast to the probabilities and mitigations of Counsel C. He states his case unequivocally; *will* (ll. 3, 4) expresses prediction and futurity here, not probability. Modification is used to strengthen, not mitigate: *extraordinary number of endangered species* (l. 1), *will be directly affected* (l. 3), *direct and clear evidence* (l. 5). His final reproach, formally worded, *with the greatest respect to my friend's comment* (ll. 3, 4), dismisses Counsel C's address as *attempts to trivialise impacts upon endangered species* (ll. 6, 7). Note how his dismissal contains a presupposition that *impacts upon endangered species* exist.

5.2   Examination of witnesses

As any viewer of films and television knows, the examination process is conducted in sequences of question-and-answer adjacency pairs in the contexts of examination-in-chief and cross-examination. In examination-in-chief, counsel examines his or her own witness; the witness is then cross-examined by the opposing counsel. Counsel also has the right to re-examine the witness, to clarify or expand on points brought up earlier. These are the interactive subcontexts of the trial or hearing.

The extracted transcripts below clearly illustrate the difference in the tactics of counsel in the contexts of examination-in-chief and cross-examination. In Transcript 3, counsel for the Protection Committee is examining the expert witness that he has called in support of the case to prevent the quarry and save the potoroo. He is examining his witness on a list of species which, it is claimed, the quarry proposal will 'significantly affect'.

Transcript 3
Examination-in-chief: Counsel W. (*For the Protection Committee. 'Save the potoroo!'*)

1 **Counsel W:** Mr P [*Expert Witness 1*] if you could turn to the table in exhibit
2 A . . . now of these species, excluding the carpet python which is no longer on
3 a Schedule 12, which of these species do you say this proposal will signifi-
4 cantly affect?
5 **Expert Witness 2:** looking at the first column?

[*1 minute later, after discussion of the effect on a number of fauna*]

75 **Counsel W:** the long-nosed potoroo?
76 **Expert Witness 1:** the long-nosed potoroo has been recorded by Miss M [*i.e.*
77 *Expert Witness 2*] in the south-eastern portion of the applicant's land . . . . that
78 record is so established and I have made a reasonable comment about that and
79 made some conjectures about home ranges, meaning the amount of area that
80 animal could be expected to utilise.

81 **Counsel W:** Mr P. you actually looked didn't you east of the road?
82 **Expert Witness 1:** that's correct, I embarked upon a tracking program and set
83 hair tube traps from\

84 **Counsel W:**   \well is this in any report?
85 **Expert Witness 1:** yes

86 **Counsel W:** in the reports of evidence?
87 **Expert Witness 1:** yes, I set a series of traps virtually parallel to the road . . . . in
88 habitat that I consider suitable for the potoroo and was unable to record any
89 potoroos in that location.

90 **Counsel W:** so at this stage you have no recording of the presence of potoroo
91 east of the road?
92 **Expert Witness 1:** no, that's correct.

93 **Counsel W:** the only recording is on the applicant's land?
94 **Expert Witness 1:** that's correct

95 **Counsel W:** Mr P would the removal of part of that habitat in the applicant's
96 land be likely to have an important effect on the potoroo?
97 **Expert Witness 1:** I believe so

98 **Counsel W:** what would the effect be?
99 **Expert Witness 1:** I think that that colony . . or that individual potoroo is
100 recorded there and nowhere else and if you take away the habitat well I
101 don't believe . . . . well I believe that it would significantly disadvantage
102 that individual.

[*Discussion for 2.5 mins on damage potential to other species*]

325 **Counsel W:** Mr P, if this quarry site is cleared . . . the areas which have been
326 identified for extraction . . . why can't these species, other than the bats, just go
327 off and carry on their business in neighbouring lands?
328 **Expert Witness 1:** well I think the frogs are particularly vulnerable . . . . you
329 know Wallum froglets are particularly vulnerable, any disruption of its aquatic
330 habitat will have an impact on the froglet, you know froglets are mobile to
331 some extent but you know individual froglets will certainly be lost. I have

332 difficulty with the idea that once you take the habitat out of somewhere the
333 animals can just jump in next door and the same difficulty was . . . . that com-
334 monly you have habitats next door that have animals in them or may have
335 animals in them, I don't know in this case we haven't got that evidence but
336 there may be sites where there's family groups that don't allow . . . . the home
337 ranges of these are large and they don't allow other animals to come in.

Transcript 3 shows that examination-in-chief is a supportive information-seeking process in which counsel and witness co-construct the testimony. Both for lay and expert witnesses, examination-in-chief is characterised by a high proportion of Wh-questions (Danet et al. 1976; Woodbury 1984; Maley and Fahey 1991) by which the witness is invited to provide information, e.g. *which of these species* (l. 3), *what would the effect be* (l. 98), *why can't these species just go off* (l. 326). Wh-questions are especially likely to be used with expert witnesses, because of the opinion and explanation-giving nature of their role. Polar questions are also used in examination-in-chief; they invite the witness to confirm or deny the question put, but, as here, the witness may be permitted to expand and explain. One very important function of polar questions in both examination-in-chief and cross-examination is to allow the counsel to state a proposition or a piece of information that he or she wishes to place in evidence as part of the overall argument or story (Maley and Fahey 1991; Jackson 1995: 419). So, here, counsel establishes that his witness had conducted a personal examination of the site (*you actually looked, didn't you?* (l. 81)). The tag question is stronger and more assumptive than a simple polar interrogative. The question establishes that his witness had already placed his report in evidence. This builds upon a frame of what establishes *good* credibility. This done, he invites opinion with a Wh-question (*what would the effect be?* (l. 98)) and gets the answer he wants, i.e. *it would significantly damage that individual [potoroo]* (l. 101). His question *why can't these species just go off . . .* (l. 326) is disingenuous, anticipating what the opposition might say, and inviting his witness to provide a full, if rambling, account of the loose boundaries and permeability of habitats (ll. 328–337).

Expert Witness 1 has a much less comfortable experience in cross-examination; the supportive environment of examination-in-chief is replaced by an openly adversarial one. Counsel C, appearing for the Council's group who wish the quarry to go ahead, confronts and challenges him directly in Transcript 4. Credibility is also an issue here, but Counsel C wishes to undermine or destroy his credibility.

Transcript 4
Cross-examination: Counsel C. (*For the Council. 'What potoroo?'*)

1 **Counsel C:** Mr P, the reports that you've prepared are advocate's documents
2 aren't they?
3 **Expert Witness 1:** they're a report prepared by me to the best of my profes-
4 sional capacity for the Protection Committee.

5 **Counsel C:** but they're an advocate's document?

6 **Expert Witness 1:** well you may interpret it as that . . . that's my answer.

7 **Counsel C:** but you see they're not a scientific document are they?

8 **Expert Witness 1:** I've documented my methodology, I've documented my
9 results . . . all of these are the standard scientific approach to these . . . to the
10 assessment of natural areas or to the assessment of lands and I've discussed . . .
11 and I've discussed and drawn upon the references of current scientific findings
12 in the field and that's in some ways why I've added such a large appendix to
13 the document

14 **Counsel C:** can I just seek to have your help because I don't want to criticise
15 you unfairly?

16 **Expert Witness 1:** mmmm

17 **Counsel C:** is it part of the scientific training that you have to cite legal proposi-
18 tions with the case references which purportedly stand for those propositions?

19 **Expert Witness 1:** I've adopted the approach given\

20 **Counsel C:**   \is that part of the scientific
21 training that you have?

22 **Expert Witness 1:** there are\

23 **Counsel C:**   \is that part of the scientific training that you have?

24 **Expert Witness 1:** part of my background?

And the counsel continues to attack the witness in this vein, seeking to throw doubt on his objectivity and competence. His opening question (l. 1), a declarative with negative tag, functions as a challenge to the witness about the objectivity of his report. It is strongly assumptive about the 'truth' of the proposition it contains, which is a challenge to the witness's credibility. Throughout this exchange (and the ones, not quoted here, that follow) he continues to use tight, closed repetitive polar questions which contrast an *advocate's document* (ll. 1, 5) with *a scientific document* (l. 7), and which attempt to coerce the witness to agree that his documents are unscientific and biased. Polar questions, particularly tagged polar questions, predominate in cross-examination because of their assumptive and coercive power and their ability to 'lead' the witness (see below) (Maley and Fahey 1991). In comparison to the tag questions used in examination-in-chief, these questions carry an unfavourable evaluation.

Counsel C's one apparently non-adversarial question (*can I just seek to have your help* (l. 14)) is a trick question, a deceptively deferential way of changing the topic before he attacks on another front. This is classic go-for-the-throat cross-examination, badgering the witness for a confirming 'yes', interrupting the witness and repeating questions in rapid-fire style. The counsel controls the topic and he constrains the scope and content of the witness's reply. Any attempt to expand or explain will be ruthlessly swept aside. Such well-known and often-used forensic tactics are intended to place doubt on the record of evidence, to contest the witness's credibility.

As the above examples show, question form is indeed very important in controlling the flow and content of evidence. All witnesses, including expert witnesses, can expect to be subjected to different questioning patterns in the courtroom process according to the context of examination, i.e. examination-in-chief or cross-examination. The question form either elicits or constrains the witness's response and the tightly controlled turn-taking sequences also shape and constrain the flow of evidence.

However, question form alone is clearly not the whole story. The form and function of the question form may constrain the shape the witness's answer, but what is said by both witness and counsel is just as important as how it is said. Depending on their content and the context of the hearing in which they are put, polar questions may be either supportive (Transcript 3, l. 81) or coercive (Transcript 4, ll. 5, 7). In both Transcripts 3 and 4, each counsel uses repetition and reformulation, one of the most common tactics in forensic rhetoric (Goodrich 1990).[7] The skill lies in choosing what to repeat or reformulate, choosing a meaning that will fit either a favourable or an unfavourable frame for the hearer, i.e. judge or jury. Thus in Transcript 3, repetition establishes that the expert witness has already submitted a full report on endangered species and the very important fact that the *only recording'* (l. 93) of the potaroo's presence is in a restricted area of land. Repetition here supports the argument of the Council, i.e. there's no real threat to the potaroo, or if there is, it can easily be contained. This conclusion follows from the evidence, but requires that the judge fit it into a particular frame which has already been set up in the opening address. In Transcript 4, repetition also has a reinforcing function, but here the meaning that the question carries, and its repetition, is unfavourable to the witness and his case. Importantly, it calls upon a wider, more general, frame; the evidence of experts is scientific and should be impartial and unbiased. Expert evidence is called in order to assist the court, not to actively advocate one course of action or serve a special interest, although it is commonly known that expert witnesses are frequently chosen for their willingness and ability to provide partisan evidence.[8] The repeated questions about the witness's scientific training also call upon the knowledge or expectation that in the institutional setting or context of the law, it is inappropriate for a non-lawyer to cite legal references.

In this hearing, both sides called expert witnesses on all relevant scientific aspects of the development proposal. This reverses the supportive and adversarial roles of the examining counsel. Counsel H, in Transcript 5 below, now examines Expert Witness 2 (Miss M), the principal expert witness appearing for the Council. This witness, an independent consultant, has submitted a number of reports about the proposed quarry. In relation to the potoroo, she has recommended that a small area of the site be 'quarantined', i.e. not used, until further surveys have been done. Counsel is examining her on this aspect of her report.

Transcript 5
Examination-in-chief: Counsel H. (*For the Council. 'What potoroo?'*)

1 **Counsel H:** [*In order to confirm a potoroo presence*] you put down some . . . do you
2 call them traps or what do you call them?
3 **Expert Witness 2:** well the hairs were put out . . . were collected from hair tubes.

4 **Counsel H:** hair tubes?
5 **Expert Witness 2:** hair tubes.

6 **Counsel H:** and you found in the hair tubes later on some hairs which you
7 believe are potoroo hairs?
8 **Expert Witness 2:** yes, we obtained one sample which . . . I mean we obtained
9 lots of samples. All were sent to the expert and she confirmed that this sample
10 was sufficient to be quite definite that it was a potoroo hair.

11 **Counsel H:** now that we have established the existence of potoroos it might be
12 time to adjourn.
13 **Her Honour:** yes and I can contemplate potoroos over my lunch hour.

LUNCHEON ADJOURNMENT

14 **Counsel H:** now Miss M, having identified potoroo hair on part of the property
15 that wasn't enough for you was it to identify whether or not it was just a visit
16 or part of the habitat or precisely what was involved?
17 **Expert Witness 2:** no, just an odd hair sample . . . it tells you that the species
18 obviously has been there.

19 **Counsel H:** has paid a visit?
20 **Expert Witness 2:** but to the extent it actually utilises that area and what sort of
21 numbers it occurs in . . . it can't tell you that.

22 **Counsel H:** your [previous] trapping program didn't show up any potoroos
23 obviously?
24 **Expert Witness 2:** no, no we caught no animals at that stage.

25 **Counsel H:** so when you carried out this tube trap if I can call it that . . . that
26 was quite unexpected, was it not, the showing of the/
27 **Expert Witness 2:**   /yes, yes I was surprised . .
28 I really didn't . . yes I was surprised.

This witness has been called by the Council who are supporting the quarry,
and who really don't want to find any endangered species on the land.
However, she has found some potoroo's hairs and has recommended that a
small area be quarantined until further investigation has been carried out.
This plan suits the Council – it cannot deny the evidence of its own witness
– for it means that the quarry will go ahead in all but this small area.
Therefore, Counsel H is content to take his witness gently and supportively
through her evidence while emphasising the uncertainties involved, i.e. *has
paid a visit?* (l. 19), *trapping program didn't show up any potoroos, obviously?*
(l. 22), *quite unexpected, was it not?* (l. 26). In comparison with the tags used
in Transcript 4, *obviously*, and *was it not?*, while requiring a confirmation,

are unchallenging, non-adversarial and assume or establish meanings favourable to his case.

These meanings reinforce the frame he and Counsel C presented in opening address; they are sceptical about a permanent presence of potoroos in the area, and wish to emphasise the paucity of evidence for their presence.

Then it is the turn of Counsel W for the Protection Committee to cross-examine the expert witness. There is no need for him to attack her, or seek to undermine her evidence, since she has already established a point important for his case; that there is evidence of potoroos on a part of the proposed quarry site.

Transcript 6
Cross-examination: Counsel W. (*For the Protection Committee. 'Save the potoroo!'*)

1   **Counsel W:** now the hair analysis is, I understand, an accepted method of iden-
2   tification by the scientific community?
3   **Expert Witness 2:** yes it is . . . . with quite a lot of qualification in that\

4   **Counsel W:**   \one
5   wouldn't list it as some kind of hypothetical ratbag method of analysis, would
6   you?
7   **Expert Witness 2:** no.

8   **Counsel W:** and therefore despite the hilarity that hair tube tracking often
9   attracts, it's considered to be a sound and proper method for field zoological
10   surveys?
11   **Expert Witness 2:** in association with other methods usually yes.

12   **Counsel W:** and confidently demonstrates presence?
13   **Expert Witness 2:** not in all cases but in some cases yes.

14   **Counsel W:** why do you say not in all cases Miss M?
15   **Expert Witness 2:** well for instance in the initial hair sample there was not
16   sufficient sample, as I stated, for the expert analyst to be totally confident that
17   it was indeed potoroo . . . you have to have sufficient quantity of hairs to, I
18   assume, allow for variation and to be certain of your identification and even for
19   a number of hairs for a number of species, even the experts cannot confidently
20   get beyond genus . . . so it is not, still not as reliable as having the animal of
21   course, but it is an accepted method\

22   **Counsel W:**   \but it is generally regarded as the accept-
23   able proof of presence?
24   **Expert Witness 2:** yes if the identification is definite yes.

25   **Counsel W:** and in this case the identification was definite?
26   **Expert Witness 2:** in the second instance yes.

In the first four exchanges of Transcript 6, Counsel W is 'leading' the witness with polar questions which allow him to make a point for his case in his own words and force the witness to answer yes or no. A leading question is 'one which tells the witness what answer he is expected to give' (Bartlett 1979: 148) and is only permitted in cross-examination.[9] Here counsel is asking for confirmation that hair tracking is an acceptable method of confirming the presence of potoroos, because counsel for the other side in his opening address (Transcription 1) had 'flippantly' suggested that potoroo hairs could be planted all round the country. In effect Counsel W is providing a favourable evaluation of the hair-tube method and asking her to confirm his evaluation. He is seeking her confirmation for a point which he himself is making. Note how the witness follows her confirmation with a qualification, but counsel in each case does not take up or explore the qualification she raises. In the fifth exchange, he does offer her a chance of explanation (*why do you say* . . . (l. 14)) but then reverts to polar questions which seek her confirmation to the point that suits his case, i.e. hair tracking produced a positive identification.

5.3   Closing addresses by counsel

When all the witnesses have been heard, counsel address the court (that is, the judge) and sum up their case. In all forensic training and in all the relevant literature, every law student and would-be advocate is impressed with the significance of the final speech in 'helping' the judge to reach a decision (Evans 1983; Napley 1975) Each counsel attempts to reinforce the version of the facts and argument that he has been promoting thus far. Each tries to frame or reframe the judge's perceptions of what has been said. On the one hand, they try to reinforce the version of facts that they have been constructing and reframe and deconstruct the opposing side's version. Here are the relevant parts of each counsel's address.

Transcript 7
Closing Address: Counsel W. (*For the Protection Committee. 'Save the potoroo!'*)

1 **Counsel W**: Expert Witness 2's evidence was that definitely the potoroo was
2 likely to be affected by the development. I think it would be fair to say that she
3 did not accept that there would be a significant effect on the environment of any
4 endangered species other than the potoroo . . . . so your Honour we would again
5 submit that there is serious concern that this proposal would give rise to likely
6 adverse impact on both the rainforest birds and the bats in both the rainforest
7 and the blackbutt areas as well as the potoroo . . . . the mitigating actions that are
8 proposed would provide no effective or substantive action to reduce these levels
9 of impact on the potoroo population.

Counsel W's closing address, like his opening address (see Transcript 2), is strong and authoritative in tenor, admitting little qualification. He reformulates the evidence of Expert Witness 2 (who appeared for the Council, the opposing side) in its strongest form (*definitely the potoroo was likely to be affected* (l. 1)). His choice of *definitely* (l. 1) before his paraphrase of the expert witness's much more modulated form *likely* (l. 2) attempts to give certainty where none was expressed. He then allies the expert witness's most favourable (to his case) testimony to his other concerns about bats and so on, expresses *serious concern* (l. 5), predicts a *likely adverse impact* (ll. 5, 6), and claims that the Council's proposed mitigating actions would provide *no effective or substantive action* (l. 8) on a *potoroo population*. (Note that neither expert witness has gone so far as to suggest the existence of a population, i.e. large numbers of potoroos.) Throughout the hearing he has maintained the frame he established in his opening address by the repetition and re-formulation of key words and phrases particularly in relation to the potoroo, e.g. *serious concern, endangered species, significant effect*. These, in addition to the steady, serious and unequivocal tenor of his language, provide cohesion (Halliday and Hasan 1976) and coherence to his argument.

In their closing addresses, counsel for the Council and the other party supporting the building of the quarry, take up again the doubting and scornful tenor which was first expressed in their opening addresses.

Transcript 8
Closing Address: Counsel C. (*For the Council. 'What potoroo?'*)

1 **Counsel C:** Your Honour it is in our respectful submission drawing a long bow
2 in the context of the reality of these applications, to suggest that the location in
3 one hair trap, I think it's called, of a hair of a potoroo, as indicating that that
4 area is one in which one can comfortably predict that destruction is going to
5 involve detriment to that species. Sorry, but it's drawing a long bow to suggest
6 that is the case . . . . Expert Witness 1 has implicated that there have been what
7 might be called valiant efforts to find the ubiquitous potoroo but with only the
8 one piece of evidence which suggests a presence however temporary that may
9 be in that locality. Now these matters do involve a balance Your Honour. If
10 there was evidence of scats or other evidence apart from the one hair which
11 might suggest a regular visit or other usage of the area then one might perhaps
12 be more cautious . . . . but given the paucity of evidence after a serious attempt
13 having been made to obtain it then it's not in our respectful submission, er it's
14 got to be a little more than that in our respectful submission if that's the evid-
15 ence that exists in this case.

Transcript 9
Closing Address: Counsel H. (*For the Council and allied party. 'What potoroo?'*)

1 **Counsel H:** and finally, the record of a probable potoroo hair sample was ob-
2 tained by Expert Witness 1. This represents the most positive . . . (not transcrib-
3 able) occurred in the locality for over two decades. So in two decades the best we
4 could find is the hair . . . we will carry out further surveys in the area, we will
5 determine whether or not this potoroo was visiting a friend that night and was
6 passing through or whether it is a significant part of its habitat

Counsel C sustains the tenor of scorn and scepticism expressed in his open-ing address (Transcript 1), by repetition of *the ubiquitous potoroo* (l. 7), *visit*

(l. 11), and the metaphor of *a long bow* (ll. 1, 5) to emphasise the *paucity of evidence* (l. 12). The modulation in *one hair trap, I think it's called* (l. 3) contrasts the doubt and probability of *I think* with the singularity of *one*. The meaning could be glossed as 'one of these things which are so unimportant I can't remember their name'. His tactics all through the hearing have been to minimise, by mitigating or scornful phrases, the possibility of the potoroo's presence in the area.

Counsel H's argument is less rhetorical but also sustains the sceptical tenor by modulation and reformulation, i.e. *in two decades the best we could find is the hair* (ll. 3, 4), *probable potoroo* (l. 1), and again raises the possibility that the *potoroo was visiting a friend* (l. 5).

In effect Counsel H and Counsel C are reformulating in its minimal form the testimony of their own witness, i.e. Expert Witness 2. They can't ignore it, but they can reformulate it to do less damage to their case. On the other hand, Counsel W has also taken the evidence of Expert Witness 2 and reformulated it in its strongest form, in order to suit his case. What Expert Witness 2 thought about the differing versions of her evidence we shall never know.

5.4 Judge's decision

So, what happened? Which side won? In effect, the Council won, since the judge decided to allow the quarry to go ahead, subject to a number of precautionary and preventative measures. In relation to the potoroo, the judge accepted the opinion of Expert Witness 2, that the area of the site *where the long-nosed potoroo might possibly be found* should be quarantined until *further bat and potoroo studies have been carried out*. Her Honour accepted the evidence of Expert Witness 2 as *more independent* compared to the evidence of the other expert witnesses. And, in fact, Expert Witness 2 had displayed rare and admirable behaviour in an expert witness: she gave evidence which, in respect to the important potoroo, was both impartial and inconvenient to the Council for whom she was appearing. Although Her Honour did not say so, the evidence of Expert Witness 2 had to some extent been favourable to both sides. She alone of the expert witnesses had actually found some potoroo hairs, which suited the Protection Committee wanting to save the potoroo. However, she had found so few hairs to raise only a suggestion of a possible potoroo habitat in a small area of the proposed development; this uncertainty allowed the Council to proceed with the quarry in all but that small area. So this witness was not at any time subjected to particularly searching or aggressive examination. However, each side did attempt to shape her testimony, even transform it, for their own case by either magnifying or minimising certain aspects. Her credibility remained unchallenged, while that of Expert Witness 1 was severely dented (see Transcript 4).

It seems likely that judges, who are usually former barristers, have the training and experience to enable them to sift through and evaluate the different versions of witness testimony and to evaluate the arguments, and frames, presented by different counsel. They are aware of the tactics being used, they have access to all documentation and reports that have been admitted to the hearing, so they are well placed to come to an independent assessment of the truth or factuality of competing versions of reality offered to them by expert witnesses. Juries, on the other hand, who are by definition lay persons, may not be so well placed. They operate at a much more visceral level and are much more subject to the influence of forensic rhetoric. So there is a real argument to be made for greater education of juries in the matter of court procedures and techniques.

The argument for information or education has even greater force in the case of expert witnesses. Again, there are many experienced and professional expert witnesses who know what to expect in court and are skilled in ways of presenting their evidence. Others, new to the scene, rely on the greater leeway offered to them in comparison with lay witnesses and are greatly disappointed when their evidence is rejected and their credibility is put at issue.[10] As the transcripts show, from our case of *the ubiquitous potoroo*, the different stages of the hearing – that is, the opening and closing addresses, examination-in-chief and cross-examination – are arenas of struggle and negotiation, as opposing counsel strive, within the constraints of the adversarial system, to place their own 'spin' or interpretive frame upon the evidence.

6   Conclusion

From the point of view of the linguist or discourse analyst who wishes to both describe and explain courtroom discourse, it is clear that concentration on surface or formal properties like sentence form or turn-taking properties may obscure the potent effect of the larger scale structural organisation of courtroom proceedings and of counsel's rhetorical framing and transformation of testimony. It is not simply a matter of extending the analysis to encompass larger stretches of interaction – important though that is. In the interpretation of legal language the analyst and interpreter must look to widening discoursal, institutional and cultural contexts and identify the ways in which counsel strive, successfully or otherwise, to establish, negotiate and maintain opposing interpretive frames during the three chief contexts or phases of the hearing or trial. The testimony of expert witnesses has special probative value in determining which of the opposing perspectives will prevail. Their opinions and evaluations are pivotal to the success of the case, and we have seen in this chapter some of the forensic tactics which counsel employ in order to support or to challenge both their personal credibility and the credibility of their evidence and opinion. These tactics are essentially discourse choices: by reiteration, selective reformulation, mitigation, evaluative words and phrases; by challenging, leading or supporting the witness; by maintaining a steady tenor towards the topic or witness, in the potoroo's case by, on the one hand, scorn and scepticism, and, on the other, firm unmodulated certainty. In these ways the culture of argument is furthered by a culture of evaluation and persuasion.

Acknowledgment

I thank Christopher N. Candlin for his comments on an earlier version of this chapter.

Notes

1. For an overview of research into the language of the law in the USA, see Levi (1994b). Jackson (1995) provides a scholarly and comprehensive account of linguistic, psychological and semiotic approaches to law.
2. There is a considerable body of legal and linguistic criticism directed at the adversarial system which argues that it does not in fact achieve fairness nor is it concerned with truth. I shall not go into these issues here, since my point is that rightly or wrongly impartiality and fair play are the explicit motivation for the laws of evidence, given the generic structural principles of the adversarial system, i.e. two contesting parties. See Maley and Fahey (1991) for metaphors of this principle. For a legal perspective, see Williams (1994).
3. For a history of the development of the law of expert evidence in English law, see Jones, T.S. in Jones, T.S. (ed.) (1994).
4. Informally, the contradictions can readily be shown. At a lecture given to about 100 magistrates in New South Wales, I asked, first, whether they took demeanour into consideration when deciding cases; second, what elements they considered constituted demeanour. Only half the magistrates said they took demeanour into account; the remainder said they preferred 'hard', i.e. testable, evidence. There was no common agreement about the necessary elements of demeanour. I followed the questionnaire with a matched guise test (five different voice styles or accents reading the same text, apparently by five different speakers but in fact by only two speakers, a man and a woman). Every one of the magistrates rated 'speakers' differently on dimensions of 'competent', 'convincing', 'likeable', 'intelligent'; so each magistrate made a value judgment on the basis of speech or accent quality. Generally the results followed research studies that non-standard, non-fluent speakers are rated less highly than standard speakers. There was a small trend towards reverse ratings in that typical Broad Australian accents were associated in male speakers with 'likeable' and 'competent'. Interestingly and alarmingly, the female 'speaker' using an aboriginal-English speech style was rated low on all criteria by about three-quarters of the group.
5. *Broken Bay Protection Committee and Peter Helman v. Byron Council and Another.*
6. In *Advocacy in Court* (Evans 1983) the author quotes, from Paterson (1982), 'an endearing observation' from the daughter of Lord Atkin, a famous British Law Lord. 'When my father used to tell us about the facts of a case', she recalls, 'it was impossible to imagine what the other side could possibly hope to achieve. It seemed that there could only be one possible outcome of the case.' Evans goes

on to say: 'There they are, a totally captive audience. All yours. Take their inter-est. Set yourself up truthfully as an 'honest guide'. Above all, talk to them and not at them.'

7. Goodrich believes that 'the principal discursive operator in courtroom dialogue is undoubtedly that of paraphrase reformulation' and goes on to make the point that its implicative power is partly dependent upon 'a pre-established discourse and meanings that are not necessarily equally available to both parties to the dialogue' (1990: 197).

8. One difficulty with the credibility of expert witnesses is that they are often perceived to be acting as 'a hired sword'. A textbook on expert witnesses com-ments: 'There is a perception among many members of the legal profession that one can always find an expert to espouse one's cause; it is just a matter of time and effort' (Freckleton 1987: 123).

9. The line between a leading and a non-leading question is often quite difficult to draw. Loftus et al. (1983: 300) provide a set of example as follows:

Leading questions: The car was red, wasn't it?; Wasn't the car red?
Non-leading questions: Was the car red?; The car was red?
Less-leading question: What colour was the car?

The difference here would seem to lie in the degree of assumptiveness; negative tagged polar questions are highly assumptive.

10. Jackson (1995: 420), commenting on the 'structural disempowerment' that expert witnesses frequently experience, refers to commercial moves in Britain to prepare witnesses, emphasising appearance and presentation skills. Important as these are, I would argue that training in answering skills should also be considered. Above all, expert witnesses should be aware of the value of impartiality.

References

Bartlett, R. (1979) *The Court is Open*. Sydney: Petty Production.

Bateson, G. (1954) *A Theory of Play and Fantasy. Steps to an Ecology of Mind*. New York: Ballantine.

Candlin, C.N. and Maley, Y. (1994) Framing the dispute. *International Journal for the Semiotics of Law* vii (19), 75–98.

Conley, J. and O'Barr, W.M. (1998) *Just Words: Law, Language and Power*. Chicago: University of Chicago Press.

Danet, B., Hoffman, K.B. and Kermish, N.C. (1976) An ethnography of questioning in the courtroom. In R.W. Shuy and A. Shnukal (eds) *Language Use and the Uses of Language*. Washington, DC: Georgetown University Press, 222–234.

Drew, P. (1992) Contested evidence in courtroom-cross-examination: the case of a trial for rape. In P. Drew and J. Heritage (eds) *Talk at Work. Interaction in Institutional Settings*. Cambridge: Cambridge University Press, 470–520.

Dunstan, R. (1980) Contexts of coercion; analysing properties of courtroom 'questions'. *British Journal of Law and Society* 7, 61–77.

Evans, K. (1983) *Advocacy in Court. A Beginner's Guide*. London: Blackstone Press.

Fairclough, N. (1995) *Media Discourse*. London: Edward Arnold.

Folger, J.P. and Jones, T.S. (eds) (1994) *New Directions in Mediation*. Thousand Oaks, California: Sage Publications.

Freckleton, Ian R. (1987) *The Trial of the Expert*. Melbourne: Oxford University Press.

Giddens, A. (1994) Elements of the theory of structuration. In *The Polity Reader in Social Theory*. Cambridge: Polity Press, 79–89.

Goffman, E. (1974) *Frame Analysis*. London: Penguin.

Goffman, E. (1981) *Forms of Talk*. Oxford: Basil Blackwell.

Goodrich, P. (1990) *Languages of Law. From Logics of Memory to Nomadic Masks*. London: Weidenfeld & Nicolson.

Goodwin, C. (1997) Contested vision: the discursive constitution of Rodney King. In B.-L. Gunnarsson, P. Linell and B. Nordberg (eds) *The Construction of Professional Discourse*. London: Longman, 292–316.

Greatbatch, D. and Dingwall, R. (1994) The interactive construction of interventions by divorce mediators. In J.P. Folger and T. Jones (eds) *New Directions in Mediation*. Thousand Oaks, Calif.: Sage Publications, 84–110.

Halliday, M.A.K. (1994) *An Introduction to Functional Grammar* (2nd edn). London: Edward Arnold.

Halliday, M.A.K. and Hasan, R. (1976) *Cohesion in English*. London: Longman.

Halliday, M.A.K. and Hasan, R. (1985) *Language, Context and Text: Aspects of Language in a Social-Semiotic Perspective*. Deakin University, Victoria: Deakin University Press.

Harris, S. (1994) Ideological exchanges in British magistrates courts. In J. Gibbons (ed.) *Language and the Law*. London: Longman, 156–170.

Hodgkinson, T. (1990) *Expert Evidence: Law and Practice*. London: Sweet & Maxwell.

Jackson, B.S. (1995) *Making Sense in Law: Linguistic, Psychological and Semiotic Perspectives*. Liverpool, UK: Deborah Charles Publications.

Jones, C.A.G. (1994) *Expert Witnesses*. Oxford: Clarendon Press.

Jones, T.S. (1994) A dialectical reframing of the mediation process. In J.P. Folger and T.S. Jones (eds) *New Directions in Mediation*. Thousand Oaks, California, Sage Publications, 26–47.

Levi, J. (1994a) Language as evidence: the linguist as expert witness in North American courts. *Forensic Linguistics* 1(1), 1–26.

Levi, J. (1994b) *Language and Law: A Bibliographic Guide to Social Science Research in the U.S.A.* American Bar Association, Teaching Resource Bulletin No. 4.

Levinson, S.C. (1988) Putting linguistics on a proper footing: explorations in Goffman's concepts of participation. In P. Drew and A.J. Wooton (eds) *Erving Goffman: Exploring the Interaction Order*. Cambridge: Polity Press, 161–227.

Loftus, E., Goodman, J. and Nagatkin, C. (1983) Examining Witnesses – Good Advice and Bad. In R. Matlon and R. Crawford (eds) *Communication Strategies in the Practice of Lawyering*. Proceedings of the 1983 Summer Conference on Communication Strategies in the Practice of Lawyering. Annandale VA: Speech Communication Association.

Maley, Y. (1987) The language of legislation. *Language in Society* 6, Cambridge: Cambridge University Press, 25–48.

Maley, Y. (1994) The language of the law. In J. Gibbons, ed. *Language and the Law*. London: Longman, 3–50.

Maley, Y. (1995) From adjudication to mediation. *Journal of Pragmatics* 23: 93–110.

Maley, Y. and Fahey, R. (1991) Presenting the evidence: constructions of reality in court. *International Journal for the Semiotics of Law* **IV**(10), 3–17.

Napley, D. (1975) *The Technique of Persuasion*. London: Sweet & Maxwell.

O'Barr, W.M. (1982) *Linguistic Evidence: Language, Power and Strategy in the Courtroom*. New York: Academic Press.

Paterson, A. (1982) *Law Lords*. London: Macmillan.

Phillips, S.U. (1984) The social organisation of questions and answers in courtroom discourse: a study of changes of plea in an Arizona court. *Text* 4, 225–248.

Phillips, S.U. (1990) The judge as third party in American trial-court conflict talk. In A.D. Grimshaw (ed.) *Conflict Talk*. Cambridge: Cambridge University Press, 197–209.

Rifkin, Janet (1994) The practitioner's dilemma. In Joseph P. Folger and Tricia S. Jones (eds) *New Directions in Mediation*. Thousand Oaks, Calif.: Sage Publications, 204–208.

Tannen, D. (1993) *Framing in Discourse*. New York: Oxford University Press.

Tannen, D. and C. Wallat (1993) Interpretive frames and knowledge schemas in interaction. In D. Tannen (ed.) *Framing in Discourse*. New York: Oxford University Press.

White, J.B. (1990) *Justice as Translation: An Essay in Cultural and Legal Criticism*. Chicago: University of Chicago Press.

Williams, C.R. (1994) Evidence and the expert witness. *Australian Journal of Forensic Science* 26, 3–7.

Wodak, R. (1985) The interaction between judge and defendant. In T.A. van Dijk (ed.) *Discourse Analysis in Society*, Vol. IV of *Handbook of Discourse Analysis*. New York: Academic Press, 181–192.

Woodbury, H. (1984) The strategic use of questions in court. *Semiotica* 48(3/4), 197–228.

Chapter 15

Whose text is it? On the linguistic investigation of authorship

Malcolm Coulthard

1 Introduction

It is now some thirty years since Jan Svartvik published *The Evans Statements: A Case For Forensic Linguistics*. In this short monograph Svartvik demonstrated that incriminating parts of a set of four linked statements, purportedly dictated by Timothy Evans to police officers, had a grammatical style measurably different from that of uncontested parts of the statements. This marked the birth of a new discipline – the linguistic investigation of authorship for forensic purposes. Initially, growth was slow; in unexpected places there appeared isolated articles in which the author, often a distinguished linguist, analysed a disputed confession or commented on the likely authenticity of purported verbatim records of interviews or identified and evaluated inconsistencies in language which had been attributed to non-native speakers (Eades 1994; Gibbons 1994; Labov 1988; Levi 1994a, 1994b).

In these early days there was, however, no attempt to establish a discipline nor even a methodology – the work was usually undertaken as an intellectual challenge and almost always required the creation, rather than simply the application, of a method of analysis. In the past fifteen years, by contrast, there has been a rapid growth in the frequency with which courts in a number of countries have called upon the expertise of linguists in cases of disputed authorship. Authorship studies has come of age and, like other mature areas of applied linguistics, is now beginning to raise new and exciting research questions for descriptive linguistics.

2 The linguistic bases of authorship identification

The linguist approaches the problem of authorship from the theoretical position that each native speaker has a distinct and individual version of the language he or she speaks and writes – a personal *idiolect*. This suggests that it should be possible to devise a method of *linguistic fingerprinting* – in other words, that the linguistic 'impressions' created by a given speaker/writer should be usable, just like a signature, as identification. So far, however, practice is a long way behind theory and no one has even begun to speculate about how much and what kind of data would be needed to uniquely characterise an *idiolect*, or how the data, once collected, would be analysed and stored – indeed work on the very much simpler task of identifying the linguistic characteristics or 'fingerprints' of whole *genres* is still in its infancy (Biber 1988, 1995; Stubbs 1996).

In reality, the concept of the linguistic fingerprint is an unhelpful, if not actually misleading, metaphor, at least when used in the context of forensic investigations of authorship, because it leads us to imagine the creation of massive databanks consisting of representative linguistic samples (or summary analyses) of millions of idiolects, against which a given text could be matched and tested. In fact such an enterprise is, and for the foreseeable future will continue to be, impractical if not impossible. The value of the physical fingerprint is that every sample is both identical and exhaustive, that is, it contains all the necessary information, whereas, by contrast, any linguistic sample, even a very large one, provides only very partial information about its creator's idiolect – a situation which is compounded by the fact that many of the texts which the forensic linguist is asked to examine are very short indeed; most suicide notes and many threatening letters, for example, are well under 200 words long.

However, the situation is not as bad as it might at first seem, because such texts are usually accompanied by information or clues which massively restrict the number of possible authors. Thus, the task of the linguistic detective is never one of identifying an author from millions of candidates on the basis of the linguistic evidence alone, but rather of selecting (or of course deselecting) one author from a very small number of candidates, usually fewer than a dozen and in many cases only two (Coulthard 1992, 1993, 1994a, 1994b, 1995, 1997; Eagleson 1994). In what follows I will use examples from real cases to illustrate some of the methods used to attribute authorship.

3   Disputed single authorship: the case of Derek Bentley

In Britain, until the late 1980s, linguistic evidence obtained by the police from interviews with witnesses and those accused of crimes, was usually collected in the form of handwritten contemporaneous records, which were later presented in court in a typewritten form. However, the fact that there were no independently verifiable records of such interactions meant that the system was open to abuse. As a result of many claims that those accused had been 'verballed' – that is, that the purported verbal records had been in part or in whole fabricated – the police have now moved over to the tape- and wherever possible video-recording of statements and interviews. However, many cases of disputed authorship, in which it is claimed miscarriages of justice have resulted, are still coming before the Appeal Court in London. I will give two examples.

The first case dates from the 1950s, but the original guilty verdict was disputed for 46 years by the Bentley family, until in 1998 the conviction was finally quashed. The salient facts are as follows: two teenagers, Chris Craig and Derek Bentley, were caught trying to break into a warehouse; in resisting arrest Craig shot and killed a policeman. Bentley, although already under arrest when the policeman was shot, was also convicted of murder and subsequently hanged. Part of the evidence against Bentley was a statement that he was said to have dictated some three hours after his arrest. At trial Bentley claimed that this statement was in fact a composite document, not only written down, but also in part authored, by police officers.

As part of the eventually successful posthumous appeal against conviction I was asked to evaluate Bentley's claim. I present the full statement below as Text 1. As you read it through bear in mind that Bentley left school at the age of 14 and was functionally illiterate – he could not even sign his own name. In my report for the court I focused on a series of linguistic features which suggested police co-authorship and which you might like to look out for: marked vocabulary choices, in particular ways of naming participants; the frequency and specificity of time and place markers; and indications embedded in the text that, as Bentley claimed at trial, it had been at least in part elicited by question and answer and therefore was not, as the police had claimed, the product of monologue dictation.

Text 1 Derek Bentley's statement with 'then' highlighted
I have known Craig since I went to school. We were stopped by our parents going out together, but we still continued going out with each other – I mean we have not gone out together until tonight. I was watching television tonight (2 November 1952) and between 8 p.m. and 9 p.m. Craig called for me. My mother answered the door and I heard her say I was out. I had been out earlier to the pictures and got home just after 7 p.m. A little later Norman Parsley and Frank Fasey called. I did not answer the door or speak to them. My mother told me that they had called and I **then** ran after them. I walked up the road with them to the paper shop where I saw Craig standing. We all talked together and **then** Norman Parsley and Frank Fazey left. Chris Craig and I **then** caught a bus to Croydon. We got off at West Croydon and **then** walked down the road where the toilets are – I think it is Tamworth Road.

When we came to the place where you found me, Chris looked in the window. There was a little iron gate at the side. Chris **then** jumped over and I followed. Chris **then** climbed up the drainpipe to the roof and I followed. Up to **then** Chris had not said anything. We both got out on to the flat roof at the top. **Then** someone in a garden on the opposite side shone a torch up towards us. Chris said: 'It's a copper, hide behind here.' We hid behind a shelter arrangement on the roof. We were there waiting for about ten minutes. I did not know he was going to use the gun. A plain clothes man climbed up the drainpipe and on to the roof. The man said: 'I am a police officer – the place is surrounded.' He caught hold of me and as we walked away Chris fired. There was nobody else there at the time. The policeman and I **then** went round a corner by a door. A little later the door opened and a policeman in uniform came out. Chris fired again **then** and this policeman fell down. I could see he was hurt as a lot of blood came from his forehead just above his nose. The policeman dragged him round the corner behind the brickwork entrance to the door. I remember I shouted something but I forget what it was. I could not see Chris when I shouted to him – he was behind a wall. I heard some more policemen behind the door and the policeman with me said: 'I don't think he has many more bullets left.' Chris shouted 'Oh yes I have' and he fired again. I think I heard him fire three times altogether. The policeman **then** pushed me down the stairs and I did not see any more. I knew we were going to break into the place. I did not know what we were going to get – just anything that was going. I did not have a gun and I did not know Chris had one until he shot. I now know that the policeman in uniform is dead. I should have mentioned that after the plain clothes policeman got up the drainpipe and arrested me, another policeman in uniform followed and I heard someone call him 'Mac'. He was with us when the other policeman was killed.

The feature I will focus on here, for exemplificatory purposes, is the word 'then'. I want to demonstrate how individual words and collocations can be significant indicators of authorship and also how corpora can be used to demonstrate that significance.

As is evident from the highlighting in bold that I have added to the statement, one of the marked features of Derek Bentley's confession is the frequent use of the word 'then' in its temporal meaning – 11 occurrences in 582 words. This may not, at first, seem at all remarkable given that Bentley is reporting a series of sequential events and that one of the obvious requirements of a witness statement is accuracy about time. However, a cursory glance at a series of other witness statements suggested to me that Bentley's usage was at the very least atypical, and thus a potential intrusion of a specific feature of policeman register deriving from a professional concern with the accurate recording of temporal sequence.

To test this hypothesis I created two small corpora, the first composed of three ordinary witness statements, one from a woman involved in the Bentley case itself and two from men involved in another unrelated case, which totalled some 930 words of text, the second corpus made up of statements by three police officers, two of whom were involved in the Bentley case, and the third in another unrelated case, which totalled some 2270 words.

The results were startling: whereas in the ordinary witness statements there is only one occurrence of 'then' in 930 words, the word occurs 29 times in the police officers' statements, that is on average once every 78 words. Thus, Bentley's usage of temporal 'then', once every 53 words, groups his statement firmly with those produced by the police officers. In this case I was fortunate in being able to check the representativeness of my 'ordinary witness' data against a reference corpus, the Corpus of Spoken English, a subset of the COBUILD Bank of English, which, at that time, consisted of some 1.5 million running words. 'Then' in all its meanings proved to occur a mere 3164 times, that is, on average, only once every 500 words, which supported the representativeness of the witness data and the claimed specialness of the data from the police and Bentley.

What was perhaps even more striking about the Bentley statement was the frequent post-positioning of the 'then's, as can be seen in the two sample sentences below, selected from a total of 7 occurrences in the 582 word text:

Chris **then** jumped over and I followed.
Chris **then** climbed up the drainpipe to the roof and I followed.

This usage has an odd feel because not only do ordinary speakers use 'then' much less frequently than policemen, but they also use it in a structurally different way – for instance, in the COBUILD spoken data 'then I' was ten times more frequent than 'I then'; indeed the structure 'I then' occurred a mere 9 times in the whole of the spoken sample, in other words only once every 165,000 words. However, the phrase occurs 3 times in Bentley's short statement, that is once every 194 words, a frequency almost a thousand times greater. In addition, while the 'I then' structure, as one might predict from the corpus data, does not occur at all in any of the three witness statements, there are 9 occurrences in just one 980 word police statement, as many as in the entire 1.5 million word spoken corpus. The average occurrence in the three police statements is once every 119 words. Thus, the structure 'I then' does appear to be a feature of policeman's (written) register. More generally, it is in fact the structure Subject (+Verb) followed by 'then' which is typical of policeman's register – it occurs 26 times in the statements of the three officers and 7 times in Bentley's own statement. Taken in combination with the other linguistic features mentioned above this evidence gave strong support to Bentley's claim that, whatever else it was, his statement was not a verbatim record of a dictated monologue.

4 Creative expansion of notes: the case of Ashley King

Ashley King was convicted, in 1986, of the murder of an old lady, solely on the basis of his own confession, which he retracted almost immediately. The evidence presented in court consisted of the records of ten interviews, nine of them apparently recorded contemporaneously as a sequence of Questions and Answers, with what each person said presented in inverted commas. In fact only one of the ten interviews was actually recorded contemporaneously, the others were 'made up' afterwards from trigger notes or simply from memory. In this case I want to demonstrate how much has been added in the process of 'making up' the trigger notes and to argue that the trigger notes authored by Mr King are significantly different from the subsequent 'dramatisations' authored by the policeman.

Let us look first at the beginning of the first interview in the form in which it was presented in court – I have indicated in **bold** those utterances which seem to derive from the trigger notes, the rest of the text appears to consist of additions by the police officer.

Text 2   Extract from 'verbatim' record of an interview with Ashley King
KING was then transported to Houghton-le-Spring Police Office where at 11.35 am
that day he was interviewed in the following manner by myself and DC Simpson.

Q.   'When we saw you last Saturday you told us that you didn't go out at all on the
     evening of Monday 4th November. Are you still saying that's true?'
A.   'Yes, I'm sure that's right.'
Q.   'It can be difficult thinking back Ash, so think very carefully, it's very important.'
A.   'Aye, I'm sure about that. I never left the house.'
Q.   'We've interviewed some people who say you were out that night?'
A.   'I don't think so.'
Q.   'Think very carefully about it, it's important.'
A.   'I think that was the night we got the tyres, is that what you mean?'
Q   'Tell us about it.'
A.   '**Billy, Berti and Melley called for** us and we went up the bank and **got some
     tyres**.'
Q.   'What time was this?'
A.   'They came for us about **six o'clock**.'
Q.   'Who's Berti?'
A.   'I don't know his second name but **he's from Shiney**.'
Q.   'When you say you got some tyres, do you mean you **stole** them?'
A.   'Aye, I think so'
                    I then cautioned KING.
Q.   'Where did you get the tyres from?'
A.   '**It's a place** next to the garage, **its near the pit**.'
Q.   'Do you know the name of the premises?'
A.   '**Tyre Services I think, but I'm not sure**.'
     (The interview record continues for 3 more pages)

It is instructive to compare this twenty-utterance conversational version of
the interview with the three lines of trigger notes on which it was based –
the capitalisation, spacing and brackets are as in the original:

6pm   Left house called for Billy Waugh & Melvin Waugh + (Berty) from
         Shiney Row
      TO TYRES Place BY PIT (TYRE SERVICES?)
      (These notes continue for 15 more lines.)

A simple prose version of these notes would be something like the following:

King said he left home at 6pm and called for Billy Waugh, Melvin Waugh and
Berty from Shiney Row. They went to the tyres place near the pit, which he
thought was called Tyre Services.

There are several points to be made about this version and those produced
by the police officers for the other interviews:

Firstly, they are much more persuasive, because they masquerade as
verbatim accounts – not only are there inverted commas implying that
these are the real words used by the participants, there are also idiosyncratic features like Mr King's apparent use of 'aye' alternating with 'yes',

see the extract above and his frequent use elsewhere of 'honest' as a reinforcer and ungrammatical usages like 'Him and Robert', 'me mam' and 'us' instead of 'me'. These are tiny features, which it is totally impossible for anyone to remember accurately, but which do give a strong flavour of authenticity to any member of a jury hearing and/or reading the evidence, a flavour which would have been totally missing had the officers chosen to produce instead a simple prose version of the trigger notes as I did above.

Secondly, significant information has been added to what is contained in the notes version; indeed there have been some factual changes:

1. The notes say that King called for the others; the interview record that the others called for him.
2. There is a reference elsewhere in the notes to a penknife, but in the interview record the fact that it was a 'small silver one' is added.
3. There is a discussion about killing, there are details about the length and width of the wood used to kill the victim, and information about the victim's clothing which are presented in the dramatised version, but for which there is no support in the notes.

Thirdly, there have been some significant changes in labelling during the conversion process: for example, where the notes have only 'Didn't visit Abbey Drive' the interview record is much more specific 'we didn't go anywhere near that old lady's house'.

Fourthly, some of the 'additions' function to worsen the reader's or listener's impression of Mr King:

1. The first 'verbatim' interview record begins, as we have seen, with Mr King denying three times that he went out at all on the Monday evening, before he eventually agrees that in fact he did go out – there is no support at all for this episode of lying in the notes, nor indeed for another episode at the end of the interview when he admits again that he had been lying. These episodes do give the reader the strong impression of King as someone from whom the truth has to be dragged out and prepare the reader for the major change of story when King later admits briefly to murder.
2. Half a page of another interview is devoted to police assertions that King has been lying – again there is no reference to these exchanges in the notes.
3. The simple phrase 'Crying when asked about Abbey Drive' in the notes is massively expanded into the following highly incriminating series of exchanges:

Text 3
Q. 'I'll ask you once again, did you go to Abbey Drive?'
R. 'Yes.'
     King started to cry
Q. 'Are you alright?'

R. 'Yes I just don't want to be charged with murder.'
Q. 'Did you kill the old lady?'
R. 'No.'
Q. 'Then we can't charge you with Murder can we?'
R. 'No, I'm alright.'
Q. 'Tell me where you went on Abbey Drive?'

4. Similarly the simple phrase 'Called at deceased's' in the notes is dramatised into the following series of highly defensive exchanges:

Text 4
Q. 'During this enquiry we have talked to everyone in Abbey Drive and we know which house you went to, do you understand?'
R. 'You meant somebody saw us.'
Q. 'Exactly.'
R. 'We didn't see anyone about.'
Q. 'I'll ask you again which house did you call at?'
R. 'We called at a few but we didn't get anything.'
Q. 'Did you call at Mrs GREENWOOD's?'
   King did not reply he looked at the ground
Q. 'Ash did you call at Mrs GREENWOOD's?'
R. 'Yes.'

In this case my task was to demonstrate that the police officer had strayed way beyond the role of scribe in making up the notes – he had in fact become a second author of the text and in so doing produced a substantially different story – and to argue that the Court should restrict itself to considering text which Mr King could be regarded more reliably as having authored, that is the trigger notes.

5 Creating one text on the basis of another: the case of the Bridgewater Four

In another famous English Court case, that of the so-called Bridgewater Four, four men were convicted of killing a teenage paper boy, Carl Bridgewater, solely on the basis of the confession of one of them, Patrick Molloy. Molloy subsequently retracted his confession, but to no avail. He admitted that he did actually say the words recorded in the confession, but insisted that he was being told all the time what to say by a policeman and that he only agreed to make the statement after being physically and verbally abused for some considerable time immediately beforehand.

However, as support for the content of the confession, the police produced the written record of an interview which they said had taken place immediately before the confession was dictated and which contained substantially the same information. Molloy denied that the interview had ever taken place – in his version he was being subjected to abuse at that time – and claimed that the interview record must have been made up later on the basis of the pre-existing confession. As is evident from a cursory glance at the extracts below, taken from the statement and interview record respectively, the similarities are such that either one of the two documents was derived from the other or both were derived from a third. In this case the same phenomenon – massive identity in phrasing and lexical choice – was seen by the lay audience as reinforcing the claimed authenticity, whereas for professional linguists it is highly suspicious:

Text 5 Extract from Molloy's statement
(17) **I had been drinking and cannot remember the exact time I was there but whilst I was upstairs I heard someone downstairs say be careful someone is coming.** (18) **I hid for a while and** *after a while* **I heard** *a* **bang** *come from downstairs.* (19) **I knew that it was a gun being fired.** (20) I went downstairs and **the three of them were still in the room.** (21) **They all looked shocked and were shouting at each other.** (22) **I heard Jimmy say, 'It went off by accident'.**

Text 6 Extract from disputed interview with Molloy
P.   How long were you in there Pat?
(18)   **I had been drinking and cannot remember the exact time that I was there, but whilst I was upstairs I heard someone downstairs say 'be careful someone is coming'.**
P.   Did you hide?
(19)   Yes **I hid for a while** and then **I heard** the **bang** I have told you about.
P.   Carry on Pat?
(20)   I ran out.
P.   What were the others doing?
(21)   **The three of them were still in the room.**
P.   What were they doing?
(22)   **They all looked shocked and were shouting at each other.**
P.   Who said what?
(23)   **I heard Jimmy say 'it went off by accident'.**

To some extent the highlighting in bold above actually understates the similarities between the two texts – there is in fact not one single word, lexical or grammatical, in Molloy's statement which does not recur in the interview record.

6   Unacknowledged textual borrowing[1]

All authors at times borrow ideas and text from other authors and there are clear rules for how to do this – indeed one of the skills all students have to learn is how to borrow legitimately by indicating their sources. Of course, there are authors who borrow text and deliberately present it as their own and risk the consequences. Mr Mackay, author of *Little Boss: A Life of Andrew Carnegie*, published in 1998, from which extract 7a is taken, was pilloried in the press and his book pulped when a journalist discovered parallels in J.F. Wall's *Andrew Carnegie* from which extract 7b is taken. (I have put in bold what is identical and in italic what is the result of paraphrase.)

Text 7a

1. The *foundation* **stone** *was not laid until* **the summer of 1907,** *in nice time for* **the opening of the Second Hague International Conference**. Actual construction of the **palace took** *a further* **six years**, delayed and exacerbated by constant *bickering* **over details,** *specifications and materials. For an entire decade* the_Peace *Palace was bedevilled by* **controversy, but** *finally,* **on 28 August 1913, the opening ceremony** *was performed.*

Text 7b

2. With all of these problems it was little short of a miracle that the 'stichting' board was ready to lay the cornerstone for the building in the summer of 1907 at the opening of the Second Hague International Conference. It then took six more years before the Palace was completed during which time there continued to be squabbles over details, modifications of architectural plans and lengthy discussions about furnishings. For ten years the Temple of Peace was a storm of controversy, but at last, on 28 August 1913, the Grand Opening ceremonies were held.

As is evident from Mackay's text, plagiarists typically use the original as a framework, maintaining the basic sequence but altering, sometimes substantially, the lexical realisations, in order to make the final text better fit their own style and chosen degree of formality/informality. This, of course, makes detection much harder as there may, as a result, be no identical strings of any length to use as irrefutable proof. However, the deceit depends on a lay belief about the degree of linguistic similarity which may occur by chance – in fact people writing on the same topic are surprisingly diverse in their choices of lexical realisations.

Johnson (1997) reports pioneering research which has led to the development of a suite of computer programs originally entitled *Vocalyse* (see Woolls and Coulthard, 1998), now called *Copycatch*, designed to identify cases where two or more students have submitted substantially the same essay without acknowledgement – the program can compare 200 essays each with all the others in less than half an hour.

The problem facing Johnson was that three students, from a group of thirty all answering the same essay question – 'Discuss the kind of policy a primary school should have towards bilingualism and multilingualism' – had produced markedly similar answers. The first paragraphs of the three texts on which Johnson worked are reproduced below. The similarity is immediately obvious, but the students concerned, while admitting they had discussed the question together, insisted that they had produced the written work independently.

Texts 8a, b, c Openings of three suspect student essays (Johnson *op. cit.*: 214)

8a. It is essential for all teachers **to understand the history of Britain as a multi-racial, multi-cultural nation. Teachers**, *like anyone else, can be* **influenced** *by* **age old myths and beliefs. However, it is only by** having an **understanding** of the **past that we can begin to** comprehend **the present**

8b. In order for teachers to competently acknowledge the ethnic minority, **it is essential to understand the history of Britain as a multi-racial, multi-cultural nation. Teachers** *are prone to believe* **popular myths and beliefs; however, it is only by understanding** and appreciating **past** theories **that we can begin to** anticipate **the present**

8c. *It is very important for us as educators to realise* that **Britain as a nation** *has become* both **multi-racial** and **multi-cultural.** Clearly it is vital for **teachers** *and associate teachers* to ensure that **popular myths and** *stereotypes* held by the wider community do not **influence** *their teaching. By* examin*ing British history* this will assist our **under-standing** and in that way be better equipped to deal with **the present** and the future

As we have seen it is possible for the plagiarist to make his/her text look very different by changing some of the lexical items. Therefore, the procedure adopted by Johnson was not to look for identical strings, but rather to focus on the 'lexical' vocabulary, that is nouns, verbs, adjectives and adverbs, on the grounds that they carry most of the content and are subject to much greater individual variation than are the grammatical words – i.e. pronouns, prepositions, auxiliary verbs, conjunctions, etc.

The research question was how similar are essays likely to be, when they have been produced independently, but on the same topic and at what point does the amount of shared vocabulary become suspicious? Johnson took three other student essays from the same batch for comparison purposes and focused on the opening paragraph(s) of the six essays, roughly the first 500 words.

What she found was that the three randomly selected essays shared only 13 lexical words, items like *policy, school, bilingual, multilingual, language(s), children*, which were central to the question set. Together the occurrences of these 13 shared lexical words constituted some 19 per cent of the total lexical tokens in the three unrelated essays. By contrast, the suspect group shared 74 lexical words, whose occurrences accounted for almost half (49.3 per cent) of all the lexical tokens. When confronted with these figures

> . . the writer of text 3 [the less similar of the two suspected of copying] admitted that collaboration was such that she could no longer say that the piece was independently written. The writers of texts 1 and 2 strongly denied plagiarism, although it transpired that text 1 was completed first and a draft of some of the text was seen by the other writers (and actually taken away on paper, says the writer of text 3). Furthermore, the writer of text 1 typed and corrected text 3 for its writer. (*op. cit.*, 233)

Recently, further empirical testing has shown that when any two students are writing answers to the same question independently, the percentage of shared lexical vocabulary is usually well below 40 per cent. For this reason significantly higher percentages are diagnostic of plagiarism, either by one student from the other or by both from a third student. In one case, when comparing essays from another university, automatically and without reading them, Woolls discovered two essays shared 97 per cent of their lexical vocabulary – and then found that the apparent 3 per cent of unique vocabulary was simply a function of the plagiarist's inability to copy correctly some of the words he had borrowed – once the spelling mistakes had been corrected the essays were seen to be identical. Worryingly, these were essays written by students who had long since graduated.

7 Computer-assisted author identification

There have long been claims that some authors, like painters, have distinctive styles and that those sufficiently sensitive can recognise the style. Several years ago the novelist Margaret Drabble, feeling that her books had come to be accepted for publication simply because they bore her name, asked her agent to send her latest novel to her usual publisher under a different name. It was speedily rejected and several more rejections followed until one publisher sent the manuscript to a reader in New York. The reader phoned the next day to ask if she was being tested, as the novel was quite obviously written by Margaret Drabble. Sadly, no one thought to ask the reader to explain the basis of her identification. However, if it is possible to recognise, there must be linguistic regularities that readers are isolating and analysing and it is these that linguists must discover. There are several that spring to mind – one is that the reader is focusing on typical or even idiosyncratic expressions, which individually or in combination identify the author.

7.1 The Unabomber

Theodore Kaczynski was eventually arrested and accused of being the Unabomber because his brother and brother's wife recognised his stylistic idiosyncrasies in the 35,000 word Unabomber document. In searching Kaczynski's wooden hut the FBI found a 300-word manuscript of a short article written 25 years earlier for submission to the *Saturday Review*, but never actually sent nor published anywhere else. An analysis produced for the FBI isolated many individual lexical items and several phrases shared by the two manuscripts. The defence ridiculed this approach as amateurish, arguing that many of the words isolated could quite easily occur in any argumentative text. They were particularly scathing about 14 items which they said could 'be expected to appear in documents of any length written in contemporary English' and which therefore could certainly not be used to argue for identity of authorship. The 'ordinary' words and phrases they picked out were:

> at any rate; clearly; gotten; more or less; presumably; thereabouts; in practice; moreover; on the other hand; propaganda; and the lemmas argue*; propose*

Prima facie this seems a reasonable claim. However, the Prosecution searched the Web and, although they found three million documents containing one or more of the 14 items, only 69 documents were found to contain all 14 – and all 69 were on-line versions of the original Unabomber manuscript. The fact is that a writer's combinations of lexical choices are more unique, diagnostic or idiolectal than people have so far been willing to believe.

7.2 Who wrote which?

A question which now arises is whether not only individual lexical choices but also patterns of lexical and grammatical choice can be distinctive. Winter and Woolls (1996) report an attempt at author identification based on this hypothesis. In this instance the challenge, for it was undertaken as an intellectual exercise and not for a case going to court, was to discover linguistic features which would distinguish between the individual styles of two authors who had jointly written a late-Victorian novel. Winter and Woolls were provided with neither the authors' names nor the whole text of the novel in question, but simply the first 1000 running words from the first five and the last six chapters (numbered 28–33) of the novel. They were also supplied with the first 2500 words of a second novel, which they were told had been written unaided by one of the two authors.

Two of the features on which Winter and Woolls focused as potentially significant were 'average sentence length' and 'lexical richness'. Both are interesting variables which are under the (usually sub-)conscious control of the writer. It has been suggested that one function of the sentence boundary is to act as an interaction point; that is, the reader allows the writer time to clarify a potentially contentious point, as I hope you are doing at this moment, until I mark by a full stop that some kind of an end has been reached and then you react, deciding whether to accept, reject or hold fire until more has been said. It is a writer's decision how much to pack into a single sentence. It is similarly a writer's decision whether to have a long sentence followed by a short one, as I have just done, because, obviously, I could equally well have chosen to make the separated short sentence a linked part of the previous one. Thus sentence length is a reasonable candidate for an objective measure of style.

A second writer decision is pace: just as some speakers articulate faster than others, so some writers cover material faster and/or in a more varied way than others. New content requires new vocabulary and thus the more rapidly a writer moves from topic to topic the more new vocabulary will be introduced. This phenomenon can be exaggerated by elegant variation, in other words the decision to mask the fact that one is talking about the same topic by choosing to relexicalise – for instance, 'system' could be rewritten as 'category' and then as 'division'. What this means for the statistics of style is that writers can vary quite widely in terms of the amount of new vocabulary they introduce over similarly sized stretches of text.

Honoré (1979), in an early study of differences in vocabulary choices, postulated that the frequency of *hapax legomena* (that is, words used only

Table 15.1 Scores for average sentence length and lexical richness

	Average sentence length	*Lexical richness*
Chapter 1	33.3	875
Chapter 3	51.4	913
Chapter 5	43.2	810
Chapter 33	30.1	928
Chapter 2	23.6	765
Chapter 4	12.5	624
Chapter 32	12.1	709
Chapter 28	13.9	832
Chapter 29	19.6	785
Chapter 30	19.4	884
Chapter 31	15.9	822
Control A	23.9	703
Control B	14.7	735
Control C	17.0	693

once) would be a significant measure of the *richness* of the vocabulary of a text. He produced a formula to measure this 'richness': $100 * \log N/(1-V_1/V)$, where N is the total length of the text in running words (tokens), V_1 is the vocabulary used only once, and V is the total vocabulary (types). What Honoré did not realise is that he was compounding the measurement of open and closed set or lexical and grammatical items. The problem with this is that there is a comparatively small number of grammatical words which are used very frequently – the four most frequent make up on average 10 per cent of all texts – and thus the larger the text the smaller the *proportion* of grammatical words which are used once only. For this reason, in order to allow comparison of texts of different sizes, Winter and Woolls resolved to measure *lexical richness*, substituting LV_1 for V_1 in the formula.

The results for the 1000 word extracts, which are presented as Table 15.1, showed a marked similarity between the sentence length and lexical richness scores for the odd numbered chapters 1, 3 and 5 and a marked difference between them and those for the even numbered chapters 2 and 4. This suggested that a stylistic difference between the two authors was being measured. When the results for the final six chapters were included, chapter 32 was found to have scores comparable with those of chapters 2 and 4, while the scores for chapter 33 seemed to fit with those for chapters 1, 3 and 5. However the scores for the remaining chapters, 28–31, fell in between and this led Winter and Woolls to suggest that the two authors may have collaborated on these chapters. The scores for the three consecutive 835 word samples from the other, single-author novel were similar to those for

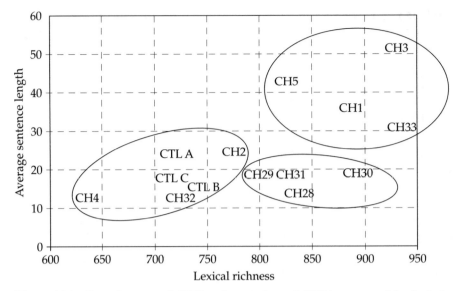

Figure 15.1 Co-written novel (CH) and control novel (CTL) compared for lexical richness and average sentence length

chapters 2, 4 and 32, and therefore it was suggested they had been written by that author.

The grounds for these decisions can perhaps be perceived more clearly in a graphical representation (Figure 15.1) which plots the lexical richness scores and the average sentence length for each chapter as a scattergraph. The locations within this two-dimensional space of the chapters from the novel under investigation are marked as CH1, CH2, etc. The three samples from the second novel are marked as CTL A, CTL B and CTL C. The graph has been divided into three segments. The left segment contains chapters 2, 4 and 32 and the three samples from the control document. The upper right segment contains chapters 1, 3, 5 and 33. The lower right segment contains chapters 28 to 31. The addition of sentence length data emphasises the divide between the authors and the graph clearly indicates the consistency of the writer marked CTL over the 2500 word stretch.

Once the analysis had been completed the jointly authored book was revealed to be *Adrian Rome* and the two authors Arthur Moore and Edward Dowson, while Dowson was also the sole author of the control text *Souvenirs of an Egoist*. An analysis of letters written by the two authors while they were engaged in writing the book confirmed that Dowson had indeed written chapters 2 and 4, and that Moore had both started and completed the novel. The authors had originally intended to write alternate chapters at the rate of one a week, exchanging their work for the other to continue the story. However, because of the dilatoriness of Dowson, the project spanned some two years and towards the end the authors had met and worked together on some of the later chapters.

To test out this method I compared the style of three of the chapters in this book – those written by Hasan, Roberts and Widdowson. I ignored the first 1000 words, on the grounds that beginnings are often atypical, concerned as they are with scene setting and therefore containing lots of references to other authors and then, after removing all quoted material, took the second 1000 and the final 1000 words from each chapter. The results were as follows:

	Average sentence length	*Lexical richness*
Widdowson 1	22	642.5
Widdowson 2	24	644.7
Roberts 1	33	703.0
Roberts 2	33	680.8
Hasan 1	26	879.3
Hasan 2	28	866.0

As can be seen, the pairs of scores for each of the three authors are close to each other and yet widely separated from those for the other two authors.[2] As mentioned above, many of the texts with which forensic linguists have to deal are quite short, so in order to see how reliable the measure of lexical richness might be when applied to much shorter extracts I took a four author article (Maley et al. 1995) and computed its lexical richness at 855.8, which ranked the style alongside that of Hasan. I then analysed the Conclusion alone, which, I was reliably informed, had been authored by Chris Candlin. The score for the 326 word conclusion was markedly different at 558.9 – but significantly, the score was very close to the score for another Candlin conclusion to a jointly written article – 327 words long with a score of 570.2. There is still much work to be done to test the validity of such stylistic measures, but in these early results we can see a marked authorial consistency between comparatively short texts.

8   Concluding remarks

There will always be texts about whose authorship the forensic linguist can say little but, as I hope I have demonstrated, we are learning more about the construction of texts all the time and honing our techniques for identifying the idiosyncrasies of authorship. The discipline in now a position to where it can begin to move towards the creation of a battery of computerised measures which will provide the forensic linguist with an initial profile of the style of both the questioned text(s) and the authenticated samples of the candidate authors.

Notes

1. I have to confess that not all of this chapter is original: some of the ideas reported here are the result of collaboration with David Woolls, who first produced Figure 15.1 for Woolls and Coulthard (1998), while some of the phrases and sentences have been shamelessly borrowed without acknowledgement from other texts I have written.
2. I did my calculations on final drafts of articles. Subsequently, the copy-editor suggested many alterations to the style of Hasan and to Widdowson – the copy-editor was particularly unhappy with Widdowson beginning sentences with 'and' and 'but'. I do not know how many of the suggestions were accepted but, such changes would make significant differences to the Widdowson sentence length score.

References

Biber, D. (1988) *Variation across Speech and Writing*, Cambridge: CUP.

Biber, D. (1995) *Dimensions of Register Variation: a Cross-linguistic Comparison*, Cambridge: CUP.

Coulthard, R.M. (1992) 'Forensic discourse analysis', in R.M. Coulthard (ed.), *Advances in Spoken Discourse Analysis*, London: Routledge, 242–257.

Coulthard, R.M. (1993) 'Beginning the study of forensic texts: corpus, concordance, collocation', in M.P. Hoey (ed.), *Data Description Discourse*, London: HarperCollins, 86–97.

Coulthard, R.M. (1994a) '*Power*ful evidence for the defence: an exercise in forensic discourse analysis', in J. Gibbons (ed.), 414–442.

Coulthard, R.M. (1994b) 'On the use of corpora in the analysis of forensic texts', *Forensic Linguistics: the International Journal of Speech, Language and the Law*, 1, i, 27–43.

Coulthard, R.M. (1995) *Questioning Statements: Forensic Applications of Linguistics*, Text of inaugural lecture, Birmingham, English Language Research.

Coulthard, R.M. (1997) 'A failed appeal', *Forensic Linguistics: the International Journal of Speech, Language and the Law*, 4, ii, 287–302.

Eades, D. (1994) 'Forensic linguistics in Australia: an overview', *Forensic Linguistics: the International Journal of Speech, Language and the Law*, 1, ii, 113–132.

Eagleson, R. (1994) 'Forensic analysis of personal written text: a case study', in J. Gibbons (ed.), 362–373.

Gibbons, J. (ed.) (1994) *Language and the Law*, London: Longman.

Honoré, A. (1979) 'Some simple measures of richness of vocabulary', *Association for Literary and Linguistic Computing Bulletin*, 7(2), 172–177.

Johnson, A. (1997) 'Textual kidnapping – a case of plagiarism among three student texts', *Forensic Linguistics: the International Journal of Speech, Language and the Law*, 4, ii, 210–225.

Labov, W. (1988) 'The judicial testing of linguistic theory', in *Linguistics in Context* D. Tannen (ed.), New Jersey: Ablex, 159–182.

Levi, J.N. (1994a) *Language and the Law: A Bibliographical Guide to Social Science Research in the USA*, Chicago: American Bar Association.

Levi, J.N. (1994b) 'Language as evidence: the linguist as expert witness in North American Courts', *Forensic Linguistics: the International Journal of Speech, Language and the Law*, 1, i, 1–26.

Maley, Y., Candlin, C.N., Crichton, J. and Koster, P. (1995) 'Orientations in lawyer-client interviews', *Forensic Linguistics: the International Journal of Speech, Language and the Law*, 2, I, 42–55.

Stubbs, M. (1996) *Text and Corpus Analysis*, Oxford: Blackwell.

Svartvik, J. (1968) *The Evans Statements: A Case for Forensic Linguistics*, Göteborg: University of Gothenburg Press.

Winter, E.O. and Woolls, D. (1996) *Identifying Authorship in a Co-written Novel*, Internal report for The University of Birmingham.

Woolls, D. and Coulthard, R.M. (1998) 'Tools for the trade', *Forensic Linguistics: the International Journal of Speech Language and Law*, 5(1), 33–57.

Index